The Glannon Guide
to Property

The Glannon Guide to Property

Learning Property Through Multiple-Choice Questions and Analysis

Fifth Edition

James Charles Smith
John Byrd Martin Chair of Law Emeritus
University of Georgia

Published by Aspen Publishing.

No part of this publication may be reproduced or transmitted in any form or by any means, electronic or mechanical, including photocopy, recording, or utilized by any information storage or retrieval system, without written permission from the publisher. For information about permissions or to request permissions online, visit us at www.AspenPublishing.com.

To contact Customer Service, e-mail customer.service@aspenpublishing.com, call 1-800-950-5259, or mail correspondence to:

    Aspen Publishing
    Attn: Order Department
    PO Box 990
    Frederick, MD 21705

Printed in the United States of America.

1 2 3 4 5 6 7 8 9 0

ISBN 978-1-5438-3931-9

Library of Congress Cataloging-in-Publication Data application is in process.

About Aspen Publishing

Aspen Publishing is a leading provider of educational content and digital learning solutions to law schools in the U.S. and around the world. Aspen provides best-in-class solutions for legal education through authoritative textbooks, written by renowned authors, and break-through products such as Connected eBooks, Connected Quizzing, and PracticePerfect.

The Aspen Casebook Series (famously known among law faculty and students as the "red and black" casebooks) encompasses hundreds of highly regarded textbooks in more than eighty disciplines, from large enrollment courses, such as Torts and Contracts to emerging electives such as Sustainability and the Law of Policing. Study aids such as the *Examples & Explanations* and the *Emanuel Law Outlines* series, both highly popular collections, help law students master complex subject matter.

Major products, programs, and initiatives include:

- **Connected eBooks** are enhanced digital textbooks and study aids that come with a suite of online content and learning tools designed to maximize student success. Designed in collaboration with hundreds of faculty and students, the Connected eBook is a significant leap forward in the legal education learning tools available to students.

- **Connected Quizzing** is an easy-to-use formative assessment tool that tests law students' understanding and provides timely feedback to improve learning outcomes. Delivered through CasebookConnect.com, the learning platform already used by students to access their Aspen casebooks, Connected Quizzing is simple to implement and integrates seamlessly with law school course curricula.

- **PracticePerfect** is a visually engaging, interactive study aid to explain commonly encountered legal doctrines through easy-to-understand animated videos, illustrative examples, and numerous practice questions. Developed by a team of experts, PracticePerfect is the ideal study companion for today's law students.

- The **Aspen Learning Library** enables law schools to provide their students with access to the most popular study aids on the market across all of their courses. Available through an annual subscription, the online library consists of study aids in e-book, audio, and video formats with full text search, note-taking, and highlighting capabilities.

- Aspen's **Digital Bookshelf** is an institutional-level online education bookshelf, consolidating everything students and professors need to ensure success. This program ensures that every student has access to affordable course materials from day one.

- **Leading Edge** is a community centered on thinking differently about legal education and putting those thoughts into actionable strategies. At the core of the program is the Leading Edge Conference, an annual gathering of legal education thought leaders looking to pool ideas and identify promising directions of exploration.

I dedicate this book to my children, Nicole and Kristin,
in recognition of all that they have taught me.

Contents

Acknowledgments

I am deeply grateful to my friend Richard Mixter, of Aspen Publishers, for presenting me with the opportunity to undertake this project, and for his encouragement and words of wisdom throughout the course of work. This culminated in publication of the first edition of this book in 2008. I'd like to thank Eric Holt, of Aspen Publishers, for his help in developing the manuscript and Sandy Doherty for her great editing of the manuscript for the first edition.

I'd also like to thank the many people who have assisted in the editing and production of subsequent editions of this book. They include Christine Hannan, Lisa Connery, Susan McClung, Paul Sobel, Gayathri Balaji, Joanne Butler, Georgia Cartmill, and Joseph Antoine.

I would also like to thank Professors Randy Beck, Paul Heald, John Kidwell, and Robin Paul Malloy for their helpful review of chapters of the manuscript.

James Charles Smith

September 2022

The Glannon Guide
to Property

1

A Very Short Introduction

*"The White Rabbit put on his spectacles. 'Where shall I begin, please
your Majesty?' he asked. 'Begin at the beginning,' the King said gravely,
'and go on till you come to the end: then stop.'"*
Lewis Carroll, *Alice's Adventures in Wonderland* (1865)

This study guide contains sets of multiple-choice questions, with accompanying introductory text, for the major topics you are likely to encounter in your basic course on Property.

This guide is organized topically. Each chapter contains clear, concise statements of the elements of property law, organized in sections that have topic headings. This content is similar to what you would find in a student text. Right after my text, there are one or occasionally two multiple-choice questions that follow up on the rules and principles. Unlike the standard student text or outline, the questions enable you to engage in active learning. After each question, I provide immediate and detailed feedback that assesses each of the multiple-choice responses. If you got the question right, your quick review of my comments hopefully will confirm your understanding; or on occasion you probably will discover that you got the question right "for the wrong reason," in which case you are able to clear things up or correct a misunderstanding.

My multiple-choice questions are designed to have a range of complexity. At the end of each chapter I've included a "Closer," which is designed to be a challenging task requiring student understanding of the material from more than one of the preceding sections in the chapters. In addition, the final chapter of this book, "Closing Closers," has a set of multiple-choice questions, many of which require an understanding of two or more discrete subject matters; for example, both covenants running with the land and the law of zoning.

You might use this book profitably in several different ways. During the semester, if you find a particular subject matter especially cloudy or difficult while you're preparing for class, it should help for you to read the text in the relevant chapter and possibly also the questions and analyses. This study guide is designed principally for use in examination review. The text may help you backstop the outline that you prepare for Property. Prior to your exam, you can take the questions in this guide as a "practice test." Even if your course exam will not include multiple-choice questions, you should find the introductory text to be useful, and the questions present many issues you will likely have to analyze in essay and short-answer questions.

Property is the oddest of the first-year courses with respect to the bundling of subject matter. There is no consensus among Property professors as to what topics must be taught. This is in contrast to Torts, Contracts, Procedure, Criminal Law, and Constitutional Law, where there is a defined core for the introductory course, with curricular diversity taking place along the edges. Some Property professors teach only real property; others include substantial coverage of various personal property topics, including intellectual property. Some professors incorporate a significant amount of land use law (typically zoning and takings). Others focus on real estate transactions (typically the recording system, contracts of sale, and deeds). A large majority of Property faculty (but not everybody) has some coverage of estates, future interests, landlord-tenant law, servitudes, and adverse possession. Here is my point, which bears on your use of this book. Some of the topics I've selected for this book probably won't be covered in your course, and conversely your course is likely to include one or two topics I haven't included in this book due to considerations of length. Let me make the unremarkable suggestion that you compare the syllabus for your course with the table of contents for this study guide. If the chapter topic is one that you are responsible for in your course, then take a careful look at the Chapter Overview at the beginning of the chapter to see whether all of the subtopics relate to what you have studied.

Although this book should be valuable for all students in all introductory property courses, my approach and objectives, not surprisingly, are a close match to those in the property law casebook that I have coauthored with Professors Edward Larson and Alejandro Camacho, *Property: Cases and Materials* (5th ed. 2022). In particular, there is substantial coverage of personal property, including intellectual property, and a focus on overarching principles that apply across a broad spectrum of property subject matters and policy choices that underlie rules and principles. Like our casebook, this book provides an overview of important rules and principles, with an emphasis on how property law has changed historically and continues to evolve. The focus is on the big picture; there is not time or space to provide a digest of property-law rules or comprehensive, in-depth treatment of specific property-law subject matters.

When I first began teaching Property in 1983, I included multiple-choice questions as part of my exam. At first, my questions only dealt with estates and future interests, an area especially suitable for the multiple-choice format when one is testing student comprehension of the complex labeling scheme that forms the backbone of the estates system. Several years later, I began drafting multiple-choice questions for other Property topic areas, a practice I have since continued and expanded upon.

I believe there are several virtues for including multiple-choice questions on law school exams. First, a normal essay exam requires the student to analyze a discrete, relatively small number of issues in detail. With an all-essay exam, large batches of material will go untested if the exam is limited to the normal three- or four-hour period. With a multiple-choice exam, the professor is able to add questions from all the areas not covered by essay-type questions. Second, to pass a bar examination most law students will have to tackle the Multistate multiple-choice questions, which include real property. Taking a multiple-choice property exam in law school is excellent practice for that important chore. Third, for combinations of reasons, some students do better answering multiple-choice questions than they do responding to essay questions under the constraints associated with the typical law school examination. Giving an exam with both types of questions helps to level the playing field for students and in my judgment produces a better overall assessment of learning performance.

One thing I am sure of is that this study guide, including the question sets, is not perfect. I find it difficult to write multiple-choice questions that are precise, challenging, and have one answer that is unassailably stronger than the other responses. If you spot a mistake or problem in the text or in any question or in my analysis of a question, I'd appreciate your letting me know by email so that I may consider fixing it for the next edition of this book. You may contact me at jim@uga.edu.

Best of luck in your study of property law, a topic I've found fascinating since my days as a first-year student at the University of Texas School of Law.

2

Finders of Personal Property

"Finders keepers, losers weepers."
Old Scottish saying

CHAPTER OVERVIEW

M ost property courses spend the majority of their time on real property subjects, but most also spend some time on personal property subjects. Of the large number of personal property topics that can be studied in the property course, the law of lost and found property (finders) is the most popular. Due to tradition and intrinsic interest, professors usually assign at least several principal cases, and students find the subject interesting and, often to their surprise, complicated.

A. The General Rule

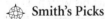

Most property casebooks lead off the subject of finders with the classic decision of *Armory v. Delamirie*, 93 Eng. Rep. 664 (1722), decided by the Court of King's Bench, sitting as a trial court in 1722. *Armory* is the font of Anglo-American finders' law. In a remarkable and remarkably short opinion, Chief

Justice Pratt stated that "the finder of a jewel, though he does not by such find-ing acquire an absolute property or ownership, yet he has such a property as will enable him to keep it against all but the rightful owner, and consequently may maintain trover."

The *writ of trover*, referred to in the *Armory* opinion, is one of the forms of action recognized at common law by the English royal courts. Trover allows an owner of a chattel to recover damages from a person who *converts* the chattel. Damages are usually measured as the full value of the chattel at the time of its conversion.

To recover in trover, the plaintiff must prove that the defendant commit-ted an act of conversion. This means that the defendant has wrongfully exer-cised dominion or control over the chattel. The defendant's interference must be significant, but it is not necessary that the defendant knows the identity of the owner or knows that she is behaving wrongfully.

The *writ of replevin* developed as an exception to an English common-law rule that an owner of converted chattels could sue only for damages. If a landlord wrongfully seized a tenant's chattels, replevin permitted a tenant to recover those specific chattels. Modern property law has expanded the scope of replevin, typically by statute, to permit an owner of a chattel to recover its possession from any wrongful possessor. Under modern law, the action for conversion has largely replaced trover and replevin.

QUESTION 1.   Watch in the park. Danny finds a valuable watch in the city park. He takes it home, places an announcement in the local newspaper disclosing his find, and after a few days he begins to wear the watch. Three months later Owen, the owner of the watch, contacts Danny and requests its return. When Owen requests his watch, Danny refuses to return it. If Owen sues Danny because of that refusal, the most probable result is

A. Owen wins if he sues in trover.
B. Owen wins if he sues in replevin.
C. Both of the above are correct.
D. Danny wins because Owen has lost title.
E. Danny wins because a finder has property rights.

ANALYSIS. A student might select Choice E based on a casual reading of *Armory v. Delamirie.* Danny did acquire a finder's property right by taking up the watch, but this is a limited property right. In the words of *Armory,* the finder has the right "to keep it against all but the rightful owner." Because Owen is the true owner, Danny does not have the right to keep the watch when Owen requests its return.

Under certain circumstances, the true owner of lost goods can lose title, thereby vesting full title in the finder. The true owner could lose title by *abandonment,* which generally requires a manifestation of intent to relinquish ownership.[1] Alternatively, a true owner can lose title by adverse possession if the finder keeps the chattel for a period longer than the statute of limitations and satisfies the other elements for adverse possession of chattels.[2] Choice **D** could point to either doctrine, but neither one would apply here. There's no evidence that Owen ever intended to relinquish ownership, and all statutes of limitation are at least several years; Owen has been out of possession for only three months.

Thus, Owen should prevail in his suit against Danny, and to pick among Choices **A**, **B**, and **C**, we need to consider remedies. Danny has converted the watch by refusing to return it to Owen, continuing that resistance after the filing of litigation. A court would grant trover if Owen requested that remedy, awarding Owen damages equal to the value of the watch. If Owen as an alternative requested replevin, the court would order Danny to return the watch. Thus, **C** is the best answer.

B.   The Public/Private Place Distinction

In *Armory v. Delamirie,* the court's opinion gives no indication of the place where the chimney sweep's boy found the jewel. English cases decided after *Armory* considered claims to chattels found on privately owned land, the two most prominent ones being *Bridges v. Hawkesworth,* 91 Rev. Rep. 850 (Q.B. 1851), and *South Staffordshire Water Co. v. Sharman,* [1896] Q.B. 44. In some of the cases, the finder prevailed over the claim of the owner of the *locus in quo,*[3] and in other cases the landowner won. The courts' opinions discussed a number of considerations, the most prominent one being a test that discriminates between an item found on premises open to the public (a "public place") and premises not open to the public. The finder is ordinarily entitled to chattels found in a public place. The landowner is ordinarily entitled to chattels found in a private place. American courts readily adopted the English public place/private place distinction, just as they had adopted *Armory.*

The public/private place test rests upon a theory of prior possession. A landowner has *constructive possession* of any lost chattels located on her real property if the landowner (1) has a general intent to exercise dominion and control over her property and (2) has engaged in substantial acts of control. Combining the two elements, the cases have sometimes said that such a landowner has a *manifested intention* to control her property. When a finder takes

---

1. Abandonment is discussed in more detail in Section D of this chapter.
2. Adverse possession of chattels (personal property) is discussed in chapter 7.
3. This is a Latin phrase used in court opinions in finders' cases to refer to the real property where the chattel is found.

up a chattel on such a private place, the chattel was already in the possession of the landowner at the moment of the finding.

Conversely, a landowner who has opened her premises to the public, by, for example, operating a store, is not in possession of chattels on her property at the moment a finder picks up the item. Such a landowner is thought to have a different intent with respect to controlling her property and has exerted different, and supposedly less extensive, acts of control. Thus, a finder who takes up lost property from such a public place is the prior possessor, as between the finder and landowner.

QUESTION 2.   Various places of finding. Rank the following places where a person has found a chattel in order of the probability that the finder may not keep the property when confronted by the claim of the owner of the locus in quo (rank from most likely that the landowner prevails to least likely).

1. In the hall bathroom of a single-family house, the finding taking place during a birthday party with 80 guests.
2. On the floor in the main lobby of a bus station, owned by a private intercity bus company, the finding taking place while the bus station is open to travelers.
3. In a fitting room of a clothing store, where customers may try on merchandise, during hours when the store is open to shoppers.
4. Next to the sofa in the living room of an apartment, while the only persons present in the apartment are the tenant and a guest of the tenant.
5. On the lawn in a small park owned and operated by the city, for which the city does not control access or charge an admission fee.

A. 3–4–1–5–2.
B. 4–3–1–2–5.
C. 4–1–3–5–2.
D. 1–4–3–2–5.
E. 4–1–3–2–5.

ANALYSIS.   Let's examine each of the five scenarios in order. (1) Under the public/private place distinction, a finding inside a single-family house normally presents a very strong claim for the homeowner. Most homeowners exercise substantial control and dominion over who may enter for what purposes. Under these facts, cutting against that claim, at least slightly, is the fact that the finding takes place during a party with a very large invitation list. The homeowner, however, has not opened her house to the public.

(2) The bus station is privately owned, but the place of finding is as open as any establishment that is open to the public. This is a very strong case for the finder.

(3) The clothing store may be just as open to the public as the bus station, but the place of finding is different. In many stores, there is some restricted access to fitting rooms, and the fitting room is to be used by customers for the limited purpose of trying on clothes. The clothing store may argue that it exercises more dominion and control over the fitting rooms than other areas of the store.

(4) The living room of the apartment, with only one guest present (who presumably is the finder) is the strongest case for the owner of the locus in quo. Some students will rank the apartment tenant's claim below that of the home-owner (number 1), but that case is weaker due to the size of the birthday party. It should make no difference that the chattel is found in an apartment rather than a single-family home (both are private residences). Likewise, it should not matter that here the "owner" of the locus in quo (the apartment) is a tenant, rather than a fee simple owner (presumably the case for the home in number 1).

(5) The city's possible claim to a chattel found in its park is the weakest because there is no evidence of the city's dominion and control. The bus sta-tion and the clothing store are closed for part of each day, and proprietors of such establishments usually monitor customers' conduct more closely than a city park department monitors the conduct of park patrons.

Putting this all together, the ranking is 4–1–3–2–5. So my answer is E. The closest call, in my opinion, is between (1) and (3). Some clothing stores have atten-dants, with customers only allowed to use a specific fitting room as directed by an attendant. That procedure certainly would reflect more control than a home-owner usually exercises when allowing a guest at a large party to use the hall bath-room. But I'm convinced that there's something special about a home as a place of finding that will steer most courts to prefer the homeowner over a guest finder.

C.   Mislaid Property

The mislaid-property doctrine is an American invention, not followed by the English courts. Property is said to be *mislaid* when the true owner intention-ally places it in a certain location, intending to retrieve it at a later time. The owner then forgets to collect the item when leaving the premises. Such mislaid property is distinguished from *lost property,* which becomes separated from the true owner without her knowledge (e.g., a small book falls out of a stu-dent's book bag while she is running to catch a bus).

The mislaid-property doctrine favors the landowner over the finder of the object. Mislaid property is not considered to be "lost property" that is open for acquisition by a finder. The landowner holds the mislaid property as bailee for the true owner, with the responsibilities that normally stem from a bailment relationship.[4] The finder has no right to take the property from the premises

---

4. Bailment is discussed in chapter 3.

and no property rights in the event the true owner never returns to reclaim her property.

QUESTION 3.   Purse on the booth seat. Candy goes to Garcia's Restaurant to have dinner. When the hostess seats Candy and her party at a booth, Candy sees a purse on the seat portion of the booth. The purse evidently had been placed there by a woman who had eaten at that table earlier in the evening. Candy picks up the purse and turns it in to Garcia, the owner of the restaurant. Garcia attempts to locate the true owner, but to no avail. Who has the better claim to the purse if the jurisdiction treats the purse as mislaid property?

A.   Candy, because her possession is what the true owner would have intended.
B.   Garcia, because his possession is what the true owner would have intended.
C.   Candy, because Garcia opened his restaurant to members of the public.
D.   Garcia, because he was already in possession of the purse when Candy picked it up.
E.   The court would order a sale of the purse with the proceeds split between Candy and Garcia.

ANALYSIS.   The most basic point to remember about the mislaid-property doctrine is that it favors the landowner over the finder. In a state that applies the lost/mislaid distinction, if the court determines that the chattel is mislaid, it awards the property to the landowner. Due to the place where Candy found the purse, on the seat of the booth, it is a reasonable inference that the purse was mislaid. This means that the true owner intentionally set it there and forgot to retrieve it when she finished her dinner and left. This question, however, does not require that you make this judgment call. It stipulates that the purse is mislaid. Thus, the purse will go to Garcia, so we can strike Choices **A, C,** and **E.** With respect to E, there are situations in which a court has determined that two or more persons have an equal claim as finders, but this has not been done with respect to mislaid property.[5]

Choices **B** and **D** offer different reasons for awarding the purse to Garcia. **D** justifies the result based on a conclusion that Garcia was in prior possession of the purse. This theory of possession is the basis of the public/private place distinction but is not part of the thinking behind the mislaid-property doctrine. Instead, the mislaid-property rule rests upon the assumption that the true owner may remember where she left her property and may return to that

---

5. Joint finders are discussed in more detail in Section E of this chapter.

location. The true owner's retrieval of her property is facilitated if the owner of the locus in quo has kept the property as a bailee for the true owner. Choice **B**, the correct answer, encapsulates this line of thought by stating that Garcia's possession fulfills the true owner's probable intent.

D.   Abandoned Property

The mislaid-property doctrine described in the previous section assumes that the true owner has retained title to the goods and that a legal rule making it more probable that the true owner will recover possession is good policy. An owner of goods, however, can lose title by abandonment. *Abandonment* is typically defined as the intentional and voluntary relinquishment of ownership. The test is aimed at ascertaining the owner's intent. In contested cases, of course, the owner (or her successor) who has been out of possession for a long time will never admit a subjective intent to surrender ownership. The issue becomes what evidence is sufficient to prove such an intent, despite the owner's protestations to the contrary? Courts commonly say that the mere fact of non-possession, even for a lengthy time period, is not sufficient by itself.

Although there are many situations when questions regarding the abandonment of goods come up, one interesting situation involves shipwrecks. When a shipwreck is discovered and the ship or its contents are salvaged (taken possession of and brought to the surface), the salvager naturally wants title to those objects. Courts, however, often apply a high bar with respect to abandonment in the shipwreck context. A good example is *Columbus-America Discovery Group v. Atlantic Mutual Ins. Co.*, 974 F.2d 450 (4th Cir. 1992), holding that insurance companies who paid claims on gold lost in an 1857 shipwreck off the coast of South Carolina did not abandon their ownership claims between the time of the loss and the time of recovery by salvagers more than 120 years later, despite the companies' inaction during that time period and the loss of many of the original records documenting their payment of insurance claims. Under maritime law, salvagers are entitled to a liberal salvage award from the owner. This may influence courts to set a relatively high standard for abandonment in the context of shipwrecks.

> **QUESTION 4.   "It's mine and I want it back."** In which of the following situations do you think a court is most likely to find that an owner of goods has abandoned ownership?
>
> **A.**   Suzie, a university student, had her backpack stolen while she was in the main library. In the backpack was a pearl necklace valued at $200. She reports the theft to the university police but takes no other measures to recover the necklace. Six years have passed since the theft.

> B. Tommy owns a condominium in a beach community, which he
>   rents out to vacationers. The condominium is fully furnished. Three
>   years ago, one of the guests took a copper kettle from the kitchen.
>   Although Tommy visits the condominium on occasion to check its
>   condition and make repairs, he has not noticed that the kettle is
>   missing.
> C. In March Ron, a college freshman, lends his DVD of the movie
>   *Inception* to a classmate, asking her to return it to him by the end
>   of the semester. She hasn't returned the movie to Ron, and Ron
>   hasn't asked for it back. It's now two years later, and they are still
>   acquaintances at the same college.
> D. Forty years ago, Isaiah, a newly wed husband, lost his wedding ring
>   in the ocean surf while vacationing with his wife. Last week a person
>   strolling along the beach found the ring and posted a description of
>   the ring's engraving on Facebook.

ANALYSIS. In some cases when a party claims that goods were abandoned, the length of time the true owner has been out of possession may be an important consideration. Here Choice **D** is quite different from the other choices. Isaiah lost his wedding ring 40 years ago, and the other three "losers" lost possession no more than 6 years ago. If this was all you had to go on, **D** would be the best choice.

But there's more to consider. With Isaiah's wedding ring, all we have is a lengthy period of non-possession, with nothing more to indicate he no longer desires to own the ring. Thus, **D** is a weak choice. **A** is also weak for the same reason. There's nothing to indicate that Suzie doesn't want her pearl necklace back. The fact that she hasn't taken any measures to recover the necklace, other than filing one police report, doesn't go far. What else, realistically, could she do? Inaction in this context does not manifest the intent to relinquish ownership.

Consider Tommy's situation in **B**. If the question were "In which situation is a finding of abandonment *least likely*?" we should pick **B**. Tommy does not yet know he no longer is in possession of his copper kettle. It may be true that he's highly unlikely to get the kettle back, but that is not the issue. It does not seem logical to say that a person intends to no longer own an object that he believes he still possesses.

This leaves **C** as a better choice than the others. In contrast to the other fact patterns, Ron has known where his property was (and who had it) all along. He voluntarily gave possession of his *Inception* DVD to a friend, who has never returned it. This is a *bailment*, and Ron continues to own the DVD for so long as the bailment continues. However, the bailment was intended to last no more than the remainder of the school year, and it's now two years later. Although it's quite possible that a court will not find abandonment here if Ron suddenly asks for "his" DVD back, it's also conceivable that a court would say that his protracted inaction evinced an intent to abandon ownership.

E.   Joint Finders

Many cases involve competing claims to finder's rights. Two or more persons assert that they found lost property. Usually the issue is resolved by asking "who is the first possessor?" among the competing claimants. The standard definition of property, which couples an intent to possess with acts of domin-ion and control, awards the lost property to the person deemed to be the first possessor. Sometimes, however, the court rules that both persons acquired possession at the same point in time. In close cases, it appears that courts may prefer the conclusion of "joint finders"; although each party wants the entire property, the outcome is a sharing of the gain, rather than "all or nothing." In *Popov v. Hayashi*, 2002 WL 31833731 (Cal. Superior Ct. 2002), a modern case contained in many property casebooks, the court held that two fans were joint owners of Barry Bond's record-setting seventy-third home-run baseball. The ball hit one fan's glove, a crowd converged, the ball fell to the floor, and the second fan picked it up.

> **QUESTION 5.   Money in the park.** Sara and Tommy, ages 11 and 14, are next-door neighbors. One day, they walk to a public park near their homes and wander next to a brook that passes an old brick fire pit. Sara notices a small piece of red cloth sticking out from under a partly burnt piece of firewood. She lifts the wood, notices it's a small dirty red bag. She picks up the bag, tosses it to Tommy, and shouts "look at this!" He throws the bag to the ground. Sara says, "Wait, there may be something inside." Tommy picks up the bag, opens it, and finds a wad of $20 bills. Sara and Tommy of course are excited. They take the bag home to Tommy's house and tell his dad. Tommy's dad takes the money to the local police precinct. The true owner of the money is never found, and the police return the money to Tommy's dad. Sara claims that she has the right to possess all the money; Tommy claims all of it should be his. If a court rejects both claims and instead rules that Sara and Tommy are joint finders entitled to equal shares of the money, the most likely reason is:
>
> **A.** Sara and Tommy together delivered the find to Tommy's father.
> **B.** Sara did not intend to possess the red bag and its contents when she first picked up the bag.
> **C.** Tommy is older than Sara and better able to ascertain the value of the find.
> **D.** Both Sara and Tommy are children, who unlike adults, lack the capacity to acquire property under the law of finders.

ANALYSIS. Conceivably, a court might hold that Sara has sole finder's rights as the first person to see and pick up the red bag, or that Tommy has sole finder's rights as the first person to discover and pick up the money. A decision that they are joint finders is quite possible. If so, the reasoning will be that neither child exhibited an intent to acquire ownership of the red bag and its contents, coupled with acts of dominion of control, before the other child. **B** is the best answer because it explains Sara's lack of the proper intent. She tossed the bag to Tommy before she knew it had valuable contents. Neither child likely would have kept the bag, had Tommy not looked inside the bag. Choice **A** may be attractive because their decision to take the money to Tommy's father in a sense points to a joint enterprise or endeavor, but it's a weak answer because that happened after they both realized the value of the find. Finder's rights, if any, should have vested earlier while they were in the park.

F. Treasure Trove

Under English common law, treasure coin consisted of coins, jewelry, and other items containing a substantial percentage of gold or silver. The treasure had to be embedded within the soil or a structure under circumstances that supported a finding that the property had been hidden or concealed for safekeeping. The treasure had to be sufficiently ancient to indicate that the owner was probably dead or incapable of identification.

In England, treasure trove belonged to the sovereign, not to the finder. Under modern British practice, treasure trove goes to a British museum, with the finder entitled to monetary compensation that is supposed to be equivalent to the market value of the treasure. In the United States, treasure trove belongs to the finder, not to the government or the landowner. There are several older cases that award treasure trove to the finder as against the owner of the land where the treasure was found, even when the finder had committed a trespass when finding and removing the treasure. There are few modern American cases, but several courts have rejected the doctrine of treasure trove, preferring the landowner rather than the finder.

> **QUESTION 6. Buried coins.** For the past 20 years John has owned and lived in a wood-frame house, originally built in 1925. He hires Rachel, age 12, to dig up an area of his lawn by the side of his house where John wants to put in a vegetable garden. John agrees to pay Rachel $7 an hour. Rachel uses a shovel, hoe, and rake. After she has been working almost two hours, she strikes something several inches under the soil with the shovel. It turns out to be a glass jar with a metal lid. The glass is broken, possibly due to Rachel's striking it with the shovel. The jar contains 41 silver dollars, which were minted between 1931 and 1944. Rachel hands the jar to John, who thanks her and says that he has never seen the jar or coins before. In most states today that recognize the doctrine of treasure trove, who has the better right to possess the silver dollars?

A. Rachel.
B. John.
C. The state where John's house is located.
D. The United States.
E. Rachel and John each should have an equal share.

ANALYSIS. This question focuses on the elements of treasure trove. The coins satisfy all the normal elements of treasure trove. They are precious metal—silver. The mint dates, together with the age of the house, suggests that someone buried the jar of coins in the yard a long time ago, satisfying the requirement of antiquity. The jar is important because (along with the large number of coins) it supports the inference that the coins were not accidentally dropped by their owner. Rather, the owner buried the coins to hide them, and for some reason failed to retrieve them subsequently.

Normally courts award chattels embedded in the soil to the owner of the locus in quo, but treasure trove is an exception. Under American common law, treasure trove goes to the lucky finder. English common law awarded treasure trove to the sovereign (probably such a rule would favor the state but conceivably the United States), but this rule was never accepted in the United States. Rachel should prevail—**A** is the best answer.

G. The Closer: Other Factors

Courts sometimes turn to a number of other factors when deciding disputes between finders and landowners. As indicated in the prior section on treasure trove, a chattel embedded in the soil or attached to a structure is sometimes placed in a special category, awarding that item to the landowner. There seems to be a feeling that the fact of attachment heightens the landowner's claim.

The nature of the relationship between the finder and the landowner also has mattered in a number of cases. Courts sometimes, but not always, disqualify a trespassing finder from keeping the chattel. When the landowner has employed the finder, or has hired the finder to perform a service at the locus in quo, the court may conclude that the finder has found the chattel on behalf of the employer/hirer. In essence, this means that there is an implied term of the contract that the person will deliver any found property to the owner.

QUESTION 7. Riding the hospital elevator. Rocky enters Big City Hospital, where he is in a hurry to visit his aunt, who is hospitalized after having undergone emergency surgery. His aunt is in a room on the fifth floor. Rocky is on the ground floor, and the regular elevator for visitors to use is far away at the end of a long hall, but he is right next to a service elevator, posted "Hospital Staff Only." Rocky asks a nurse's aide, who is standing nearby, if he may use the service elevator. She gives him permission, and they enter the elevator together. Rocky looks down and spots two $20 bills on the floor of the elevator. He picks them up and shows them to the aide, who asks him to turn the bills in to the hospital's lost and found after he visits his aunt. Rocky, an honest lad, does so. The true owner never appears to reclaim the cash. Who has the better claim to the $40?

A. Rocky, because the $20 bills are treasure trove.
B. Rocky, because the nurse's aide gave Rocky permission to ride the service elevator.
C. The hospital, because the $20 bills are mislaid property.
D. The hospital, because the service elevator is not normally used by visitors.
E. The hospital, because it employed the nurse's aide.
F. The federal government (United States Treasury).

ANALYSIS.   This is a tough question when we get down to the two "better" answers. Let's eliminate the weaker choices first. Choice **A** is improbable. There are a few American cases that expand treasure trove to include currency when its nature and location satisfies the other elements of the treasure trove doctrine. Here there is no evidence that the bills are old; they clearly have not been on the elevator floor very long; and no one would intentionally place the bills there for safekeeping.

Likewise, Choice **C** is weak. The bills are not likely to be classified as mislaid property. Almost certainly someone who had been taking the service elevator accidentally dropped the two bills, perhaps from a pocket or an open bag or purse. Who would have intentionally laid them on the elevator floor, even for a short time period?

The nurse aide's employment status, referred to in Choice **E**, will not help the hospital. If the aide were the finder, the hospital could argue that she found the bills on the hospital's behalf, but Rocky found them.

Choice **F** also is improbable. When they were first printed, the bills were United States Treasury property but obviously they were placed in circulation. Nor does the government have a claim to lost money by escheat.

Our two final contenders are **B** and **D**, which both revolve around the public/private place distinction. Rocky will claim that the hospital is generally open to the public and that he found the bills in a public place. The hospital may concede that many areas of the hospital are open to the public, but it will argue that the service elevators are generally not open for use by a visitor such as Rocky. Rocky will respond that the nurse's aide gave him permission to use the elevator, and that he reasonably believed that she had the authority to extend permission. The issue is close, but the hospital has the better argument, so **D** is preferable. Even if the aide had actual or apparent authority to let Rocky ride the elevator once, she did not (and presumably could not) make the service elevator generally available for use by all hospital visitors.

 ## Smith's Picks

1.	Watch in the park	**C**
2.	Various places of finding	**E**
3.	Purse on the booth seat	**B**
4.	"It's mine and I want it back"	**C**
5.	Money in the park	**B**
6.	Buried coins	**A**
7.	Riding the hospital elevator	**D**

3

Bailments

"A borrowed mule soon gets a bad back."
Syrian proverb

CHAPTER OVERVIEW
A. The Nature of Bailments
B. Whom Does the Bailment Benefit?
C. The Bailee's Standard of Care
D. Divisible Bailments
E. The Closer: Who Has My Car?
◈ Smith's Picks

Bailment is a common, everyday occurrence. A *voluntary bailment* is created whenever a person rents a car, checks luggage on an airline, takes clothes to the cleaners, borrows a book from a classmate, or leaves a pet with a friend during a trip. For many commercial transactions, the terms of the bailment are expressed in a writing, often in a standardized contract or in very small print on a receipt. Commercial bailments are typically characterized as bailments for the mutual benefit of the bailor and bailee, and are often called a *bailment for hire*. A bailee, like a finder, has a limited property right. In the following cases, notice the role played by the concept of possession.

A. The Nature of Bailments

Like most legal terms, courts and commentators have defined bailment in a number of different ways. The core idea relates to possession of goods (chattels). A person other than the true owner is in possession of the goods. Most courts and many commentators define bailment by using one or more contract-law elements. Here's a typical example: A "bailment is the delivery of property for some purpose upon a contract, express or implied, that after the purpose has been fulfilled, the property shall be redelivered to the bailor, or otherwise dealt with according to his directions, or kept until he reclaims it." *Toll Processing Servs., LLC v. Kastalon, Inc.*, 880 F.3d 820, 827 (7th Cir. 2018).

Long ago contracts scholar Samuel Williston provided a much broader definition: "A bailment may be defined as the rightful possession of goods by one who is not the owner." Samuel Williston, 2 *The Law of Contracts* §1032 (1920). Though contained in a contracts treatise, this definition includes none of the basic elements of contract, such as mutual intent, offer, or acceptance. Instead, it views bailment through the lens of property. Williston's property-law definition simply says bailment is all rightful possession of goods by a person other than the owner.

Does it matter whether a court follows a contract definition or a property definition of bailment? Consider the following question.

QUESTION 1.   Becky finds a dog. Becky takes a walk in a neighborhood, and a collie follows her home. The dog has no collar or identifying tag, but the dog is well behaved and appears to be in good health. For the next seven days Becky cares for the dog at her home, feeding the dog each day, and occasionally letting the dog inside her house. The dog sleeps on the screened porch at the back of her house each night. The best argument that Becky is not a bailee with respect to the dog is:

A.   Becky has not intended to take possession of the dog.
B.   Becky has not taken dominion and control of the dog.
C.   Becky's possession of the dog is not rightful.
D.   The owner of the dog has not delivered possession to Becky.

ANALYSIS.   Choices **A** and **B** both revolve around the core question whether Becky is in possession of the dog. Neither choice is a plausible conclusion to draw from the facts. Although Becky may not have intended that the dog follow her home, she chose to feed the dog and allow it into her house. She is treating the dog exactly like a normal pet owner treats a dog. Likewise, these are sufficient acts of control and dominion so that it can be said that she has actual possession.

Choice **C**, like Choices **A** and **B**, focus on the property-based definition of bailment as "the rightful possession of goods by one who is not the owner." Assuming that the dog has a true owner, Becky's possession is either rightful or wrongful. Under these facts, "rightful" seems highly probable. Although one might criticize Becky for not attempting to locate the true owner, under these facts it's not clear what steps she might have taken, and she is not concealing the dog.

So this leaves Choice **D** as the best answer. Unlike the other choices, Choice **D** uses typical language for a contractual definition of bailment. The true owner of the dog, though probably aware that the dog is missing, does not know whether anyone has found the dog. Plainly the owner did not deliver the dog to Becky "for some purpose." Thus, a court that adopts a contract definition of bailment may decide no bailment exists.

B.   Whom Does the Bailment Benefit?

Many bailments benefit both parties, the bailor and the bailee. A bailment for the mutual benefit of both parties fits squarely within the contract model of bailment, with consideration going in both directions.

But mutual benefit is not required. Many bailments benefit only one party, either bailor or bailee. A *gratuitous bailment* is defined as a "bailment for which the bailee receives no compensation," benefitting only the bailor. Black's Law Dictionary (11th ed. 2019). Likewise, a bailment may benefit only the bailee; for example, you borrow something without payment or other compensation to the owner. This is a *bailment for the sole benefit of the bailee*. Most authorities distinguish this from a gratuitous bailment (benefitting only bailor), reserving the term "gratuitous bailment" only for the transactions that solely benefit the bailor. But a few authorities define "gratuitous bailment" to cover both types of bailments that benefit only one party. E.g., *Mezo v. Warren County Public Library*, 2010 WL 323302 (Ky. Ct. App. 2010) ("When a bailment benefits only one party and no consideration is given, the bailment is gratuitous"; holding that library patron who checks out books is gratuitous bailee).

> **QUESTION 2.   Becky finds a dog revisited.** Under the facts of Question 1 above, if Becky is a bailee in possession of the dog, what type of bailment is most likely?
>
> **A.** A gratuitous bailment.
> **B.** A mutual-benefit bailment.
> **C.** A bailment for the bailee's sole benefit.

ANALYSIS. This question is not as easy as it may first appear. Let's look at Choice **C** first. Choice **C** means that only Becky is benefitted by her decision to take possession of the dog. But if a bailment exists, it's necessarily the case that someone else still owns the dog. That person (the bailor) is obviously benefitted by the care given by Becky. Absent Becky's action, the dog might still be lost, wandering about, and unfed. So we can strike Choice **C**.

Choice **A** is right if this is a "bailment for which the bailee receives no compensation." The dog owner has not paid Becky to take care of the dog. In the event the owner locates the dog and takes it back, the owner may reimburse Becky or pay a reward, but in most states this is optional. So Choice **A** is the better answer. Becky is a volunteer, and is gaining nothing from her act of kindness in caring for a lost dog.

But can we find a mutual benefit, justifying Choice **B**? Possibly, if we try hard enough. The facts don't tell us anything about Becky's motivations. Maybe she is a "dog person" who truly enjoys canine companionship. If so, and it's making her happy to take care of this dog, is this enough of a benefit to make this a mutual-benefit bailment? This is a stretch argument, which I don't think a court is likely to endorse—but it has some plausibility. If these facts came up in an essay question, a good student answer would spot the issue and argue both sides.

C.   The Bailee's Standard of Care

What happens when goods subject to a bailment are damaged or lost? Generally, the bailee's liability to the bailor depends upon fault, measured under a negligence standard. For a bailment for the mutual benefit of both parties, a bailee has a duty to exercise reasonable care to protect the property. For bailments that benefit only one party, the traditional rule alters the negligence standard based on whom the bailment benefits. For a gratuitous bailment, benefitting only the bailor, the bailee a duty to exercise slight care, and thus is liable only for gross negligence. For a bailment benefitting only the bailee, the bailee has a duty to exercise great care, and thus is liable for slight negligence. Some courts reject the traditional three-tiered standard for a single standard of reasonable care under the circumstances.

The parties may modify the bailee's standard of care by agreement. The bailee may undertake complete liability for loss or damage, regardless of fault. For example, rental car agreements usually obligate the renter to pay the company for damage or loss of the vehicle, regardless of the cause. Or a bailment contract may exculpate the bailee from liability. When the property subject to the bailment is covered by insurance, the parties to the bailment should consider the relationship between insurance coverage and the parties' rights and liabilities with respect to damage or loss.

QUESTION 3.   Borrowing the neighbor's car. Kareles and Haley are next-door neighbors and good friends. Last week Kareles's car incurred severe damage from a hailstorm. His car is presently at an auto body shop, undergoing repairs. Haley owns and drives a recent model year Honda Accord sedan. At 3 PM in the afternoon, Kareles borrows Haley's

Accord to make a short trip. Consider the following three versions of the story:

1. Haley is sick with the flu, and Haley asks Kareles to drive the Accord to her pharmacy, located within a nearby supermarket, to buy several over-the-counter cold and flu pharmacy products for Haley.
2. Kareles is hungry and out of groceries, and he asks Haley to borrow the Accord so he can shop at the nearby supermarket.
3. Kareles is hungry and out of groceries, he asks Haley to borrow the Accord so he can shop at the nearby supermarket, Haley agrees but tells Kareless she also needs a few things, which Kareless agrees to purchase for her.

All three stories have the same sad ending. Kareles is in a hurry when he arrives at the supermarket. He parks in a regular parking space, dashes into the store, while leaving the Accord unlocked with the keys on the front passenger seat. He quickly shops, but when he returns to the parking lot, the Accord is gone. Maybe the car thief will be identified, or the car recovered, but this has not happened yet. What standard of care will apply to determine if Kareles is liable to Haley for the loss of the Accord?

A. Slight care for 1, extraordinary care for 2, and reasonable care for 3.
B. Slight care for 1, reasonable care for 2, and extraordinary care for 3.
C. Reasonable care for 1, extraordinary care for 2, and slight care for 3.
D. Reasonable care for 1, slight care for 2, and extraordinary care for 3.
E. Extraordinary care for 1, slight care for 2, and reasonable care for 3.
F. Extraordinary care for 1, reasonable care for 2, and slight care for 3.

ANALYSIS. This one is straightforward. It tests whether you understand the traditional three-tiered standard of care developed by courts to determine when the bailee is liable to the bailor for loss or damage to the bailment property. To get the answer, you do not have to reach a conclusion on how bad (negligence) or blameless Kareles's conduct was in leaving the car keys in an unlocked car. It's only necessary to determine which of the three standards applies to each of the three transactions. This is a matching question.

Transaction (1) is plainly a gratuitous bailment, benefitting only Haley. Kareles is going to the supermarket solely as a favor to Haley, to shop for her. He must be slightly careful (i.e., he is liable only for gross negligence). In transaction (2), the favor goes in the other direction. Haley is gaining nothing by letting Kareles use her car to shop for himself. He must be extraordinarily careful (i.e., he is liable for slight negligence). In transaction (3), there is mutual benefit. Kareles is shopping for himself, but buying a few things for Haley, saving her from making a trip to the supermarket. He must be reasonably careful (i.e., he is liable for ordinary negligence). So the right answer is **A.**

D.   Divisible Bailments

Bailments frequently involve an object that has contents. A traveler checks luggage with a common carrier. A hotel patron turns over his Lexus sedan to the hotel valet parking attendant. A woman mislays her purse in a restaurant,[1] which is found by a restaurant employee. It's quite possible that all three items (luggage, sedan, purse) contain valuable contents. In most transactions, thankfully, the nature and value of the contents never becomes important. When the bailment ends, the bailee redelivers possession to the bailor, with the container and all contents in the same condition as they were before.

But sometimes there is a problem with the contents. All or some of the contents are missing or damaged. Is the bailee liable for the loss or damage? Courts usually try to solve the problem by resorting to contract rules (what did the parties agree to?), tort rules (did the bailee exercise proper care, or was there negligence?), or a combination of both rules. Under the contract approach, the issue is: What were the parties' reasonable expectations with respect to the contents? A contract-based definition of bailment may excuse the bailee for liability if the presence of valuable contents was not known by the bailee, or reasonably foreseeable to the bailee. This gives rise to the doctrine of *divisible bailment*. For example, a bailment might cover the purse, but not its contents, thus relieving the bailee for liability for loss or damage to the contents.

> **QUESTION 4.   "Don't whine over lost wine."** Peter owns an expensive yacht, the Silver Slipper, which he kept at a marina. Peter made plans to spend the next six months in Europe. He gave his set of keys to the yacht to his friend Karl, who lived near the marina. Peter told Karl that he could use the Silver Slipper; he also asked Karl to take good care of it. For the next three months, Karl used the yacht several times a week, always returning it to the marina at the end of his day on the bay and the ocean. Near the end of the third month, Karl forgot to lock the cabin door one evening, and thieves broke in and stole two cases of exceptionally fine French wine that Peter had stocked in the yacht bar area. The wine has a market value of $12,000. Karl, not a drinker, had never went near the bar area, and was not aware of the wine's presence before the theft. Peter demands that Karl compensate him for the loss of the wine. If Karl prevails, the most likely reason will be:
>
> **A.** No bailment was created because Karl was not paid for taking care of the yacht.

---

1. For a refresher on the mislaid-property doctrine, see Section C of chapter 2.

> **B.** A bailment was created, but Karl did not owe Peter a duty to take care of the bailed property.
> **C.** A bailment was created, but it covered the yacht but not the wine.
> **D.** A bailment was created, but it continued only for the time periods when Karl was present on the yacht.

ANALYSIS.   Let's look at the choices in order. Choice **A** is flatly wrong. This is clearly a voluntary bailment, which all courts would recognize, even those who embrace a contract-law definition of bailment. Peter intended to transfer possession of the yacht to Karl, Karl intended to accept possession, and that's what happened. The lack of payment to Karl might justify a conclusion that this is not a mutual-benefit bailment (although it seems Karl enjoyed sailing the yacht); but if so, it's still a bailment — a gratuitous bailment.

Choice **B** is flawed. The first premise — a bailment was created — is right. But the second premise flunks. Karl owed Peter a duty of care, either a duty of reasonable care or a duty of slight care (the latter if this is a gratuitous bailment, and the jurisdiction follows the traditional three-tier calibration for the bailee's duty of care).

Choice **C** correctly finds a bailment, but excludes the wine from the scope of the bailment. This reflects the concept of divisible bailment. It's not certain that this is a winning defense for Karl. Despite his lack of knowledge that the yacht contained wine, and it was expensive wine, a court may conclude that the loss was a reasonably foreseeable consequence of his failure to lock the yacht. But nevertheless this is a plausible defense for Karl.

Choice **D** is a clever argument for Karl. This issue is whether the bailment is continuous, lasting until Peter returns home from Europe; or whether it persists only for the days and hours Karl takes physical possession of the yacht. Under some facts, it's possible that a bailment can start, stop, restart, stop again, etc. So our only two decent choices are **C** and **D**. I believe **C** is the best defense from the choices given. Because Karl retained the keys at all times, and Peter never returned to the marina until after the theft, a court almost certainly would rule that Karl's possession is continuous. If need be, the court could say he was in constructive possession when he wasn't on the yacht or at the marina.

E.   The Closer: Who Has My Car?

Litigation concerning motor vehicles frequently involves bailment issues. Whenever the owner is not in immediate physical possession of her vehicle, it's possible that another person may be deemed to be a bailee.

QUESTION 5.   Park and walk away. Rank the following fact patterns involving a car owner parking her car in order of probability that a bailment is created (the car owner would be the bailor and the owner or operator of the parking lot or garage would be the bailee).

1. Ariel drives up to a shopping mall, parks in the mall's parking lot, and enters a department store.
2. Bob drives up to a hotel, notices that a sign reading "Valet Parking, $40 per day," exits his vehicle, hands his keys to the smiling valet, tells her to park his car, and enters the hotel lobby.
3. Carry parks her car on a public street, ignoring a "no parking" sign, and leaves her car. A parking officer notices the violation and directs a towing company to take the car to the company's impound lot.
4. Doug enters a multi-level parking garage by taking a ticket from a machine, which opens a gate allowing entry into the garage. He parks his car on level 2, takes his keys, and heads to a local restaurant. Payment is to take place later at an exit gate, where an employee who sits in a kiosk collects the appropriate parking fee.

A.   2-3-1-4.
B.   2-3-4-1.
C.   2-4-3-1.
D.   4-2-3-1.
E.   1-2-3-4.

ANALYSIS.   Let's take a look at each of the four scenarios in order.

(1) There's no plausible argument of a bailment here. Whoever owns the shopping mall probably also owns the parking lot, but there are no facts pointing to that person exercising any dominion and control over Ariel's car, or any of the other cars in the lot.

(2) In contrast, this must be a bailment. Bob has voluntarily given up complete dominion and control of his car to the hotel's employee, who has accepted possession and driven it to wherever valet parking is located.

(3) Now it's getting harder. The towing company has full dominion and control of Carry's car, although this is not what Carry intended, and she may not yet know that her car is not where she parked it. Quite possibly, this is a constructive or involuntary bailment. Many courts attach this label to a fact pattern like this, in order to make the possessor subject to a standard of care with respect to the property.

(4) Like (3), a ruling of either "bailment" or "no bailment" is plausible. The latter is more probable because Doug selected his parking space and has his car keys. The parking garage owner has exercised some dominion and control, unlike the surface parking lot in (1), but not much. No employee has

driven or touched the car. Dominion and control appear limited to the entry and exit gates, which prevent Doug from leaving with his car without paying the parking fee, and the presence of one employee (who, however, is supposed to leave Doug's car alone).

Where does this leave us? The best ranking is 2-3-4-1. This shows up as Choice **B**.

 ## Smith's Picks

1. Becky finds a dog   **D**
2. Becky finds a dog revisited   **A**
3. Borrowing the neighbor's car   **A**
4. "Don't whine over lost wine"   **C**
5. Park and walk away   **B**

4

Gifts of Personal Property

"It is more blessed to give than to receive."
Acts of the Apostles 20:35

CHAPTER OVERVIEW
A. The Basic Elements
B. Physical Delivery
C. Constructive and Symbolic Deliveries
D. Acceptance
E. Gift Causa Mortis
F. The Closer: Gifts of Future Interests
❖ Smith's Picks

Many property courses include some coverage of the law of gifts as part of the introduction to personal property. Part of the appeal of the subject is that all students have prior experiences as givers and recipients of gifts, although few students have considered the legal implications of attempted gift giving prior to law school. This chapter covers the basics of gifts of personal property, with most of the attention devoted to chattels. Additional, more complicated issues sometimes arise with respect to gifts of intangible personal property, such as stocks, bank accounts, and intellectual property.

A. The Basic Elements

The three requirements for a valid gift are

- **Donative intent.** The donor must intend to give the property to the donee.

- **Delivery.** The donor must deliver the subject matter of the gift to the donee. Delivery may be physical, constructive, or symbolic, as discussed in the next two sections of this chapter.
- **Acceptance.** The donee must accept the gift.

When an alleged gift is disputed, the donee has the burden of proof for all three elements.

Every gift is an inter vivos gift or a gift causa mortis.[1] An inter vivos gift is complete when the three elements are satisfied, and at that time the gift is generally irrevocable.[2] This means that the donee has title, and a donor has no right to change her mind and retrieve the chattel.

QUESTION 1.   Last-minute birthday present. Today is Johnnie's birthday. It is 6 PM and his friend Sarah has forgotten to shop for a present. Sarah is about to leave town on a business trip. She telephones Johnnie, wishes him "Happy Birthday" and tells him that his present is a porcelain vase, which Johnnie previously saw at her house and admired. She tells Johnnie that he can pick it up next weekend. Before Sarah returns home from her trip, she changes her mind about the birthday present. Who presently owns the vase?

A.   Johnnie, because Sarah expressed a definite intent to make a gift.
B.   Johnnie, because he relied upon Sarah's expression that the vase was his.
C.   Johnnie, because he allowed Sarah to retain possession of the vase temporarily.
D.   Sarah, because she expressed an intent to make a gift in the future.
E.   Sarah, because the requirements for making a gift were not satisfied.

ANALYSIS.   This is a relatively simple question that tests understanding of the three basis elements for a gift of a chattel: intent, delivery, and acceptance. From the description of the telephone conversation, it appears that Sarah expressed a present intent to give the vase to Johnnie as his birthday present. For this reason, Choice **D** is wrong.

Choice **B** asserts that Johnnie relied upon Sarah's gift (or Sarah's promise to make the gift). Under certain circumstances, the donee of a failed gift may prevail with reliance by using the contract law doctrine of promissory estoppel, but there are no facts supporting the assertion of reliance by Johnnie.

Sarah should prevail because there was no delivery of the vase. Choice **A** is incorrect because a definite expression of present donative intent is not sufficient. It must be coupled with a delivery. Choice **C** would be correct had Sarah

---

1. The gift causa mortis is discussed in Section E of this chapter.
2. In many states, there is an exception for engagement rings and other engagement gifts. Engagement gifts are often revocable if the wedding does not take place.

completed the gift with a delivery and then Johnnie had agreed to let Sarah keep possession temporarily, but this did not happen. **E** is the correct answer; the delivery requirement was not satisfied.

B.   Physical Delivery

Donative intent is usually established through the donor's written or spoken words. Often the words alone are not conclusive as to what the alleged donor really intended to accomplish. They may be ambiguous or incomplete, and this is one reason why the law requires delivery in addition to manifested intent.

Normally delivery means the actual physical transfer of possession of the chattel to the donee. This is sometimes called *manual transfer* of the chattel. This transfer of possession is seen as strong evidence that the donor intended to make an irrevocable gift.

> **QUESTION 2.   Mom may read the book first.** Suzuki came home from college over the holidays to visit her parents. The three of them unwrapped presents together next to the Christmas tree. Suzuki gave her parents a framed photograph of their favorite daughter (Suzuki). Her parents gave Suzuki a just published bestseller, for which she thanked them. Suzuki was going to be too busy to read the book during the first part of the semester back at college, and she knew that her mom also wanted to read the book, so she left the book with her mom when she returned to college. Has there been a completed gift?
>
> **A.** Yes, because the parents delivered the book to Suzuki.
> **B.** Yes, because the photograph, given in exchange for the book, furnishes consideration.
> **C.** No, because Suzuki's transfer of the book to her mother revoked the delivery.
> **D.** No, because the parents did not intend to make a present transfer of ownership to Suzuki.
> **E.** No, because Suzuki made a valid gift of the book to her mom.

ANALYSIS.   First let's tackle the three responses that do not expressly address the delivery requirement for gifts. Choice **B** invokes contract law, arguing that Suzuki has a property right to the book because she gave the photograph to her parents. This does not fly. Suzuki did not bargain for her parents to give her the book by offering to give them the photograph. Exchanges of gifts are exchanges of gifts; they are not contracts in which parties bargain for promises or performances.

Choice **D** is wrong based on the facts. Normally holiday exchanges of gifts are complete when the recipients open their presents, and there is no indication here that the parents expressed any unusual idea or condition that the book was not to be Suzuki's immediately.

Choice **E** might be plausible. Someone who receives a gift may decide to give the object, right away, to another person.[3] But the facts state that Suzuki "left the book with her mom," implying a loan (bailment) of the book. **E** is weak.

The two responses dealing with delivery are **A** and **C**. The latter choice states that Suzuki's bailment of the book to her mom, one of the donors, revoked delivery. A gift, once completed with all three elements satisfied, is irrevocable. Neither the donee nor the donor may revoke. Thus, a delivery may not be revoked once donative intent and acceptance have taken place to complete the gift.

A is the right answer. The parents made an actual physical delivery of the book to Suzuki, and her subsequent delivery to her mom as a bailment does not invalidate the gift.

C.   Constructive and Symbolic Deliveries

Instead of a physical, manual delivery of the chattel, a donor may deliver to the donee a writing or another object that represents or refers to the chattel. Delivery of that thing may suffice to validate the gift if the court recognizes a constructive or symbolic delivery. This type of delivery is not always allowed. Courts often say that the donor must make the "best delivery possible" under the circumstances. A constructive or symbolic delivery is allowed as a substitute only if there is some reason why it was not practical for the donor to make a physical delivery of the chattel.

Some courts use the terms *constructive delivery* and *symbolic delivery* as synonyms, but there is a recognized distinction between the two terms. A constructive delivery provides the donee with the *means of access,* allowing the donee to acquire physical possession. Under the law of some states, a constructive delivery is preferred to a symbolic delivery (just as a manual delivery is preferred to a constructive or symbolic delivery). Some courts are more willing to allow a constructive delivery, compared to a symbolic one, because with a constructive delivery the donor has done all that is necessary to allow the donee to acquire possession of the chattel. Without anything further from the donor, the donee is able to obtain dominion and control over the chattel.

---

3. This phenomenon, called "regifting," sometimes takes place when the recipient doesn't want the item. The practice has its defenders (efficiency grounds) but is seen by some as a serious breach of etiquette.

QUESTION 3. A gift of an automobile. Homer wants to make a gift of an automobile to his niece. He has a certificate of title for the automobile, as required by the certificate of title act for the state where Homer resides. Which of the following statements is true?

A. Delivery of the certificate of title is a constructive delivery.
B. Delivery of the certificate of title is an actual delivery.
C. Delivery of the automobile itself is a symbolic delivery.
D. Delivery of the keys to the automobile is a constructive delivery.
E. Both A and D are correct.

ANALYSIS. This question tests the ability to distinguish the three types of delivery (actual, constructive, and symbolic), including the rule that a constructive delivery provides the donee with an object that furnishes the means of access. Actual delivery of the automobile is what you would think it is. Homer allows his niece to take possession of, and drive, the auto. Thus, **B** and **C** are wrong.

For Choice **A**, the question to ask is whether the niece, if she receives only the certificate of title, has the means to take possession of the car and drive it. She does not have the means, even if the certificate is properly endorsed by Homer. Without the keys, she cannot unlock the car or drive it. Delivery of the certificate of title is a symbolic delivery, but not a constructive delivery.

Delivery of the keys, on the other hand, is a constructive delivery. She can go to wherever the automobile is located (probably Homer's home) and take it. **D** is the right answer.

D.   Acceptance

Acceptance by the donee is required, but this element seldom poses a problem. Courts have often said that acceptance is presumed or implied if the gift has value. In the absence of affirmative evidence that the donee rejected the gift, an attempted gift is not likely to fail for lack of acceptance.

QUESTION 4.   A gift of a pit bull. Babe, the owner of a pit bull dog named Roscoe, is planning to move to another state far away. Roscoe, a purebred, has a market value of $300. Babe decides not to take Roscoe with her. She thinks her friend, Marcus, may want Roscoe. After loading up her U-Haul trailer, she drives to Marcus's house on the way out of town, but Marcus is away at the moment. She ties Roscoe to a post on the front porch of Marcus's house, leaving a note that reads: "I'm giving Roscoe to you. I know you'll take good care of him. Love, Babe." Marcus returns home and does not want Roscoe. He takes Roscoe to a local dog rescue shelter, which accepts possession of Roscoe. The shelter has a policy of charging $30 to the owner of any dog that the shelter is unable to place for adoption within 30 days. The shelter, not having placed Roscoe within 30 days, bills Marcus. Is he liable for the charge?

A. Yes, because Marcus accepted the gift by taking Roscoe to the shelter.
B. Yes, because the law presumes acceptance by Marcus.
C. Yes, because Marcus acted as Babe's agent in taking Roscoe to the shelter.
D. No, because Marcus never accepted the gift.
E. No, because Babe's delivery of Roscoe was not sufficient.

ANALYSIS.   This question concentrates on the requirement of acceptance by the donee. First let's knock off the two choices that do not discuss acceptance. C is wrong, even if we assume that the dog rescue shelter would be justified in billing an agent who delivered a dog on behalf of the owner, because there are no facts to support a finding of agency. Babe did not know that Marcus took Roscoe to the shelter.

Delivery, referred to in **E,** is not open to question. Babe left Roscoe at Marcus's house. This would accomplish actual, physical delivery, making a completed gift provided there was donative intent and acceptance.

Acceptance in the law of gifts, just as in the law of contracts, depends upon a person's intent. As in contracts, in gifts a court may focus on *manifested intent.* A presumption of acceptance typically applies to solve a timing problem, when an alleged donee who wants the property first learns of the purported gift after the donor has died. Here the presumption will not apply because the facts indicate that Marcus does not want to own Roscoe. Choice **A** is a better pick than **B** but is also weak. Marcus might accept the gift by conduct, acting as if he were Roscoe's owner. The facts are sparse here, but there's no indication that he pretended to be Roscoe's owner or misled the shelter. Choice **D** is the best answer. Marcus decided not to accept Babe's offer of gift.

E.   Gift Causa Mortis

A gift causa mortis is a special type of gift made by a donor who is in apprehension of imminent death. Just as for inter vivos gifts, a gift causa mortis requires donative intent, delivery, and acceptance. The delivery (manual, constructive, or symbolic) must take place before the donor dies.

With respect to donative intent, the donor does not always expressly refer to the possibility of pending death. This can raise a question as to whether an alleged donor intended to make a gift inter vivos or a gift causa mortis.

Courts will infer an attempted gift causa mortis when the surrounding circumstances indicate that the donor acted while in apprehension of possible imminent death.

A gift causa mortis takes effect immediately when all three required elements are present. The gift, however, is revocable. The donor has the right to revoke prior to death, assuming the donor has remained mentally competent. Moreover, revocation occurs automatically if instead of dying the donor recovers from the perceived peril. This timing distinguishes the gift causa mortis from a testamentary transfer, which takes place at the moment of the donor's death. Sometimes an attempted gift causa mortis fails because the court determines that the donor attempted a testamentary transfer, which could only be accomplished by the donor making a valid will.

QUESTION 5.   The diamond ring. In January, Mary made a will, which bequeathed her diamond ring to her daughter, Alice; her Ford Mustang convertible to her daughter, Brenda; and all the rest of her property to her husband, David. In April, Mary learned that she had a serious heart defect. The evening before she went into the hospital for surgery, she handed her diamond ring to Brenda, telling her, "This is yours, darling, you've always been so good to me." No one else was present when Mary handed Brenda the ring. Mary died during the surgery. Who has the better claim to the diamond ring?

A. Alice, because a gift causa mortis cannot revoke a will.
B. Alice, because there were no witnesses to the alleged gift causa mortis other than Brenda.
C. Alice, because delivery was not the best possible under the circumstances.
D. Brenda, because Mary adequately expressed her intent.
E. Brenda, because Mary made an effective symbolic delivery of the ring.

ANALYSIS.   Students may be drawn to Choice **A** because the question clearly involves an attempted gift causa mortis and Choice **A** is the only response that uses the term. But **A** is wrong. A will is revocable and operates only at the moment the testatrix dies. If the will includes a specific bequest and the testatrix no longer owns that property when she dies, the legatee has no claim to that property.

Choice **B** makes a good point. With no independent witnesses, there is a risk that Brenda has not described the transaction accurately. She may have even committed fraud. But this is an inherent problem with the gift causa mortis doctrine, and there is no requirement that a donee provide additional corroborating evidence.

Choices **C** and **E** both discuss delivery, with flaws. Delivery is not a problem here because Mary handed the diamond ring to Brenda. This is an actual delivery, not a symbolic delivery (which is a delivery of a symbol in lieu of the chattel), and an actual delivery, when it is made, is always the best delivery possible.

We're left with Choice **D**, the right answer. **D** is only a partial explanation for why Mary should win: we can also say that this is a valid gift causa mortis, with a proper delivery, which was accepted by Brenda. **D** is the best answer because it is the only choice without a flaw.

F.   The Closer: Gifts of Future Interests

A promise to make a gift is generally unenforceable. Under property law, the explanation is that the promisor still has title and ownership. Contract law analysis leads to the same conclusion. The lack of consideration given to the promisor makes the promise unenforceable.

Although a promise to make a future gift is unenforceable, a gift of a future interest in property is valid. At first consideration, this may seem anomalous if not contradictory. But there is a distinction of substance. A promise to make a gift in the future does not transfer any property right to the promisee at the time the promise is made. In contrast, a gift of a future interest vests the donee with title to the future interest at the moment the gift is made. Like other inter vivos gifts, a gift of a future interest is irrevocable when made. The donee's right to possession is deferred until the point in time when the present estate expires. This deferral of possession and enjoyment is not the result of a special condition that the donor has sought to impose on the gift. Instead, such deferral follows from the nature of future interests. By definition, every future interest represents deferred enjoyment of property.

> **QUESTION 6.   Future interest in a computer.** Travis, 94 years old, just bought a new computer system. He wrote a letter to Junior, his great-grandson, which stated in pertinent part: "I love my new Multi Gig Byte Deluxe computer. When I die you may have it along with all the add-ons." Junior received the note through the mail and sent a thank-you card to Travis. Three months later Travis died of natural causes. Travis died intestate, and his sole heir is his wife, Woodsy. Who has the better claim to the computer system?
>
> **A.** Junior, because Travis made a gift causa mortis of the computer system.
> **B.** Junior, because Travis made a gift of a future interest in the computer system.

> **C.** Woodsy, because Travis made no delivery of any kind.
> **D.** Woodsy, because there is not adequate evidence that Travis intended to make a present gift.
> **E.** Junior and Woodsy should share the computer system because they are both heirs of Travis.

ANALYSIS.   Some students may be tempted by Choice **A**, given that many people as old as Travis do have an appreciation of pending mortality. But old age by itself does not qualify a person to make a gift causa mortis, and the facts state that Travis died of natural causes.

Choice **C** is incorrect because the letter from Travis can qualify as a symbolic delivery. If Travis has made a proper expression of donative intent, delivery is probably sufficient. Acceptance is no problem; not only is it presumed, but Junior sent a thank-you card.

Choice **E** is wrong because it is contradicted by the facts, which state that Woodsy is Travis's sole heir. In many states, Woodsy and Junior would both be heirs, but here the facts stipulate otherwise.

We're left with **B** and **D**, which forces you to decide whether Travis has made a present gift of a future interest in the computer system to Junior. Travis is able to make such a gift, and a letter written to Junior would be an appropriate mechanism to accomplish such a gift. A famous case contained in many property casebooks, *Gruen v. Gruen,* 496 N.E.2d 869 (N.Y. 1986), validated a gift of a remainder interest in a painting, made by a letter sent by a father to his son. But here there's a problem with Travis's expression of intent. By saying "When I die you may have [the computer]" Travis has indicated that Junior is to acquire an ownership interest at the time of Travis's death. This is too late. A property owner can transfer property at his death only by making a valid will, and the letter cannot qualify as a will. **D** is the best answer.

 # Smith's Picks

1.	Last-minute birthday present	**E**
2.	Mom may read the book first	**A**
3.	A gift of an automobile	**D**
4.	A gift of a pit bull	**D**
5.	The diamond ring	**D**
6.	Future interest in a computer	**D**

5

Intellectual Property

"The ancients stole our best ideas."
Mark Twain

CHAPTER OVERVIEW
A. Patents
B. Copyrights
C. Trademarks
D. Trade Secrets
E. Misappropriation
F. Right of Publicity
G. The Closer: Distinguishing among the IP Categories
✦ Smith's Picks

Only recently have property teachers begun to include intellectual property ("IP") in the basic property course. The core topics of intellectual property law consist of patents, copyrights, and trademarks. The term "intellectual property" is not a term of art, and so its boundaries are not well defined. Nearly all lawyers and academics would also classify trade secrets and misappropriation as part of the law of intellectual property, and many would also add the emerging law governing the right of publicity.

In property courses with a traditional curriculum, students will receive little or no introduction into the subject matters that comprise intellectual property. In other property courses, students will encounter a substantial amount of materials dealing with intellectual property topics, although due to time constraints thorough coverage is not feasible. Detailed study is left to the upper-level curriculum; most law schools offer a variety of upper-level intellectual property course offerings. This chapter attempts to provide a rudimentary sketch of the best known intellectual property topics.

A.   Patents

The federal Constitution empowers Congress to "promote the Progress of Science and useful Arts" by granting to "Inventors the exclusive Right to their . . . Discoveries" for a limited time. U.S. Const. art. I, §8. Since passing the first patent statute in 1790, Congress has exercised this power, which the Supreme Court has interpreted as preempting any conflicting state laws, foreclosing the states from issuing patents or adjudicating patent rights.

The federal patent statute requires that an inventor apply for a patent from the United States Patent Office. Today a patent lasts for 20 years from the date of the application for the patent, an increase made by Congress in 1994 from the previous term of 17 years.

The constitutional terms "useful arts," "inventor," and "discoveries" are the foundation of the scope of what is protectable under patent law. Patents are limited to the classes of subject matter set forth in the patent statute. The earliest statute defined the appropriate subject matter as "any useful art, machine, manufacture or composition of matter, or any new and useful improvement [thereon]." Today's subject matter has changed remarkably little. The patent statute now authorizes patents for

1. A process.
2. A machine.
3. An article of manufacture.
4. A composition of matter.
5. An improvement of any of the previous items.

35 U.S.C. §101.

Most patents are *utility patents.* In addition to coming within one of the listed subject matters, the applicant for a patent must establish that the invention has the following three characteristics:

- **Novelty.** The invention must be a new process or thing. If the "invention" already exists, an applicant may not obtain a patent. The test sounds easy, but its application sometimes requires a careful examination of the "prior art" (information previously available to the public). Novelty is defeated if the process or thing was known or used by other persons in the United States or patented or described in a printed publication anywhere in the world. 35 U.S.C. §102. Use by others includes all commercial uses, even uses that are nonpublic and secret. If the public has already had the benefit of the claimed invention, then a patent is no longer available.
- **Utility.** This is a relatively easy standard to meet. The invention must have the prospect of producing a direct benefit for people. The utility requirement does not mean that the claimed invention must be superior to comparable products or processes. One could successfully patent a mousetrap that was inferior in every way to those in the prior

art. If the invention is frivolous or harmful, it lacks utility. In the patent application, the inventor must be able to explain the use of the invention.

- **Non-obviousness.** The invention, at the time it was made, must not have been obvious to a person having ordinary skill in the art to which the subject matter pertains. 35 U.S.C. §103. The person having ordinary skill is a hypothetical person who, although having only ordinary skills, also has a comprehensive knowledge of the prior art. It is hard to imagine a real person having only ordinary skills in the art but encyclopedic knowledge of that art.

The America Invents Act of 2011 made a number of important changes to patent law and the patent issuance process. The most sweeping change is to transform the United States from a "first to invent" to a "first to file" system, which conforms U.S. law to the standard presently followed by virtually all other countries. Under the new law, the first inventor to file, subject to a grace period, is entitled to a patent regardless of another's prior invention.

The patent statute also encourages prompt filing of the patent application. The so-called *statutory bar rule* provides that even if an applicant was the first inventor to file, the application will be denied if certain disabling events occurred within the year preceding the application. 35 U.S.C. §102(b).

A *design patent* is available for an article of manufacture that embodies an ornamental feature. To qualify for a design patent, the invention must meet the requirements of novelty and non-obviousness, just as for a utility patent—though some could argue that these criteria are more difficult to apply than in the case of utility patents. The most important limitation, distinguishing the design from the utility patent, is that the claimed design feature must be primarily ornamental. The design patent is based solely upon the appearance of the item. If the claimed feature can be shown to be "primarily functional," then no design patent can issue. A design patent has a shorter term than a utility patent; it lasts for 15 years from the date the Patent Office issues the patent (extended from 14 to 15 years in 2015).

QUESTION 1. Requisites for a design patent. To be eligible for a design patent, the patented feature of the invention must

A. Be novel.
B. Be non-obvious.
C. Have a practical advantage.
D. Have no practical advantage.
E. Both A and C.
F. Both A and D.
G. All of A, B, and C.
H. All of A, B, and D.

ANALYSIS.   Novelty is required for both utility patents and design patents. Thus, Choice **A** is correct. Similarly, a design patent must be non-obvious, so Choice **B** is correct.

Choices **C** and **D** pose the question: Should the invention have a practical advantage? If the feature for which the design patent is sought has a "practical advantage," then that feature goes beyond being ornamental; it has some functional value. This makes the invention ineligible for a design patent. Thus, **H** is the right answer.

B.   Copyrights

Federal copyright law, like patent law, is authorized by the Constitution, which authorizes Congress to grant to "authors . . . the exclusive right to their . . . writings." U.S. Const. art. I, §8. The first copyright statute, passed in 1790, protected only "maps, charts and books." Subsequently Congress expanded the subject matter eligible for copyright to include almost every form of expression. Although Congress is limited by the Constitution to the protection of a "writing," the Supreme Court has defined the word as any physical manifestation of a person's intellectual labor. This allows copyright for virtually all literary, artistic, and visual works. This includes songs, photographs, movies, video recordings, computer programs, sculptures, and building architecture. The only limitation is that the work of authorship must be reduced to a tangible form.

Since the Copyright Act of 1976, copyright arises as soon as a work is rendered in a tangible form. Federal copyright protection automatically extends to all qualifying works, whether or not the author has published the work. No formal steps, including the affixation of a copyright notice, are required to obtain or maintain a copyright. An author may register a claim to copyright in the United States Copyright Office. Registration and putting a copyright notice on the work are often advantageous, but neither is essential. United States citizens must register as a prerequisite to bringing suit for infringement in federal court.

Copyrights, like patents, are not perpetual. The Constitution allows Congress to grant an exclusive right only "for limited times." The principal justification espoused for the recognition of copyrights and patents is utilitarian. The exclusive right is intended to encourage authors to write and inventors to discover. Absent grants of protection, society would suffer from insufficient investment in the creation of works. In theory, Congress should establish the duration of patents and copyrights based upon an assessment of how long a period is necessary to spur writing and inventing. Today copyrights last for much longer than previously. For most works under the Copyright Act of 1976, the copyright persists for the life of the author plus 70 years.

One important limitation on copyright is what is known as the idea/expression dichotomy. The copyright statute provides: "In no case does copyright protection for an original work of authorship extend to any idea, procedure, process, system, method of operation, concept, principle, or discovery, regardless of the form in which it is described, explained, illustrated, or embodied in such work." 17 U.S.C. §102(b). This section codifies in part the rationale of Baker v. Selden, 101 U.S. 99 (1879), which refused to protect a ledger form that embodied a new bookkeeping system from alleged infringement. The Court stated that the author had no right to prevent others from adopting the author's bookkeeping system. To the extent that the bookkeeping system required the use of a similar ledger form, others could copy the form. They could use and publicize the author's ideas or methods without being guilty of copyright infringement. Only the author's *expression* of ideas or methods, as distinct from the ideas or methods themselves, is copyrightable.

Only an *original* work is entitled to copyright. In *Feist Publications Inc. v. Rural Telephone Co.*, 499 U.S. 340 (1991), the Court explained that originality is required not only by the copyright statute but also by the Constitution; the requirement is implicit in the word "Authors." In *Feist Publications*, the Court denied protection for telephone directory white pages because the publisher's compilation of facts was unoriginal. The directory contained only alphabetized names, addresses, and telephone numbers—the same organization followed by all publishers of white pages. The Court explicitly rejected the publisher's argument, which had some support based on prior case law, that its "sweat of the brow" in collecting the data for the directory justified a claim to copyright.

QUESTION 2. Baseball statistics. Serena, an avid baseball fan, has decided to write and publish a book of statistics on the World Series, the championship series played each October between the two best teams in the National League and the American League. Serena wants as much of the content of her book as possible to be protected by the copyright laws. Which of the following strategies is most likely to improve her prospects for obtaining such protection?

A. Arrange the statistics in a format that is not used in other publications.

B. Add a statement to the book providing that no part of the book may be reproduced or transmitted in any form or by any means, electronic or mechanical.

C. Obtain the permission of the Commissioner of Major League Baseball to publish the book.

D. Make the book more comprehensive than any existing baseball statistics books by including more data, such as the numbers of batters faced by each pitcher.

E. None of the above will help because compilations of statistics are not eligible for copyright.

ANALYSIS. This is a hard question that tests the student's understanding of *Feist Publications.* Choice **E** is wrong. A compilation of statistics, like other compilations, is copyrightable, but the author must demonstrate that her work has the requisite originality.

Choice **C** is not likely to help Serena. The statistics that Serena will assemble and publish are an arrangement of facts—events that happened during World Series games. Facts are not copyrightable. In other words, Major League Baseball does not own the facts or statistics that Serena wants to publish. She does not need the permission of the Commissioner of Baseball to publish her book, and if a third party republishes the statistics from her book, having the Commissioner's permission will not strengthen her claim of copyright infringement.

Likewise, inclusion of the notice described in Choice **B** does not help Serena. Such notices, which are commonly included in printed materials, do not make the materials subject to copyright. One cannot get a copyright simply by announcing that you have one.

We're left with Choices **A** and **D**, both of which have some plausibility. **A** proposes that Serena find a unique format or arrangement for the statistics. **D** proposes that Serena differentiate her book from other publications by including more statistics. Serena needs to be able to make the case that her World Series book, unlike the telephone directory in *Feist Publications,* is original. Either method appears helpful. But **D** poses some risk. If she makes her book of statistics "complete," the court may say that she made no choices with respect to what to include and what to leave out. A lack of selectivity counts against originality. A unique format or arrangement of the statistics, in contrast, does not have this potential vice. Thus, **A** appears to be the better answer, though I confess this is a close call, which some may see the other way.

C.   Trademarks

A trademark is any symbol or device (a "mark") used to identify a product. The identifying mechanism becomes protectable as a trademark when it is distinctive; that is, it points to a particular manufacturer or seller as the origin of the product. Trademark rights develop through usage, as consumers of products learn to associate the mark on a product with a single source.

The rationale for protecting trademarks is different from the rationale for protecting patents and copyrights. There is not thought to be a societal interest in promoting the creation of more trademarks per se. Rather, the goal is to prevent consumer deception. When consumers see a product bearing a certain trademark (such as Nike shoes or Samuel Adams beer), they should be able to expect that the product was made by the manufacturer with whom they are already familiar and with whom they associate the mark.

Trademark law began as part of the common law of torts as an offshoot of the law of deceit. In 1870 Congress passed a statute providing for the registration of trademarks. The Supreme Court struck down the statute because it purported to be an exercise of Congressional power under the Copyright and Patent Clause, and the Court held that trademarks were not within the scope of that clause. *The Trademark Cases*, 100 U.S. 82 (1879). The following century Congress passed new legislation based on the Commerce Clause.

The modern federal law of trademarks is based on the Trademark Act of 1946, popularly known as the Lanham Act, and amended many times. The Lanham Act was first seen as providing for the federal registration of rights created under state law. Trademarks are registered in the United States Patent and Trademark Office. Modern trademark law is a blend of state and federal law. Now the Lanham Act is increasingly understood as the primary locus of substantive trademark law. Suits under the Act may be filed in either federal or state court to protect both registered and unregistered marks.

QUESTION 3.   Two restaurants with the same name. Vicky, a resident of Metropolis, has an idea for opening a new restaurant, where she will cook and serve "down-home" food. She plans to call her establishment "Vick's Vittles." In June, she forms a corporation named "Vick's Vittles Inc." and negotiates to rent a building along the main highway leading into Metropolis. She enters into a lease, takes possession of the premises, installs trade fixtures, and orders furniture. At the same time, she plans her menu and goes to a printing firm and has the menu printed. By mid-August, Vicky's preparations are nearly complete. She plans to open "Vick's Vittles" on September 1.

Antonio owns and operates an existing restaurant, "Antonio's Place," in Metropolis. In mid-August, from a friend he hears somebody is making plans to open a restaurant to be called "Vick's Vittles." Antonio likes this name a lot as he is a big fan of a former National Football League (NFL) star quarterback named Michael Vick. He decides to use the name. On August 28, he changes the name of his restaurant to "Vick's Vittles," immediately changing the exterior signage and the menus. Vicky opens her restaurant on September 1, featuring a menu of very tasty food. Antonio's restaurant serves lower-quality food than Vicky's. On September 10 Vicky sues Antonio for trademark infringement. Who is likely to prevail?

A. Vicky, because she decided to employ the name before Antonio.

B. Vicky, because she used the name before Antonio used the name.

C. Vicky, because she formed the corporation before Antonio used the name.

D. Antonio, because he changed the name for his restaurant before September 1.

E. Antonio, because he acted in good faith.

ANALYSIS.   Vicky is "first in time" with the idea of opening a restaurant in Metropolis named "Vick's Vittles." It may seem that this should be enough for Vicky to receive protection against an interloper like Antonio, but trademark law does not provide the avenue. A trademark is created only by actual use in the marketplace. Choice **A** is wrong because Vicky's state of mind or intention is not relevant to actual use. She didn't reserve the mark by filing an intent-to-use application with the Patent and Trademark Office, something which is permitted since a 1988 amendment to the federal trademark statute. Nor does it matter that Vicky formed a corporation named "Vick's Vittles Inc." before Antonio changed the name of his restaurant to Vick's Vittles. A person cannot obtain trademark rights by incorporating under the name of an intended trademark.

Choice **B** is wrong on the facts once we realize that "use" for trademark law means actual use consisting of sales of the product to consumers. In a different sense, Vicky "used" the name before August 28 (when Antonio opened under Vick's Vittles) by forming the corporation, renting a building, and printing menus, but these preliminary steps are not the type of use that is sufficient to create a trademark.

So Antonio should win. Why? **D** is a better answer than **E**. Good faith is not the point, and arguably Antonio did not act in good faith because he "stole" Vicky's idea. Antonio successfully defends the trademark infringement claim because he began using the trademark (Vick's Vittles) in the relevant market (Metropolis) before Vicky.

D. Trade Secrets

The law of trade secrets protects valuable information that a person has chosen not to disclose publicly. The trade secret may be an invention (a tool or mechanism), a process (the use of a chemical compound), a business plan (an advertising scheme), or a compilation of data (a list of customers). The trade secret must be information that is not generally known. If generally known, of course it is not a "secret." The recipe for the soft drink Coca Cola is said to be a trade secret. A trade secret has value because it confers a competitive advantage. If competitors obtain the trade secret, they are likely to decide to use it for their own products or line of business. Then the trade secret owner will no longer enjoy a market advantage.

To qualify as a trade secret, the owner must make reasonable efforts to guard against disclosure. This generally means that some form of physical security is required. Also, the owner generally must notify persons who are given access to the information that they must keep the information confidential.

There is some argument over whether trade secret law is a form of intellectual property or whether it is a tort law concept grounded principally on confidential relations. Many but not all of the trade secret cases involve alleged disclosures made by employees of the company that owns the secret. In that case, and in similar cases involving disclosures by other persons connected with the company, such as agents and partners, the wrong is readily described as breach of contract or breach of confidential relations.

Unlike the protection afforded by a patent, ownership of a trade secret does not ensure that a competitor may not use the trade secret. A competitor who discovers the trade secret on its own may use it. It is commonly said that a trade secret is protected from use by a competitor who discovers it by improper means. The Restatement of Torts proposes a broad view of improper means, which a number of courts have followed. It provides:

> *Improper means of discovery.* The discovery of another's trade secret by improper means subjects the actor to liability independently of the harm to the interest in the secret. Thus, if one uses physical force to take a secret formula from another's pocket, or breaks into another's office to steal the formula, his conduct is wrongful and subjects him to liability apart from the rule stated in this Section. Such conduct is also an improper means of procuring the secret under this rule. But means may be improper under this rule even though they do not cause any other harm than that to the interest in the trade secret. Examples of such means are fraudulent misrepresentations to induce disclosure, tapping of telephone wires, eavesdropping or other espionage. A complete catalogue of improper means is not possible. In general they are means which fall below the generally accepted standards of commercial morality and reasonable conduct.

Restatement of Torts §757, comment *f* (1939).

A trade secret has no set duration. It lasts as long as the secret has value and secrecy is maintained. With respect to inventions, trade secret law and patent law are alternate, mutually exclusive, methods of protection. A patent application, subject to some exceptions, requires disclosure to the Patent Office of the invention, and then to the public 18 months after filing, foreclosing any possibility that the invention remain a trade secret. Due to the cost of the patent process and the limited term for patents (20 years), some inventors decide to rely on the law of trade secrets if the invention has a nature that allows realization of its value without making the secret readily ascertainable.

QUESTION 4.   Duplicating a new recipe. Three months ago the famous chef, Chef Fumer, invented a masterpiece named "Strawberry Squid Linguine," which he served to great acclaim at his restaurant, Fumer's Fire. A competing restaurant, Borrowdale, wanted to add the dish to its menu. Borrowdale's chef phoned Chef Fumer, asking him if he would share the recipe with Borrowdale. Chef Fumer refused. Borrowdale sent one of its employees to dine at Fumer's Fire. The employee ordered Strawberry Squid Linguine, ate part of the dish, and then asked the waitress to put the rest in a "to go" box. The waitress said that no one had ever made that request before—"they always finish our most delectable dish" — but she complied. Borrowdale then subjected the remaining portion of Strawberry Squid Linguine to chemical analysis and succeeded in replicating the dish. Fumer's Fire lost business to Borrowdale after the latter restaurant added Strawberry Squid Linguine to its menu. Fumer's Fire brings an action against Borrowdale, seeking to recover for the wrongful appropriation of its trade secret. Who should prevail?

A. Fumer's Fire because Borrowdale obtained the recipe by improper means.

B. Fumer's Fire because it lost revenues due to Borrowdale's appropriation of the recipe.

C. Fumer's Fire because Borrowdale knew that Fumer's Fire did not want Borrowdale to obtain the recipe.

D. Borrowdale because Fumer's Fire publicly disclosed the recipe.

E. Borrowdale because Fumer's Fire did not take sufficient measures to safeguard the recipe.

ANALYSIS. Let's start with Choice **B**. Proof of lost revenues is important to Fumer's Fire because it demonstrates that the secret recipe has commercial value. This choice is plausible *if we conclude that Fumer's Fire should win* because they can establish all the elements for a wrongful taking of a trade secret.

Choice **C** asserts that it is relevant that Borrowdale knows that Fumer's Fire wants to keep the recipe secret. It is not. A person is allowed to use a competitor's trade secret if the person acquires that secret by lawful means, and this is true even if the person knows that the competitor desperately wants to maintain sole possession of the secret.

Let's look at **A**. Did Borrowdale obtain the recipe by improper means? There is no confidential relation present here. Chef Fumer and Borrowdale's chef had a telephone conversation. They were not fiduciaries; they were dealing at arm's length. It was Borrowdale's employee, not Fumer's Fire's employee, who took the sample to Borrowdale to be tested. Nor does it appear that Borrowdale's employee deceived the waitress. The waitress undoubtedly assumed that the diner wanted to finish eating the dish later, at home, but the employee made no express promise. The means by which Borrowdale obtained the secret recipe seem proper. What Borrowdale did was a type of *reverse engineering* (discovering the composition or technology of an object by analysis of its structure, function, and operation), which is considered a legitimate way for a person to learn a competitor's trade secret.

If we had a choice opposite to **A**, which said "Borrowdale should prevail because it obtained the recipe by proper means," we would pick it as the best answer. But alas we don't. Borrowdale should win. Given the two remaining choices we do have, which is better? Choice **D** says Borrowdale wins because Fumer's Fire publicly disclosed the recipe. This is wrong factually. There is no indication that Fumer's Fire ever told the recipe to anyone outside of the restaurant, and the waitress's letting Borrowdale's employee take the uneaten portion is not public disclosure *of the recipe*.

Only **E** is left standing. It's debatable whether Fumer's Fire took reasonable and sufficient measures to safeguard the recipe. To their credit, they did not publicly disclose the recipe. Conceivably Fumer's Fire could have better guarded the secret by not letting customers take an uneaten portion of Strawberry Squid Linguine home with them. This may have rankled some customers as a violation of a norm customarily followed by restaurants. But if Fumer's Fire foresaw the risk of reverse engineering and cared enough about keeping the recipe secret, they could have adopted such a policy and instructed their waitstaff to enforce it. **E** is the best of the choices out there.

E.   Misappropriation

Misappropriation is a type of unfair competition claim. The common law action of misappropriation was birthed by the famous case of *International News Service v. Associated Press*, 248 U.S. 215 (1918), which holds that a news service has a "quasi-property" interest in the news that it collects, which continues after publication of the news for a short time period, while that news still has commercial value. Thus, the defendant International News Service (INS), a rival news service, could not take that news and republish it for its subscribers. Such conduct constituted the "misappropriation" of the first publisher's work, the plaintiff Associated Press (AP).

Since *International News Service* was decided, the doctrine of misappropriation has had a checkered history. The elements of the action are vague. No clear rules define when the borrowing of another person's information, practices, or ideas is inappropriate. Some commentators have criticized misappropriation as unnecessary and counterproductive, given the parameters of the better-defined realms of patent, copyright, trademark, and trade secret. A number of courts have refused to extend *International News Service* beyond its news gathering setting. *International News Service* is no longer part of federal law since the Court's subsequent decision in *Erie Railroad v. Tompkins*, 304 U.S. 64 (1938) (holding federal courts must apply state law, not federal common law, in diversity cases).

Nevertheless, a number of states still follow the misappropriation theory of *International News Service* as part of their common law. Complicated preemption issues arise when the state misappropriation claim intersects with federal patent law or federal copyright law. If the work is patented, due to preemption the infringer can be liable only for patent infringement; not also for state law misappropriation. Under certain circumstances, preemption applies if the work is patentable (but not patented) or it meets the requirements for a federal copyright.

> **QUESTION 5.   Duplicating a new recipe revisited.** Assume all the facts of Question 4 are the same, except that Fumer's Fire brings a different cause of action. Instead of suing for the wrongful use of a trade secret, Fumer's Fire claims that Borrowdale has misappropriated its recipe. The action is brought in a jurisdiction that follows *International News Service*. Who should prevail?
>
> A.   Fumer's Fire because it has a "quasi-property" interest in the recipe.
> B.   Fumer's Fire because competitors are not allowed to imitate the products of others.
> C.   Borrowdale because it acquired the recipe by proper means.
> D.   Borrowdale because Fumer's Fire publicly disclosed the recipe.
> E.   Borrowdale because Fumer's Fire did not take sufficient measures to safeguard the recipe.

ANALYSIS.   This question is designed only for students who have read the case of *International News Service*. Misappropriation is difficult to test in a multiple-choice format because it is open-ended and amorphous. Asking "who should prevail" in the abstract would be appropriate for an essay exam question, but it would be impossible (i.e., unfair) in a multiple-choice question that gave you only two choices, the parties' names, with no accompanying rationales.

In an attempt to make this question work, I've limited the field by stipulating that the jurisdiction follows *International News Service*. That is something, but it leaves much still open. A jurisdiction could "follow" the case but read it narrowly; or it might embrace the underlying rationale wholeheartedly, applying it to a wide-ranging host of different settings.

I've tried to give weak rationales for all three of the "Borrowdale prevails" choices. All three point to elements of the law of trade secrets. They do not address the contours (admittedly vague) of the misappropriation doctrine or the principled criticisms of misappropriation that are commonly made. Choice **C** asserts that Borrowdale acquired the recipe by proper means. That's not a defense to misappropriation. In *International News Service*, the INS acquired the AP's news by buying newspapers and by reading news on AP's published bulletins, which was proper. As for Choice **D**, Fumer's Fire probably did not publicly disclose the recipe, but even if it did, that would not necessarily foreclose a misappropriation claim because AP publicly disclosed its news before the INS appropriated it. Likewise, Choice **E** appears to be beside the point because *International News Service* allows a person to disclose information publicly and yet stop a competitor from taking advantage of the value of that information.

So if Fumer's Fire wins on its misappropriation claim, what's the best reason? Choice **B** is way too broad. As a general matter, competitors are allowed to imitate the products of others. Otherwise the first person to come out with a new product, service, or business plan would have a monopoly, which presumably might last forever. The misappropriation doctrine is an exception to the principle that normally we allow competition based on latecomers imitating the first firm.

We're left with Choice **A**, which is conclusory but tracks the explanation given in the majority opinion of *International News Service*. The Court said that the AP had a "quasi-property" interest in the news it gathered, which justified an injunction prohibiting the INS from appropriating that news while it still had market value. Similarly, if Fumer's Fire prevails, one could say it has a "quasi-property" interest in the recipe, making it wrongful for Borrowdale to profit by using the same recipe without the consent of Fumer's Fire.

F.   Right of Publicity

During the latter part of the twentieth century, courts began to recognize the right of publicity, which many people consider to be a new form of private property. The right of publicity was derived from an earlier creation of tort law, the right to privacy. Advertisers sometimes used a person's picture or name without the person's consent, and some courts began awarding relief based on the idea that this was an invasion of privacy, which harmed the person's dignity or reputation. The plaintiffs were generally not celebrities; they were persons who could be presumed to want to maintain a zone of privacy.

The right of publicity cases that followed were different from the privacy cases. Plaintiffs in the early publicity cases were celebrities who were commercially exploiting some feature of their persona, such as their name, picture, image, or voice. They were earning money by exploiting their persona, either directly or by contracting with other entities, such as advertising and merchandizing firms. They could not plausibly claim to be seeking to maintain a private sphere for their lives. Rather, they sought to stop persons with whom they had not contracted from exploiting their persona. Courts in a number of states recognized a cause of action for invasion of the right of publicity.

Tort law traditionally has considered privacy rights to be personal in that they end when the person concerned dies. At first courts struggled with the question whether the right of publicity should end at the person's death or instead pass by will or by intestate succession to the heirs. The early cases were split, but eventually a large majority of courts decided in favor of inheritability of the right of publicity. Also, many states, including California, passed publicity-rights statutes, which codify and modify the common-law right of publicity and make the right inheritable and devisable for a fixed period of time after the owner's death (70 years in California).

QUESTION 6.   Graffiti art. The world-famous graffiti artist Bankhead was paid $500,000 to paint a mural on the wall of a commercial building in downtown Los Angeles, California. The mural includes caricatures of four famous actors and actresses, including film star Bonnie Parks. All observers instantly recognize Park's likeness in the mural. Parks did not consent to Bankhead's use of her image. She brings a cause of action for damages against Bankhead. If the court holds in favor of Parks, the most likely reason is that defendant has interfered with her:

A. Trademark.

B. Real property.

C. Right of privacy.

D. Copyright.

E. Easement rights.

F. Intangible property.

ANALYSIS.   This is an easy question, which will not trip up students who have a decent understanding of the right of publicity. The fact pattern resembles the Tiger Woods case, found in some property casebooks, in which the court rejected Woods' right of publicity claim brought against an artist who produced limited-edition art prints commemorating Woods' victory at the Masters Golf Tournament. *ETW Corporation v. Jireh Publishing, Inc.*, 332 F.3d 915 (6th Cir. 2003). The court found that the print had original creative content added by the artist and that a celebrity's publicity right is limited by the public interest in promoting freedom of expression.

A student would expect to find "Right of Publicity" as one of the answer choices, but alas it's not there! So the point is to decide whether "right of publicity" fits within one of the choices given. The two IP answers (Choice **A** trademark, Choice **D** copyright) are wrong. Parks does not have a trademark in her image, and she has not authored anything that the defendant might be infringing. Choice **C** might look attractive because the right of publicity evolved from the earlier tort-law concept of the right of privacy. However, Parks is a famous actress, and her claim has nothing to do with wanting to keep her image or other aspects of her life or persona private.

This leaves Choice **F** as the correct answer. The right of publicity is one type of intangible personal property, like the other forms of IP.

QUESTION 7.   War heroine. During the war in Iraq in 2003, United States Special Forces staged a dramatic rescue of Private Jessica Lynch, who had been taken prisoner by the enemy. Almost instantly, the media turned its spotlight on Lynch, canonizing her as a war hero. Shortly thereafter, a company named All-American T-Shirts began producing and selling Jessica Lynch t-shirts without her permission. The shirt bears a photograph of Lynch in uniform, which All-American obtained by downloading an image from a news website account of her rescue. Under the photograph, the shirt has the words, "Jessica Lynch, All-American Fighting Angel." Lynch files an action against All-American, asserting that All-American has interfered with her right of publicity. If you were arguing on behalf of All-American, which of the following facts would best support your argument?

A. All-American obtained the permission of the Government to sell the shirts.

B. All-American did not act with malice and did not charge in excess of a reasonable price for the shirts.

C. All-American obtained Lynch's photograph in good faith from a reputable source.

D. Lynch did not intend to become famous.

E. Lynch did not intend to benefit her heirs.

ANALYSIS. Choices **B** and **C** are variations of an argument that All-American acted in good faith and did not knowingly interfere with Lynch's right of publicity. But intention to cause harm is not one of the elements of a case for interference with the right of publicity. A defendant may be held liable for interfering with a person's publicity rights even if the defendant reasonably believed its actions were legal or privileged.

Choice **E** is flawed because Lynch is alive; she is the plaintiff. If she has a publicity right based on the events in Iraq that made her famous, it does not matter whether the jurisdiction views the right of publicity as inheritable or noninheritable.

Choice **A** may be attractive to students. It rests upon the premise that the government, and not Lynch, is the owner of any publicity rights associated with Lynch's military service and rescue. The government employed Lynch, and the events took place during a military action. But the claim has weaknesses. Although the government may have the right to disclose to a private entity such as All-American the story of the rescue and to authorize the display of some government-owned objects associated with the rescue, All-American has used Lynch's photograph on the shirt. When employers use photographs of their employees for the employer's commercial gain, usually they expressly bargain for the right.

Choice **D** at first doesn't sound like a right answer, but it's the best of the five arguments for All-American to make. Cases developing the right to publicity involve celebrities who clearly intended to become famous. A large part of the rationale for recognition of the right of publicity is to protect expectations formed while the person is building a career and to encourage investment in enterprises that exploit publicity values. Lynch became famous due to luck, not due to ambition or a plan. Although a few courts have extended publicity rights to persons who became famous unintentionally, this is not universally accepted. Arguably Lynch has no right to publicity. Though she should have a right to privacy, that's not the claim she has brought.

G.   The Closer: Distinguishing among the IP Categories

It is challenging, especially for beginning students, to distinguish among the various intellectual property categories when presented with a fact situation that doesn't telegraph the relevant category. When confronted by such a fact pattern in an essay exam, a number of students head off on tangents by discussing several IP subject matters, even though some make little sense. But when confronted by such a question cast in the multiple-choice format, the student must decide. There is no opportunity to waffle.

> QUESTION 8.   A hotel guide. Bill visits all of the hotels in Big City, putting down the names, addresses, telephone numbers, types of rooms and suites, amenities, and room rates for each establishment. At each place he also inquires as to the discount programs that are available. Bill includes all of the above information in a booklet, which he labels "Bill's Hotel Guide." Bill then sells the booklet to the public for $15 per copy. Judy buys one booklet for $15. She uses her scanner to prepare a computer file that has the entire contents of the booklet. She then uploads this file to her website, where she sells the information to anyone who pays her $6. Each buyer is allowed to download the file. Bill finds out about this and sues Judy. Bill's best claim is based upon his ownership of a:
>
> A. Trademark.
> B. Trade secret.
> C. Copyright.
> D. Patent.
> E. Right of publicity.

ANALYSIS.   The three weakest choices are trade secret, patent, and right of publicity. A compilation of data could become a trade secret, but the compiler must make reasonable efforts to maintain the secrecy of the data. Here Bill has done the opposite. Rather than guard the data from disclosure, he has chosen to sell it to members of the general public.

Bill has not filed a patent application and for good reason. His booklet is not eligible for a patent. The patent statute limits patents to an "invention or discovery," which not surprisingly are construed not to include books and other printed materials.

Bill may have a right to publicity (this is more likely if he is famous), but even if he does, Judy is not exploiting Bill's publicity value. Judy's customers are not paying money to obtain a picture or image of Bill. They are buying the data Bill created to facilitate their purchases of hotel rooms in Big City.

We're left with trademark and copyright. The title of Bill's booklet, "Bill's Hotel Guide," may be eligible for protection as a trademark. It may become sufficiently distinctive if an association develops. Members of the public might associate Bill's name with his hotel guide. This would become more likely if Bill publishes other guides, such as "Bill's Hotel Guide for Little City." Bill's complaint, however, does not seem to be trademark infringement. Judy is not selling her own hotel guide under the name "Bill's Hotel Guide." Rather, she is selling Bill's information on her website, and it isn't clear whether she is displaying the title "Bill's Hotel Guide" or whether she has stripped that heading.

Choice **C**, copyright, is the best answer. Judy has copied all of Bill's information, without modification or rearrangement, and is selling it. This is the core of copyright infringement. Judy may have a defense; perhaps Bill's work is not sufficiently original to merit copyright protection. But if Bill is to prevail in an action against Judy, almost certainly his claim has to be based on copyright.

 ## Smith's Picks

1. Requisites for a design patent   **H**
2. Baseball statistics   **A**
3. Two restaurants with the same name   **D**
4. Duplicating a new recipe   **E**
5. Duplicating a new recipe revisited   **A**
6. Graffiti art   **F**
7. War heroine   **D**
8. A hotel guide   **C**

6

Adverse Possession of Real Property

"A thing which you have enjoyed and used as your own for a long time,
whether property or an opinion, takes root in your being and cannot be torn
away without your resenting the act and trying to defend yourself,
however you came by it."
Oliver Wendell Holmes, *The Path of the Law,*
10 HARV. L. REV. 457, 477 (1897)

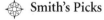
The law recognizes a number of different methods for the acquisition of property. Usually a person acquires title to previously owned property through a transaction in which the prior owner voluntarily relinquishes ownership. Sales and gifts are effective based upon the actual or presumed intent of the seller or donor. Similarly, transfers at death, whether by devise or inheritance, rest upon the decedent's actual or presumed intent.

The doctrine of adverse possession is also a method for the acquisition of title, but it is radically different. Under the law of adverse possession, a person who takes possession of property without the consent or permission of the owner and thereafter maintains possession for a long time may acquire title. The prior ownership is extinguished.

Almost every property course spends some time on the law of adverse possession. The topic is interesting and challenging. With respect to land, adverse possession disputes are often litigated, generating a substantial body of case law in all states. This chapter addresses the standard elements for adverse possession of real property. The next chapter treats adverse possession of personal property.

A.   The Basic Concept: Wrongful Possession

Wrongful possessors of property, by definition, have liability to the true owner. For real property, the true owner may bring a trespass action. For chattels, the owner may recover in replevin or trover. All states have statutes of limitation, which require that the owner file the action within a specified period of time. The doctrine of adverse possession is based upon the running of that statute. The law of adverse possession determines when the statute of limitations has expired. It also serves to transfer ownership to the wrongful possessor, who is treated as the recipient of a new title to the property. The new title is a fee simple absolute, with one exception. When the title to the property was divided between a present estate and a future interest before the adverse possession began, the adverse possessor acquired only the interest of the present possessor.

The core of the doctrine of adverse possession, not surprisingly, is the concept of possession. In the law of property, "possession" is fundamental but evasive. Not every trespasser is in "possession" of land, even when the conduct that constitutes the trespass is repeated. At least some physical occupation of the land is necessary. The precise minimum amount of physical presence cannot be quantified. The *actual possession* requirement means that the claimant's conduct or activities must be extensive enough to rise to the level of "possession." It is commonly said that the trespasser must establish actual possession of the property in question.

> **QUESTION 1.   Laying down a mobile home.** Elsie finds an unoccupied one-acre tract of rural land. She buys a used mobile home, which she places near one of the front corners of the tract. Elsie uses the mobile home as her residence, living there continually with the exception of infrequent, short vacations. Immediately adjacent to the home she plants

a small area with grass and flowers, which she thereafter maintains in a neat and attractive condition. Elsie has two dogs, which she lets run loose whenever she lets them outside her home. They wander throughout the one-acre tract. Elsie notices that along the rear boundary of the tract there are wild blackberry bushes. They bear fruit annually, and each year she picks berries, which she eats and shares with friends and relatives. Assuming that Elsie's activities continue for a period longer than the relevant statute of limitations, Elsie may obtain title by adverse possession to the following part of the tract:

A. None of the tract.
B. The area on which the mobile home rests.
C. The area on which the mobile home rests and the area with grass and flowers.
D. The area on which the mobile home rests, the area with grass and flowers, and the area with the blackberry bushes.
E. All of the tract.

ANALYSIS.   Elsie may acquire title only for those parts of the tract that she has possessed. That limitation is implicit in the name of the doctrine — title by adverse *possession*. The land physically covered by a substantial improvement, such as a home, obviously qualifies as "actual possession." That it is a "mobile home" makes no difference. Our facts assume that Elsie keeps the home in a single location for longer than the statutory limitations period.

Planting grass and flowers by itself might not qualify as actual possession. A one-time planting, with no subsequent use of the area or maintenance, clearly would be insufficient. But the facts state that she has maintained it, which necessarily requires regular use. Presumably Elsie uses the area as a homeowner normally uses her yard. She should be considered in actual possession of this space.

Elsie's activities with respect to the remainder of the tract are not sufficient. She did not plant the blackberry bushes, and picking berries would involve occasional entries over no more than several weeks per year. Passage over other parts of the tract by Elsie's dogs is a less intensive use than picking berries and does not support a conclusion that she has taken possession of the entire tract. **C** is the right answer.

B.   Standard Elements and Policies

The statute of limitations for the recovery of land usually just states the number of years within which the action must be filed. The courts, however, have specified a number of elements that the adverse possessor must prove in order to gain the protection of the statute. The five traditional ingredients of adverse possession are

- Actual possession (previously discussed in Section A)
- Open and notorious possession
- Hostile and adverse possession
- Exclusive possession
- Continuous possession

The courts evaluate the necessary elements over a continuum of time. All the elements must both exist and continue for the number of years specified by the statute of limitations.

Some states impose additional requirements. In several jurisdictions, the subjective good faith of the adverse possessor is required, expressly or by implication. Other states require that the possessor have "color of title" to the property or prove that the possessor has paid the real estate taxes, either across the board or for a particular type of adverse possession claim.

Courts and commentators have offered several policy justifications for the doctrine of adverse possession:

- First, there is a public interest in "quieting title" to land by cutting off old claims.
- Second, landowners who neglect to assert their property rights for a period longer than the statute of limitations merit punishment. They are negligent stewards who have "slept" on their rights.
- Third, there are reliance interests to protect. Due to the length of time, either the adverse possessor or other persons who have dealt with the adverse possessor are justifiable in relying on a continuation of the status quo. With respect to the adverse possessor, the reliance rationale is especially strong when the claimant took possession with a good faith belief that he had acquired good title.
- Last, an efficiency rationale is based upon the goal of promoting land development. Those persons who use and improve land and cause it to be productive are rewarded because they have added to the community's resources. Along with the reliance rationale, the efficiency perspective can support a conclusion that the adverse possessor has "earned" ownership rights.
- Some of these policies overlap, and some may be more persuasive than others. However, the outcomes in litigated cases often turn upon which policy or policies the court seeks to apply.

QUESTION 2.   Requiring payment of taxes. Under the present adverse possession laws of State X, payment of taxes by the true owner or the adverse possessor has no bearing on whether the statute of limitations has expired, vesting the adverse possessor with title. The state legislature is considering passing a statute that will require that the adverse possessor pay real estate taxes for a period of at least five years as a condition to obtaining title. Which of the following policy rationales for adverse possession best supports the proposed statute?

A. A possessor who fails to pay taxes cannot have a good faith belief that the possessor had title.
B. The possessor's payment of taxes ensures that the true owner has notice of the possessor's claim.
C. The requirement of payment of taxes ensures that the possessor has made valuable improvements to the property.
D. The possessor who pays taxes has a stake in the property that is worth protecting.
E. Third parties have an interest that is worth protecting because they are likely to rely on the possessor's payment of taxes.

ANALYSIS.   There is a logical connection between the payment of taxes and the possessor's beliefs about ownership. Usually a person who pays real estate taxes will have a good faith belief that she is paying taxes on property that she owns. But Choice **A** is wrong because it states this idea absolutely ("cannot have a good faith belief"). In mistaken boundary cases, it is common for the adverse possessor to pay taxes on a tract she owns but not on the part of the neighbor's tract being claimed by adverse possession. Also, a person can fail to pay taxes unwittingly; for example, due to simple neglect or a mistaken belief that someone else such as a lender or a relative would pay.

Similarly, **B** is a weak answer because of its categorical language. The possessor's payment of taxes might tip off the true owner that there is a problem. If both the true owner and the possessor make payment, the taxing authority may notify the true owner of the duplicate payment. If the true owner doesn't pay the taxes and learns, surprisingly, that there is no delinquency (nothing is due), the true owner may learn who paid the taxes. But this is not certain to happen. Thus, a statutory requirement that an adverse possessor pay taxes would not "ensure" that the true owner receives notice of the adverse possessor's claim.

C is wrong. Real estate taxes are due whether or not the adverse possessor adds new improvements to the land. The possessor may pay taxes whether the land is unimproved, contains old improvements, or contains new improvements added by the possessor.

Both **D** and **E** invoke the reliance theory of adverse possession. **E** identifies a reliance interest of third parties, but this is unlikely. Third parties may rely upon the general appearance that an adverse possessor has title. Such reliance, however, does not depend upon the possessor's payment of taxes and is not likely to be enhanced by tax payment. **D** simply states that a taxpaying adverse possessor has a stake or interest that merits protection. By paying taxes the possessor is making an investment in the property, much the same as when the possessor adds improvements. In so doing, the possessor can be said to rely upon the expectation of continued ownership. **D** is stronger.

C. Adverse Possession and Record Title

The law of adverse possession as applied to land has two substantial impacts on the recording system, which contains records used to establish title. First, adverse possession strengthens record titles by barring the potential claims of persons who are not in possession of a parcel of land after a specified period of time has elapsed, provided that certain conditions are met. By extinguishing old claims, the record title of the present possessor is enhanced.

The second impact is a drawback with respect to the quality of the land records. Adverse possession often modifies the boundary line between neighbors when the parties' actual possession has diverged from the true boundary line as reflected by deeds and other records. The consequence is that the boundary line shown by the records is no longer accurate because the fact of adverse possession is not displayed by any public record prior to the initiation of litigation between the parties.

> **QUESTION 3.** **A problematic chain of title.** Three years ago Kabeer bought a single-family house on a half-acre lot. Kabeer is considering selling his house, and in preparation he has ordered a title search for his property. The search has revealed a warranty deed in the chain of title, executed and recorded 14 years ago, that contains a discrepancy. The typed part of the deed identifies as the grantor "James Charles Smith," but the signature on the deed appears to read "Jamie Smith." Kabeer has consulted a lawyer, who advises Kabeer that there is some risk that a person named "James Charles Smith" might appear and claim that he did not sign the deed in question. The lawyer also advises that there is a good possibility that if this happens the law of adverse possession would bar such a claim by Smith. If litigation is commenced and a court holds that the law of adverse possession bars Smith's claim, what effect will this judicial action have on record title to Kabeer's property?
>
> A. It will improve the quality of Kabeer's record title because the court will order the warranty deed in question removed from the public land records.
> B. It will improve the quality of Kabeer's record title because a purchaser from Kabeer will not be able to raise an objection to marketable title.
> C. It will diminish the quality of Kabeer's record title because title acquired by adverse possession is generally not considered to be marketable.
> D. It will diminish the quality of Kabeer's record title because the court's judgment transfers to Kabeer land that was owned by Smith.
> E. It will have no effect because the warranty deed in question will still be part of the public land records.

ANALYSIS. Choices **A** and **E** both contain propositions directed to the status of the 14-year-old warranty deed as a recorded instrument. Once an instrument is recorded, it remains a part of the public land records even if subsequent events, including litigation, demonstrate that the instrument has a defect or there is some other problem associated with it. Even when a court rules that a recorded deed has no operative legal effect, the deed still remains in the records. Thus, **A** is wrong.

Although **E** contains a correct statement as to the status of the warranty deed in the records, it is wrong for a different reason. The adverse possession litigation has an effect on the quality of Kabeer's title to the property. The judgment means that Smith no longer has an ownership interest. Does this judgment improve or detract from the quality of Kabeer's title? **C** asserts that it diminishes the quality of Kabeer's record title. It is generally true that a title founded on adverse possession is not marketable, but what is meant by that statement is that title based on adverse possession is unmarketable in the absence of litigation decided in the favor of the adverse possessor. Here a court has held against Smith, who has an old claim based upon the records, and in favor of the adverse possessor, Kabeer.

Choice **D** is incorrect. A plausible interpretation of the judgment is that it transfers or confirms an interest held by Smith to Kabeer, but if so, this strengthens rather than diminishes Kabeer's record title.

We're left with **B** as the best answer. After the conclusion of the litigation with Smith, a buyer of Kabeer's property will not be able to raise a meritorious title objection based on the discrepancy in the signature on the warranty deed. This has made Kabeer's title marketable. It is important to realize that it is marketable because the court's judgment has become a record. A new title search will retrieve the judgment, with the title searcher concluding that the judgment has a beneficial effect on Kabeer's title.

D. Color of Title and Constructive Adverse Possession

Color of title consists of a deed or other instrument that purports to transfer title to the adverse possessor. The deed or instrument constituting color of title is invalid or defective for some reason, and this induces the grantee to rely upon adverse possession in order to overcome the defect. Color of title serves two roles. First, in many states, a statute expressly requires color of title for certain adverse possession claims. Some states, for example, allow a shorter period of limitation for a claimant with color of title.

Second, color of title allows the adverse possessor to use the doctrine of constructive adverse possession. Constructive adverse possession is an exception to the requirement that the claimant must be in actual possession of all of the disputed land. If the claimant has actual possession of part of the land described in the color of title, the claimant also gains title to the unoccupied part. The adverse possessor is said to be in "constructive possession" of the entire parcel. To use the doctrine, the possessor must have had a good faith belief in the validity of the color of title (the deed purporting to convey title).

QUESTION 4. Four lots in a row. Fourteen years ago, Ophelia inherited the fee simple ownership of four contiguous subdivision lots, labeled on the subdivision map as Lots 1, 2, 3, and 4 (see diagram below). Each lot is the same size. Ophelia did not take possession of any of the property. Twelve years ago, Francine, who had no legitimate claim to any of the lots, signed and delivered to Pedro a warranty deed that purported to convey Lots 1, 2, and 3 to Pedro. That year Pedro took possession of the front half of Lot 2 and built a cabin, and since then he has remained in possession. Occasionally he has parked his truck on part of Lot 3 next to the street. The statute of limitations for the recovery of real property is ten years.

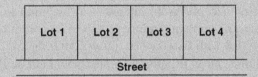

Pedro has gained title by adverse possession to

A. Lots 1 through 4.
B. All of Lot 2.
C. All of Lots 2 and 3.
D. All of Lots 1, 2, and 3.
E. The part of Lot 2 that he possessed.

ANALYSIS. This question deals with the concept of constructive possession under color of title. The deed from Francine to Pedro is invalid because Ophelia, not Francine, owns all the lots. Because there is no indication in the facts that Pedro knew the deed was invalid, he is entitled to the benefit of constructive possession.

Without color of title and constructive possession, **E** would be the correct answer. But Pedro is claiming under color of title. Building the cabin on part of the land described in his deed is sufficient to include all of the land described in the deed. Some authorities indicate that to use constructive possession, (1) all the land must be contiguous and (2) the occupied part cannot be extremely small compared to the remainder, but neither of these rules presents a problem with respect to Pedro's claim. Pedro cannot acquire Lot 4 because it was not included in the deed. Parking the truck on Lot 3 on occasion does not rise to the level of possession, and it makes no difference to the outcome in this question. The only reason Pedro obtains Lots 1 and 3 is because of their inclusion in the deed. **D** is the right answer.

E.   Open and Notorious Possession

The claimant's activities must provide some form of visible evidence that the property is being adversely used. If they provide visible evidence of adverse use, then they are said to be "open and notorious" acts of possession. This enables a true owner, who acts diligently, to discover the trespass before the statute of limitations expires and take appropriate action.

Courts generally use the terms "open" and "notorious" as synonyms, but each word has a distinctive flavor. Openness is from the standpoint of the wrongful possessor. A possessor acts openly if there is no attempt to conceal or hide the activities.

Notoriety, on the other hand, implies some level of community awareness or knowledge of the possessor's actions. The physical acts must be of a nature that imparts notice to the local community and thus to the true owner, who is presumed to be an interested member of that community.

QUESTION 5.   Nighttime parking. For longer than anyone can remember, Joe has worked the night shift at Joe's Bar & Grill, which is open 24 hours a day. He arrives at work at 10 PM and leaves for home at 6:30 AM. Joe's Bar & Grill does not have a parking lot. Next door to Joe's Bar & Grill is an office building, which has a row of parking spaces along the boundary separating the two neighboring parcels. The office building and the parking lot are almost completely empty every night. Despite a sign that warns parking is only for office tenants and their guests, Joe parks in the office building parking lot every night and always in the same space (the one closest to Joe's Bar & Grill). Joe's parking practice continues for more than ten years, which is the statutory period for adverse possession in the jurisdiction. The best argument that Joe has **not** acquired title by adverse possession to the parking space he has used is

A. Joe lacks color of title to the parking space.
B. Joe did not take actual possession of the parking space.
C. The owner of the office building did not have actual knowledge of Joe's use of the parking space.
D. Joe's use of the parking space was not hostile or adverse.
E. Joe did not take open possession of the parking space.

ANALYSIS.   Choice **A** asserts that Joe does not have color of title to the parking space. It is true that Joe lacks color of title—there is no deed or another writing that purports to give him the right to possess or use that space. But this answer is weak because a person like Joe may acquire title by adverse possession without having color of title. There are advantages for an adverse possessor who has color of title, but a meritorious claim is possible without color of title.

Let's turn to Choice **C**. It may be true that the owner of the office building is not aware of Joe's nighttime parking (the facts say nothing about this either way). But the true owner's actual knowledge of the adverse use is not required for the adverse possessor to gain title.

Choice **D** is wrong because a sign prohibits Joe from parking at the office building. There is no indication that the owner of the office building consented, expressly or by implication, to Joe's use. A court should find that his parking is hostile and adverse.

We're down to our final two choices, **B** and **E**. Is it more likely that a court would say Joe's nighttime parking is not *actual* possession or that it is not *open* possession? The occasional parking of a car, even if it is always in the same space, might not rise to the level of the parker "possessing" the space. A person may trespass without being in possession of the area where the trespass occurs. Joe, however, is parking in the same space, evidently every night, and leaving his car there for many hours. This probably rises to the level of "possession." Even though his parking amounts to actual possession, a court could logically say it is not open possession because it is visible only to a person inspecting the parking lot at night. Joe may win the case, but if he loses, a likely explanation is that his possession was not open. **E** is the best answer.

F.   Hostile and Adverse Possession

The possession must be "adverse" or "hostile," which are often but not always understood as synonymous. At a minimum, this requirement means that the person was in wrongful possession, not rightful possession, of the land. If the possession was wrongful, then by definition the true owner had a cause of action for trespass. Possession is adverse only if it is without the authority or permission of the true owner of the land. If the possession is rightful during a particular period of time, then the true owner could not have filed a complaint and the statute of limitations was not then running. A rightful possessor, if that person is in fact in "possession," is necessarily some type of tenant.

Many cases have required more than this, interpreting "hostile possession" to require that the possessor have a certain state of mind. The possessor must "intend" to acquire title to the disputed property. This intent component of hostility has frequently arisen in the mistaken boundary cases. The basic issue is whether the adverse possessor's subjective intent may serve to cause the possession to be deemed nonhostile and, thus, insufficient. The Connecticut rule, presently followed in the large majority of states, adopts an objective view of hostility. The possessor's subjective intent while trespassing is not relevant. Only actions are evaluated. The competing Maine rule considers the possessor's subjective state of mind. The possessor must intend to possess his neighbor's land in order to be in hostile possession. A neighbor who occupies beyond the boundary through mistake, while intending only to possess his own land, does not satisfy the hostility requirement.

QUESTION 6.   An encroaching fence. Alyssa and Peter own neighboring farms, each being 160 acres in size. The boundary line between their two properties was never properly determined or clearly known to Alyssa and Peter. In 2002, Alyssa built a wooden fence where she thought the boundary lay, but in fact the fence encroached on Peter's land by ten feet along the entire boundary. In 2007, Peter gave up farming and moved to another state. That year and all following years he leased his farm to a nearby farmer, Ralph. In 2014, Peter died, and his executor, preparing to sell the farm, hired a surveyor who discovered the encroachment. The executor demanded that Alyssa move the fence. She refused, and in 2014 he filed suit to quiet title. The statute of limitations for the recovery of real property is ten years. The most probable result is

A. Plaintiff wins because Alyssa lacks color of title.
B. Plaintiff wins because Alyssa's claim cannot affect Peter's reversion under the lease to Ralph.
C. Plaintiff wins because Peter impliedly consented to the location of the fence.
D. Plaintiff wins because Alyssa cannot demonstrate hostile possession.
E. Alyssa gains title by adverse possession.

ANALYSIS.   Here's a sketch of the facts. For complicated fact patterns on exams, you should get in the habit of making a sketch on scratch paper, just as you should be doing when you brief difficult cases for class preparation. For most people this helps in developing a clear picture of what's going on. On an exam sometimes the professor includes a sketch for you as part of the exam question, but frequently that's not the case. The facts here aren't all that complicated, but here's a sketch anyway.

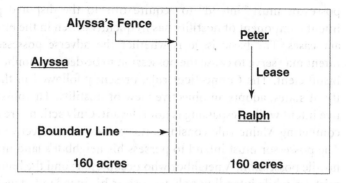

It is true that Alyssa does not have color of title to the ten-foot strip enclosed by her fence, but in most states a person can gain title by adverse possession without having color of title. The description of the statute of limitations in the facts does not indicate that color of title is required. Thus, **A** is not a likely outcome.

B is wrong. Peter's decision to give up farming and lease his farm has no legal effect upon Alyssa's claim of title by adverse possession. Peter and his executor are not entitled to extra time to sue by virtue of Peter giving up possession and leasing the property. Alyssa is able to gain adverse possession title to Peter's fee simple estate because her trespass began before Peter leased his farm to Ralph.

If Peter consented to Alyssa's fence when she built it, then Alyssa's possession would not be adverse or hostile, and she could not acquire title by adverse possession. But there are no facts given that support a finding of implied consent. Courts generally presume that a neighbor's encroachment across a boundary line is not due to permission and is a trespass in the absence of evidence to the contrary. **C** is not a likely outcome.

Choice **D** implicates the competing Connecticut and Maine rules, which bear on the state of mind of the alleged adverse possessor. Under the Maine rule, if Alyssa built the fence under a mistaken belief that she had located it on her property, and the evidence shows that she did not then intend to claim title to any of Peter's property, then Peter would win. But the Maine rule is a minority rule, followed only in a few states. Under the majority Connecticut rule, Alyssa's state of mind makes no difference.

E is the right answer. Alyssa gains title to the ten-foot strip by adverse possession because the facts indicate that she has met all the requirements (possession that is actual, open, exclusive, and continuous for longer than the statutory period).

G. Exclusive Possession

The claimant must have exclusive possession of the land. This requirement is not taken literally. First, a group of persons, such as a married couple, may qualify as joint adverse possessors of land. If the group collectively has exclusive possession and meets the other legal requirements, then the group will obtain an adverse possession title as cotenants. Second, the claimant's possession may be shared with third parties, provided that the nature of that sharing is consistent with how an owner of land generally behaves. For example, an adverse possessor may lease the property to a tenant or grant a license that allows entry onto the property, and still be considered to be in exclusive possession.

When a claimant fails to satisfy the exclusive possession test, usually the problem consists of simultaneous use by the claimant and the true owner. Frequent use or even occasional entries by the true owner will defeat the adverse possessor's claim. It is open to question whether any physical entry by the true owner defeats exclusive possession. A number of courts have indicated that the entry or entries must rise to a certain minimum level of permanence or significance. The latter view appears sound. A claimant's possession should be sufficient, even if not absolutely exclusive, if it is of the character that one would expect of an owner of the type of land in question.

When applying the exclusive possession test, care must be taken to concentrate only on the tract of land claimed by the adverse possessor. Exclusivity of possession is not destroyed where the adverse claimant possesses part of a tract of land, asserting title thereto, and the true owner has possession of the remainder of the tract, to which the claimant is not asserting title. The true owner's possession of contiguous land is irrelevant. This rule is essential for the principle of adverse possession to function properly in mistaken boundary cases.

QUESTION 7.   A dastardly brother. Kevin had fee simple ownership of an unimproved lot in a distant mountain community. His brother, impersonating Kevin, sold the lot to Dana, who paid valuable consideration. Dana took possession and built a cabin. After living there for four and one-half years, she moved elsewhere and immediately rented the cabin to Teresa for a term of one year at a rent fairly reflecting market value. When the one-year term ended, Dana and Teresa extended the lease for a second year. During that year Kevin discovered his brother's wrongdoing and the presence of the cabin and Teresa. In the litigation that follows Dana asserts title by adverse possession. A five-year statute of limitations for the recovery of real property applies when the person in possession makes a claim of right under color of title. The most probable outcome is

A. Kevin prevails because Dana was not in open possession.
B. Kevin prevails because Dana was not in exclusive possession.
C. Kevin prevails because Dana is not making a claim of right under color of title.
D. Kevin prevails because Dana was negligent in not determining that she was buying from an imposter.
E. Dana prevails.

ANALYSIS.   Choice **A** is wrong. Building a cabin on the lot is an act of actual, open, and continuous possession. Apparently Dana at first, and then Teresa, occupied the cabin with no significant gaps when the cabin was vacant.

Students who decide that Kevin should win this case are most likely to conclude that Dana's possession is not exclusive due to her lease to Teresa. This is incorrect because in renting the property Dana is behaving like a true owner of this type of property. She is not sharing possession with Kevin, and she is not allowing an outsider to share possession with her in a fashion that suggests that she is not the property's owner. Thus, **B** is wrong.

C is wrong because Dana has color of title. The deed from Kevin's bad brother qualifies. A forged deed, such as this one, may constitute color of title. A court may require that Dana have a good faith belief that the forged deed was valid, but under our facts that appears to be the case.

Choice **D** takes us out of the realm of the law of adverse possession, offering a tort law argument for Kevin. So far courts have not imposed a duty of reasonable care on adverse possessors. In many cases adverse possessors have gained title under circumstances suggesting that their carelessness led to the problem. A reasonable care requirement would be inconsistent with the standard rule allowing an intentional wrongdoer, as well as a mistaken wrongdoer, to gain limitation title.

We're left with **E** as our best answer. Dana probably wins this case, as it appears that her acts satisfy all the standard requirements for adverse possession.

H.   Continuous Possession and Tacking

Continuous possession means the claimant's possession must persist unbroken for the entire duration of the period of years specified by the statute of limitations. Although the test is easily stated, it is tricky in application. No person physically remains on a tract of land continuously with no travel whatsoever to other places. Vacations and other short occasional absences do not rise to the level of interruption of continuous possession. When courts evaluate continuity, they have to decide whether a claimant's absences were substantial enough to justify the conclusion that the claimant abandoned possession of the property for a period of time. In so doing, courts pay attention to factors such as

- The location and value of the land.
- The actual use or uses made of the land.
- Other uses for which the land is suitable.
- How long the claimant was absent and for what reasons.
- Whether the claimant made improvements to the land which remained in place when the claimant was absent.

Seasonal possession (for example, growing a summer crop) has proven troublesome. Some courts require occupation that is essentially year round, but other courts have allowed seasonal possession to qualify as continuous where the land, due to its nature, is both suitable and normally used for seasonal endeavors.

Other acts, in addition to breaks in the adverse claimant's physical occupation and use, sometimes destroy the continuity of possession. A claimant's verbal statements or other conduct that operates as a *disclaimer of title* will interrupt the continuity of possession. Very similar is recognition by the claimant of the true owner's title to the land. This type of conduct merits denial of the adverse possession claim when there is the risk of deceiving the true owner. The owner who hears of the disclaimer of title or *recognition of title* is likely to conclude that there is no need to bring judicial action against the possessor or otherwise interrupt the possession.

The concept of tacking modifies the requirement of continuous possession. Under American law, successive adverse possessors are allowed to "tack" (this means add together) their periods of adverse possession provided they are in privity. This allows the acquisition of title by adverse possession, even though there is no single adverse possessor who maintained possession for a time as long as the relevant period of limitations. English law does not require privity. If the true owner remains out of possession for longer than the statutory period, the owner is barred, regardless of the nature of the relationship between consecutive adverse possessors.

Privity exists if there is a sufficient nexus or connection between the consecutive possessors. Usually privity rests upon a conveyance, with the former possessor delivering a deed or a similar instrument that purports to convey title to the land. As indicated earlier in this chapter, such a writing is called "color of title." It does not matter whether the conveyance stems from a sale of the land or a gift. Succession at death, whether by inheritance or a devise in a will, also supplies privity.

Privity functions only to permit the addition of the consecutive time periods of possession of successive occupants. Each possessor whose occupancy is tacked must meet all of the ordinary elements of adverse possession, except for continuity for the whole period of the statute of limitations.

Moreover, the parties in privity must be successive possessors of the land. There cannot be a tacking of periods of adverse possession between two parties who are in privity with each other if someone not in privity with both of them possessed the land for a period of time between their two possessions.

A special tacking problem arises in adverse possession disputes over contested boundary lines. When an adverse possessor claims title to a part of her neighbor's land, usually the adverse possessor lacks color of title to the disputed area. Some early courts held against the adverse possessor, interpreting privity strictly to bar claims to land adjoining but outside of the parcel described in the possessor's chain of title. The modern trend, however, is to permit tacking if the evidence indicates that both parties intended to transfer possession to the disputed area.

QUESTION 8. Seizing an open tent. Tree Company owns a 10,000-acre tract of pineland. Franklin clears a quarter-acre parcel deep in the midst of Tree Company's property, where he puts up a large tent and an outhouse, plants a vegetable garden, and builds a chicken coop. Franklin lives there for just over eight years, when one day his life changes. He wins a multi-state lottery prize worth $6 million. He decides to buy a luxury yacht, where he'll live from now on. On the way out of town, he stops at the tavern and converses with Wendy, a casual acquaintance. Franklin tells Wendy that he's left his tent and some other possessions behind and expects he won't return. Wendy still lives with her parents, an arrangement that became "old" long ago. Wendy immediately goes to Franklin's parcel and moves in. After Wendy is in possession for three years, Tree Company discovers her oasis and brings an appropriate action for dispossession. The statute of limitations for the recovery of real property is ten years. The most probable result is

A. Tree Company wins because Wendy cannot claim the benefit of Franklin's period of possession.
B. Tree Company wins because Franklin and Wendy were not in open possession, as one-quarter acre is a miniscule percentage of Tree Company's tract.
C. Tree Company wins because when Franklin entered he lacked color of title to the quarter-acre parcel.
D. Wendy wins because she relied on Franklin's promise that she could occupy the quarter acre.
E. Wendy wins because her period of possession added to Franklin's period of possession is greater than ten years.

ANALYSIS. The real issue in this question is whether Wendy is entitled to the benefit of tacking, and Choices **A** and **E** present opposite conclusions on this issue. The other choices head off in other directions. Tree Company may try to argue the fact mentioned in Choice **B** as an "equitable" consideration. As a timber company with a huge tract, Tree Company may assert that it is not feasible to inspect all of its timberland to spot a minor incursion such as this. Thus, Tree Company was not "sleeping on its rights." Under standard analysis, however, Tree Company should lose. Franklin and Wendy's acts were "open" in the sense that they were not concealed, and would have been visible to a person entering the quarter-acre parcel at any time during the ten-year period.

Choice **C** correctly observes that Franklin lacked color of title, but an adverse possessor is allowed to gain title by adverse possession even if she does not have the benefit of color of title. This will limit Wendy's claim to the quarter-acre parcel that she and Franklin have actually occupied, but that is all she apparently is claiming.

Choice **D** is wrong on the facts. There is no indication that Franklin said Wendy could take over the property, or that Wendy announced to Franklin that she was thinking of doing so. Had there been a promise, conceivably a court that has a broad view of privity may have allowed Wendy to tack Franklin's eight years of possession.

We're down to Choices **A** and **E**, and it's time to resolve the tacking question. Generally, privity is satisfied when there is a consensual transfer of a property right from the first possessor to the next possessor. Here Franklin did not attempt to sell or give his interest to Wendy. Franklin and Wendy are not strangers, but a court will require a "reasonable connection" between them that makes them something more than successive trespassers. Franklin's statements, which suggested to Wendy that she might be able to take possession with no objection from Franklin or Tree Company, is probably not enough of a connection. **A** is the better response.

I.   Disability Provisions

In most states, certain owners are protected from the loss of their land by disability provisions set forth in statutes. When a disability provision applies, the adverse possessor will not prevail, even though that person has met all of the standard elements with respect to the nature and quality of possession. The statutory period is "tolled" (i.e., extended) due to the disability. The idea is one of fairness. In the normal case, the owner who loses title by adverse possession can be said to be at fault, for having "slept on his rights." But an owner who is subject to disability has a diminished ability to monitor his property, to check for possible trespasses, and to bring a lawsuit in time.

Consider Texas Civil Practice and Remedies Code §16.022, which provides

> (a) For the purposes of this subchapter, a person is under a legal disability if the person is:
>> (1) younger than 18 years of age, regardless of whether the person is married;
>> (2) of unsound mind; or
>> (3) serving in the United States Armed Forces during time of war.
> (b) If a person entitled to sue for the recovery of real property or entitled to make a defense based on the title to real property is under a legal disability at the time title to the property vests or adverse possession commences, the time of the disability is not included in a limitations period.

QUESTION 9.   Give the kid a break. In 2010, Judy, age 13, inherited Blackacre from her father. At the time of his death Blackacre was vacant, unimproved land, but four months later, Carl took possession and built a house on Blackacre. Thereafter Carl maintained open, continuous, and exclusive possession of the entire parcel. Judy graduated from high school at age 17 and decided to enlist in the United States Army. She made the necessary arrangements and commenced active service on her eighteenth birthday. She served in the Army for four years; that entire period was considered to be a "time of war" for the United States. Under the Texas statute reproduced above, assuming that a ten-year statute of limitations applies, when will Carl acquire title by adverse possession?

A. 2015.
B. 2020.
C. 2025.
D. 2029.
E. When Judy dies.

ANALYSIS.   A is plainly bad. Judy will turn 18 in 2015, but a ten-year statute applies. A person with no disability gets until 2020 to sue, and the only issue here is whether Judy is entitled to extra time.

The key to this question is to read the Texas statute carefully. The statute excludes "the time of the disability" from the limitations period if a person such as Judy "is under a legal disability at the time title to the property vests or adverse possession commences." The Texas statute is consistent with most American disability provisions. The disability must exist at the time the adverse possession begins. An owner who becomes disabled later is not given extra time to bring an action. Such an after-occurring or *intervening disability* has no effect. Judy qualifies because at the moment Carl entered, she was under 18. This disability ends on her eighteenth birthday, in the year 2015. Thus, ignoring her military service, the limitations period begins to run then, and she must bring the lawsuit by 2025.

But Judy is in the Army, and the Texas statute treats her military service as a "disability." Does this entitle her to an additional four years, extending the period to 2029 (Choice **D**)? No, it does not. It is commonly said that no tacking of disabilities is allowed. We can spot this rule from a close reading of the Texas statute. The limitations period is tolled for "the time of *the disability*," which refers back to the owner having "a legal disability *at the time . . . adverse possession commences.*" Because Judy's military service started after Carl entered into adverse possession, it is disregarded. Thus, the statute will expire in 2025. The right calculation is **C**.

J.   The Closer: State of Mind

Some of the toughest problems with the law of adverse possession deal with the possessor's state of mind. It appears that courts intuitively seek to avoid conferring title on an adverse possessor who is an intentional wrongdoer or has acted dishonestly. Some courts have observed that "squatters" do not merit the protection of the statute of limitations. Due to the amorphous nature of the standard adverse possession elements, courts sometimes appear to manipulate findings and conclusions to deny title to intentional trespassers.

A minority of states, by judicial decision or statute, go further. They explicitly require that the adverse possessor have a good faith belief that she actually owned the property in question. Recall from our discussion in Section F of this chapter ("Hostile and adverse possession") that in boundary cases, a few states have reached a diametrically opposite conclusion. Under the Maine rule, a neighbor who intentionally trespasses across the boundary may gain limitation title, but a good faith trespasser may not if that good faith trespasser admits to having had no desire to invade the neighbor's property.

> **QUESTION 10.   Mistake with the fence.** Barbara and Dale are neighboring homeowners. Barbara puts up a chain-link fence separating her backyard from Dale's. By mistake, she places the fence three feet onto Dale's lot. The three-foot strip is covered by grass, and after constructing the fence, Barbara continues to mow the grass on the strip, just as she does for the rest of her back lawn. Dale is away when the fence is built, and he never says anything to Barbara about the fence. Thirteen years later, Dale orders a survey of his lot and discovers that the fence encroaches. Dale sues Barbara for trespass. The jurisdiction has a ten-year statute of limitations to recover possession of real property. What is Dale's best argument that his action is timely?
>
> **A.**   He does not have to prove actual harm because even a nominal trespass is actionable.
> **B.**   Barbara did not build the fence in good faith.
> **C.**   Barbara did not intend to possess any of his lot.
> **D.**   Because he didn't object to the fence, Barbara was not in hostile possession.
> **E.**   Barbara was negligent in not getting a survey when she built her fence.

ANALYSIS.   Choice **A** correctly recites the nominal trespass rule (a landowner may obtain relief, damages, or an injunction for a trespass even if actual harm cannot be proven), but this is beside the point. If the owner does not bring the action in time, it is barred by the statute of limitations, whether the claim is for a nominal trespass or a trespass causing real injury.

In some states Barbara will lose if she did not build the fence in good faith, but the facts state that she located the fence where she did "by mistake." This suggests good faith, and no other facts cut the other way. **B** is a weak choice.

Choice **E** imports tort analysis, arguing that Barbara's negligence in putting the fence on Dale's lot justifies a refusal to protect Barbara as an adverse possessor. Whether or not she was negligent, adverse possessors are not ordinarily disqualified due to the failure to exercise reasonable care when locating improvements.

Choices **C** and **D** are both plausible. **C**, which states that Barbara did not intend to possess any of Dale's lot, seems weak. It (1) gives a conclusion with no reasoning and (2) appears unlikely. Doesn't it seem like Barbara, when mowing grass and treating the three-foot strip as part of her yard, took possession and intended to do so? But **D** has its own problem. Usually courts presume hostility rather than permission—that a person's unexplained entry on her neighbor's property is a trespass. There are some cases where courts have implied permission, usually due to particular facts bearing on the parties' personal relationship (they may be relatives or close friends). Here we have no evidence to suggest Dale gave implied consent or implied permission. Let's go back to Choice **C**. Though the response sounds strange, it reflects the reasoning that underlies the Maine rule, which in a few states may preclude a good faith possessor, such as Barbara, from gaining limitation title. Her good faith means that she did not subjectively intend to possess *Dale*'s property, even though she did intend to possess the three-foot strip. Only students who have a sophisticated understanding of the Maine rule will grasp this point. This is a tough, tough question. The last time I used this question on an exam, 49 percent of the students picked **D** and 42 percent took **C**. Test scoring, however, showed a very high "discrimination index" (i.e., students who did well on the exam as a whole got this one right). I'm not convinced that **C** is better than **D** by a wide margin, but I think it's fair.

 ## Smith's Picks

1.	Laying down a mobile home	C
2.	Requiring payment of taxes	D
3.	A problematic chain of title	B
4.	Four lots in a row	D
5.	Nighttime parking	E
6.	An encroaching fence	E
7.	A dastardly brother	E
8.	Seizing an open tent	A
9.	Give the kid a break	C
10.	Mistake with the fence	C

Adverse Possession of Personal Property

"Your neighbor's apples are the sweetest."
Yiddish proverb

CHAPTER OVERVIEW
A. Adverse Possession Elements
B. Discovery Rule
C. Demand and Refusal Rule
D. The Closer: True Owner Obtains Possession Extrajudicially
 Smith's Picks

The last chapter explored the law of adverse possession of real property, which has a very long history and is well established. This chapter turns to the law of adverse possession of personal property. Cases concerning chattels are much less frequent, but many property casebooks reproduce the leading case, *O'Keeffe v. Snyder,* 416 A.2d 862 (N.J. 1980), which deals with an attempt by the famous American painter Georgia O'Keeffe to recover three of her paintings.

Statutes of limitation for the recovery of personal property are usually much shorter than for land. For the conversion of goods, typical periods are three to six years, which apply whether the true owner seeks replevin (return of the item) or trover (damages). California's statute is typical:

Cal. Civ. Proc. Code §338
The Time of Commencing Actions Other Than for the Recovery of Real Property

Within three years: . . .
(c)(1) An action for taking, detaining, or injuring any goods or chattels, including actions for the specific recovery of personal property.

Note that this statute mentions neither of the historic terms *replevin* and *trover*, but plainly reaches such actions by referring broadly to "taking, detaining, or injuring" chattels and then mentioning "specific recovery" (i.e., replevin) to remove any doubt that the statute is limited to actions for damages.

A. Adverse Possession Elements

For personal property, courts traditionally have tended to apply the rule set they developed for the adverse possession of land. Under this approach a wrongful possessor of a chattel becomes immune from a conversion action brought by the true owner if the possessor's holding is characterized as adverse (hostile), open (notorious), exclusive, and continuous for the requisite statutory period. Following the land cases, most states allow tacking by successive adverse possessors.

In the cases involving chattels, the issues that come up most frequently are adversity and openness. Just as for land, the statute of limitations cannot run unless the possessor is a wrongdoer. A person in possession with the express or implied consent of the owner (usually that person is a bailee) cannot acquire title. The requirement that the possessor hold openly and notoriously, as in the land cases, may serve two distinct purposes. Thieves and other knowingly wrongful possessors are often found to hold covertly, not openly, so as not to reward their misconduct. Second, openness may protect the true owner by requiring a possession that gives the owner a fair chance of discovering the location of her property and asserting her rights.

> **QUESTION 1. Who gets the portrait after more than 50 years?**
> Redmond, the owner of a valuable portrait of Captain James Lawrence, a hero of the War of 1812, died in 1887. Her will bequeathed the portrait to her son with a provision that if he should die leaving no descendants, it should go to the New Jersey Historical Society. At the time her son was 14, so her executors delivered the painting to the Historical Society. Later the son married and had children, but the Historical Society kept possession of the portrait. In 1938 the son died, bequeathing his property to his children. They promptly demanded that the Historical Society turn over possession of the portrait. When the Historical Society refused, the children brought an action for replevin. The state has a six-year statute of limitations. What is the children's best argument that they should prevail?
>
> **A.** The statute began to run when the Historical Society refused the children's demand for the portrait in 1938.
> **B.** The Historical Society converted the portrait when it accepted possession from Redmond's executors.

> **C.** The Historical Society's possession of the portrait was not of an open nature.
>
> **D.** The Historical Society did not pay valuable consideration for the portrait.

ANALYSIS. This question presents a slightly modified version of the facts in a New Jersey case, *Redmond v. New Jersey Historical Society*, 28 A.2d 189 (N.J. E. & A. 1942), discussed in the subsequent New Jersey case of *O'Keeffe v. Snyder*. The *Redmond* court held in favor of the children, reasoning that the transaction between the executors and the Historical Society was a "voluntary bailment," with its possession not becoming adverse before the children demanded possession in 1938. (Until the terms of Redmond's will, presumably the son could have demanded possession — especially after he became a father — but there was no evidence he ever did so.)

So Choice **A** is the right answer. Choice **B** is wrong because finding a conversion in 1887 would support the Historical Society's adverse possession case.

Let's look at **D**. True, there's nothing in the facts indicating that the Society paid for the painting or gave other consideration. This is why the *Redmond* court called the transaction a bailment. Although many adverse possessors take the property under a transaction of sale and purchase that is tainted, this is not a requirement of the law of adverse possession. So **D** helps the children little if at all.

Choice **C** is stronger than **B** or **D**; it's the second-best answer. A judicial conclusion that the Society did not hold the portrait openly would help the children by tolling the statute of limitations. But there are no underlying facts in the question that support this conclusion, so **A** is more plausible than **C**.

B.   Discovery Rule

A competing approach is the *discovery rule*, developed by the court in *O'Keeffe v. Snyder*, 416 A.2d 862 (N.J. 1980). Under the discovery rule, the cause of action accrues when the owner knows of the location of the chattel or the identity of its possessor or when the owner should have known of the location or identity through the exercise of *due diligence*. The owner has the burden of proving that she has exercised due diligence in seeking to recover the property. Under adverse possession, the wrongful possessor has the burden of proof for the elements of adverse possession. Dissenting judges in *O'Keeffe* criticized the majority for shifting the burden to the true owner, contending that the need to prove diligence to retain ownership was unfair.

What constitutes due diligence depends upon the facts, including the nature of the property and its value. For example, for a stolen chattel filing a police report might be sufficient, but if the chattel has high value and there are additional steps that a prudent owner would take, then more is necessary to toll the running of the statute of limitations.

The *O'Keeffe* court stated that under the discovery rule, just as under adverse possession principles, a subsequent possessor would receive the benefit of tacking, and expiration of the statute would confer title upon the possessor.

Under the logic of the discovery rule, it would seem to make no difference whether the chattel is possessed by a knowing wrongdoer (such as a thief) or a good faith purchaser, but in *O'Keeffe* the dispute was between the true owner, Georgia O'Keeffe, and a merchant who bought the paintings, apparently in good faith.

Several courts outside of New Jersey have adopted the *O'Keeffe* discovery rule, and a California statute calls for a type of discovery rule for the conversion of fine art and articles of "historical, interpretive, scientific, or artistic significance." Cal. Civ. Proc. Code §338(c)(2). In most states, there is no modern law, cases or statutes, dealing with adverse possession of personal property.

QUESTION 2.   **"Stolen once, stolen twice."** In January 2012, Brian steals a diamond ring from Alice's house, and one month later travels to another state, where he sells the ring to Carlos, for valuable consideration. In June 2017, Denise steals the ring from Carlos' house and two weeks later sells it to Evelyn, for valuable consideration. The following statute is in force in the jurisdiction whose law applies to determine property rights in the ring: "Actions of replevin and all other actions for taking, detaining, or injuring goods or chattels shall be commenced within six years after the cause of action accrues, and not afterwards." In 2020, Alice discovers that Evelyn has the ring. Alice confronts Evelyn with her claim to ownership and, without litigation, Evelyn voluntarily returns the ring to Alice. That same year Carlos sues Alice in replevin. His best argument would be:

A.   Evelyn transferred no rights to Alice because Evelyn had none.
B.   Alice had no rights prior to the transfer from Evelyn because Alice had not diligently searched for the ring.
C.   Carlos had adversely possessed the ring for the statutory period.
D.   Carlos should win because Brian had good title.

ANALYSIS.   This is a tough one, as none of the choices look really good. The weakest two are **C** and **D**, so we'll start there. Choice **C** falls down on the facts. The statute bars replevin after six years, Carlos bought the ring in February 2012 and lost it due to theft in June 2017. That's less than six years.

Choice **D** says Brian had good title. True, if he did, then Carlos as purchaser from Brian would acquire good title, but Brian is a mere thief. His possession was clearly inferior to the original true owner, Alice—not good title.

Choices **A** and **B** both have some appeal. Choice **A** claims to support Carlos by positing that Evelyn didn't transfer any property right to Alice because Evelyn had none. It assumes that Alice's defense to Carlos' action will rely on that transfer, rather than upon Alice's original title. Evelyn's rights (prior to the transfer) were likely less than full, good title, but she at least had limited property rights (for example, a better right than Denise, who sold the ring to her). So **A** is flawed, due to the assumption and the mischaracterization.

Left standing is Choice **B**. It assumes, in contrast to Choice **A**, that Alice's defense will rely on her original title. It invokes the discovery rule, stating that she had not exercised due diligence in seeking to recover the ring. The facts say nothing that points in favor, or against, that conclusion. Still, it's possible, and if true, Carlos should win. Choice **B** does not complete the loop by saying that Alice didn't acquire any right from Evelyn that would be superior to Carlos' claim. That would be part of a more complete explanation. However, **B** is the only answer without major flaws.

C.   Demand and Refusal Rule

New York rejects both the adverse possession doctrine and the discovery rule for chattels. Its courts apply the *demand and refusal rule,* which delays the accrual of the cause of action when the chattel is held by a good faith possessor (a person who believes she has good title). That person's possession of the chattel is considered not to be wrongful until the true owner demands its return and the possessor refuses. The leading case is *Solomon R. Guggenheim Foundation v. Lubell,* 569 N.E.2d 426 (N.Y. 1991), which like *O'Keeffe* involved stolen art work. The Guggenheim museum made a "tactical decision" not to report the theft to the police or to take any other affirmative steps based upon its "belief that to publicize the theft would succeed only in driving the gouache further underground and greatly diminishing the possibility that it would ever be recovered." Reaffirming the New York demand and refusal rule, the *Guggenheim* court explained:

> To place the burden of locating stolen artwork on the true owner and to fore-close the rights of that owner to recover its property if the burden is not met would, we believe, encourage illicit trafficking in stolen art. Three years after the theft, any purchaser, good faith or not, would be able to hold onto stolen art work unless the true owner was able to establish that it had undertaken a reasonable search for the missing art. This shifting of the burden onto the wronged owner is inappropriate.

The *Guggenheim* court emphasized that the demand and refusal rule only applies to a refusal by a good faith possessor, and that the statute of limitations runs when "the stolen object is in the possession of the thief." The court indicated that under some circumstances a good faith possessor might prevail under the affirmative defense of laches, if the plaintiff delayed unreasonably in bringing the action to the prejudice of the possessor.

QUESTION 3. Warhol painting stolen long ago resurfaces. Seven years ago Alonso bought an Andy Warhol painting of the actress Marilyn Monroe ("Marilyn") painting from a private collector, Guido, for $10.2 million. Alonso prepared a short memorandum of sale, which Guido signed, and did not make any inquiries of Guido as to how long he had owned "Marilyn" or where he got it. He thought it odd that Guido closed the deal in an abandoned warehouse late at night, and rejected Alonso's tender of a cashier's check, insisting that he pay cash. But Alonso had fallen in love with "Marilyn," and so what if Guido was a tad eccentric? Last month, the Museum of Long-Lost Art contacted Alonso. It presented evidence indicating that it had received "Marilyn" as a charitable donation in 2000 and that "Marilyn" was stolen from its collection in 2003. The thief was never apprehended. The Museum formally demanded that Alonso turn over possession of "Marilyn." One week after Alonso refused, the Museum commenced a replevin action against him. Assume that the jurisdiction whose law governs has a four-year statute of limitations and follows the demand and refusal rule. Alonso's best defense would be:

A. After the theft of "Marilyn" the Museum did not exercise due diligence in attempting to recover the painting.

B. When Alonso purchased "Marilyn" he hung the painting on a wall in the parlor of his private residence, where it remained until the Museum made its demand.

C. When Alonso purchased "Marilyn" he had inquiry notice that his seller may have lacked the right to sell "Marilyn."

D. When Alonso purchased "Marilyn" he followed the customary practice of the art industry in not requiring the seller to provide documentary evidence of ownership.

ANALYSIS. This question tests basic understanding of the New York demand and refusal rule. Let's take a look at the answers in order. Choice **A** gives the conclusion that Alonso would need under the discovery rule — that the Museum as true owner did not act diligently in seeking to recover its property. But the demand and refusal rule is an alternative rule, not an overlay. In *Guggenheim* the court expressly stated that the museum did not have to prove diligence to recover its stolen art.

Choice **B** explains what Alonso did with "Marilyn" after his purchase. It's hazy as to what legal rule this might relate to — perhaps the traditional adverse possession elements, suggesting that Alonso had open possession of "Marilyn"; possibly the discovery rule, although from our facts it's hard to see how Alonso's display of "Marilyn" in his residence should have led to the Museum's discovery of its whereabouts. At any rate, nothing in **B** ties to the elements of the demand and refusal rule.

Choices **C** and **D** both consider Alonzo's behavior when he bought "Marilyn" from Guido. Choice **D** may rest on a truthful predicate—a custom in the art industry for buyers of high-end art not to press their sellers to prove ownership. See in addition to the *O'Keeffe* case, *Lindholm v. Brant*, 925 A.2d 1048 (Conn. 2007) (purchaser of Andy Warhol's "Red Elvis" painting acted in good faith notwithstanding failure to investigate seller's claim of title). But this supports the Museum's case: its claim that Alonzo was a good faith purchaser and good faith possessor of "Marilyn." Instead, to escape the demand and refusal rule, Alonzo needs to impugn his good faith. So **C** is the right answer. Alonzo needs to introduce evidence that he acted in bad faith. This should strike you as perverse. It is, and this highlights a major policy flaw in the rule.

D.   The Closer: True Owner Obtains Possession Extrajudicially

For real property, it is universally held that expiration of the statute of limitations extinguishes the original owner's title and vests the possessor with a new title. This is also widely accepted for personal property, even though statutes of limitation for conversion rarely have any express language suggesting that result. Without this doctrine, rights to the property in question would be separated and uncertain, with the adverse possessor being immune to a judicial action brought by the title owner, but the owner apparently retaining some rights, such as the right to recapture the property by self-help.

> **QUESTION 4.   A trade-in that doesn't work.** Ace Electronics is a dealer in new and used televisions. In 2015, Badge breaks into Ace Electronics one night after the store is closed and steals a television. Badge uses the television in his home, and in 2012, he sells it to Camilla for $800. In 2020, Camilla decides she no longer wants the television. She takes it to Ace Electronics, where Ace's clerk tells her that the television is worth $400 as a trade-in. She selects a new television, but because there are none in stock she is to return in three days to pick up her new television. She leaves the old television with Ace. When she returns in three days, Ace tells her that they have run the serial number on the old television, that it was stolen from Ace in 2015, that Ace will keep it, and that they will not give her a trade-in allowance in any amount. The following statute is in force: "Actions of replevin and all other actions for taking, detaining, or injuring goods or chattels shall be commenced within four

years after the cause of action accrues, and not afterwards." Camilla immediately sues Ace in trover. The most probable result is:

A. The action will fail because Camilla is not allowed to tack Badge's period of possession to her own.
B. The action will fail because Ace Electronics is not the plaintiff and thus is not subject to the statute.
C. The action will succeed because Ace Electronics made an enforceable promise to give Camilla a trade-in allowance.
D. The action will succeed if Ace Electronics failed to take appropriate measures to recover the television.
E. The action will succeed if Camilla purchased in good faith.

ANALYSIS.   Choice **A** raises tacking, which is important here. Courts, how-ever, consistently allow tacking in personal property limitations cases, whether they apply traditional adverse possession rules or the discovery rule. The New York demand and refusal rule would deny Camilla the benefit of tacking, but this is a minority rule, and you are asked to pick the "most probable result." Thus, you should not pick **A** as the best answer unless all the other choices have greater flaws.

Choice **B** is attractive. Literally the statute is inapplicable. Camilla is the plaintiff, and if she has a cause of action against Ace Electronics, it accrued in 2020, the same year she filed the action. But for personal property, just as for adverse possession of land, expiration of the statute of limitations is deemed to transfer title from the prior possessor to the present possessor. This means that a person like Ace, who recovers possession without needing to go to court, can be forced to relinquish possession.

Choice **C** gives a contract law explanation for why Camilla might prevail. Although the explanation may sound plausible, it fails under standard con-tract law analysis. A seller of goods makes an implied warranty that she is able to convey title to those goods (this comes from U.C.C. §2-312). If Camilla has not acquired title by virtue of expiration of the statute, Ace Electronics has the right to rescind the trade-in contract because Camilla lacks title.

Choices **D** and **E** are alike in that they give conditional answers — Camilla wins, based on limitation title, only if additional facts are found. Choice **E** is grounded on the premise that Camilla needs to prove she is a bona fide purchaser, or good faith purchaser, to prevail. But under standard analysis, Camilla can obtain limitation title even if she knowingly purchased stolen goods, whether the court applies adverse possession rules or the discovery rule.

Choice **D**, the best answer, is a correct statement of the discovery rule, as announced in *O'Keeffe v. Snyder* and applied by a good number of other courts. If since the time of the theft in 2015, Ace Electronics has acted with due diligence to recover its television, then the statute of limitations has not expired and it has the right to keep the television. Alternatively, the failure to exercise due diligence means that Camilla's action will succeed.

 ## Smith's Picks

1. Who gets the portrait after more than 50 years?   **A**
2. "Stolen once, stolen twice"   **B**
3. Warhol painting stolen long ago resurfaces   **C**
4. A trade-in that doesn't work   **D**

8

Fee Simple Estates

"Land is the only thing in the world that amounts to anything, for
'Tis the only thing in this world that lasts,
'Tis the only thing worth working for,
worth fighting for—worth dying for."
Margaret Mitchell, *Gone With the Wind* (1936)

CHAPTER OVERVIEW
A. Some Basic Principles
B. Creation of Fee Simple at Common Law: Words of Inheritance
C. Creation under Modern Statutes: Presumption of Fee Simple
D. Rebutting the Presumption of Fee Simple
E. The Closer: Dying without Heirs
✦ Smith's Picks

The system of estates has terrified generations of law students. At least it has that reputation, though many students, once they have mastered the subject, have come to appreciate the subject matter. The law of estates is written in a technical language developed in feudal England, where its chief purpose was to define relationships among the monarchy, the landed nobility, and other persons who held land as tenants under the nobles. The system consists of a set of elaborate rules—perhaps the most technical rules that you will encounter in the basic law school curriculum, although the federal tax code will prove to be a worthy rival. It is a logical system, developed by courts and legislatures over centuries. To appreciate its logic and internal consistency, hard study on your part to learn the basic concepts and terminology is essential. If you do the work, you'll be able to master this stuff. Compared to other legal materials that you must learn, there are two advantages: (1) there is a closed set of rules to consider—the body of knowledge you're studying is not open-ended; (2) there are definite answers—each basic question you'll see on an exam has an answer that is clearly "right" with other responses being clearly "wrong."

A.   Some Basic Principles

Learning estates in land is like learning a foreign language. The vocabulary and concepts, deeply rooted in English history, sound alien to the modern ear. To get off to a good start, consider the following basic principles:

- **The estates system is a method of carving ownership over time.** An *estate* is the ownership of a particular parcel of land. All the estates are alike in that they entitle the owner to possess the mythical plot known as Blackacre. By definition, an estate is a possessory interest in land. The distinctions between the estates turn on duration—on how long the estate will or might last.

- **The estates system is a closed set.** There are four and only four estates recognized at common law: the fee simple, the fee tail, the life estate, and the leasehold. The fee tail is obsolete. Most states do not recognize the fee tail at all, and in states where it can exist, there are procedures for converting the fee tail to a fee simple (this is called *disentailing* the estate). A deed or a will should clearly point to the type of estate that is being created. If the author of a deed or will uses ambiguous language, the court will select one of the four recognized estates. There are no hybrids, and parties are not allowed to invent a new estate. As a practical matter, this limitation is not very important today because the estates system, as it has developed, has great flexibility. An owner can accomplish virtually any legitimate goal by using one or more of the three estates of modern significance (fee simple, life estate, and leasehold).

- **Each estate may be a present or future estate.** The estates system facilitates the temporal division of ownership of any tract of land. The owner is allowed to carve up ownership into segments of time. Each of the four estates may be a present estate or a future estate. The owner of a present estate is in actual possession of the land now or has the immediate right to possession. The owner of a future estate (also called a future interest) does not have a present right to possession. A future interest is a property right that will or may become possessory at some point in the future.

- **Each estate may be indefeasible or defeasible.** An estate is indefeasible if it cannot be cut short. On the other hand, an estate is defeasible if it can be cut short. To decide whether the estate is indefeasible, you look at the language used to create the estate. If there is no language pointing to defeasance, the estate is indefeasible. Defeasible estates are considered in more detail in chapter 9.

- **There are three ways to transfer an estate.** First, the owner may convey her estate. This is also called *alienation*. For freehold estates, the statute of frauds requires a writing, and typically the owner uses a *deed* to convey a fee estate.

Second, the owner may *devise* the property by naming the next owner in a *will*. A will does not take effect until the person making the will (the *testator*) dies and the will is probated in court. Thus, it is possible that the person named in the will to get the land (the *devisee*) will never get Blackacre. The owner might change her mind and either convey Blackacre to someone else before she dies or revoke her will.

Third, the owner of an inheritable estate may die without a valid will, in which event her *heirs* inherit the estate. The heirs are said to acquire the property by *descent*. The decedent is said to have died *intestate* (without a testament, or will) and is often called the *intestate*. Historically in England, the term "heirs" referred to persons who took real property through inheritance. Personal property went to an intestate's *next of kin*, which also were relatives but were determined under different rules.

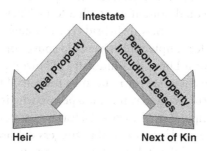

Today in the United States, the word "heirs" is used to refer to persons taking any property by intestate succession without making a distinction between real and personal property.

All estates are inheritable except a life estate measured by the life of its owner.

QUESTION 1.   Dividing the ranch over time. Ophelia, the owner of a large ranch, Northfork, is getting on in years and is beginning to think about her estate planning. She has decided that at her death she wants Northfork to go to her son, Elmer, for his lifetime, and then when he dies, she wants Northfork to go to the children of her sister, Sarah, who are then to acquire complete ownership. Ophelia may best accomplish her objective by using which of the following estates or combinations of estates?

A. Fee simple in Elmer, with Sarah's children having a right to protected inheritance.
B. Fee simple in Elmer, defeasible at his death, followed by a fee simple in Sarah's children.
C. Fee tail in Elmer, followed by a fee simple in Sarah's children.
D. Life estate in Elmer, followed by a fee simple in Sarah's children.
E. Leasehold in Elmer, followed by a fee simple in Sarah's children.

ANALYSIS. A landowner like Ophelia can use the estates system to achieve a wide variety of objectives with respect to her property. Ophelia wants to retain possession of Northfork for the time being. The easiest way for her to go forward is to provide for Elmer and Sarah's children in her will. In her will, she should give a present estate to Elmer because he is to have possession immediately at her death. Then Ophelia's will should provide for Sarah's children to have a future estate. Elmer is to have the land for the rest of his lifetime, and the straightforward, logical way to manage this is to give him a life estate. (The life estate is studied in detail in chapter 10.) Next, transferring "complete ownership" to Sarah's children is accomplished by giving them a fee simple. Therefore, **D** is the best answer.

A does not work because the estates system does not recognize creation of a right to "protected inheritance." Sarah's will might contain language that says at Elmer's death that Northfork has to pass by inheritance to Sarah's children, but courts would not enforce such a term. They would see this as an invalid attempt to create a new or hybrid type of estate. The outcome would be that Elmer has a fee simple, which he could convey or devise to anyone. We should also note that if Elmer dies intestate, still owning Northfork, Sarah's children (his first cousins) may turn out to be his heirs, but they may not be his heirs because his survivors may include a person who is more closely related to him.

In principle **B** might work. Defeasible estates are allowed, and a person's death can be made the event that triggers defeasance. However, a fee simple by definition is inheritable, at least under some circumstances, by the heirs of the present owner, and this would not be the case here. Ophelia intends for Elmer to have no chance to pass Northfork at his death to someone other than Sarah's children. This means that Elmer should have no more than a life estate.

C is not a good choice because the fee tail is obsolete and is only created in the United States today when a drafter of a deed or will accidentally uses the traditional language that at common law conjured up the estate (most directly, "to Elmer and the heirs of his body"). In addition to this flaw, the concept of the fee tail does not fit with Ophelia's plan anyway. If Elmer had a fee tail, Northfork should pass to his children or other lineal descendants at Elmer's death, which is not what Ophelia wants to happen.

E is the second-best answer in the sequence. At first, the idea of giving Elmer a leasehold does not seem plausible. The most common type of leasehold is a term of years, which lasts for a fixed number of years. We don't know and can't predict how long Elmer will live. But recall that any estate can be made defeasible, and a person's death can be the triggering event for defeasance. Thus, Ophelia's will could devise Northfork "to Elmer for 99 years, but the leasehold shall terminate if Elmer dies before expiration of the 99-year term; and upon termination of the leasehold, to Sarah's children and their heirs." This works (our assumption is that Elmer is already old enough that he's not likely to live for 99 more years), but it is convoluted, whereas devising a life estate to Elmer is direct and straightforward.

B.   Creation of Fee Simple at Common Law: Words of Inheritance

When a fee simple estate is not defeasible, it is called a *fee simple absolute*. Because the large majority of fee simple estates are not made defeasible, lawyers often just say *fee simple* or *fee estate* when they mean fee simple absolute. The fee simple absolute is the fullest form of land ownership recognized in our system. When a natural person owns a fee simple absolute, she can keep the property for the remainder of her lifetime or convey it by sale or gift. If not conveyed prior to death, she may devise the property by will. If she dies intestate, it passes to her heirs. The fee simple absolute, which may last forever, may be represented by the following timeline.

The fee simple absolute ends only if the owner dies intestate without discoverable heirs. Then the property *escheats* to the state.

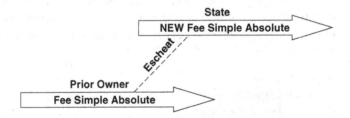

At common law, a deed had to use particular language to create a fee simple. The deed had to convey "to Anne and her heirs" or "to Aaron and his heirs." In the examples given above, the words "to Anne" and "to Aaron" are called *words of purchase*. They indicate who is receiving the estate. The phrase "and her heirs" are called *words of limitation* because they limit, or define, the estate being created.[1] Using the word "heirs" was essential. The failure to use the term "heirs" in a deed meant that the grantee always received just a life estate. The rationale dates back to medieval England. The grantor had to show expressly that an estate of inheritance was intended. At first after the Norman Conquest, inheritable estates were exceptional. Life estates instead of fee estates were usually created. Using words of inheritance showed that the new owner was getting a special deal. He could pass the estate on to his heir, and that heir could pass on to his heir, and so on. The fee simple created a potentially infinite chain of title through inheritance.

---

1. They are also called *words of inheritance* because they signify that the estate is to be inheritable.

The common law recognized several exceptions to the formal requirement that the word "heirs" be used. The two most important ones involved wills and organizational grantees. First, the Statute of Wills was adopted in 1540 long after the rule crystallized for deeds, and courts chose not to extend the rule to wills. Nevertheless, to devise a fee simple at common law, the will still had to include some language manifesting an intent to give a fee simple. Otherwise a life estate was presumed. Second, only a natural person can have "heirs." Because an organization like a corporation cannot have "heirs," courts did not require use of an inapt term. A deed to a corporation passed a fee simple in the absence of language pointing to a lesser estate.

QUESTION 2.   A law student's help. Cassal owns a fee simple absolute estate in Blackacre. She tells her friend, Marcy, who is in law school, that she would like to make a gift of Blackacre to Cassal's sister, Susan. She says that she wants to give away all of her ownership rights, retaining nothing. Marcy tells Cassal that she can find an appropriate deed form in the law library. Marcy supplies Cassal with a deed form, which Cassal completes. She signs the deed and delivers it to Susan. The deed properly describes Blackacre, and the granting clause in the deed purports to convey Blackacre "to my sister, Susan, and her assigns forever." **Assume that traditional common-law rules apply to determine the legal effect of Cassal's deed.** What present estate, if any, does Susan own in Blackacre?

A. A life estate.
B. A defeasible life estate.
C. A fee simple absolute.
D. A defeasible fee simple.
E. Susan does not own a present estate in Blackacre because there are no words of limitation.

ANALYSIS.   To answer this question, our first step is to ask ourselves a simple question: does the deed refer to Susan's heirs? At traditional common law, there must be words of inheritance (i.e., the word "heirs" is present) to create a fee simple. If the magic word is missing, end of game. The grantee cannot have a fee simple. The deed says to "Susan, and her assigns forever." A person's "assigns" are not the same as her heirs. If Susan conveys the estate she receives, those grantees are "assigns." Insertion of the term in the deed signifies that Susan's estate is to be assignable, but this is an inherent characteristic of all estates in land. Therefore, Susan cannot have a fee simple, and both **C** and **D** are wrong.

From the remaining answers, we have two basic choices. **A** and **B** indicate that Susan has some type of life estate, and **E** states that Susan has no estate at all. Let's focus on **E**. This answer asserts that "there are no words of limitation."

This isn't true because the deed indicates that Susan and her assigns are to have Blackacre "forever." Thus, we have words of limitation, although the law will not enforce them fully. The more basic claim made by **E** is that Susan should have no estate in Blackacre because the deed violates the requirement that a deed refer to the grantee's heirs to convey a fee simple. Although it might be plausible to penalize Cassal and Susan for the deed's shortcoming, this is not what the law has done. Instead, Susan is allowed to take a lesser estate (a life estate). This way she gets something, rather than nothing at all. Although this defeats Cassal's intent by not allowing her a fee simple, it does not override intent as much as it would if Susan had no ownership whatsoever.

But which type of life estate does Susan have — a life estate (**A**) or a defeasible life estate (**B**)? Remember that "defeasible" means that the estate can be cut short, and there must be express language in the deed that tells us what event will accomplish that shortening. There is nothing here of that nature. If Susan transfers her life estate to an "assign," that does not cut short the estate. The life estate continues with the assignee as its new owner.[2] The life estate will last until Susan dies. Her eventual death does not make the life estate defeasible. At her death, the life estate ends, but we say that it *expires naturally*. It is not what we call defeasance. Therefore, **B** is wrong. We are left with **A** as the best answer. The choice for **A** could have been a more complete explanation, saying an "indefeasible life estate" or even a "life estate absolute," although that latter term (parallel to fee simple absolute) is rarely seen. Nevertheless, **A** is the only correct answer.

As this question demonstrates, law students ought to be especially careful when relatives and friends ask them for legal assistance or legal advice. Marcy has not committed malpractice, but she is off the hook only because she is not yet a lawyer, and by definition only a lawyer can commit the wrong of "malpractice." A tremendous amount of litigation is generated from deeds of conveyance that contain flaws and ambiguities. Often the problem arises because the document was drafted by one of the parties or a layperson, such as a real estate broker, instead of an experienced lawyer.

C.   Creation under Modern Statutes: Presumption of Fee Simple

Almost all states have eliminated the common-law rule that a deed must have words of inheritance to convey a fee simple estate. Only a handful of states cling to the old rule. The large majority of states accomplished the reform by statute, often a long time ago. The reform recognizes that most people who own and transact with respect to real estate want a fee simple estate. It is by far

---

2. Life estates are considered in chapter 10.

the most common form of land tenure. The Georgia statute, enacted in 1863, is typical. Georgia Code Ann. §44-6-21 provides:

> The word "heirs" or its equivalent is not necessary to create an absolute estate. Every properly executed conveyance shall be construed to convey the fee unless a lesser estate is mentioned and limited in that conveyance. If a lesser estate is expressly limited, the courts shall not, by construction, increase such estate into a fee but, disregarding all technical rules, shall give effect to the intention of the maker of the instrument, as far as the same is lawful, if the intention can be gathered from the contents of the instrument. If the court cannot gather the intention of the maker from the contents of the instrument, it may hear parol evidence to prove the maker's intention.

Under the modern approach, we come up with a different answer to Question 2. The conveyance of Blackacre "to my sister, Susan, and her assigns forever" gives Susan a fee simple absolute, not a life estate. Let's move on to look at another problem with deed language.

QUESTION 3.   Conveying to a grantee and her successors. Lucia and Arastas are lifelong friends. Arastas owns Blackacre, a tract of rural timberland located in Georgia, in fee simple absolute. They often use Blackacre together for camping and other recreational pursuits. Arastas is planning to move out of state and is willing to sell Blackacre to Lucia for an extremely generous low price. In exchange for the price, Arastas signs and delivers a deed that purports to convey Blackacre. The granting clause of the deed provides: "Arastas hereby grants, conveys, and bargains and sells said timberland to my friend Lucia and her successors, to have and to hold." Under modern American law, as reflected by the Georgia statute, this grant creates

A. A fee simple absolute in Lucia.
B. A life estate in Lucia and a fee simple absolute in her successors.
C. A fee simple determinable in Lucia.
D. A tenancy in common in fee simple absolute in Lucia and her successors.

ANALYSIS.   The primary point of this question is to focus on what language is needed to create a fee simple estate under the rules applicable in most states today. Notice that the deed lacks words of inheritance: the magic word "heirs" is missing. Prior to the widespread adoption of statutes dispensing with the need for a deed to include words of inheritance, Lucia would have taken only a life estate. But today we have a different result. There is a presumption that a deed creates a fee simple. In the words of the Georgia statute, every conveyance "shall be construed to convey the fee unless a lesser estate is mentioned and limited in that conveyance."

The presumption can be rebutted. We need to examine the deed to see if there is any language that points to "a lesser estate," but there is none. The extra language we have consists of (1) a reference to the property being timberland, (2) the grant going not only to Lucia but also to "her successors," and (3) the odd phrase "to have and to hold."[3] None of these references suggest that Lucia might have only a life estate or a leasehold (or a fee tail where permitted). Thus, Lucia takes a fee simple. This means that **B** is wrong.

The other three choices force us to consider (1) whether Lucia's estate is determinable or absolute and (2) whether the estate is owned solely by Lucia or whether her "successors," whoever they may be, have an interest. As to the first point, the "timberland" reference does not make Lucia's estate determinable so **C** is incorrect. One can draft a deed that makes an estate end if the owner cuts trees, thereby changing the nature of the property to something other than timberland. But here no language restricts Lucia's ownership or takes away her estate if a certain event happens. Rather, the word "timberland" just describes the land as it now is.

The second and final point to consider is whether the deed's conveyance "to Lucia and her successors" may give her successors a property right. The term "successors" is close in meaning to "assigns," which we analyzed in Question 2. Its legal meaning can vary according to context. Narrowly, a person's successors are her heirs, but more generally it can mean anyone who follows or takes the place of another person. Whichever view we take, in this deed "successors" shows an intent that Lucia's estate is capable of being transferred. Therefore, **D** is wrong. (And this is an additional reason why **B** is wrong. Her successors do not have a future interest in the property.)

So by the process of elimination we are left with **A** as the right answer. Lucia owns a fee simple; it is not defeasible (thus it is a "fee simple absolute"), and she is the sole owner of the estate.

D.   Rebutting the Presumption of Fee Simple

Many cases have struggled with how specific language must be to rebut the presumption that the grantee or devisee takes a fee simple. No one would argue about the following examples:

- A deed conveys Blackacre "to Maria for life."
- A will devises Greenacre "to Carlos until he dies, and then to Fernanda and her heirs."

The first instrument uses the traditional formula, "to X for life." It is a term of art and cannot be misunderstood (by lawyers). It is not necessary, however,

---

3. These words customarily appear in the part of the deed known as a *habendum clause*. Their location here is atypical but harmless.

to use the words "for life" to create a life estate. They are not magic words, like the need to say "heirs" to create a fee simple at traditional common law. It works if the language of the grantor or testator, whatever it is, clearly shows the intent to create an estate to last for the life of a designated person or persons.

The test is flexible, and thus judicial outcomes are hard to predict. Courts often say the issue turns on the facts of each case, looking not only at the entire instrument but also the surrounding circumstances, which may shed light on what the grantor or testator hoped to accomplish. It is a question of judgment as to whether particular language is strong enough to overcome the presumption of a fee simple, leaving a life estate.

QUESTION 4.   The Alpine cottage. Ludwig dies, survived by his brother, sister, and five nephews and nieces. Of the nephews and nieces, his favorite was Latte, the only one who regularly visited Ludwig in his assisted-living complex. At his death Ludwig owned an Alpine cottage, where he had lived for part of every year until five years ago, when he went into assisted living. For the past five years, he has rented the Alpine cottage to tenants to generate income. Latte is a ski bum who loves the Alps and idolizes the lifestyle of American skier Bode Miller. As Ludwig knew, Latte would like nothing better than to have the means to continue his idyllic ski bum existence. Ludwig's will devised the cottage to "my nephew Latte so he will have a place to live in." The best argument that Latte takes a life estate under the will is

A. Under modern law, a life estate is presumed when the deed is ambiguous.
B. Latte will not need a place to live after he dies.
C. This is no restraint on Latte selling the property.
D. If the conveyance is a fee simple, it violates the Rule against Perpetuities.

ANALYSIS.   Cases conflict as to whether language such as this creates a fee simple or a life estate. There is no rule for you to memorize. It's likely that your property casebook has at least one case of this variety. Two principal cases commonly studied are *White v. Brown*, 559 S.W.2d 938 (1977) (fee simple created by will that devised house with words, "I wish Evelyn White to have my home to live in and not to be sold"), and *Williams v. Estate of Williams*, 865 S.W.3d 3 (1993) (life estate created by will devising house to three daughters "to have and hold during their lives, and not to be sold during their lifetime"). Note that both cases are decided by the same court, have similar (but not identical) language, yet they come out the opposite way. The question does not ask you to make the call as to whether Latte is likely to get a fee simple or a life estate. What you ought to be able to do is make reasoned arguments for either side.

A is plainly wrong. Modern law presumes a fee simple, not a life estate, when the will or deed is ambiguous as to the nature of the estate created.

In *White* and *Williams*, one issue was what to make of the apparent restriction on the sale of the home. Arguably in both cases the express restraint points in favor of a life estate because a restraint of this type imposed on a fee simple is legally unenforceable. At least in some states, a restraint on the transfer of a life estate is valid. This argument was weak in *White* and *Williams*: the presence or absence of a restraint on alienation would not indicate whether Ludwig was trying to convey a fee simple or life estate to Latte. But regardless of the strength of the argument, here there is no restraint. So **C** is not a good answer.

D is wrong. If the grant creates a fee simple, it would be a fee simple absolute, with no one holding a future interest. If no one has a future interest, there cannot possibly be a violation of the Rule against Perpetuities.[4]

This leaves us with **B** as our best answer, even though at first blush it doesn't sound like a right answer, perhaps because it is so obvious (no one needs a house in this world after death) and it includes no legal terms. For most students, this question would be easier if instead response **B** stated something like "From the will's language it appears that the testator intended Latte to have only a life estate." That would sound more like a court's analysis, but observe that such a statement is a conclusion, with no indication of the reasoning that supports such a conclusion.

E.   The Closer: Dying without Heirs

Recall that a primary characteristic of the fee simple estate is that when the owner dies, the property is inheritable by the owner's heirs. To create a fee simple, it is traditional and customary for a deed or will to include the words "and his heirs" or "and her heirs" after the name of the grantee or devisee. But what happens when the instrument includes the word "heirs" but in a different formulation? One form used with some frequency gives the grantee's name and then states what happens with the property if that person "dies without heirs." Assuming as courts generally do that the grantor meant "heirs" according to its technical legal definition, the expression signifies that the grantee has died with no relatives who qualify as "heirs" under the state statute of inheritance. As mentioned above, that person's property would escheat to the state, but that outcome would not follow for the property conveyed in the instrument if the language pointed to a different outcome.

---

4. For discussion of the Rule against Perpetuities, see chapter 13.

QUESTION 5. Dying without heirs at common law. Karen, the owner of Blackacre in fee simple absolute, conveyed the property "to my favorite niece, Cedilla, but if she dies without heirs, then said property shall go to the Goodnight Corporation and its successors and assigns." Assume that this conveyance creates no problem with respect to the Rule against Perpetuities and that it does not create a fee tail estate. **At traditional common law,** who owns what interests in Blackacre?

A. Cedilla has a fee simple and the Goodnight Corporation has a life estate.

B. Cedilla has a fee simple and the Goodnight Corporation has a fee simple.

C. Cedilla has a life estate and the Goodnight Corporation has a life estate.

D. Cedilla has a life estate and the Goodnight Corporation has a fee simple.

ANALYSIS. At traditional common law Cedilla can have a fee simple only if the grant is made to her "and her heirs." Although the granting clause contains the word "heirs" and it clearly means Cedilla's heirs, it is included as part of a defeasance provision, not as an indication of the quality of the estate Cedilla is to take. Even though it appears that Karen intended that Cedilla would have an inheritable estate, the common law required use of the word "heirs." Cedilla has only a life estate.

We might conclude the Goodnight Corporation also has only a life estate at common law because the conveyance does not say to the Corporation "and its heirs." But a corporation cannot have heirs, and therefore recall that the common law presumes that a conveyance to a corporation passes a fee simple in the absence of language to the contrary. **D** is our answer.

QUESTION 6. Dying without heirs today. For the conveyance given in Question 5, who owns what interests in Blackacre under modern law?

A. Cedilla has a fee simple and the Goodnight Corporation has a life estate.

B. Cedilla has a fee simple and the Goodnight Corporation has a fee simple.

C. Cedilla has a life estate and the Goodnight Corporation has a life estate.

D. Cedilla has a life estate and the Goodnight Corporation has a fee simple.

ANALYSIS.   Under modern law, a deed does not have to refer to the grantee and her "heirs" to pass a fee simple. The fee simple is presumed in the absence of language pointing to a lesser estate. Here the conveyance does have a take-away provision, but is that provision extensive enough to leave Cedilla with only a life estate? If Cedilla dies with heirs, she keeps the property (to be precise, we mean that at her death her estate acquires the property, and it passes to her heirs if she dies intestate or to her devisees if she dies testate). The Goodnight Corporation also has a fee simple, just as it did at traditional common law. Our answer is **B**.

 ## Smith's Picks

1.	Dividing the ranch over time	**D**
2.	A law student's help	**A**
3.	Conveying to a grantee and her successors	**A**
4.	The Alpine cottage	**B**
5.	Dying without heirs at common law	**D**
6.	Dying without heirs today	**B**

9

Defeasible Estates

"If your Riches are yours, why don't you take them with you to t'other world?"
Benjamin Franklin, *Poor Richard Improved* (1751)

CHAPTER OVERVIEW
A. The Nature of Defeasible Estates
B. What Language Makes an Estate Defeasible?
C. The Fee Simple Determinable
D. The Fee Simple Subject to Condition Subsequent
E. The Fee Simple Subject to Executory Limitation
F. The Closer: Distinguishing Cutting Short an Estate and the Natural
Expiration of an Estate
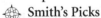 Smith's Picks

The last chapter introduced some basic elements of the estates system and focused on the fee simple absolute estate. Every estate is either indefeasible or defeasible. The fee simple absolute is not defeasible. This chapter considers defeasible estates, of which there are several types: (1) an estate that is *determinable,* (2) an estate that is *subject to condition subsequent,* and (3) an estate that is *subject to executory limitation.*

The purpose of a defeasible estate is to allow the person who creates the estate to retain an element of control over the land after the transfer. We can say that such an estate is "defeatible"—it can be defeated by the person who is given the right of control. An owner of a farm or another type of rural property may want that land to become a park or a nature sanctuary, with the opportunity to regain the land if those wishes are not followed. Similarly, an owner may be willing to donate land to a school or a nonprofit organization only if the recipient improves and uses the land in a specified way. The law allows the creation of defeasible estates to accomplish such objectives. Defeasible estates date back to the early days of English common law, and they remain widely used today.

A. The Nature of Defeasible Estates

An estate is defeasible if the language indicates that the estate can end before the normal expiration for that type of estate. To determine whether an estate is defeasible, we need to pay careful attention to the language of the instrument that created the estate. The question is not whether the estate can expire, or end. Every estate can expire. A fee simple absolute, which is the largest estate and is indefeasible, can end. The language that makes an estate defeasible must cause the estate to expire *prematurely*; that is, before the time a normal estate of that type, which has no special language in the instrument, would expire.

A defeasible estate is an estate that will or may terminate early based upon the happening of a future event. There are three types of defeasible fee simple estates:

- The fee simple determinable
- The fee simple subject to condition subsequent
- The fee simple subject to executory limitation

At this point, we are not concerned with the distinctions among these three types.[1] Rather, our focus is on a basic point common to all three. What words in a deed or will are sufficient to make the estate defeasible? We start with a strong presumption that an estate is indefeasible. Language of defeasance has to be expressed. It cannot be implied. This protects the grantee by giving the grantee as much ownership as possible. The law disfavors all limits or conditions on estates in part because they restrict the present use and future development of land. Although no precise language is required to create a defeasible estate, the instrument must clearly express the intent that the estate shall end upon a specified event.

A defeasible fee simple, which may last forever but which may be defeated, is represented by the following timeline.

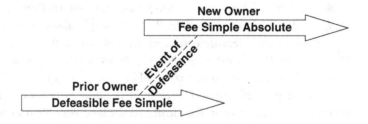

Notice that this diagram shows the initial present estate as "Defeasible Fee Simple" but after the event of defeasance, the "New Owner" is shown as having a "Fee Simple Absolute." This is normally what happens. Defeasance terminates the control (the limitation or condition) so that it does not bind the new owner. This depends, however, upon a reading of the language of the

---

1. The distinctions are explored in the following sections of this chapter.

instrument. The instrument can be drafted so that when defeasance causes a transfer of ownership, the new owner takes subject to the same control and acquires a defeasible estate, the same as her predecessor had.

QUESTION 1.   Defeasible or not? Which of the following conveyances create defeasible estates?

1. Owner conveys Blackacre "to Ahab, and at Ahab's death Blackacre shall go to Ishmael and his heirs so long as Ishmael is alive at the time of Ahab's death."
2. Owner conveys Greenacre "to Franklin for 20 years, but if Franklin fails to maintain the stone fence along the northern boundary of Greenacre, Owner shall have the right to terminate Franklin's estate and reenter Greenacre."
3. Owner conveys Whiteacre "to Whitney for life so long as Whitney remains a resident of the City of Chicago, and at the termination of Whitney's life estate to Wasco and his heirs in fee simple absolute."
4. Owner conveys Redacre "to Abigail and her heirs; provided that if Abigail dies while she still owns Redacre, and she dies intestate, and she dies without heirs, then this estate shall end and Redacre shall escheat to the state in which Redacre is situated."

A. All of the above.
B. 1, 2, and 3.
C. 3 only.
D. 2 and 3.
E. 2, 3, and 4.

ANALYSIS.   Let's go down the list in order. For conveyance 1, we need to decide whether either Ahab's estate or Ishmael's estate is defeasible. Ahab has a life estate. Is there any language in the conveyance indicating how it might end before Ahab's death? There is not: Ahab is to own Blackacre until he dies. Ishmael's remainder sounds like it's defeasible due to the words "so long as Ishmael is alive at the time of Ahab's death," but this is a trick. The words "so long as" often point to a defeasible estate, but here the phrase represents a condition precedent to the vesting of Ishmael's remainder. If Ishmael survives Ahab, he will take a fee simple absolute. So there are no defeasible estates in conveyance 1.

In conveyance 2, Franklin has a 20-year term for years, but it can be cut short if Franklin fails to maintain the fence. A term for years can be defeasible, and this one is.

Similarly, conveyance 3 imposes a requirement that Whitney remain a Chicago resident. If she moves, her life estate ends then. This is a defeasible life estate.

Conveyance 4 stipulates that if Abigail dies without heirs, the property shall escheat to the state. The language certainly describes a method by which her estate may end, but escheat is an inherent limitation on every fee simple estate. The language does no more than express this implied limit. Thus the language does not add any restriction to what Abigail acquired as a grantee of a fee simple. She still has a fee simple absolute. So our right answer is **D** because only conveyances 2 and 3 include defeasible estates.

B.   What Language Makes an Estate Defeasible?

So we've learned that to have a defeasible estate, the deed or will must contain clear language that points to defeasance. In actual cases, the real problem is deciding "how clear is clear enough"? An informed drafter will use time-honored language, tested by long lines of cases, which clearly suffices. The most cautious approach is to have language that does three things unequivocally:

- Uses the traditional language that signals the type of defeasible present estate;
- Refers specifically to the holder of the future interest, using the proper traditional language; and
- Includes a statement that names the type of estate created by the instrument.

For example, consider a plan to create a fee simple subject to condition subsequent where the grantor wants the land to remain as timberland. Suppose that the relevant parts of the deed state:

> to Grantee on the condition that the land shall be used and maintained at all times as timberland. Provided, that if at any time in the future, the land shall be used for a purpose other than timberland, Grantor or his heirs shall have the right to reenter the property . . .
>   This deed is intended to create a fee simple subject to condition subsequent and to reserve a right of entry in Grantor.

This is pretty good. A court will necessarily hold that this language creates what it says it does, assuming there is no language elsewhere in the deed that is arguably inconsistent and assuming that the court will not hear extrinsic evidence to the contrary that a party may seek to introduce.

Often parties have failed to use such clear language. When the parties to a deed employ ambiguous language concerning the grantee's use of the property, there are four possibilities:

- The deed creates a defeasible fee simple (one of the three types listed above).
- The deed creates a fee simple absolute, with a promise by the grantee to use the land only for certain purposes. This promise may be personal

to the parties, or it may bind and benefit their heirs and assigns. If the promise has the latter effect, it is called a covenant that runs with the land (formally called either a *real covenant* or *equitable servitude,* depending on technicalities of its creation). Breach of a covenant will entitle the grantor or his successors to contract remedies (damages or an injunction) but not to recovery of the land.[2]

- The deed creates an unrestricted fee simple absolute. The language is precatory or merely recites the parties' reasons for entering into the transaction. The grantee is free to do as it pleases, and the grantor has no legal right to object.
- It is possible that an ambiguous deed does not convey an estate at all, but only an *easement* which gives the grantee the right to use the land for a limited purpose.[3] The grantor then retains his fee simple, but it is subject to the granted easement. This frequently happens in situations where a landowner conveys a strip of land for a "railroad right-of-way" or a "road right-of-way."

QUESTION 2.   Keep up the fence. In 1980, Grover conveyed to Cleveland a 20-foot-wide strip of land that passes along the north side of Grover's property. The grant enabled Cleveland to access a highway. The deed conveyed "on the condition that said Grantee shall build a stone fence to separate the conveyed parcel from said Grantor's remaining land and forever maintain the fence in good condition." Ten years later Cleveland died, survived by his sole heir, Alexander. Cleveland had timely built the fence and maintained it in immaculate condition, but over the next decades, the fence weathered substantially and Alexander did nothing in the way of repairs. Grover, now an old man, sued Alexander to recover possession of the 20-foot strip. Alexander's best defense is:

A. The grant should be interpreted as having granted an easement to Cleveland.

B. The obligation to maintain the stone fence is an unreasonable restraint on alienation.

C. The grant should be interpreted as a covenant by the grantee to build and maintain the stone fence.

D. The obligation to maintain the stone fence violates the Rule against Perpetuities.

E. The obligation does not apply to Alexander because the deed only required "Grantee" to build and maintain the stone fence.

---

2. For discussion of covenants, see chapters 26 and 27.
3. For discussion of easements, see chapters 24 and 25.

ANALYSIS.   This question focuses on arguments that mere language of condition is insufficient to create a defeasible fee. There is a presumption under modern law that every deed creates a fee simple absolute. The best answer is **C**, even though it reflects a conclusion, rather than the thought process needed to arrive at that conclusion. Alexander wants to argue that the parties' use of the word "condition" is not enough, in and of itself, to make the obligation a "condition subsequent" so that the deed creates a fee simple subject to condition subsequent. Alexander points to the lack of any language indicating what should happen if the fence isn't maintained as evidence that the parties did not want the grantee to lose ownership if that happened. Thus, Alexander is arguing that the obligation should be labeled a covenant for the purpose of limiting Grover's remedies. Alexander is willing to concede, in this litigation, that Grover may be able to sue him for damages or injunctive relief based on Alexander's failure to maintain the fence,[4] but that should be Grover's only recourse, not actual loss of the land.

   A is not a strong answer, even though the assertion that the grant should create an easement is plausible. Because the original purpose was to give Cleveland access to the highway, all Cleveland needed was a right-of-way easement. Most neighboring landowners would solve the need for a person to gain access across a neighbor's property by granting an easement, not by conveying a strip of land in fee simple. However, the question states that Grover conveyed "a strip of land," and this descriptor points to fee title rather than an easement. More importantly, it doesn't help Alexander if he has an easement. He still has the same problem as to whether failure to maintain the stone fence ends the grant. Instead of an easement with perpetual duration, he may have a defeasible easement (in other words, an easement subject to a condition subsequent).

   B is wrong. The doctrine of restraints on alienation applies if language in the instrument denies the grantee the power to convey by sale or gift or to pass the property to the grantee's heirs or devisees. Here nothing in the deed purported to restrict any attempt by Cleveland to transfer the strip of land to a new owner, and Alexander took the strip by inheritance, with no language in the deed purporting to interfere with that succession. As a practical matter, land is less alienable if the grantee has a defeasible fee simple, but the doctrine of restraints on alienation does not preclude the creation of defeasible fee simple estates.

   There is no Rule against Perpetuities violation, so **D** is not correct.[5] It is true that the condition to maintain the fence may persist longer than 21 years after lives in being (that is, after the latter to die of Grover and

---

4. Such relief would stem from construing the language as creating a real covenant or equitable servitude. For discussion, see Part C of chapter 26.
5. For discussion of the Rule against Perpetuities, see chapter 13.

Alexander), but the Rule against Perpetuities does not apply to a right of entry. If the condition makes the conveyance a fee simple subject to condition subsequent, then Grover has a right of entry. Rights of entry, like possibilities of reverter, have always been considered immune from the Rule against Perpetuities.

E is the second-best answer of the sequence. Deeds are often drafted to impose an obligation on the "Grantee, his heirs and assigns," but here that language is lacking. Thus, arguably the obligation was personal to Cleveland, and does not apply to his heir, Alexander. However, a court is likely to fill in the gap, holding that the fence obligation runs with the land, whether it is a covenant or a true condition subsequent. The parties to the deed used the word "forever" and therefore appeared to want to ensure that the stone fence would be maintained for a very long time. This intent is defeated if a court reads the deed as not binding Cleveland's heirs and assigns. If all Cleveland had to do to get out of the fence obligation was to convey the strip to someone else, then Cleveland's performance was optional. This plainly is not what Grover would have intended when he put this language in the deed.

C.   The Fee Simple Determinable

A fee simple determinable may last indefinitely, but its continuance depends upon the occurrence or nonoccurrence of a specified future event or state of affairs. The future event that terminates a fee simple determinable is called a *limitation*. The future interest retained by the grantor or the testator's estate is called a *possibility of reverter*.

If the limitation for a fee simple determinable is triggered, then the estate ends automatically. The grantor does not have to give notice to the possessor under the fee simple determinable estate or take any action to regain title.

The traditional words used to create a fee simple determinable are:

- until
- so long as
- as long as
- during

Generally the incorporation of these words in the part of the instrument indicating how long the estate should continue is sufficient to create a fee simple determinable. To remove possible doubt, a careful drafter will also (1) specifically state that the property is to revert to the grantor or to the grantor's successors upon the specified contingency and (2) name the interests created—for example, a fee simple determinable to the grantee and a possibility of reverter to the grantor.

QUESTION 3.   Is it determinable? Which of the following conveyances create fee simple determinable estates?

1. Owner conveys Blackacre "to Ames and his heirs so long as the old stone cottage situated on Blackacre remains in place and in good repair."
2. Owner conveys Greenacre "to Burundi and her heirs, but if alcoholic beverages are ever sold on the premises, Owner has the right to reenter Greenacre."
3. Owner conveys Farmacre "to Carlo and his heirs for the purpose of growing soybeans."

A. None of the above.
B. 1, 2, and 3.
C. 1 only.
D. 1 and 3.
E. 2 only.

ANALYSIS.   Let's review the conveyances in the order they're given. Conveyance 1 uses the magic words "so long as," which point to a fee simple determinable. Because there is no language that conflicts with this indicator or creates ambiguity, this suffices.

Conveyance 2 does create a defeasible estate, but the key words "but if" point to a fee simple subject to condition subsequent, not to a fee simple determinable.

Conveyance 3 expresses a purpose, which generally is not sufficient in and of itself to create a defeasible estate of any type. The grantee, Carol, has a fee simple absolute. Thus our answer is **C.**

D.   The Fee Simple Subject to Condition Subsequent

A fee simple determinable has a sibling: the fee simple subject to condition subsequent. Like the former estate, the fee simple subject to condition subsequent may last forever, but it may end based upon what happens after its creation. The future event that terminates a fee simple subject to condition subsequent is called a *condition.* The future interest retained by the grantor or the testator's estate is known as a *right of entry* or a *power of termination.*

Unlike a fee simple determinable, a fee simple subject to condition subsequent does not end automatically when the triggering event takes place. The grantor or her successor has the right to terminate the estate but must take action to accomplish a termination. If the right of entry is not exercised or enforced, the estate continues uninterrupted.

To create a fee simple subject to condition subsequent, the instrument usually includes explicit language of condition placed after the language that grants the property. The condition often reads as if it were an "afterthought" in the mind of the grantor or testator. The traditional words used to point to fee simple subject to condition subsequent are

- but if
- provided that
- on condition that
- subject to the condition that
- however

Under modern law, it is dangerous to use these words alone if the grantor wants to create a defeasible estate. A number of courts have interpreted instruments with such phrases as creating a fee simple absolute in the absence of additional evidence that a fee simple subject to condition subsequent was intended. An express reference to the right of the grantor or her successors to reenter the property or to terminate the estate is highly advisable.

> **QUESTION 4.   Which estate should the grantor pick?** Courts have often said that the fee simple determinable (where the estate ends automatically upon the triggering of the limitation) is more onerous for the grantee than the fee simple subject to condition subsequent. This has led to a standard rule of construction. When there is doubt or ambiguity as to which estate was intended, the grantee should have the fee simple subject to condition subsequent. This tends to suggest that an informed grantor is likely to want to create a fee simple determinable, rather than a fee simple subject to condition subsequent. Is this invariably true? Compared to a fee simple determinable, why might a grantor prefer the fee simple subject to condition subsequent?
>
> A. The grantor has more flexibility in deciding what to do when a triggering event takes place if the grantee has a fee simple subject to condition subsequent.
> B. The grantor will find it easier to regain actual possession of the land if the grantee has a fee simple subject to condition subsequent.
> C. The grantor's future interest will have a higher market value if the grantee has a fee simple subject to condition subsequent.
> D. The grantor will not have to compensate the grantee for the value of improvements added by the grantee if the grantee has a fee simple subject to condition subsequent.
> E. All of the above.

ANALYSIS. Let's begin with Choice **B**. If a triggering event takes place and the grantee is in actual possession of the land, the grantor has the same practical and legal problem in regaining possession, whichever type of defeasible estate exists. If the grantee will not vacate possession voluntarily, the grantor probably will have to commence a lawsuit.

C suggests that a right of entry might have a higher market value than a possibility of reverter for the same property, with the same triggering event. There is no reason to suppose this would be the case. Under modern law, in most states both interests are capable of inter vivos transfer by deed, but there are no active markets in which such interests are traded or exchanged.

D raises the issue of what happens if the grantee has added valuable improvements to the property. For either type of defeasible estate, improvements may become the grantor's property upon an ending of the estate, or the court may choose to protect the improver. It is not likely that the nature of the underlying estate will affect the court's willingness to favor the grantee.

A posits that the fee simple subject to condition subsequent confers flexibility upon the grantor. This is correct. With a fee simple determinable, the grantor automatically is given title to the property if the specified event occurs. Because future circumstances may not be what the grantor envisions when she creates the estate, it is possible that the grantor may not want to get the property back for a given violation. The simple subject to condition subsequent gives her a choice, letting her make that decision when and if the time comes.

E. The Fee Simple Subject to Executory Limitation

Like the two other defeasible fee simple estates, the fee simple subject to executory limitation can last indefinitely. Also like them, its continuance depends upon a future act or event. The distinction between the fee simple subject to executory limitation and the two other defeasible fee simple estates is where the property goes when the triggering act or event occurs. Unlike the fee simple determinable and fee simple subject to condition subsequent, the property goes to an alternative grantee named in the deed or will. Whenever there is a fee simple subject to executory limitation, by definition there is a grantee who holds an executory interest. An executory interest is a future interest, held by a grantee, that divests (or cuts short) a present estate before its natural end.

Executory interests are of two basic types:

- The springing executory interest. This type divests the grantor of her estate in the future. It is called springing because it springs out from the grantor.
- The shifting executory interest. This type divests an earlier grantee of her estate in the future. It is called shifting because it shifts the estate from an earlier grantee to an alternative one.

The executory interest resembles the possibility of reverter, which is held by the grantor in that an executory interest becomes possessory automatically upon the happening of a triggering condition or limitation. As the following chart indicates, our system does not recognize an executory interest that allows its holder the option to terminate the prior estate.

Who Holds Future Interest	Automatic Termination	Optional Termination
Future Interest in Grantor	Possibility of Reverter	Right of Entry
Future Interest in Grantee	Shifting Executory Interest	Not Allowed
Future Interest in Grantor	Springing Executory Interest	Not Allowed

No particular language is required to create a fee simple subject to executory limitation. The instrument may use language of limitation, the same as a fee simple determinable, or it may use language of condition, the same as a fee simple subject to condition subsequent. In either case, the interests created are labeled the same: a fee simple subject to executory limitation, followed by an executory interest.

QUESTION 5. Spot the executory interests. Which of the following conveyances create a fee simple subject to executory limitation (and thus also create an executory interest)?

1. Owner conveys Blackacre "to Omar and his heirs when and if he marries." Omar, single at the time of the conveyance, remains unmarried.
2. Owner conveys Redacre "to Amelia and her heirs, but if the property is devoted to a use other than a wildlife park before the expiration of 21 years after Amelia's death, to Brian and his heirs."
3. Owner conveys Greenacre "to Circes and her heirs so long as the ginkgo tree presently growing on the property remains alive and in place."

A. All of the above.
B. 1 only.
C. 2 only.
D. 3 only.
E. 1 and 2.

ANALYSIS.   Let's consider the three conveyances in order. Conveyance 1 calls for a transfer of Blackacre from Owner to Omar if he marries. Owner presently has a fee simple subject to executory limitation, and Omar has an executory interest. Although it's generally true that a fee simple subject to executory limitation involves two grantees, this conveyance illustrates an exception. Omar cannot have a remainder because his estate, if it vests, will not follow the expiration of a life estate, a leasehold, or (where permitted) a fee tail. Omar's estate will cut short the grantor's ownership. Thus, Omar has to own an executory interest (more precisely, a springing executory interest in fee simple). Because Owner's fee simple is subject to that executory interest, we attach the label fee simple subject to executory limitation.

Conveyance 2 uses conditional language to take the property away from Amelia if the land use is changed. Amelia has a fee simple subject to executory limitation, and Brian has an executory interest.

Conveyance 3 calls for Circes's estate to end upon the death or destruction of the ginkgo tree. This creates a defeasible estate, but it's not a fee simple subject to executory limitation. Greenacre will revert to Owner or Owner's successors when the tree is no longer. Circes holds a fee simple determinable. So our answer is **E**.

F. The Closer: Distinguishing Cutting Short an Estate and the Natural Expiration of an Estate

An executory interest must divest, or cut short, a prior estate. The prior estate does not have to be a fee simple. It may be a life estate, a leasehold, or (where allowed) a fee tail estate. But the executory interest must cut short that estate. If the future interest follows the natural expiration of the prior estate, the future interest is a remainder, not an executory interest. This can get tricky.

> **QUESTION 6. Let's stay married.** Owner conveys Blueacre "to Sedalia so long as she remains alive and married, and when she dies or becomes unmarried, to Rapunzel and her heirs." Sedalia is married to Brutus, and was so at the time of the conveyance. This conveyance probably creates
>
> **A.** A defeasible life estate and an executory interest.
> **B.** A defeasible life estate and a remainder.
> **C.** A defeasible life estate, an executory interest, and a remainder.
> **D.** A defeasible fee simple and a springing executory interest.
> **E.** A defeasible fee simple and a shifting executory interest.
> **F.** A fee simple determinable and a possibility of reverter.

ANALYSIS.   The first step for all estates and future interest questions is to label the present estate, which typically means an examination of the first words of the grant. Although the words "to Sedalia so long as she remains alive and married" do not explicitly say "life estate" or the traditional formula, "to Sedalia for life," we should conclude that she has a life estate. Owner has clearly expressed the intent that at the end of her life, even if she remains married to Brutus for her entire life, Blueacre is to go to Rapunzel. Thus we've eliminated Choices **D**, **E**, and **F**.

Should we pick **A**, **B**, or **C**? Blueacre will go to Rapunzel at the first to occur of Sedalia's death or the ending of Sedalia's marriage (presumably by death of her husband or by divorce). It looks like Rapunzel has an executory interest, and a number of students will reach this conclusion. But this is the wrong path. Rapunzel's future interest will not cut short Sedalia's estate, even if it becomes possessory due to the ending of Sedalia's marriage. The language "so long as she remains married" is considered as marking the time of natural expiration of her estate. Thus, Rapunzel has a remainder, not an executory interest, and **B** is the correct answer.

 Smith's Picks

1. Defeasible or not?	D
2. Keep up the fence	C
3. Is it determinable?	C
4. Which estate should the grantor pick?	A
5. Spot the executory interests	E
6. Let's stay married	B

10

Life Estates

"Waste not, want not."
English saying, eighteenth century

CHAPTER OVERVIEW
A. The Nature of the Life Estate
B. Legal and Equitable Life Estates
C. The Doctrine of Waste
D. The Closer: Continuing an Ongoing Activity
✦ Smith's Picks

The life estate is an ancient form of property ownership. In our Anglo-American legal system, the life estate dates back to the tenurial system established in England after the Norman Conquest. At first, nobles held land of the King for their lifetime. After the invention of the fee simple, that newer estate became popular and eventually became the most common form of land ownership.

The life estate, however, has persisted because it still serves a useful purpose. A person's economic needs last for that person's lifetime and no longer. The advantage to fee simple ownership is the right to specify who shall own the property after the present owner has died. While this is a valuable right, it is not central to satisfying a person's present needs. Family wealth, land as well as financial assets, is often placed in life estates. Life estates are usually created by gift, devise, or bequest, initiated by an owner who wants to provide for a spouse, children, grandchildren, or other relatives. Today in the Unites States, most life estates are held in trust, with trustees managing the property for beneficiaries, who receive the trust income for their lives.

A. The Nature of the Life Estate

As its name implies, a life estate lasts only so long as the grantee or devisee (known as the life *tenant*) lives. Upon the life tenant's death, the property reverts to the original grantor or her successors, or it shifts to another grantee designated in the deed or will. Almost always that next grantee holds a future interest called a remainder. A life tenant has the exclusive right to possess and enjoy the property until death, but the life tenant cannot pass it to her heirs or devisees. A life tenant may convey the property during her lifetime, but the grantee only succeeds to the possessory rights of the original life tenant. A life tenant's conveyance cannot extend the duration of the life estate. In practice, very few people buy or sell life estates.[1]

We may represent the creation of a simple life estate, followed by a remainder, by the following timeline diagram.

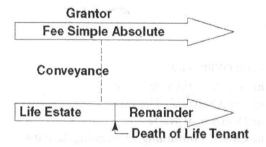

When a life estate is transferred to another, it is called an estate *pur autre vie*, from old French words meaning "for another's life." An estate *pur autre vie* may also be created directly when an owner conveys property to a grantee for the lifetime of another specified person.

The traditional language used to create a life estate is to a person or to a class of persons (such as my children) "for life" or "for their lives." These words do not have to be used. Any language that evinces the intent that the grantee or devisee should have the property for her lifetime is sufficient.

Today fee simple estates in land are much more commonly used than life estates. This has led to a rule of construction, usually mandated by state statute, which favors the fee simple absolute over a life estate when there is ambiguity or doubt as to the intent of the grantor or testator.

---

1. One reason is the risk stemming from the uncertainty as to how long a life estate will last. Consider the story of a French woman, Jeanne Calment, who died in 1997 at the age of 122, having reached the longest confirmed lifespan in history. In 1965, when she was a mere 90, she sold her condominium to a lawyer in exchange for an annuity (monthly payments to her until she died). The purchaser paid dearly — at the time of the sale, the value of the condominium was equal to ten years of payments.

QUESTION 1.   Conveying more than the life tenant owns. Sue owned an oceanfront condominium in fee simple absolute. At her death, a will was found. A devise in Sue's will provided

> Because my dear friend, Sam, and his family have always enjoyed vacationing at my Ocean Beach condominium, I devise that property to Sam for the remainder of his life and then to his children.

Two years after Sue's death, Sam, strapped for cash, sold the condominium to Paula with the deed conveying "to Paula and her heirs." Paula owns what interest in the condominium?

A.   A fee simple absolute because the language in the deed she took from Sam has no restrictions or limitations.
B.   A defeasible fee simple, which will terminate when Sam dies.
C.   A life estate, which will terminate when Sam dies.
D.   A life estate, which will terminate when Paula dies.
E.   A life estate, which will terminate after Paula and her heirs have all died.

ANALYSIS.   Whenever you have a question that includes multiple transfers of the same tract of land, you should analyze the ownership interests step by step. Here we must consider the will before we think about the deed. The will's language is obvious: "to Sam for the remainder of his life" plainly creates a life estate. Although the language does not incorporate the most commonly used phrase to create a life estate ("to Sam for life"), Sue's intent is crystal clear.

Sam's attempted sale of the condominium to Paula muddies the water. The facts imply that he did not disclose to her that he owned only a life estate, and the deed that he gave her purported to convey "to Paula and her heirs." This means that she should have a fee simple absolute, but he cannot convey more than he owns. Paula cannot qualify as a bona fide purchaser because Sue's will is a link in Sam's chain of title. If Paula had obtained a title search, it would have revealed Sam's lack of ownership of the fee. Therefore, **A** is wrong.

B is incorrect for a similar reason. Sam's deed transferred his life estate to Paula, and there is no reason to relabel it as a defeasible fee simple.

Choices **C**, **D**, and **E** are all in the right ballpark inasmuch as they recognize that Paula owns a life estate. The choices differ by assigning alternative times for the life estate to expire. The right answer is **C**. When a life estate is transferred, there is no change made with respect to the measuring life. Sam owned a life estate measured by his own life, and now Paula owns a life estate measured by Sam's life. The time when Paula and her heirs die has no impact on the duration of the life estate.[2] This type of life estate is known as an estate *pur autre vie.*

Let's try a variation on the last scenario. What should happen with an apparent devise of a life estate if no remaindermen are around?

QUESTION 2.   Premature death of potential remaindermen. Recall from Question 1 that Sue's will devised her condominium "to Sam for the remainder of his life and then to his children." Suppose at the time that Sue made her will, Sam was married and had two children. One week before Sue died, both of Sam's children tragically died in a boating accident. Does this change our conclusion from Question 1 that the will devised a life estate to Sam, which was all he could transfer to Paula?

A.   No, because the language of the will indicates Sam should have a life estate.

B.   No, because Sam may have another child before he dies.

C.   Yes, because Sam takes the remainder that his children would have owned.

D.   Yes, because the remainder is read out of the will and Sam is presumed to take a fee simple.

ANALYSIS.   **C** and **D** are alike in that both attribute significance to the new fact regarding Sam's children and conclude that Sam acquired more than a life estate. **D** directly gives Sam a fee simple by applying the presumption that in the absence of contrary evidence, a will passes a fee simple to a devisee. However, there is no good reason for a court to award more than a life estate to Sam, regardless of the status of his children at any point in time. The will is clear that Sam should have a life estate. **D** is wrong because the failure of the remainder creates a reversion; it does not upgrade Sam's life estate.

Similarly, **C** is wrong. The remainder was to go to Sam's children, and their untimely deaths do not transfer an interest to Sam.

This leaves us with **A** and **B**, which both limit Sam, and Paula as his successor, to a life estate, notwithstanding the new fact. It is true that Sam might have one or more children before he dies, and those children would take the remainder in fee simple. But this is not the reason why Sam has only a life estate. Even if the remainder ultimately fails because Sam has no additional children, Sam should have no more than a life estate. If the remainder fails, then Sue's estate has retained a reversion, and at Sam's death the condominium will go to whomever acquired that reversion through Sue's estate. Thus, **A** is the right

---

2. If Paula dies before Sam, under modern law Paula's heirs or devisees will own the life estate.

answer. Because Sam still has only a life estate, that is all he can transfer in a sale to Paula.[3]

B.   Legal and Equitable Life Estates

One classification of property rights, applicable to many different forms of property, distinguishes between legal interests and equitable interests. Every life estate is either a *legal life estate* or an *equitable life estate*. The former term means there is only one owner. Conversely, an equitable life estate arises when property is held in trust, and a beneficiary of the trust has an ownership interest measured by her lifetime. The trustee who manages the trust has legal title to the property, and such a beneficiary has an equitable life estate. Today it is much more common for property owners to create equitable life estates by forming a trust, rather than creating legal ones. A trust affords its creator wide discretion to accomplish a number of objectives, including protection of beneficiaries, preservation and maintenance of trust property, and professional management by individual or institutional trustees.

> **QUESTION 3.   Spot the equitable interests.** Claudio conveys Blackacre "to Teresa, to hold and manage said property for the sole benefit of Richard for the duration of his life, and at his death said property shall be distributed to Richard's children for the duration of their lives; and upon the death of the last of Richard's children, said property shall go to the XYZ Church." Who owns equitable life estates?
>
> A.   Richard.
> B.   Richard and his children.
> C.   Richard, his children, and the XYZ Church.
> D.   Teresa.
> E.   Teresa, Richard, his children, and the XYZ Church.

ANALYSIS.   Let's go step by step. Claudio's conveyance says that Teresa must hold and manage Blackacre for Richard's benefit "for the duration of his life." Although the word "trust" or "trustee" does not appear, it's plain that Teresa is not entitled to benefit personally from her ownership of Blackacre. So she is trustee, with legal title. Richard does not have legal title, so he has an equitable

---

3. There is another possibility with respect to the fate of the remainder, but it has no effect on the reasoning process needed to answer this question. The doctrine of lapse applies when a devisee dies after the testator makes the will but before the testator dies. Under state anti-lapse statutes, the property goes to the descendants of the deceased devisee under certain circumstances. In many states, if Sam's children had descendants, they would qualify as owners of the remainder.

life estate. He is the beneficiary of the trust created by Claudio. We've eliminated **D** and **E**.

Richard's children and XYZ Church own future interests in Blackacre. To pick among **A**, **B**, and **C**, we must determine whether their interests are equitable life estates. Richard's children have a life estate, but is it equitable or legal? Claudio could have provided that Teresa would continue to serve as trustee after Richard's death for the benefit of his children, but he specified the opposite. The conveyance states that at Richard's death "said property shall be distributed" to the children. Thus, the children have a legal life estate (no separation of legal and equitable title). Similarly, XYZ Church's interest is legal, not equitable. (In addition, XYZ Church's future interest is not a life estate. It has a fee simple absolute.) So **A** is the answer.

C.   The Doctrine of Waste

The doctrine of waste, developed by courts at common law, protects the holder of the future interest from conduct by the life tenant that may destroy or damage the property. The doctrine of waste does not apply to property held in fee simple absolute because its owner has an economic interest in preserving and protecting the property value. The fee simple owner can realize the future value of the property beyond her lifetime by making a present sale or by specifying the new owner in her will. In contrast, a life tenant has no innate economic interest in preserving or protecting property beyond her lifetime. She cannot sell its future value beyond her own life expectancy. For this reason, the law of waste steps in to protect the future interest owner.

The modern law of waste seeks to achieve a balance between the rights of the possessor and the rights of the other owners. The basic goal is to preserve the economic value of the property for the future owners. Thus, a life tenant ordinarily cannot remove a house or cut valuable timber. Yet the possessor is entitled to make reasonable use of the property, and often reasonable use requires the making of some changes to the property. For example, trees may have to be removed or an old building may require drastic structural renovations or even demolition. The old common law view of waste that developed in agrarian England barred such changes, generally preventing the possessor from making any substantial physical change to the property. The aim was to preserve the property in its present physical form for successive owners. Today waste is much more flexible. Instead of concentrating on the physical substance of the property, the focus is on preserving and protecting economic value for the successive owners. Thus, clearing trees and making major changes to buildings are often permitted. It depends on whether such changes are reasonable and prudent, which in large part hinges on their effect on property value.

The law of waste has two branches. First, the life tenant must not commit *affirmative waste* by engaging in conduct that removes, destroys, or damages the property, such as tearing down a valuable building or selling timber. Affirmative waste is sometimes called *voluntary waste* because it sanctions intentional conduct that substantially diminishes the value of the property. Second, the law of waste also imposes affirmative duties on the life tenant by labeling certain failures to act as *permissive waste.* This means that the life tenant's failure to act has diminished the property value. The most common type of permissive waste is the failure to make ordinary and necessary repairs to buildings and other structures. In addition, other acts that jeopardize the future owner's interests in ways that are unrelated to the physical condition of the property may constitute waste. For example, failure to pay real estate taxes may be permissive waste because it creates the risk that title to the property will be lost by a tax foreclosure sale.

The doctrine of waste empowers the holder of a reversion or remainder in the property to force the life tenant to preserve its capital value intact. The remedies for waste vary but can include an injunction, monetary damages, and forfeiture of the property.[4]

QUESTION 4.   Let's cut some trees. Aunt Judy's will devised 200 acres of virgin woodland property "to my dear sister Edith for life, and then to my favorite niece, Natalie, and her heirs." Two years after Judy died, Edith discovered that the timber on the land was worth lots of money, and she promptly began negotiating with Tree Reapers, Inc., a local lumber company, to sell the standing timber. Natalie believes the property should be left in its natural state, with no cutting of the trees. She objects to Edith making any deal with Tree Reapers. In spite of Natalie's objection, Edith continues to negotiate with Tree Reapers. It appears that Edith is on the verge of selling her entire interest in the property to Tree Reapers for $300,000. Natalie brings an action against Edith and Tree Reapers. Which of the following outcomes is most likely?

A.   The court will enjoin the sale if Natalie proves that Tree Reapers, as buyer, customarily has failed to replant seedlings after cutting mature timber.

B.   The court will enjoin the sale unless Tree Reapers submits a bona fide, feasible plan to replant seedlings on all of that property after it cuts the timber.

---

4. Life tenants are not the only people protected by the law of waste. The owners of future interests that follow defeasible fee simples (possibility of reverter, right of entry, and executory interests) may bring an action for harm to the property if defeasance of the estate is imminent. The waste doctrine also protects mortgage lenders from conduct that impairs the value of the real property that serves as collateral. See Section C in chapter 22.

C. The court will enjoin the sale regardless of Tree Reaper's conduct in prior harvesting.
D. Natalie could not have the sale enjoined, but she could recover damages from Edith.
E. Natalie could not have the sale enjoined, but she could obtain an injunction prohibiting Edith and Tree Reapers from cutting any trees.

ANALYSIS. Of the five responses, the first three propose that, at least under some circumstances, the court will enjoin Edith's proposed sale of the timberland. A life tenant such as Edith has the right to convey her life estate to anyone she pleases. A remainderman such as Natalie has no right to block a conveyance, no matter how objectionable she views the proposed grantee. Thus, **A**, **B**, and **C** are all infirm answers.

This leaves us with **D** and **E** as the remaining candidates for the best answer. The first clause in **D** is correct (the sale will not be enjoined), but can Natalie recover damages from Edith? Certainly, she cannot recover damages based on the sale alone, but what if Tree Reapers commits affirmative waste shortly after the sale by cutting trees? Might Edith, in addition to Tree Reapers, bear liability for damages? The issue is a close one, but I consider it unlikely that Natalie will prevail. It is rare to impose liability in tort on a person in Edith's position who has fully parted with the property before the tortious conduct commences.

So we're left with **E** as the correct answer. Because it appears probable that Edith and Tree Reapers will strike a deal allowing Tree Reapers to commit waste by harvesting timber, Natalie may obtain an injunction prohibiting such waste.

D. The Closer: Continuing an Ongoing Activity

One exception to the doctrine of waste applicable to life tenants is known as the *open mine doctrine*. Ordinarily, the law of waste prohibits a life tenant from taking minerals, timber, or other depletable natural resources from the property. The owner of the reversion or the remainder has the right to those assets. The open mine doctrine allows the life tenant to continue resource extraction that was taking place when the grantor or testator created the life estate. Granting this privilege to the life tenant is thought to be consistent with the probable intent of the grantor or testator who was engaging in the resource extraction, either directly or by authorizing another person to do so.

QUESTION 5.   **Selling soil.** Five years ago, Homer tired of farming his 640 acres, on which he had grown soybeans for more than 30 years. He decided to accept federal crop subsidies in exchange for not growing crops. His farm has rich topsoil. The next year he augmented his income by selling topsoil to a company, which paid him $6 per ton of topsoil. Homer and the company entered into an annual contract with no renewal rights. Nevertheless, the parties negotiated a new annual contract at the same rate for the following two years. The contract expired two months before Homer died. Homer and the company had negotiated over the terms of a new contract but failed to reach an agreement. Homer wanted a royalty of $7 per ton, which the company refused to pay. Homer had executed his will seven years before his death. His will devised his farm "to my daughter Edie because she needs financial support since her husband died." His will says nothing more about his farm, and it contains no residuary devise. Homer's heirs are his three children: Edie and her two younger brothers. One year after Homer died, Edie remarried. Her new husband is a surgeon with a substantial income. Shortly after the couple's honeymoon, Edie reached an agreement to sell topsoil to the company her father dealt with, calling for a royalty of $6.60 per ton. The brothers have brought an action against Edie. If the brothers prevail, the most likely reason will be

A. Edie has not acted in good faith by negotiating the topsoil contract without including her brothers.
B. After Edie's remarriage she no longer needed financial support due to her changed circumstances.
C. At the time when Homer made his will there was no contract in place for the sale and removal of topsoil.
D. At the time when Homer died there was no contract in place for the sale and removal of topsoil.
E. There is a presumption that Homer's will devised a fee simple, rather than a life estate, to Edie.

ANALYSIS.   This is a toughie. Before we examine our choices, let's start out by identifying the major issues. First, does Homer's will grant Edie a life estate or a fee simple? Under modern law, a fee simple is presumed in the absence of language that clearly points to a lesser estate. Here the only possible reason for finding a life estate is Homer's statement of purpose. Probably this isn't sufficient to limit her estate, but the brothers can make a plausible argument that Edie's need for "financial support" will not extend beyond her lifetime. A dead person does not need to consume economic resources.

The second major issue concerns the open mine doctrine. Assuming that Edie has a life estate, is she privileged to sell topsoil? Normally a life tenant's sale of a natural resource like topsoil is waste. There is an exception, however, if the creator of the life estate, Homer, has opened the property for that use. Homer engaged in topsoil sales for years prior to his death, but there was no contract in place when he died. This may make application of the open mine doctrine problematic.

Now let's review the choices. **A** asks us to consider Edie's good faith. This is a red herring. Either she has a legal right, based on her property ownership, to sell topsoil, or she does not because her brothers own a property right in the farm that conflicts with Edie's claim. Good faith and bad faith have nothing to do with it.

B has something going for it. As indicated above, the will's language concerning Edie's financial circumstances may be a reason for deciding that she has only a life estate. But if she has a life estate, it must have been a life estate when Homer died. Her estate couldn't change from a fee simple to a life estate upon her favorable marriage. Thus, **B** is somewhat weak.

Let's move on to **E**. A presumption of a fee simple does apply, but this cannot help the brothers. The brothers have a much better chance of prevailing if they convince the court that Edie took only a life estate. Conceivably the brothers might win if Edie took a defeasible fee simple and defeasance took place when she married, but this is unlikely. Moreover, **E** fails to express the core of this argument.

C and **D** both invite us to apply the open mine doctrine. They are distinguished by the time at which we should measure Homer's intent. Because a will becomes operative not when executed, but only at the testator's death, we should consider Homer's probable intent about Edie's use of the farm from the time perspective of his death. So we're left with **D** as the strongest answer of the set.

 ## Smith's Picks

1. Conveying more than the life tenant owns   **C**
2. Premature death of potential remaindermen   **A**
3. Spot the equitable interests   **A**
4. Let's cut some trees   **E**
5. Selling soil   **D**

11

Reversions and Remainders

"Faith, and so we should;
Where now remains a sweet reversion:
We may boldly spend upon the hope of what
Is to come in:
A comfort of retirement lives in this."
William Shakespeare, *Henry IV*, Part 1, Act IV, Scene 1

CHAPTER OVERVIEW
A. Distinguishing Reversions and Remainders
B. Types of Remainders
C. Distinction between the Contingent Remainder and the Vested
    Remainder Subject to Complete Divestment
D. Alternative Contingent Remainders
E. The Closer: Stripping the Share of a Deceased Grantee
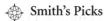 Smith's Picks

A t common law, reversions and remainders are two of the primary future
interests. Both are alike in that they are future estates that follow lesser
estates. Whenever an estate is less than a fee simple, there has to be at
least one reversion or remainder. We can visualize property ownership as a pie,
where the whole pie represents a fee simple absolute. If we carve the pie and
identify one slice as a life estate or a leasehold or (where permitted) a fee tail,
there has to be something left. That "something left" is a reversion or remainder.

A. Distinguishing Reversions and Remainders

When a person owns an estate in land, she may convey her entire ownership
interest to a grantee, or she may convey less than she owns. A *reversion* is a

future interest retained by a grantor when the grantor conveys an estate that is less than the estate that she owns. Historically, the term reversion signified that *seisin*[1] should revert to the grantor when the lesser estate expired. A reversion can never be created in a grantee or a third party. Most of the time when a reversion is created the grantor begins with a fee simple and grants a lesser estate, such as a life estate or leasehold (or where permitted, a fee tail). A person, however, who owns less than a fee simple can also retain a reversion by granting a lesser estate.

A *remainder* is a future interest conveyed to a third party that will or may become possessory after the expiration of a preceding estate. The preceding estate must be less than a fee simple. The term "remainder" signifies that seisin should *remain* away from the grantor after expiration of the prior estate. A remainder can only be created in a transferee. A grantor cannot retain a remainder.

> **QUESTION 1.   What follows the life estate?** Abigail owns Blackacre in fee simple absolute. She conveys Blackacre "to Byron for life." Who owns what future interest in Blackacre?
>
> **A.** Abigail owns a reversion.
> **B.** Abigail owns a remainder.
> **C.** Byron's heirs own a remainder.
> **D.** The state owns a future interest under the doctrine of escheat.
> **E.** No one has a future interest in Blackacre.

ANALYSIS.   Let's start with considering Byron's interest. The language plainly indicates that he gets a life estate. This will expire when he dies. There is no mention of Byron's heirs in the conveyance, and thus the property cannot go to them when Byron dies. **C** is wrong.

D is also wrong. Escheat only applies when an owner of property dies without ascertainable heirs. Here no one has died so escheat is not possible.

E may sound plausible. Looking at the conveyance, there is no visible future interest. The brief language in Abigail's deed speaks only about Byron's life estate—that's it. But Abigail started with a fee simple, and something must happen with respect to Blackacre when Byron dies. Although no words in the conveyance express the idea of Abigail keeping a future interest, this is the

---

1. A simple definition of "seisin" is possession of an estate in land coupled with a claim of ownership. The concept of "seisin" played a key role in medieval England land law, but the historic nuances are not important in order for you to grasp the basic operation of the modern estates system. The term roughly correlates to the modern conception of "title to property."

result of what she has done. She keeps all the property rights she starts with except to the extent that she has manifested an intent to convey rights to others.

So we're left with **A** and **B**. Abigail must own a future interest that will become possessory when Byron's life estate runs out. When a person conveys less than she owns, the consequence is that she retains a future interest in the land. Is Abigail's future interest a reversion or a remainder? She can't have a remainder because that interest can only be created in a third party, not a grantor. She owns a reversion because she conveyed a lesser estate than she started with, which was a fee simple absolute. **A** is our answer.

QUESTION 2. Two grantees. Abigail owns Blackacre in fee simple absolute. She conveys Blackacre "to my brother, Byron, for life, and at his death said property shall go to his daughter, Heather, and her heirs." Who owns what future interest in Blackacre?

A. Heather owns a reversion.
B. Heather and her heirs own a reversion.
C. Heather owns a remainder.
D. Heather and her heirs own a remainder.
E. Byron owns a remainder if Heather is less than 18 years old.

ANALYSIS. To analyze a conveyance that may create future interests, the first step is to label the present estate, so we should pay attention to Byron's interest. Here Byron has a life estate, which is indefeasible (no stated event can terminate his life estate prior to his death). **E** indicates that Byron also owns a remainder. Is this possible? No, because the language directly says the property should go to Heather at his death. Her age is immaterial. She may own a future interest even if she is an infant.

The other answers in the series deal with two variables: is the future interest owned by Heather or by Heather and her heirs, and is the future interest a reversion or a remainder? The future interest goes to "Heather and her heirs." This is not an attempt to give an interest to Heather's heirs, whoever they may turn out to be. The words "and her heirs" are words of limitation, which signify that her future interest is to be an estate in fee simple.[2] Thus **B** and **D** are wrong.

This leaves us with **A** and **C**. Does Heather own a reversion or a remainder? A reversion is a future interest created in the grantor, who is Abigail, so Heather cannot have a reversion. A remainder is a future interest created in a third party, like Heather. **C** is our answer.

---

2. We discuss words of limitation and the term "heirs" in chapter 8 if you would like a refresher.

B.   Types of Remainders

Every remainder is either contingent or vested. A contingent remainder is a remainder for which (1) there is no ascertainable owner or (2) there is a condition precedent that must be satisfied before the remainder can become possessory.

There are three types of vested remainders. An *indefeasibly vested remainder* (often just called a "vested remainder") is not subject to either of the uncertainties that make a remainder contingent and it is not subject to a reduction in share.

A *remainder subject to open* has at least one ascertainable owner and is ready to become possessory, but it is subject to more owners acquiring a share in the property. This type of remainder is also called a vested *remainder subject to partial divestment*.

A *remainder subject to complete divestment* has an ascertainable owner and is ready to become possessory, but it is subject to termination by another future interest. The language in the instrument that may cause termination is called a condition subsequent. The distinction between a condition precedent, which makes the remainder a contingent remainder, and a condition subsequent, which makes the remainder vested subject to complete divestment, is subtle. It has plagued generations of students.

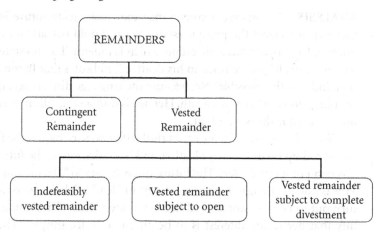

QUESTION 3.   **Not yet a parent.** Aaron conveys Blackacre "to Rachel for life, then to Rachel's children." At the time of the conveyance Rachel has no children. What future interest, if any, is owned by Rachel's children?

A.   An indefeasibly vested remainder.
B.   A vested remainder subject to open.
C.   A contingent remainder.
D.   Nothing, because Rachel has no children.

ANALYSIS. The future interest given to Rachel's children follows a life estate, so it must be a remainder. Is the remainder contingent or vested? To call it vested, we must be able to identify at least one person who presently owns the remainder. Because Rachel hasn't had any children yet, there is no one to point to. Because the remainder has no ascertainable owner, it cannot be vested. **A** is wrong.

For the same reason **B** is wrong. To label a remainder vested subject to open, there has to be at least one identifiable member of the class. Here there isn't one because Rachel hasn't had a child.

D may seem to be a good answer. Rachel is presently childless, so how can her children own a remainder? How can people who do not exist, and may never be born, own anything? However, this is an instance where the law of property, strange as it may seem, attributes ownership to a person (or persons) who may never come into being. Rachel's possible future children are conceptualized as owning, right now, a contingent remainder. One reason a remainder may be contingent is the inability to ascertain a present owner, which is what we have here. Thus, **C** is correct.

QUESTION 4. What's left for Aaron? In Question 3 above, does Aaron have any remaining property right in Blackacre after he has conveyed "to Rachel for life, then to Rachel's children"? Again, assume Rachel has no children.

A. Yes, Aaron has a remainder.
B. Yes, Aaron has a reversion.
C. Yes, Aaron has a possibility of reverter.
D. No, Aaron owns nothing.

ANALYSIS. Remember, we have to account for who should own Blackacre under all of the logical possibilities. Here, Rachel has a life estate, and the variable comes into play at her death. The two logical possibilities are that she will have had children (one or more) or not. If not, Blackacre must go somewhere. Aaron's conveyance does not tell us what to do if this happens, but we apply the axiom that he has kept whatever property rights he has not given away. Thus, **D** is wrong. Aaron owns the future right to possess Blackacre if Rachel dies childless.

So how do we label Aaron's future interest? It's not a remainder (Choice **A**) because that interest can only be created in a third party. It's not a possibility of reverter (Choice **C**)—that can be created in a grantor like Aaron, but a possibility of reverter divests a fee simple determinable. Rachel has only a life estate. So we're left with **B**, the right choice. Aaron has a reversion. It is not certain to become possessory; that depends upon a future event—whether Rachel ever has a child.

> **QUESTION 5.   One child.** In Question 3 above, suppose that when Aaron delivered the deed of conveyance to Rachel, which conveyed a remainder to "Rachel's children," she had one child, Rocky, age seven. What future interest, if any, is owned by Rocky?
>
> A.   An indefeasibly vested remainder.
> B.   A vested remainder subject to open.
> C.   A contingent remainder.
> D.   A vested remainder subject to complete divestment because Rocky might die before Rachel.
> E.   Nothing, because Rocky might die before Rachel.

ANALYSIS.   First we need to decide whether the remainder is contingent or vested. The remainder is presently owned by Rocky, an ascertained person. There is no language in the deed that can be construed as a condition precedent, or for that matter as any type of condition. Thus Rocky has a vested remainder. **C** is wrong.

But what type of vested remainder does Rocky have? Is it subject to complete divestment? It's possible that Rocky might die before his mother, Rachel. But this will not destroy the remainder. The deed has no express condition that requires that Rocky survive his mother for the remainder to be good. The law does not imply survival as a condition. If Rocky dies before Rachel and has not previously conveyed his remainder to someone, then the remainder will go through Rocky's estate to his heirs or devisees. **D** is wrong, and for the same reason **E** is wrong.

So Rocky has either an indefeasibly vested remainder or a vested remainder subject to open. Which is it? If it's indefeasibly vested, this means that Rocky's share of the property, presently 100 percent, will never be decreased. What should happen if Rachel has another child? That sibling also is included in the words of purchase ("Rachel's children") used in Aaron's deed, and thus the two children together will own the remainder. This is called a vested remainder subject to open, so **B** is the correct answer.

Does Aaron own anything? No. Our conclusion that Rocky's remainder is vested means that there is no logical possibility that Blackacre will ever return to Aaron.

> **QUESTION 6.   More children.** Suppose instead that Aaron's deed conveyed Blackacre "to Rachel for life, then to Rachel's child, Rocky." At the time of the conveyance Rocky was seven years old. One year later Rachel gave birth to a daughter, Rosette. Who owns which future interest in Blackacre?
>
> A.   Rocky owns an indefeasibly vested remainder.
> B.   Rocky owns a contingent remainder.

> **C.** Rocky owns a vested remainder subject to complete divestment.
> **D.** Rocky and Rosette own a vested remainder subject to open.
> **E.** Rocky and Rosette own a contingent remainder.

ANALYSIS. This modification makes a critical change in the words of purchase. Now the deed conveys the remainder "to Rachel's child, Rocky." Rosette is not named in the deed, either directly by stating her name or by a broader reference (such as "Rachel's children" or "Rocky's sisters") that includes her. There is absolutely no evidence that Aaron intended that Rocky should share the remainder with anyone else. This eliminates choices **D** and **E**.

What type of remainder does Rocky own? There is no condition precedent, and we know who Rocky is, so the remainder has an ascertainable owner. The remainder is not contingent, so **B** is wrong. Is Rocky's remainder indefeasibly vested or vested subject to complete divestment? There is nothing that will take Rocky's remainder away from him. It is unlikely that Rocky will die before his mother, but this could happen. We don't usually think about a young child having "heirs," but every person does, even a baby. Thus if Rocky predeceases his mother, the remainder will go to his heirs or devisees. So **A** is the right answer.

C. Distinction between the Contingent Remainder and the Vested Remainder Subject to Complete Divestment

The law would be tidier if all conditions attached to a remainder made the remainder contingent, but this is not the system we have. If the language results in what is called a condition precedent, then this condition must be satisfied before the remainder can become possessory. The remainder is a contingent remainder for so long as the condition remains unsatisfied.

Conversely, if the language results in what is called a condition subsequent, we do not have a contingent remainder. Instead we visualize the remainder as vested but subject to the risk that it may be taken away if the condition takes place. This is what we call a vested remainder subject to complete divestment.[3]

Often there is a functional difference between the contingent remainder and the vested remainder subject to complete divestment. The event of divestment is capable of occurring after the remainder becomes possessory. With a

---

3. It is sometimes called a vested remainder subject to complete defeasance. Also, sometimes you will see the adjective "total" instead of "complete," and sometimes the adjective is dropped (for example, a "vested remainder subject to defeasance").

condition precedent, this is not possible. When there is a contingent remainder, the remainderman is not allowed to take possession before the condition is met. Consider the following diagram, which shows satisfaction of a condition precedent taking place after expiration of a preceding life estate. Suppose we have a remainderman, Carlos, who is subject to the condition that he graduate from law school. Imagine that he graduates one year after the death of the life tenant.

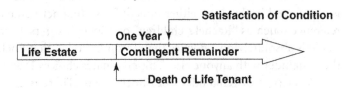

Carlos is not entitled to take possession when the life tenant dies because he has not yet satisfied the condition precedent. Under modern law, the contingent remainder remains in existence, and he is allowed to take possession after one year, when he graduates.

In the above example, there is a functional difference between a condition precedent and turning the graduation requirement into a condition subsequent, which would allow Carlos to take possession but strip him of ownership if he did not graduate by a specified date after the life tenant's death. Sometimes, however, there is no functional difference between a condition precedent, which creates a contingent remainder, and a condition subsequent, which creates a vested remainder subject to complete divestment. Due to the nature of the condition, it necessarily will be satisfied or fail no later than the earliest time that the remainder may become possessory. In this situation, the labeling of the remainder as contingent or vested is wholly a matter of form.

A long time ago, English courts preferred calling remainders vested rather than contingent because they had more stability. This preference has continued into modern law. Courts make the choice between vested and contingent based on how the words of condition are placed in the document. If in the relevant sentence the words of condition *precede* the words of purchase (the words describing the owner of the remainder), they amount to a condition precedent. Also, if the words of condition immediately follow the words of purchase, both appearing in a run-on phrase with no punctuation separating the two parts, then they are a condition precedent. With a run-on phrase, the thinking is that the condition is an integral part of the description of the remainder owner.

Conversely, if the words of condition *follow* the words of purchase (and they aren't in a run-on phrase), then they create a condition subsequent, making the remainder subject to complete divestment. The condition is a takeaway provision. We visualize the grantor as having had a two-step thought process. First, she wanted the grantee to have a solid (vested) remainder. Then it occurred to the grantor that if something happened (the condition), that solid property interest ought to be taken away and go to some other person.

> **QUESTION 7.   Taking it away if the student doesn't graduate.** Teresa conveys Blackacre "to Roberto for life, then to Sallie and her heirs, provided that if Sallie fails to graduate from law school before her fortieth birthday, Blackacre shall go to Thomas and his heirs." At the time of the conveyance, Roberto was 84 years old and Sallie, a first-year law student at the Paper Chase School of Law, was 27 years old. Three months later, Sallie dropped out of law school. What future interest does Sallie presently own in Blackacre?
>
> A. An indefeasibly vested remainder.
> B. A vested remainder subject to open.
> C. A contingent remainder.
> D. A vested remainder subject to complete divestment.
> E. Nothing, because Sallie has withdrawn from law school.

ANALYSIS.   Let's consider **E** first. It's unfortunate, perhaps also sad, that Sallie has quit law school. If it were now impossible for the condition to be satisfied, **E** would be the best answer. But Sallie is only 27 and may decide to return to the Paper Chase School of Law or someday (before she is 40) attend another law school. Thus it's possible that she may satisfy the condition. It doesn't matter that it may appear unlikely that she will do so. **E** is not a good answer.

Is Sallie's remainder contingent or vested? Clearly there is an ascertainable owner of the remainder (Sallie), so the lack of an ascertainable person to take the property is not a ground for calling the remainder contingent. Is the law-school-graduation requirement a condition precedent or subsequent? Textually it follows the words of purchase ("to Sallie and her heirs"), so it's subsequent and Sallie's remainder is vested. **C** is incorrect.

What type of vested remainder does Sallie have? She can't have a vested remainder subject to open because the remainder is given to her personally, not to a class (like someone's children) that may increase in size. **B** is incorrect.

This leaves us with **A** and **D**. Because Sallie has not yet graduated from law school, the condition is still operative. We can't call the remainder indefeasibly vested. **D** is the right answer.

> **QUESTION 8.**   The student must graduate. Now Teresa has used different language to express her intentions with respect to the gift to Roberto, Sallie, and Thomas. Her deed conveys Blackacre "to Roberto for life; then if Sallie has graduated from law school and was less than 40 years old on the date of graduation, to Sallie and her heirs; and if Sallie fails to graduate from law school before her fortieth birthday, Blackacre shall go to Thomas and his heirs." At the time of the conveyance Roberto was 84 years old and Sallie, a first-year law student at the Paper Chase

School of Law, was 27 years old. At the time of the conveyance, what future interest does Sallie own?

A.   An indefeasibly vested remainder.
B.   A vested remainder subject to open.
C.   A contingent remainder.
D.   A vested remainder subject to complete divestment.
E.   Nothing, because the condition is against public policy.

ANALYSIS.   Sallie, presently in law school, has not yet satisfied the condition, so she cannot have an indefeasibly vested remainder. So **A** is wrong.

Let's dispose of **E**. There's nothing wrong with Teresa's condition from the standpoint of public policy. Although courts will refuse to enforce some types of conditions for reasons of public policy (such as a condition providing an incentive for the remainderman to engage in illegal conduct), this is not one of them.

Is Sallie's remainder vested or contingent? Here the language of condition *precedes* the words of purchase ("to Sallie and her heirs") where we first read Sallie's name. This means the remainder cannot be vested. **A** and **B** are wrong. Sallie has a contingent remainder so **C** is the right answer.

QUESTION 9.   You get it if you survive.   William executes a deed of gift, which conveys Blackacre "to Francis for life, then to Gracie and her heirs if Gracie survives Francis." What future interest does this create in Gracie?

A.   An indefeasibly vested remainder.
B.   A vested remainder subject to open.
C.   A contingent remainder.
D.   A vested remainder subject to complete divestment.

ANALYSIS.   Gracie has a remainder, and there is a survival condition attached to it. She must outlive Francis, the life tenant. This means **A** cannot be right due to the express condition.

Likewise **B** is wrong. Gracie is not a member of a class that may increase in size so she cannot have a remainder that is subject to open.

We're left with **C** and **D**. We must decide whether the survival condition is a condition precedent or a condition subsequent. This is one of the tougher labeling problems you may encounter. Textually, the conditional language appears after the words of purchase, which name Gracie and tell us that her remainder is to be a fee simple estate. But the run-on phrase, "to Gracie and her heirs if Gracie survives Francis," is interpreted as one clause and thus amounts to a condition precedent. Gracie has a contingent remainder. Thus **C** is correct.

QUESTION 10.   You don't get it if you don't survive. Suppose William uses slightly different language in his deed of gift. The deed conveys Blackacre "to Francis for life, then to Gracie and her heirs; but if Gracie fails to survive Francis, the property shall revert to Grantor or his heirs." Now what future interest does Gracie have?

A. An indefeasibly vested remainder.
B. A vested remainder subject to open.
C. A contingent remainder.
D. A vested remainder subject to complete divestment.

ANALYSIS.   Just as in Question 9, Gracie has a remainder subject to a survival condition. **A** is wrong due to the express condition. **B** is also wrong because this is not a class gift.

Our choices come down to **C** and **D**. Is survival a condition precedent or a condition subsequent? The conditional language appears after the words of purchase, naming Gracie, and they are set off from those words of purchase by punctuation and the word "but." This makes the term a condition subsequent, so the remainder is not contingent. **C** is wrong. The right answer is **D** because Gracie has a vested remainder subject to complete divestment. Notice that functionally there is no difference between the way the condition works in this question and in Question 9. In both cases, Gracie's remainder will become possessory if, and only if, she survives Francis. This illustrates the highly formalistic nature of the distinction between a contingent remainder and a vested remainder subject to complete divestment.

D.   Alternative Contingent Remainders

A deed or will may provide for *alternative contingent remainders*. You should apply this label when you spot a contingent remainder *and* subsequent language calls for the property to go to another person (or class of persons) if that first contingent remainder fails to vest. Usually when there are alternative contingent remainders they are a pair, but there may be more than two alternative contingent remainders in a series. This may happen when the plan of the grantor or testator is complicated.

QUESTION 11.   Survival is the hinge. Patricia conveys Blackacre "to Able for life, then if Carol survives Able, to Carol and her heirs; but if Carol has not survived Able, to David and his heirs." What future interests are created by this conveyance?

> **A.** Carol has an indefeasibly vested remainder.
> **B.** Carol has a vested remainder subject to complete divestment.
> **C.** Carol and David own a remainder subject to open.
> **D.** Carol has a contingent remainder and David has a different type of future interest.
> **E.** Carol and David own alternative contingent remainders.

ANALYSIS. The first step is to label Carol's future interest. She has a remainder, which may become possessory when Able's life estate expires. Due to the survival condition, the remainder cannot be indefeasibly vested. **A** is wrong.

But is Carol's remainder vested or contingent? Here the text of the survival condition precedes the words of purchase, "to Carol and her heirs," so we have a condition precedent. **B** is wrong.

Let's dispose of **C**. Two things are wrong with this choice. First, as we just noted, Carol has a contingent remainder, and a remainder subject to open is a species of vested remainder. Second, a remainder subject to open means two or more people may share the same future interest, with the possibility in the future of a shared right to possess the property. Here that cannot happen. The language indicates that Blackacre must go to Carol or David, one or the other—both cannot acquire it together.

We're left with **D** and **E**. The distinction between these two answers turns on how we label David's interest. His interest qualifies as a contingent remainder. The condition is that Carol's remainder does not vest. Thus he has an alternative contingent remainder, and **E** is the right answer.

E. The Closer: Stripping the Share of a Deceased Grantee

As mentioned above, when a living person owns a future interest, the normal rule is that the person's death prior to expiration of the preceding estate does not defeat the future interest. The common law does not imply a survival requirement.

If the language of the will or conveyance expressly "takes away" the future interest based on a failure to survive, then that language is enforced. But there is a corollary to the "no implied survival" rule. Courts will construe "takeaway" provisions strictly. If the language, carefully read, does not mandate awarding the property (or the share of the property) to someone else, then the future interest continues. It must go through the deceased owner's estate to the person's heirs or devisees.

Read the next problem *very* carefully. It's a toughie.

> **QUESTION 12.   A deceased child's share.** Catherine executed a warranty deed, conveying Blackacre "to my son Ross for and during his natural life only, at his death to his children, the child or children of any deceased child of Ross to have and receive their deceased parent's share." At the time of delivery of the deed, Ross had two children, Susan and Thomas. Two years later Ross had a third child, Usha. Later while Ross was still alive, Susan died, survived by one child, Sabrina. And also while Ross was still alive, Thomas died childless. His heir was his widow, Trudie. Ross has just died. Blackacre is now owned by:
>
> **A.**   Sabrina one-half and Usha one-half.
> **B.**   Sabrina one-half and Trudie one-half.
> **C.**   Usha owns the entire property.
> **D.**   Sabrina one-third, Trudie one-third, and Usha one-third.
> **E.**   Sabrina one-third, Catherine one-third, and Usha one-third.

ANALYSIS.   Let's start by labeling the interests. Once we accomplish that task, we should be able to determine where the property ought to go at the death of Ross, the life tenant. After the life estate, the next words are "at his death to his children." This is a gift to a class, and if we stopped here (visualize putting a period after "children" and deleting the remaining words), we would have a vested remainder subject to open. Susan and Thomas would own this remainder initially, and it would open to include baby sister Usha upon her birth. This means that **B** is wrong; Usha should have a share.

The next phrase ("the child or children of any deceased child of Ross to have and receive their deceased parent's share") shows Catherine's intent that if Ross's child dies before Ross, that child's share should go to the deceased child's children. Is this take-away provision a condition precedent or a condition subsequent? Because it's separated from the words of purchase ("at his death to his children") by punctuation (a comma), it probably should be viewed as a condition subsequent. There's no run-on phrase. Thus, the remainder to Ross's children is vested subject to complete divestment.

Let's consider Sabrina's position. The condition plainly assigns the share of her mother, Susan, to Sabrina because Susan died before her father, Ross. Thus **C** is wrong.

Now let's move on to Trudie's claim. Trudie is Thomas's widow. Thomas, like Susan, died before their father, but Thomas died childless. What should happen to his share? The take-away provision ("the child or children of any deceased child of Ross to have and receive their deceased parent's share") says nothing about what should happen if a child of Ross dies without having children. We apply the rule that survival is not an implied condition, and thus Thomas continued to own his share of the remainder at his death. This puts his share into his estate, where it passes to Trudie, his widow and heir. This means that **A** is wrong (it gives no share to Trudie) and **E** is wrong (Trudie should have a share, and there is no basis for assigning a share to the original grantor, Catherine). We've made it to the end. **D** is right.[4]

 ## Smith's Picks

1.	What follows the life estate?	A
2.	Two grantees	C
3.	Not yet a parent	C
4.	What's left for Aaron?	B
5.	One child	B
6.	More children	A
7.	Taking it away if the student doesn't graduate	D
8.	The student must graduate	C
9.	You get it if you survive	C
10.	You don't get it if you don't survive	D
11.	Survival is the hinge	E
12.	A deceased child's share	D

---

4. This problem is based on the deed in *Kost v. Foster*, 94 N.E.2d 302 (Ill. 1950), where the court held this language created vested remainders in the children that were both subject to open and subject to complete divestment.

12

Executory Interests

"He gives with one hand, and takes away with the other."
Old English saying

CHAPTER OVERVIEW
A. The History of Executory Interests
B. Active Trusts
C. Distinction between Springing and Shifting Executory Interests
D. The Divesting Effect of Executory Interests
E. The Closer: Taking Away a Trust Beneficiary's Interest
✤ Smith's Picks

A future interest in a grantee may be either a remainder or an executory interest. Once you have a firm understanding of remainders, you're ready to tackle executory interests. A bit of history is necessary to understand why we have two different categories for future interests in grantees. This chapter gives you just enough for you to understand the historical basis of our modern law and its terminology.

A. The History of Executory Interests

At early common law, a grantor could not create an estate that would arise at a specified time in the future unless the conveyance first created a present life estate or fee tail ("springing interests" were said to be void). Similarly, a grantor could not divest an estate by providing for its transfer to a third person ("shifting interests" were void). These limitations were overcome in equity when the Court of Chancery developed the *doctrine of uses*. When one person agreed to hold title to land (technically, "seisin") for the use and benefit of another person, the Court used its power to require the holder to comply with the agreed terms. Creation of a use split ownership between the holder of seisin, who had legal title, and the owner of the use. Landowners were allowed to create "springing uses" and "shifting uses." Today the word "use" has become archaic. We now say "equitable title" or "equitable ownership" with the same meaning. The institution of uses is the foundation for the *law of trusts*. We call the holder of legal title the "trustee" and the holder of the equitable interest the "beneficiary."

In medieval England, the monarchy raised substantial revenues through its land tenure rights, which developed after the Norman invasion in 1066. Owners of legal estates owed services or money to the Crown under certain circumstances, but these obligations did not attach to uses. This distinction caused a substantial loss of revenues, and in 1535 at the insistence of Henry VIII, Parliament passed the *Statute of Uses* for the purpose of restoring Crown revenues. The statute did not take the direct approach of abolishing the separation of title to land. Instead, the statute said that whenever one person is seised to the use of another person, that second person shall have seisin. In other words, the statute transferred seisin from the legal titleholder to the use holder, leaving the former with nothing. The use was said to be "executed" by the statute: hence the term "executory interest" means a future interest operated upon by the statute. Executory interests quickly became an important part of the law of estates, and their importance has not waned. They remain prevalent today in the United States, which has incorporated the Statute of Uses as part of its property law.

QUESTION 1.   Declaration of trust. Thomas, owner of Blackacre in fee simple absolute, conveys Blackacre "to Wayne and his heirs for the benefit and use of Glory and her heirs." What interests does Thomas intend to create by using this language?

A. Wayne should own a fee simple and Glory should own nothing.
B. Wayne and Glory should own a fee simple as cotenants.
C. Wayne should own a present fee simple estate and Glory should own a remainder.
D. Wayne should own an equitable fee simple and Glory should own a legal fee simple.
E. Wayne should own a legal fee simple and Glory should own an equitable fee simple.

ANALYSIS.   A would be correct only if the words "for the benefit and the use of Glory and her heirs" were ineffective and thus were read out of the conveyance. But the law allows a grantor to designate a trust, thereby splitting title between grantees such as Wayne and Glory.

If Wayne and Glory are cotenants, as **B** states, then they would have coequal rights to use and possess Blackacre. Here the intent is different. Glory is to have real and beneficial ownership, so they are not cotenants.

C is partially right because Wayne does have a present fee simple estate, but **C** is also partially incorrect. Glory does not have a remainder or any other type of future interest. She should have the immediate beneficial use of Blackacre.

D and **E** both recognize the idea behind a trust: splitting ownership with one person having legal title and the other getting equitable title. Who has which? The person who has the use, Glory, has equitable title. Wayne is to hold legal title for her benefit. It would also be proper to say that Wayne is a trustee. **E** is the right answer.

QUESTION 2. Impact of Statute of Uses. In Question 1 above, assume that the Statute of Uses applies to "execute the use." Who owns what interests in Blackacre by virtue of Thomas's conveyance "to Wayne and his heirs for the benefit and use of Glory and her heirs"?

A. Wayne owns an equitable fee simple and Glory owns a legal fee simple.
B. Wayne owns a legal fee simple and Glory owns an equitable fee simple.
C. Wayne owns a fee simple and Glory owns nothing.
D. Wayne owns nothing and Glory owns a fee simple.

ANALYSIS. Here the Statute of Uses applies to "execute" the use. This defeats Thomas's intent. There is no longer a separation of legal and equitable title. For this reason **B** is wrong, and **A** is "doubly wrong" because apart from the statute Wayne would have legal title and Glory equitable title, not vice versa.

The statute unifies the title that was to be fragmented. Both **C** and **D** show a unified title. Who gets the unified title? The statute transfers Wayne's seisin (legal title) to Glory, so our answer is **D**, not **C**. She owns a complete legal fee simple, and Wayne is out of the picture.

B.   Active Trusts

If the Statute of Uses executes uses, how can we still divide legal and equitable interests? In principle, an overbearing application of the statute might have prevented the law of trusts, with its separation of legal and equitable title, from developing. But early on, courts decided that the statute did not apply in certain situations, one of which was the *active trust*. An active trust results if under the trust instrument the trustee has some duties with respect to the property. The trustee retains title (it is not executed by the statute) so she may perform her responsibilities.

The term *passive trust* is in contrast to an active trust. With a passive trust, the trustee does not manage the property and has no duties. The trustee's only role is to serve as titleholder and to convey the property when asked to do so by the beneficiary. Today it is possible to create passive trusts for real or personal property, even though the Statute of Uses will execute certain passive trusts for real property, depending upon the language used in a deed of conveyance.

QUESTION 3.   A busy trustee. Omar wants to make a gift of Blackacre in trust for his daughter, Emily. He conveys "to Zion and his heirs in trust for Emily and her heirs," directing Zion to collect the rents and profits accruing from the land, to pay real estate taxes charged against the land out of such rents and profits, and to distribute the net amount of such rents and profits to Emily on each June 1. Assume that the Statute of Uses applies to Omar's conveyance. Who owns what interests in Blackacre?

A.   Zion has a legal fee simple absolute and Emily has an equitable fee simple absolute.

B.   Zion has a legal fee simple absolute and Emily has a future interest that enables her to receive profits on every June 1.

C.   Zion has an equitable fee simple absolute and Emily has a legal fee simple absolute.

D.   Zion has nothing and Emily has a fee simple absolute.

E.   Zion and Emily are cotenants owning a fee simple absolute.

ANALYSIS.   D is correct if we apply the Statute of Uses to this conveyance, but should we? Zion is plainly given duties other than serving as a mere holder of the legal title. He is to manage Blackacre, at least to the extent of collecting rents and profits, paying taxes, and properly accounting for the revenues and payments. This is enough to make this an active trust. Only passive trusts are executed by the statute. **D** is wrong.

E is badly flawed. Although both Zion and Emily are mentioned in the conveyance, they clearly are not cotenants, who would both have the right to use and enjoy the property. A trustee and a beneficiary both own interests in the same property at the same point in time, but they are never considered to be cotenants.

A and **B** claim that Zion has legal title, but **C** asserts that Zion has equitable title. Which is it? The fundamental concept of this chapter is that the beneficial owner has what we call "equitable title" and the trustee has what we call "legal title." Strike **C**.

The difference between **A** and **B** turns on how we label Emily's interest. Does she have a present equitable fee simple or a future interest that enables her to get an annual distribution of money? Some students will pick **B**. Her right may seem to be in the nature of a future interest because she does not have the right to take possession of Blackacre and do whatever she would like with the property. It may be that she can visit Blackacre, but her presence there should not interfere with Zion's efforts to manage the property so as to generate rents and profits. However, this fact does not make her rights as beneficiary into a future interest. Throughout the year, not just on June 1, she has beneficial ownership of Blackacre. In order for her to own a future interest, there would have to be another person who has the present right to beneficial ownership and distributions of net income, and there is no such person. **A** is right.

C. Distinction between Springing and Shifting Executory Interests

There are two basic types of executory interests. A springing executory interest may divest the grantor in the future. We can visualize the interest springing out from the grantor.

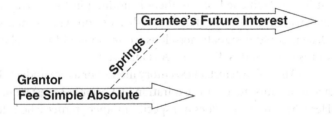

The second type, a shifting executory interest, divests an initial grantee in favor of a second grantee. We visualize this interest as shifting from one grantee to another.

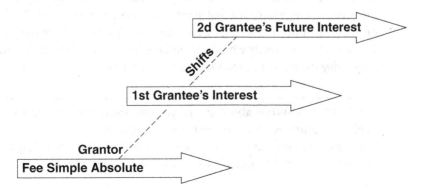

> **QUESTION 4.** **Wait until you're 21.** Octavia plans to make a gift of Blackacre, which is her residence where she lives with her teenage daughter, Amelia. She conveys Blackacre "to Amelia and her heirs upon Amelia becoming 21 years of age." Amelia is 18 at the time of the conveyance. At the time of the conveyance what interest does Amelia own?
>
> **A.** An equitable interest in fee simple.
> **B.** A springing executory interest in fee simple.
> **C.** A shifting executory interest in fee simple.
> **D.** A remainder in fee simple.
> **E.** A life estate.

ANALYSIS. Does Amelia own a type of fee simple, as stated by Choices **A** through **D**, or does she have a life estate? The conveyance contains the words "and her heirs." Remember, these are *words of limitation*, which we translate to mean that Amelia has a fee simple. So **E** is wrong.

Is Amelia's interest legal or equitable? **A** states that she owns an equitable interest, and Choices **B** through **E** all indicate legal interests. Although it does not say "legal" in **B** through **E**, this is implied because there is no qualification by using a term like "equitable." When we describe a property right, the normal assumption is that the right is legal unless otherwise stated. Amelia's interest is not equitable because there is nothing in the conveyance that suggests the creation of a trust. The only other person who is mentioned is Octavia. Octavia could designate herself as trustee to hold for Amelia's benefit, but no words point in this direction. **A** is incorrect.

Is Amelia's interest an executory interest or a remainder? To be a remainder, her estate must follow the expiration of a prior lesser estate in another grantee. Here the conveyance does not specify another grantee who is to take possession for the next three years. Octavia has retained the right to possess Blackacre until Amelia turns 21. Amelia cannot have a remainder, so we strike **D**.

So Amelia has an executory interest. Is it springing or shifting? The words sound similar, but we need to keep them straight. **C** is incorrect. A shifting executory interest moves from a first grantee to a second grantee. Here we have only one grantee, Amelia. A springing executory interest moves from the grantor to a grantee, which is exactly what happens here. When Amelia turns 21, ownership is to *spring* from the grantor, Octavia, to Amelia. **B** is the right answer.

> **QUESTION 5. What about the next three years?** In Question 4 above, we learned that Amelia has a springing executory interest in fee simple. At the time of the conveyance she was only 18. What should happen with respect to the right to possess and use Blackacre for the next three years?

> **A.** Octavia and Amelia should share possession and use until Amelia turns 21, at which time Amelia should have the right to sole possession and use.
> **B.** Octavia should retain possession and use until Amelia turns 21.
> **C.** Amelia should have the immediate right to possession because the conveyance is silent and ambiguity is construed against the author of the conveyance.
> **D.** Blackacre should be placed in trust, with Octavia and Amelia as beneficiaries for the next three years and Amelia as sole beneficiary when she turns 21.
> **E.** Blackacre should be placed in trust, with Octavia as the sole beneficiary for the next three years and Amelia as sole beneficiary when she turns 21.

ANALYSIS. This may be a hard question. Let's dispose of the trust angle first. **D** and **E** envision the creation of a trust, the difference being whether the trust benefits both Octavia and Amelia during the next three years or only the grantor, Octavia. The problem with both responses is that Octavia's deed doesn't show any intent to create a trust. This is why we rejected the suggestion of "equitable interest" in Question 4.

For some students **C** will prove to be an attractive answer. In other contexts, ambiguity is construed against the drafter of an instrument. Here, however, a different norm applies. When a grantor does not expressly allocate a segment of time to a grantee, by implication the grantor has kept that interest. A deed only conveys the property rights described in the deed. Whatever else the grantor happens to own stays with the grantor. Amelia should not get possession of Blackacre before she's 21.

For the same reason, **A** is not sound. Octavia could have granted Amelia an ownership interest as cotenant for the next three years, followed by sole ownership when she turned 21. But no language points to that result. I've muddied the waters a bit by making Blackacre Octavia's residence and stating that she and her daughter live there. So they might continue to live there for the next three years, but the question asks who has the "right to possess and use Blackacre" for this time period. This plainly calls for you to determine rights based on the language of the conveyance, rather than to make a prediction based on family relationship as to where Amelia will live. **B** is right.

QUESTION 6. What do we call the grantor's interest? So we've seen that Octavia owns the right to possess and use Blackacre for the next three years, until her daughter turns 21. What label do we attach to Octavia's retained rights?

> **A.** Defeasible life estate.
> **B.** Fee simple absolute.
> **C.** Fee simple subject to executory limitation.
> **D.** Term for three years.
> **E.** Tenancy at will.

ANALYSIS. Octavia no longer owns a fee simple absolute because she has conveyed a future interest to Amelia. Strike **B**.

A has a grain of truth—Octavia's estate is defeasible—but it's a small grain. She started with a fee simple absolute, and her conveyance has not reduced her interest to a life estate, even though it's probable (but not certain) that she will still be alive in three years when Blackacre is to go to Amelia.

Both **D** and **E** are leasehold estates, and Octavia has not converted her interest to either one. A tenancy at will is terminable at any time by the landlord or the tenant, and Octavia has a right to possession for three years that cannot be taken away from her. **D** will be attractive to some students. Functionally her position is much like ownership of a lease with a term of three years. But she did not purport to convey a fee simple to Amelia with the reservation of a term or leasehold. Moreover, there is a functional difference. Amelia's future interest is contingent. If she dies before reaching 21, Octavia's fee will not be divested. Thus she owns more than a three-year term.

C is correct. Octavia owns a fee simple subject to executory limitation. It would also be correct to say that she owns a fee simple subject to the springing executory interest held by Amelia.

D. The Divesting Effect of Executory Interests

Springing and shifting executory interests look very much like remainders, but they are different historically. As a result, some different rules have applied to them. The key distinction between an executory interest and a remainder is the effect it has on the preceding estate when the future interest becomes possessory. An executory interest divests (or cuts short) a present estate or vested future interest before its natural end. A remainder cannot cut short a prior estate. It must wait for that estate to expire before it becomes possessory. Thus, a remainder can only follow a lesser estate: a life estate, a leasehold, and (where recognized) a fee tail.

What happens to an executory interest when the divesting event takes place? For future interests created in the grantor, recall that a right of entry gives the grantor the choice to regain title. The grantor must assert her rights; otherwise, the previous estate continues. In contrast, when a grantor has a possibility of reverter, divestment of the fee simple determinable takes place automatically.[1] One might expect to find the same distinction for executory interests, but we do not. All executory interests become possessory automatically upon the happening of a triggering condition or limitation, like a possibility of reverter but unlike a right of entry.

QUESTION 7. No buildings. Romper conveys Blackacre, a rural tract of land, "to Alice and her heirs, but if any building or other improvements are added to the land before the expiration of 21 years after Alice's death,[2] then the land shall go to Brian and his heirs." What interest does Brian have in Blackacre?

A. A vested remainder.
B. A contingent remainder.
C. A right of entry.
D. A springing executory interest.
E. A shifting executory interest.

ANALYSIS.   Brian can have a remainder only if the remainder follows the natural expiration of Alice's estate. Due to the words "Alice and her heirs," we're certain that Alice is to have a fee simple estate. Thus Brian's future interest, if it becomes possessory, will divest Alice's fee simple. So we eliminate **A** and **B**.

Let's consider **C**. The "but if" language of the conveyance is language of condition, which can be used to create a fee simple subject to condition subsequent, which is paired with a right of entry. But a right of entry can only be created in the grantor, who is Romper. Instead a grantee, Brian, takes Blackacre if improvements are made, so Brian cannot have a right of entry.

We're down to **D** and **E**. Does Brian's executory interest spring or shift? If Blackacre is improved, ownership will leave the grantee, Alice. Brian has a shifting executory interest, so **E** is our right answer.

E.   The Closer: Taking Away a Trust Beneficiary's Interest

Most trusts are not perpetual. They are created for a duration specified by the grantor. When a trust ends, legal title and equitable title are reunited. Here's a conveyance that couples a trust with a take-away provision.

---

1. For the nature and operation of these two future interests, see chapter 9.
2. This 21-year time limitation avoids a problem with the Rule against Perpetuities. For discussion of the Rule against Perpetuities, see chapter 13.

> **QUESTION 8. Don't get divorced.** Gary has made a gift of Blackacre. Acme is Gary's elderly sister. Brenda is his daughter. She is married to Robert. Camilla is Acme's daughter (Gary's niece). Gary conveys "to Acme for life, then the property shall go to Robert, who is instructed to manage said property for the benefit of Brenda and her heirs; but if Brenda and Robert ever divorce, then said property shall be distributed to Camilla and her heirs." What interest does Brenda have in Blackacre?
>
> A. Legal remainder.
> B. Equitable remainder.
> C. Shifting executory interest.
> D. Equitable executory interest.

ANALYSIS. Gary has created an active trust by instructing that Robert shall manage the property after Acme's death. This means we have no concern that the Statute of Uses upsets this arrangement by executing the "use." Thus **A** and **C** are wrong. Brenda's future interest is equitable, not legal.

Our two "equitable" choices are **B** and **D**. Brenda's interest is a remainder if it does not divest the preceding life estate. There is no divestment here — there is no take-away provision attached to Acme's life estate. Brenda's interest begins at the natural expiration of that life estate. **B** is right.

> **QUESTION 9. When the divorce happens.** In Question 8 above, what interest does Camilla have in Blackacre?
>
> A. Equitable remainder.
> B. Alternative contingent remainder.
> C. Springing executory interest.
> D. Shifting executory interest.
> E. Equitable executory interest.
> F. Nothing, because the restraint on divorce is void as contrary to public policy.

ANALYSIS. Let's start as we did in Question 8 by determining whether Camilla's interest is legal or equitable. Here, if there's a divorce, the conveyance states that the property "shall be distributed to Camilla." This instructs Robert, the trustee, to terminate the trust at this point in time. Camilla therefore has a legal interest, not an equitable one. **A** and **E** are out.

F asks us to consider whether the condition is probably valid. Courts sometimes invalidate restraints on marriage on public policy grounds, but they have not yet invalidated restraints that encourage someone to stay married. **F** is not a strong answer.

We're down to **B**, **C**, and **D**, all of which correctly identify Camilla's future interest as legal. The distinction is whether Brenda and Camilla have alternative contingent remainders (**B**) or whether Brenda has an equitable vested remainder that is subject to complete divestment by Camilla's executory interest. To decide, we have to determine whether the "no divorce" condition operates as a condition precedent or condition subsequent.[3] Here the words of purchase ("to the use of Brenda and her heirs") appear before the divorce language, and they are separated by punctuation. This makes it a condition subsequent. Camilla's future interest can be a remainder only if it follows a preceding estate without divesting that estate. Here it will divest Brenda's equitable fee simple. So **B** is incorrect.

Now we're left with asking whether Camilla's interest springs or shifts. Here it's a shifting executory interest because it cuts short the estate of a prior grantee, Brenda. So at last we're at the end—**D**'s right.

 ## Smith's Picks

1.	Declaration of trust	**E**
2.	Impact of Statute of Uses	**D**
3.	A busy trustee	**A**
4.	Wait until you're 21	**B**
5.	What about the next three years?	**B**
6.	What do we call the grantor's interest?	**C**
7.	No buildings	**E**
8.	Don't get divorced	**B**
9.	When the divorce happens	**D**

---

3. This is reviewed in Section C of chapter 11.

Rule against Perpetuities

"I set out on this ground, which I suppose to be self evident, 'that the earth belongs in usufruct to the living': 'that the dead have neither powers nor rights over it.'"
Letter from Thomas Jefferson to James Madison (Sept. 6, 1789),
in *The Papers of Thomas Jefferson*, vol. 15, p. 392
(Julian P. Boyd, et al., eds., Princeton U. Press 1950)

CHAPTER OVERVIEW
A. Background to the Rule
B. Future Interests That Are Subject to the Rule
C. The Basic Concept: An Event That May Take Place Far in the Future
D. The Concept of Measuring Lives
E. Class Gifts: The Problem of the Afterborn Person
F. Statutory and Judicial Reforms
G. The Closer: Who Graduates from High School?
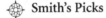 Smith's Picks

ThischapterprovidesabriefintroductiontotheRuleagainstPerpetuities. The rule is highly complex in its application. Property courses vary markedly in the degree of attention given to the rule by professors. Many professors devote substantial attention to both the common law Rule against Perpetuities and the most popular reforms to the rule adopted by a number of states. Other professors choose to cover only a few basic points. Here I've taken a middle ground, setting out the fundamentals and dealing with several of the complexities.

A. Background to the Rule

Professor John Chipman Gray stated the Rule against Perpetuities as follows:

> No interest is good unless it must vest, if at all, not later than twenty-one years after some life in being at the creation of the interest.

John Chipman Gray, *The Rule against Perpetuities* §201, at 191 (4th ed. 1942). Gray's succinct description of the rule, subsequently reproduced by numerous courts and commentators, has come to be considered as the classic statement of the rule.

Although the rule sounds like legislation, courts themselves developed the Rule against Perpetuities. After the Statute of Uses, executory interests that were indestructible arose. Their creation allowed title to land to be tied up indefinitely. The rule, first stated in the *Duke of Norfolk's Case* in 1681, 2 Eng. Rep. 931 (Ch. 1681), was designed to promote the marketability and development of estates in land and to limit the dead-hand control of grantors over future interests. The rule turned out to be a success. After more than 300 years, most American states have retained the Rule against Perpetuities in some modified form, despite having abolished many other formal rules of English property law.

QUESTION 1. Why do we have the Rule against Perpetuities? Which of the following are primary purposes of the Rule against Perpetuities?

1. To preserve revenues payable by landowners to the government.
2. To make land more readily alienable.
3. To allow for the creation of new types of future interests.
4. To encourage landowners to put lands in trust.

A. All of the above.
B. 2 only.
C. 4 only.
D. 2 and 3.
E. 1 and 4.

ANALYSIS. Let's consider the choices in order. One may argue in favor of 1 although there is no direct evidence that judges who developed the Rule against Perpetuities considered the impact on the English government's collection of revenues. If the rule has the consequence of increasing wealth by allowing the improvement and development of land, free of certain future interests that would persist beyond the perpetuities period, then government revenues might increase. But this line of argument is attenuated.

Choice 2 is clearly correct. Due to the rule land is more marketable, or alienable, when future interests subject to the rule are invalidated. Choice 3 is wrong. The rule does not expand the types of future interests allowed. Rather, within three types of future interests (discussed in the next section) it invalidates certain interests that may vest too remotely. Choice 4 is also wrong. The Rule against Perpetuities applies to future interests in trust, just as it does for legal future interests. This means **B** is the best answer. We don't actually have to decide whether 1 is a plausible choice because we're not given the choice of 1 and 2 only.

B. Future Interests That Are Subject to the Rule

Professor Gray's statement of the Rule against Perpetuities does not tell us what interests must be tested for compliance for the perpetuities time period. Generally, all contingent future interests created in third parties are subject to the rule. This includes contingent remainders, powers of appointment, and most executory interests. Interests not subject to the rule are

- Present estates
- Future interests in the grantor, including possibilities of reverter and rights of entry
- Vested remainders except for vested remainders subject to open (the special rules applicable to these remainders are discussed below in the section Class Gifts)
- Charitable trusts
- Resulting trusts

Most applications of the Rule against Perpetuities involve donative transactions; in other words, the interest in question is created by will or by deed of gift. There is a split of authority as to whether the rule applies to commercial transactions. In many states, the Rule against Perpetuities applies to options and to rights of first refusal to purchase land that are not incident to a lease for years. An option gives its holder, the optionee, a contract right to buy a particular tract of land at a fixed or ascertainable price and thus resembles a future interest. A right of first refusal gives its holder a contract right to buy a particular tract of land at the price offered to the owner by another potential buyer. The rationale for applying the rule to bargained-for rights such as options and first refusals is that, like contingent future interests, they may inhibit the marketability and development of property.

Here is a chart showing what interests are subject to evaluation under the Rule against Perpetuities.

Type of Interest	Does the Rule apply?
Contingent remainder	Yes
Executory interest	Yes, if the executory interest is subject to a contingency
Vested executory interest	No
Vested remainder (indefeasibly vested)	No
Vested remainder subject to complete divestment	No
Vested remainder subject to open	Yes
Reversion	No
Possibility of reverter	No
Right of entry (power of termination)	No
Present estate	No
Charitable trust	No
Option to buy property	Yes, in many states
Right of first refusal to buy property	Yes, in many states
Easements and profits	Yes, if subject to a contingency
Real covenant	No
Equitable servitude	No

QUESTION 2. Testing an option. What is the best argument for applying the Rule against Perpetuities to an option to buy a tract of land?

A. Society has an interest in the addition of improvements on the land.
B. Society has an interest in the preservation of the land in its natural state.
C. Application of the rule advances the original intentions of the parties to the option contract.
D. Application of the rule protects the optionor from selling the land at a price substantially below market value.
E. Both B and D are correct.

ANALYSIS. Let's start with **C**, which asks about the intent of the parties to the option contract. The Rule of Perpetuities, when it applies to void an interest, typically is intent-defeating, and that's the case here. An optionee typically pays consideration to obtain the option, and the optionee would not do so if she believed she was not obtaining an enforceable right due to risk that the optionor would refuse to perform based upon the rule. The optionee would draft the option contract in a fashion that did not violate the Rule against Perpetuities or not enter into the transaction. Likewise, in almost all cases, the optionor would also be ignorant of the possible application of the Rule against Perpetuities at the time the parties reached their bargain.

D may be an attractive answer. If the option price is a fixed amount of money and the option period is lengthy, the land value may rise over time, resulting in a significant gap between market value and price. This may discourage the landowner-optionor from improving the property.

A and **B** both posit that other people besides the parties have an interest in what happens to the land. If we apply the rule to invalidate a long-term option, will that increase the probability that the land will be improved or that it will remain in its existing possibly natural state? Application of the rule to options is grounded on the belief that the landowner-optionor will choose not to undertake economically valuable improvements to the land due to the risk that the optionee will exercise the option and thereby appropriate the value of the improvements. Thus, the rule in this context is pro-developmental and anti-conservationist. **A** is our best answer. **D** is second-best. This may be a close call, but **D** is weaker because our concern is not protecting one of the parties to the option contract, but it is the perceived public interest in having land improved and developed. Notice that **E** is incorrect because it does not pair the two best answers, **A** and **D**.

C.   The Basic Concept: An Event That May Take Place Far in the Future

The common law Rule against Perpetuities is a rule of logical proof. If, by any possibility, an interest cannot vest or fail within the 21-year limit, then the devise is void for remoteness. The traditional Rule against Perpetuities imposes a maximum time limit on the potential duration of a contingent future interest. Under the rule, the future interest cannot possibly last longer than 21 years beyond the death of the last relevant person alive at the time of its creation. The future interest must be certain to vest, close, become possessory, or fail within this period. If we are not certain, then the future interest is void from the moment of its creation.

It is necessary to pay careful attention when a future interest is made contingent upon the happening of a future event, and it is not certain when (or even if) that event will take place. If the event could happen after the perpetuities period, then the future interest is void. It is often said that the future interest is void *ab initio*. This phrase means that it does not matter what actually happens after the time of the grant or devise. We are to analyze the possibilities only as they appeared at that one vantage point, considering what might have happened rather than what actually happened later.

> **QUESTION 3.** Keep the library open. Fifteen years ago the Reading Corporation made a gift of land to Literate City for use as the site for a city library. The deed provided that "if at any time the city shall cease to use the land for library purposes, then title to the land shall pass to Fred and Floy." Fred and Floy are the sole shareholders of Reading Corporation. Literate City promptly constructed a library on the site. The library opened to the public 14 months after delivery of the deed to the city, and it has remained open ever since. What is the status of the future interest granted to Fred and Floy under the Rule against Perpetuities?
>
> **A.** The rule does not apply because Fred and Floy have a future interest that is not subject to the rule.
> **B.** The future interest is valid because Fred and Floy's future interest will necessarily vest during their lifetimes.
> **C.** The future interest is valid because the city timely performed by constructing and opening the library.
> **D.** The future interest is invalid because the city has not expressly promised to keep the library open for more than 21 years.
> **E.** The future interest is invalid because the city might close the library at some point in the future.

ANALYSIS. The first step is to analyze the deed to determine what type of future interest is held by Fred and Floy. Although they are shareholders of the Reading Corporation, they are distinct persons. Thus, they do not have a reversionary interest, such as a possibility of reverter, that is exempt from the Rule against Perpetuities. Nor do they have a vested remainder because their future interest will divest a prior fee simple and cessation of library use is a condition precedent to the vesting of their interest. Fred and Floy have a shifting executory interest, which is subject to the rule. **A** is wrong.

What about **B**? Will Fred and Floy's interest necessarily vest during their lifetimes? Their executory interest is inheritable, and the city might operate the library for a lengthy period and close it more than 21 years after the last to die of Fred and Floy. **B** doesn't work.

Let's continue down the list. **C** focuses on the city's quick construction of the library, but this is not relevant. The issue is how distant into the future it might be when the city ceases to use the site for library purposes, not when it started.

Suppose the city closes the library 50 years from now. It's true, as **D** suggests, that this conduct will not violate an express promise made by the city. But whether the event that triggers the vesting of a future interest is a breach of obligation does not matter for perpetuities analysis. A future interest may be invalid under the rule even if the grantor or the holder of a future interest could make an alternative argument that the owner of the present estate is liable for breaching an obligation.

This leaves us with **E**, which is worded somewhat vaguely, but it is correct. Because the city might close the library more than 21 years after Fred and Floy die, the future interest given to Fred and Floy is invalid at the outset. It does not matter that only 15 years have passed since the grant.[1]

D. The Concept of Measuring Lives

Here are the guts of the Rule against Perpetuities: **All contingent future interests must be certain to vest within 21 years plus a life in being.**

A "life in being," also called a measuring life, is a natural person who was alive when the interest was created (when the deed was delivered or when the testator died). The instrument must identify a person or persons who can serve as the measuring life or lives. You cannot rely on what an ordinary life span may happen to be. Ordinarily the "life in being" will determine whether and when the future interest will vest or fail.

Corporations and other fictive entities are of course not living beings. When there is no human validating life to add to the equation, the perpetuities period is a flat 21 years.

A period of gestation may be added to the 21 years. A fetus in existence at the time of the conveyance or devise is deemed to be a life in being for all purposes of the rule.

> **QUESTION 4.   A devise to surviving children.** Noah died testate. His will devised Blackacre "to Carole for life, then to such of Carole's children and their heirs as survive her; and if no child of Carole survives her, then to Dominic and his heirs." At the time of Noah's death, Carole has one child, Saber. Under the Rule against Perpetuities, Dominic's interest is
>
> A. Valid, because Noah can serve as a measuring life.
> B. Valid, because Carole can serve as a measuring life.
> C. Valid, because Dominic can serve as a measuring life.
> D. Valid, because either Carole or Dominic can serve as a measuring life.
> E. Invalid, because Dominic may die more than 21 years before Carole dies.

ANALYSIS.   The first step is to label Dominic's interest to find out whether it is subject to the Rule against Perpetuities. To label Dominic's interest, we must first label the preceding interests mentioned in the will. Carole has an

---

1. This question is based on *City of Klamath Falls v. Bell*, 490 P.2d 515 (Or. App. 1971), a case that is often reproduced in property law casebooks.

ordinary life estate. What about the remainder given to Carole's children? Even though there is presently an ascertainable owner of this remainder (Carole's son, Saber), the remainder is contingent because survival by Saber and any siblings he might have in the future is a condition precedent. What will happen if the contingent remainder given to Carole's children fails to vest because no child survives Carole? The property is to go to Dominic. Thus, Dominic has an alternative contingent remainder. Contingent remainders are subject to the Rule against Perpetuities, so it is now necessary to decide whether Dominic's remainder is certain to vest within 21 years plus a life in being.

Let's go in order, first testing Noah, the testator, as a potential measuring life. Because he is the testator, by definition Noah died at the moment his will became effective. Nevertheless, it's permissible to use him as a measuring life. Since he is no longer a "life in being," the equation means that we have a flat perpetuities period of 21 years from the date of his death to consider. Is Dominic's contingent remainder certain to vest within 21 years after Noah's death? Dominic's remainder cannot vest until Carole dies, and we have no idea how old Carole presently is. Even if we did know her age and she was elderly when Noah died, we would assume that she may live for more than 21 years after Noah died. Thus, Noah is not a valid measuring life.

Now let's consider Carole as a measuring life. When Carole dies, what is to happen to Blackacre? If Saber or any future-born children of Carole survive Carole, Blackacre goes to the person or persons. If no child of Carole survives Carole, Blackacre goes to Dominic. Thus, both contingent remainders are certain to vest no later than the time of Carole's death. Carole is a valid measuring life. We don't need the extra 21-year period in this case.

Moving on to Dominic, is he a valid measuring life? Many students will think he is. Up until now, we've been talking about Blackacre going either to Carole's surviving children or Dominic, so won't Dominic be alive at Carole's death when that decision has to be made? Not necessarily. Dominic has a contingent remainder in fee simple (notice the will says "to Dominic and his heirs"). This means that his remainder is inheritable and, in most states today, devisable. Dominic might not only die before Carole, he might die more than 21 years before Carole dies. This means that Dominic is not a valid measuring life. E is wrong. Carole is a valid measuring life, and we need only one to validate Dominic's contingent remainder. **B** is our answer.

E. Class Gifts: The Problem of the Afterborn Person

A *class gift* is a devise or conveyance to a described group of persons whose identity is not ascertainable at the time the devise or conveyance is made. Gifts to someone's "children" are the most common class gifts, but gifts to a person's grandchildren, brothers and sisters, nephews and nieces, and other classes of relatives are also frequent. A vested remainder subject to open is one type of class gift.

Class gifts present special problems under the Rule against Perpetuities because they often allow an *afterborn person*[4] to become a member of the class. In order to determine the effect of the rule on a class gift, we must know how to determine the membership. We do this by looking at two separate points in time. First, the class is measured when the instrument becomes legally operative. This establishes the minimum size of the group, assuming there is no condition of survival.

The second point in time determines the maximum size of the class under a rule known as *class closing*, or the *rule of convenience*. The class closes when two events have occurred:

1. Someone qualifies for distribution of the property, and
2. The property is available for distribution. When the class gift is a future interest, this means that any prior estates have expired.

Once the class closes, no afterborn persons are eligible to share in the gift (except for a fetus who was conceived at the time of class closing). The policy is efficiency. If the class did not close, title could not vest completely in the devisees who presently qualify. It would be "inconvenient" if their shares were uncertain in amount for the remainder of the parent's lifetime.

Class closing does not mean that each member of the class must meet any condition precedent specified by the language of the instrument. The class may close, with its maximum size thus established, but we may not know until some point in the future, after class closing, whether all of the class members have satisfied the condition.

The last point to keep in mind is what's called the *all or nothing* rule. If the interest of one potential afterborn member of the class violates the Rule against Perpetuities, the entire class gift is struck down. This is what "all or nothing" means: every class member stands or falls together.

QUESTION 5.   Mount Everest. Teresa, a mountain climber, shared that hobby with her son, Juan. In 1995, Teresa made a will, which devised Blackacre "to my daughter, Miranda, for life, and at her death the property is to go to all of the children of my son, Juan, who have completed a climb of Mount Everest." At the time, Juan had two children, Jacaranda and Maria. Five years later, in 2000, Teresa and Juan died in an avalanche while they were mountain climbing. When Juan died his wife was pregnant. Five months after Juan's death his widow gave birth to Fernanda. Under relevant law Teresa and Juan are considered to have died

---

4. By "afterborn person" we mean a person who is born after the delivery of the deed or the death of the testator.

simultaneously. It is now 2022. Miranda is still alive, and so are all three of Juan's children, but none has climbed Mount Everest. Is the remainder to Juan's children valid?

A. Yes, because Juan's three children are measuring lives.
B. Yes, because the remainder must vest or fail within 21 years after Miranda's death.
C. No, because Fernanda was born after Teresa made her will.
D. No, because Fernanda was born after Teresa and Juan died.
E. No, because one of Juan's children might climb Mount Everest more than 21 years after Miranda's death.

ANALYSIS.   The remainder to Juan's children is a class gift, and notice that it is subject to a condition precedent. Each member of the class must climb Mount Everest to qualify. Notice that there is no time limitation attached to a child's satisfaction of the condition.

The key to this question is to focus on the maximum size of the class. When Juan dies, he can have no more children. Well, that isn't literally accurate because we know that he had Fernanda posthumously, but recall that Fernanda is considered to be a life in being at the moment of Juan's death. This makes **D** incorrect.

Let's take care of **C**, which attributes significance to Fernanda being born after Teresa made her will in 1995. This is not material because a will is considered legally effective when the testatrix dies, not when the will is made. This sequence does not make Teresa an afterborn child for purposes of the Rule against Perpetuities.

B and **E** both deal with the possibility that a child might climb Mount Everest more than 21 years after Miranda's death. **B** is wrong because there is no language in the devise that requires the children to accomplish the mission within that 21-year period. In contrast, **E** is accurate: one of Juan's children might climb Mount Everest more than 21 years after Miranda's death. In theory, he or she could wait until they are an octogenarian, although that would make the task awfully difficult.[5]

E would be the right answer if the best we could do in selecting a measuring life was to pick Miranda as our measuring life. Jacaranda, Maria, and Fernanda are all lives in being at Teresa's death. The class cannot get larger than the three of them. There are no potential afterborn children. We'll know whether the remainder fails or vests no later than the time the last of the three children dies. Thus, **A** is our right answer.

---

5. The oldest person to make the ascent was 64, according to *www.mnteverest.net/history.html* (last visited May 5, 2022).

F.   Statutory and Judicial Reforms

Only a few states today apply the Rule against Perpetuities in its traditional common law form. Courts and state legislatures have intervened to override the rule in circumstances in which its application was perceived to be harsh or inflexible. There are three primary reforms.

First, in some states, but not a majority, courts possess the authority to reform future interests so as to bring them within the perpetuities period. This authority is called *cy pres*, which means "as near as possible." The object is to carry out the intentions of the parties "as near as possible" under the rule. When a court uses cy pres, it implies a time limit within which the relevant event must take place. In states that recognize the cy pres doctrine, all future interests subject to the rule are eligible for salvation through this approach.

Second, either a court or a legislature may adopt a *wait-and-see* approach. The traditional Rule against Perpetuities requires the analysis to be made at the time the instrument becomes effective, based only on what is known and considered to be possible at that time. Under wait-and-see, contingent future interests remain valid throughout the perpetuities period and are voided only if the contingency is not resolved by the end of the period.

The third reform consists of the Uniform Statutory Rule against Perpetuities (USRAP), adopted by a majority of state legislatures since its promulgation in 1986. Under USRAP, contingent future interests are valid for either the common-law perpetuities period or 90 years, whichever is longer. Thereafter, courts are empowered to reform the interest so as to bring it within this extended perpetuities period. Further, USRAP exempts options to purchase and other commercial transactions from all perpetuities limits.

A few states that initially adopted USRAP later abolished the Rule against Perpetuities altogether or at least as applied to perpetual trusts. Some other states have skipped the intermediate step by simply abolishing the Rule against Perpetuities. As a result, the Rule against Perpetuities now survives in its traditional form only in a handful of states. But it also survives in its traditional form on law school exams and on state bar examinations. It is also worth emphasizing that most of the reforms to the rule cannot be comprehended without an understanding of the traditional rule.

> **QUESTION 6.   A woman as president.** In 2006, Susan devises Blackacre "to Julia for life, then to the first female president of the United States of America." Assume that the first female president is elected in November 2048, that she was born in the year 2007, and that Julia dies in 2030. The remainder is valid under which of the following perpetuities reform measures?
>
> 1. The cy pres doctrine.
> 2. Wait-and-see.

3. USRAP.
4. Abolition of the rule as applied to perpetual trusts.

A. All of the above.
B. 1 and 3.
C. 2 and 3.
D. 3 only.
E. 1, 2, and 3.

ANALYSIS. Let's study our choices in order. Under the cy pres doctrine, the court reforms the will to impose a time limitation on when the remainder must vest or fail. Because Julia is a measuring life, the appropriate time limitation would be to require that the remainder vest or fail no later than 21 years after Julia's death. Julia died before the election of the first female president, so the remainder is valid under cy pres.

Now let's look at the wait-and-see approach. Here this yields the same result as cy pres. The remainder actually vested less than 21 years after Julia's death, so it's valid.

USRAP validates all contingent future interests that vest within 90 years of their creation. Here the remainder vested 42 years after the 2006 devise, so it's valid under USRAP.

The devise does not create a perpetual trust — it doesn't create any type of trust. Thus, statutory abolition of the Rule against Perpetuities for perpetual trusts has no effect here. This makes E the right answer.

G. The Closer: Who Graduates from High School?

Here's a tough question dealing with a class gift. To handle this one, you need to think carefully about what might conceivably happen with respect to existing class members after the making of the conveyance.

QUESTION 7. Stay in high school. Orestes conveys Blackacre "to Amanda for life, remainder to all of Brad's children who graduate from high school." Brad presently has three children, two having graduated from Pine Valley High School and one who is a 15-year-old freshman. The remainder to Brad's children is

A. Valid, because Brad can serve as a measuring life.
B. Valid, because Amanda can serve as a measuring life.
C. Valid, because Orestes can serve as a measuring life.
D. All of the above are correct.
E. Invalid.

ANALYSIS.   I've given this question a number of times, and students have struggled with it. The most recent time I put this on an exam, 47 percent got it right.

We start by paying careful attention to the language creating the remainder. This is a class gift because it goes to all persons who come within the description "all of Brad's children." Orestes's deed could have named Brad's existing three children and conveyed Blackacre to them. This would not be a class gift, and legally it would have different consequences. Because Orestes used the term "all of Brad's children," he is deemed to have included afterborn children (that is, children born to Brad after he made the conveyance).

When will the class of Brad's children close? When the conveyance is made, Brad has two living high-school graduates, so the first prong of the class closing rule is satisfied. These two children qualify for distribution of the property. When will the property be available for distribution? It is not presently available because Amanda has a life estate. When she dies, the class will close. Were Amanda to die right now, shortly after the conveyance, the class would close, and it would consist of Brad's three children. The two graduates would have the right to present possession of Blackacre, and the freshman would have the right to share with the siblings if and when the freshman graduated.

Now we're far enough along that we can just about see the problem. Suppose Brad has a fourth child who is born while Amanda is still alive. This afterborn child will enter the class because the class will not close until Amanda's death. We need to ask ourselves whether this afterborn child's interest is certain to vest or fail within 21 years after the death of a measuring life. Let's start testing the possible measuring lives.

Will Brad work? Recall we should hypothesize that anyone can die at any time, in any sequence. Brad might die soon after the birth of his last child. Can we tell for sure whether this child will graduate from high school no later than 21 years after Brad's death? No, we can't. We don't deal with probabilities for perpetuities analysis. If anything could conceivably happen, assume that it will. Few high school graduates are more than 21 years old, but it's possible for someone to languish in the school system for more than 21 years and then graduate.[2] Thus, Brad is not a valid measuring life.

Let's move on to consider Amanda as a possible validating life. We have the same problem. Just as Brad's fourth child, the afterborn, might graduate from high school more than 21 years after Brad's death, the child might also graduate more than 21 years after Amanda's death. And we don't do any better using Orestes as a measuring life. The choices given to us do not include trying to use Brad's existing children as measuring lives. We're allowed to try, but that doesn't solve the problem either. All three of the older siblings could die suddenly, more than 21 years before the fourth child's graduation.

---

2. Most dropout students who later on obtain high school credentials do so by passing the General Educational Development (GED) test. I don't think it's necessary for purposes of the Rule against Perpetuities to decide whether Orestes's intent was to include children who obtained GED credentials within the class.

So the class gift is invalid, leaving **E** as our right answer. Under the all or nothing rule, the remainder to Brad's children is struck down, even though the class included two children whose interest was already vested at the time the deed was made. It seems cruel, which is why the Rule against Perpetuities has been said to apply "remorselessly."

Can we see a way to save the class gift in Orestes's deed by redrafting? The problem, again, is that the class closes too late due to the possibility of an after-born fourth child. Orestes could have closed the class by saying "to Amanda for life, remainder to all of Brad's children *now living* who graduate from high school." By adding these two words, "now living," Orestes specifies that only the three existing children are eligible to take shares. Now there's no perpetuities violation. The children are valid measuring lives; the interest of each will vest or fail during their respective lifetimes.

 ## Smith's Picks

1. Why do we have the Rule against Perpetuities?   **B**
2. Testing an option   **A**
3. Keep the library open   **E**
4. A devise to surviving children   **B**
5. Mount Everest   **A**
6. A woman as president   **E**
7. Stay in high school   **E**

14

Cotenants

"Share everything."
Robert Fulghum, *All I Really Need to Know I Learned in Kindergarten* (1988)

CHAPTER OVERVIEW
A. Right to Shared Possession
B. Ouster
C. Tenancy in Common
D. Joint Tenancy
E. The Closer: Tracing Cotenancy Interests through the Generations
⟡ Smith's Picks

Most property courses pay some attention to the law of cotenancy. A cotenancy is present when multiple persons have the right to possess, use, and enjoy an item of property. The owners, who are called *cotenants*, have rights that are concurrent in time.

Cotenancy is the oldest form of shared ownership recognized in the Anglo-American legal system. It dates back to the earliest days of English common law. The principles of cotenancy were developed by courts for ownership of estates in land, but they also apply to personal property (both goods and intangible personal property). Today shared ownership, especially in business settings, is often accomplished by the formation of corporations or other entities, which take title to the property, but cotenancy is of enduring significance. Married couples and relatives own much of their property as cotenants, and not infrequently property used in a trade or business or held for investment is also placed in cotenancy.

This chapter addresses the general nature of cotenancy and two types of cotenancy: the tenancy in common and joint tenancy. The third type of cotenancy that has modern significance is the tenancy by the entirety. The tenancy by the entirety is a form of marital property, and it is discussed in the next chapter.

A. Right to Shared Possession

The core of cotenancy is that each cotenant has a right to use and possess the entire property. Putting aside until the next chapter tenancy by the entirety, each cotenant also has the right to transfer his right of possession. This may be accomplished by a complete transfer of the cotenant's interest. For land, the cotenant accomplishes such a transfer by execution and delivery of a deed of conveyance. A cotenant also has the right to make a limited transfer. For example, the cotenant may transfer a right to possession by leasing her interest, may grant a licensee the right to use the property, or may mortgage her interest. A transfer by one cotenant affects the nontransferring cotenant in the sense that there is a new owner with whom the property must be shared.

The law of cotenancy does not require that each cotenant use or take possession of the commonly owned property. A cotenant, just like any other property owner, may choose to ignore her property. When one or more of the cotenants are out of possession, they may desire compensation from the occupying cotenant. The parties may contractually agree to such an arrangement, but in the absence of agreement, the majority rule is that nothing is payable. A cotenant is entitled to take sole possession, with no duty to account to the other cotenants. An exception is made if there is an *ouster*. If the possessing cotenant excludes the other cotenants, preventing them from entering and also enjoying the property, then there is an actionable wrong. The ousted cotenants may recover damages and obtain injunctive relief.

The situation is distinguishable when one cotenant, instead of taking possession personally, uses the property to obtain rents or profits from third parties. That cotenant has a duty to account for rents and profits to her cotenants pursuant to a rule that dates back to the Statute of Anne, passed by the English Parliament in 1705. This duty may be enforced by an action for an accounting brought by the cotenants who have not received their proper share.

A cotenant may terminate the cotenancy relationship by using a procedure called *partition*. This is a safety valve that enables a cotenant to end a property relationship that may no longer serve a useful purpose or may be impaired by personal friction among the owners. Every cotenant (except a tenant by the entirety) has the right to a partition. There are two types of partition. With a *partition in kind*, a court divides the property between the cotenants according to their respective percentages of ownership. When the property is a tract of land, the property is subdivided, with each cotenant ending up with a separate parcel. The cotenants become neighboring landowners.

With a *partition by sale*, the property is sold and all of the cotenants take a share of the net sales proceeds according to their respective ownership percentages. Usually the court effectuates a partition in kind by ordering a public sale by auction. At the auction, an outsider may turn out to be the high bidder, but often one of the existing cotenants (usually the plaintiff) bids the most and purchases the property. Thus, partition by sale can function as a court-supervised buy-out procedure.

The law has a preference for partition in kind rather than partition by sale. If any cotenant asks for partition in kind, the court will grant that remedy if it can make a "fair and equitable" division of the property. Due to the nature of some types of property (both real and personal property), partition in kind is sometimes not feasible or appropriate.

An agreement among the cotenants may restrict or modify the right to partition. Courts, however, often refuse to enforce such agreements if they are unlimited in time or have other provisions that appear unreasonable. When a court invalidates a partition restriction, usually it is on the basis that the agreement constitutes an improper "restraint on alienation."

QUESTION 1.   The old family home. Victor and Patricia were the sole heirs of their mother, who died two years ago. Victor and Patricia inherited the family residence, a house where their mother had lived, which had been in their family since 1910. Patricia lived in an apartment in the city where their mother's house was located. Her brother Victor lived in a neighboring state with his family. Shortly after their mother's death, Patricia cancelled her apartment lease and moved into the house, where she has resided since. Four months ago, Patricia rented a room in the house to Bob, while she continued to reside in the house herself. Victor and Patricia have made no agreement with respect to Patricia's occupancy of the house or her rental to Bob. In an action for damages brought by Victor against Patricia, the most probable outcome is:

A. Victor can recover damages based on the rental value of the entire house since the time Patricia took possession, including the portion rented to Bob.

B. Victor can recover damages based on the rental value of the house since the time Patricia took possession, excluding the portion rented to Bob since he took occupancy of his room.

C. Victor can recover damages based on the rents paid by Bob, but cannot otherwise recover based on the rental value of the house.

D. Victor cannot recover any damages based on Patricia's possession of the house or her rental to Bob.

E. Instead of ruling on Victor's claims for damages, the court will convert the action into one for partition of the property.

ANALYSIS. Let's start at the end with choice **E**, which discusses partition. The facts state that Victor has brought an action for damages, and the facts say nothing about Victor, or Patricia as defendant, seeking partition (either partition by sale or partition in kind). Remember, an operating rule for all exam questions (including multiple-choice questions) is: *never assume facts that are not stated*. In civil litigation, the court will not grant relief for which neither party has asked. A person in Victor's situation would usually couple a claim for partition with his claim for damages, but he has not chosen to do so. The court will adjudicate Victor's claim for damages and will not order or consider partition.

In most American states, a cotenant like Patricia is entitled to take sole possession of the property without compensating an absent cotenant, like Victor. This is subject to the exception of ouster, but here there are no facts suggesting that Patricia may have ousted Victor. The fact that Victor all along has lived in another state and thus presumably does not want to move into the house does not constitute an ouster. There is no evidence that if Victor (with or without his family) had shown up at the house and asked to move in, Patricia would have attempted to exclude him. Thus, Patricia owes Victor nothing with respect to her occupancy of the house since the time of their mother's death. So we should strike **A** and **B** as wrong answers.

Patricia's rental of a room to Bob is another matter. In most American states, she has an obligation to share the rents paid by Bob with her cotenant, Victor. Our right answer is **C**.

B. Ouster

Let's think a bit more about ouster. In Question 1, Patricia did not oust Victor from the house owned in cotenancy because Victor never attempted to enter or move into the house.

An *ouster* is present when a cotenant engages in acts of possession or other conduct that is inconsistent with the rights of other cotenants. Proof of ouster by an excluded cotenant may include statements made by the cotenant in possession that show an intent to exclude, but conduct alone (such as changing the locks) may suffice.

> **QUESTION 2. "You better find a place to live."** After Cathy's divorce, she moved 500 miles back to her hometown, where she moved in with her older sister, Anna, an unmarried woman. Anna's place was too small, so the sisters bought a larger home, each paying one-half of the purchase costs. They agreed to share all the expenses of homeownership, but one year later Cathy lost her job, causing Anna to shoulder most of the expenses. Soon they began bickering. This went on for six months, with

the sibling relationship steadily deteriorating. One day Anna told Cathy that she was putting the house up for sale and that she "better find a place to live." Cathy promptly moved out. Anna remained in possession and listed the house for sale with a real estate broker, but the market was terrible. Anna sold the house ten months after Cathy departed. Anna sent Cathy a check for one-half of the net proceeds of the sale, but Cathy wanted more money. She sued for damages based upon Anna's use of the house for the ten months prior to the sale. The most probable result is:

A. Cathy may recover damages because Anna enjoyed sole possession of the house.

B. Cathy may recover damages because Anna ordered Cathy to leave.

C. Cathy cannot recover damages because she left the house voluntarily.

D. Cathy cannot recover damages because she defaulted in her obligation to pay one-half of the expenses.

ANALYSIS. This question tests your understanding of "ouster," although neither the facts nor the responses use the word. Cathy's claim is based on the allegation that her sister has ousted her from the house. **A** is wrong because Anna's sole possession, by itself, is not sufficient to impose liability for damages. If Cathy chose to leave, Anna is entitled to remain in sole possession without having to pay.

D is wrong, even though it is true that Cathy's loss of employment does not excuse her from the obligation to pay one-half of the house expenses. In the litigation, Anna has the right to assert a counterclaim based on Cathy's failure to pay expenses. But this isn't a defense to Cathy's claim.

We're down to **B** and **C**, both of which are plausible. If Cathy decided to leave the house voluntarily after their conversation, then there is no ouster. On the other hand, if Anna stated that she must leave, then there is an ouster. A court is unlikely to find "no ouster" just because Anna did not use physical force to get Cathy out of the house. So let's look closely. For months the personal relationship was troubled, and Anna said her sister "better find a place to live." This seems much more direct than suggesting that Cathy might move if she wanted to. **B** is the better answer.

C. Tenancy in Common

The tenancy in common is the most typical form of cotenancy used in the United States. At traditional common law, the joint tenancy was the preferred form of concurrent ownership. When a deed or will created a cotenancy (and the cotenants were not a married couple — we're not presently concerned with the tenancy by the entirety), a joint tenancy resulted in the absence of language pointing to a tenancy in common. Today the presumption is the opposite. State statutes create a presumption that favors the tenancy in common. The Arkansas statute is typical:

> Every interest in real estate granted or devised to two (2) or more persons, other than executors and trustees as such, shall be in tenancy in common unless expressly declared in the grant or devise to be a joint tenancy.

Ark. Code §18-12-603.

With a tenancy in common, each cotenant owns a separate, undivided interest in the property. Unequal shares are permitted. In other words, one tenant in common may have a greater fractional share in the property than another tenant in common. Don't let this confuse you. The allowance of unequal shares does not override the basic principle that each tenant in common has a right to use or possess all of the property. A tenant in common with a small fractional share still has the right to make personal use of all of the property. The smallness of a particular share becomes significant only when the property is partitioned or when there are rents and profits to divide among the tenants in common.

In contrast to the joint tenancy, a tenant in common has no survivorship rights without respect to the commonly owned property. When a tenant in common dies, the decedent's entire share goes into the decedent's estate to be distributed to her heirs or devisees.

QUESTION 3. The conveyance of Disneyacre. Snow White conveyed Disneyacre "to my dear friends, Mickey, Minnie, and Daffy and their heirs, to have and to hold and to enjoy together forever." One year later Mickey sold his entire interest to Donald for 1,000 imperial doubloons. Six months later both Mickey and Daffy died (one day apart, in that order). Neither Mickey nor Daffy made a last will and testament. Daffy's only heir is Donald. Mickey's only heir is Minnie. Who owns what interests in Disneyacre?

A. Minnie has one-third and Donald has two-thirds, with their interests held in tenancy in common.

B. Minnie has one-third and Donald has two-thirds, with their interests held in joint tenancy.

C. Minnie has two-thirds and Donald has one-third, with their interests held in tenancy in common.

D. Minnie has two-thirds and Donald has one-third, with their interests held in joint tenancy.

E. Minnie and Donald each have one-third, and Mickey retains his one-third because Mickey did not have the right to convey his interest. All these interests are now held in tenancy in common.

ANALYSIS.   First we need to determine the effect of the first conveyance, the deed from Snow White. The words after the grantees' names, "to have and to hold and to enjoy together forever," suggest a type of unity of purpose that's consistent with a joint tenancy. However, there is no express reference to a "joint tenancy," to "joint tenants," or to the grantees having a right of survivorship. The language in the Snow White deed is not enough to rebut the presumption of a tenancy in common. Therefore we start with a tenancy in common owned by Mickey, Minnie, and Daffy.

Next we have the sale from Mickey to Donald. Although Snow White expressed a wish that the three grantees would have and hold and enjoy the property "together forever," this is not sufficient to make the interests inalienable. The law disfavors restraints on alienation. A clear restraint on alienation for a limited time period might be enforceable, but the deed language does not rise to this level. Thus **E** is wrong. After the sale, Minnie, Daffy, and Donald each own one-third as tenants in common.

Our last transfer is Donald's inheritance from Daffy. Now Donald has a two-thirds share, having acquired the original shares held by Mickey and Daffy. Donald holds this with Minnie, who still has her one-third. They're tenants in common, so our answer is **A**.

D.   Joint Tenancy

At common law, joint tenancy was characterized by four unities, which the joint tenants shared:

- **The unity of title.** Each joint tenant acquired his interest by the same document (deed or will) or act of inheritance.
- **The unity of time.** Each joint tenant acquired his interest at the same point in time.
- **The unity of interest.** Each joint tenant obtained the same fractional share.
- **The unity of possession.** Each joint tenant has the same undivided right to possess the property.

All four unities were necessary to create a joint tenancy. The California joint tenancy statute reflects this history but modifies it to allow the creation of a joint tenancy by a person who already owns the property. Other states have enacted similar reforms. The California statute provides:

Joint tenancy; definition; method of creation. A joint interest is one owned by two or more persons in equal shares, by a title created by a single will or transfer, when expressly declared in the will or transfer to be a joint tenancy, or by transfer from a sole owner to himself or herself and others, or from tenants in common or joint tenants to themselves or some of them, or to themselves or any of them and others, or from a husband and wife, when holding title as community property or otherwise to themselves or to themselves and others or to one of them and to another or others, when expressly declared in the transfer to be a joint tenancy, or when granted or devised to executors or trustees as joint tenants. A joint tenancy in personal property may be created by a written transfer, instrument, or agreement.

Cal. Civ. Code §683(a).

The four unities gave rise to the doctrine of *severance*. Once a joint tenancy is created, the unities must persist intact for the joint tenancy to continue. This means that if one joint tenant conveys her interest to a grantee, the joint tenancy is severed (that is, terminated) as to the interest that is conveyed.

QUESTION 4. Disneyacre redux. Snow White conveyed Disneyacre "to my dear friends, Mickey, Minnie, and Daffy and their heirs, to have and to hold and to enjoy together forever as joint tenants." One year later Mickey sold his entire interest to Donald for 1,000 imperial doubloons. Six months later both Mickey and Daffy died (one day apart, in that order). Neither Mickey nor Daffy made a last will and testament. Daffy's only heir is Donald. Mickey's only heir is Minnie. Assume that the California joint tenancy statute applies. Who owns what interests in Disneyacre?

A. Minnie has one-third and Donald has two-thirds, with their interests held in tenancy in common.

B. Minnie has one-half and Donald has one-half, with their interests held in tenancy in common.

C. Minnie has two-thirds and Donald has one-third, with their interests held in tenancy in common.

D. Minnie has one-half and Donald has one-half, with their interests held in joint tenancy.

E. Minnie owns all of Disneyacre (100 percent).

ANALYSIS. The first step, again, is to figure out the effect of Snow White's deed. Here the final three words, "as joint tenants," are sufficient to create a joint tenancy among Mickey, Minnie, and Daffy.

Mickey's sale to Donald is valid because a joint tenant is allowed to convey his interest in the property, and the deed lacks an effective restraint on alienation. Mickey's conveyance amounts to a severance of the joint tenancy, but to what extent? When there are more than two joint tenants, a conveyance severs the joint tenancy only as to the interest conveyed. Therefore, after the conveyance Donald holds one-third as a tenant in common, and Minnie and Daffy continue to hold their one-thirds as joint tenants with each other.

When Daffy dies, his one-third goes to the surviving joint tenant, Minnie. At his death the joint tenancy ends (Minnie cannot be a joint tenant with and by herself). Now Minnie owns two-thirds of Disneyacre. So this leads us to our correct answer, **C**.

E. The Closer: Tracing Cotenancy Interests through the Generations

When property passes from one generation to the next, children and grandchildren often obtain fractional shares, which they hold as cotenants. Joint tenancies, when they are formed and are not dissolved by severance or by other actions, consolidate ownership when owners die. Conversely, tenancies in common fragment ownership. Because tenancies in common are more popular in the United States, the intergenerational transmission of wealth tends to result in the creation of large groups of owners, whose shares are often unequal. This phenomenon spawns problems for searching title to real property and for the effective management and use of the property.

> **QUESTION 5. Follow the bouncing ball.** Freddie delivered a deed that conveyed Blackacre "to Gary and Hattie and their heirs and assigns, share and share alike." One year later, Gary died, devising "all of my right, title, and interest in Blackacre to my daughters, Sarah and Tristan, jointly." Two years after that conveyance, Sarah died intestate. Sarah's heirs are her three children, Dickie, Dobby, and Drago. Next Tristan died, with her will devising all of her property "to my two sons, Edward and Emanuel as joint tenants." Finally, Hattie died, devising "an undivided one-third interest in all of my property to my niece Ursa, and an undivided two-thirds interest in all of my property to my nephew Victor." Who owns what interests in Blackacre?
>
> A. Ursa owns one-third and Victor owns two-thirds as tenants in common.
> B. Ursa owns one-sixth and Victor owns one-third as tenants in common; and Edward and Emanuel each own one-quarter as joint tenants.
> C. Ursa owns one-quarter and Victor owns one-quarter as tenants in common; and Edward and Emanuel each own one-quarter as joint tenants.
> D. Ursa owns one-sixth and Victor owns one-third as tenants in common; and Edward and Emanuel each own one-quarter as tenants in common.
> E. Ursa owns one-sixth and Victor owns one-third as tenants in common; Dickie, Dobby, and Drago each own one-twelfth as tenants in common; and Edward and Emanuel each own one-eighth as joint tenants.

ANALYSIS. Law students are notorious for their math anxiety. Though I recognize that phobia, I do not cater to it unduly. Although the math in this question involves nothing more complicated than fractions, this question is about as far as I'll go on an exam in requiring students to trace fractional shares.

Whew! A diagram for this one sure helps. You should try to chart this out on scratch paper. Here's a text description of the steps, with the diagram at the end of this analysis.

First step: Gary and Hattie take as tenants in common, each with a one-half interest. The words "share and share alike" really add nothing of legal significance. They do not create a joint tenancy.

Second step: Gary's devise to his two daughters "jointly" might conceivably create a joint tenancy, but the courts that have addressed this issue have ruled to the contrary. Although "jointly" may sound like "joint tenancy" or "joint tenants," the word has a popular meaning that means they own together. Therefore, Sarah and Tristan are tenants in common. They split their father's one-half share, so they each own one-quarter.

Third step: Sarah dies, survived by her children, Dickie, Dobby, and Drago (the "Three Ds"). They split their mother's one-quarter share, so each "D" owns one-twelfth as a tenant in common.

Fourth step: Tristan dies, devising her property to Edward and Emanuel. They split their mother's one-quarter share, so each owns one-eighth as a joint tenant.

Fifth (and thankfully last) step: Hattie dies, with her will making an unequal division between Ursa and Victor. Ursa gets one-third of Hattie's one-half (that's one-sixth), and Victor does twice as well (two-thirds of Hattie's one-half equals one-third). The dust has settled, and **E** is our answer.

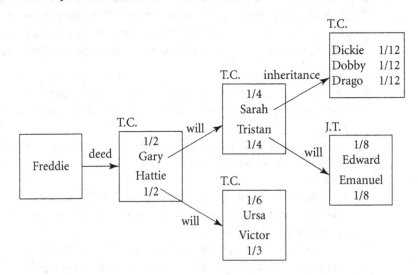

Smith's Picks

1. The old family home   **C**
2. "You better find a place to live"   **B**
3. The conveyance of Disneyacre   **A**
4. Disneyacre redux   **C**
5. Follow the bouncing ball   **E**

15

Marital Property

"What's yours is mine, and what's mine is mine, too."
American idiom
(variation of an expression of generosity:
"What's yours is mine, and what's mine is yours.")

CHAPTER OVERVIEW
A. Tenancy by the Entirety
B. Death
C. Divorce
D. Community Property
E. The Closer: Treatment of Real Property Held by Both Spouses at
   Divorce
 Smith's Picks

Most property courses pay at least some attention to marital property, although the degree of emphasis and the selection of which topics to study can vary widely. Often the subject of marital property is grouped with the standard cotenancies (the tenancy in common and the joint tenancy) under the title "Concurrent ownership," which we studied in the preceding chapter.

A.   Tenancy by the Entirety

A tenancy by the entirety arose under English common law as a form of cotenancy limited to a married couple. It resembled the joint tenancy in that each owner had a right of survivorship. The surviving spouse succeeded to the share of the deceased spouse, with no interest passing to the decedent's heirs or devisees. The tenancy by the entirety also resembled the joint tenancy by incorporating the requirement of four unities: the spouses must have the same *title*, acquired at the same *time*; they must have the same *interest*; and they must have a shared right to *possession*. In addition, for the tenancy by the entirety, there was said to be a fifth unity—the unity of the *person*. A joint tenant was considered to own a separate share for some purposes, but a tenant by the entirety had no separate ownership interest. The tenancy was conceptualized as ownership by the marital unity (apparently a fictive entity), not by the individual spouses. While the marriage lasted, the husband had full management rights over the entirety property by virtue of a concept known as the husband's estate *jure uxoris*.

In England, a conveyance of land to a married couple always created a tenancy by the entirety. A couple was not allowed to take title as joint tenants or tenants in common. Thus, a deed or will did not have to use any particular language to create a tenancy by the entirety.

Today in the United States approximately one-half of the jurisdictions recognize the tenancy by the entirety. The tenancy is modified to afford wives and husbands coequal management rights over property held in this form. In states recognizing the tenancy by the entirety, a couple may choose a joint tenancy or tenancy in common as an alternative. When a deed or will does not clearly indicate the type of cotenancy that is intended, most states presume a tenancy by the entirety if the language refers to the takers as "husband and wife."

In most states, an individual spouse cannot convey any interest in the property to an outsider. The spouses must act together to sell, lease, or mortgage the property. In a few states, one spouse acting alone is allowed to transfer that spouse's right to possession, right to income and profits, or contingent survivorship right. Such a transfer has no effect upon the survivorship right of the nonparticipating spouse.

A tenancy by the entirety provides a survivorship right that is much more durable than that afforded by a joint tenancy. Severance generally requires the consent of both spouses or the ending of the marriage by divorce. *United States v. Craft*, 535 U.S. 274 (2002), recognized an exception to the general rule. In *Craft*, a husband failed to pay a significant federal income tax liability. He and his wife owned real estate as tenants by the entirety. The Internal Revenue Service filed a notice of federal tax lien. The husband subsequently conveyed his interest in the property to his wife. When the wife later sold the property, the government claimed a share of the sales proceeds. The wife argued that under state law her husband never owned a separate property interest and thus there was no property to which the tax lien could attach. The Court, with three justices dissenting, held for the government. It concluded that a lien attached because, notwithstanding the nature of the tenancy by the entirety, each spouse had sufficient individual property rights, including the survivorship right and the right to share in rents and profits.

In all states recognizing tenancy by the entirety, spouses can elect to own real property in that form. As to personal property, states differ. Some restrict the tenancy by the entirety to real property, and others extend it to personal property.

QUESTION 1.   Mortgaging the station. Susan and Bob own a gasoline station, where Susan works, as tenants by the entirety. Bob pursues his occupation elsewhere. He is a real estate attorney. Susan borrowed money from her bank, which required that she grant the bank a mortgage on the gasoline station as collateral. She did so. Bob didn't sign or agree to the mortgage. Susan then defaulted in paying the bank loan. In most states that recognize a tenancy by the entirety, what rights does the bank have under the mortgage?

A. The bank can foreclose its mortgage on the entire property because each spouse has the authority to bind the other's interest.
B. The bank has no rights in the property as long as Susan and Bob are alive.
C. The bank can foreclose its mortgage to gain Susan's right to possession and her contingent right to survivorship.
D. The mortgage destroyed the spouses' rights to survivorship and the bank can foreclose its mortgage to gain Susan's undivided one-half.

ANALYSIS.   Let's start with **A.** It is possible that Susan might have obtained Bob's permission to grant a mortgage on the gasoline station. If so, Susan may have acted as Bob's agent with respect to his share when she signed the mortgage. But we have no facts supporting this agency theory. It is not a feature of the tenancy by the entirety that one spouse automatically has authority to bind the other spouse's interest. **A** is a weak answer.

In a few states, **C** is correct. In those states, Susan by herself can transfer her interest, and only her interest, to a grantee. Bob would be protected in those states in that his survivorship right and his present right to possession would not be impaired by Susan's transfer. But this is a minority rule, and the question asks for the outcome in "most states."

D is the weakest answer so far. The main purpose of the tenancy by the entirety is to give each spouse an indestructible survivorship right. Bob's survivorship right cannot be prejudiced by Susan's unilateral decision to attempt to mortgage the property.

B, our correct answer, states that the bank as mortgagee has no rights while both spouses are alive. In most states, a spouse by herself cannot transfer any property rights, including a mortgage, to an outsider. Note that the answer hedges with respect to what may happen when Bob or Susan dies. It is possible that the bank will have an enforceable right as mortgagee if Bob dies before Susan, thus ending the tenancy by the entirety.

———————————

To make sure you understand the key differences between the tenancy by the entirety and the joint tenancy, let's consider what would happen if one spouse by herself mortgages property held in joint tenancy.

> **QUESTION 2. Mortgaging a joint tenancy property.** With our facts from Question 1 above, assume instead that Susan and Bob had owned the gasoline station in joint tenancy. Now what rights does the bank have under the mortgage?
>
> **A.** The bank can foreclose its mortgage on the entire property because each spouse has the authority to bind the other's interest.
> **B.** The bank has no rights in the property as long as Susan and Bob are alive.
> **C.** The bank can foreclose its mortgage to gain Susan's right to possession and her contingent right to survivorship.
> **D.** The bank can foreclose its mortgage to gain Susan's right to possession.

ANALYSIS.   We're faced with the same set of answers as in Question 1. For **A**, there is no change in what we concluded with respect to agency and the lack of implicit authority of one spouse to bind the other spouse's interest. **A** is still weak.

B is now wrong. An individual joint tenant may make a unilateral transfer of his or her interest. The bank definitely has rights in the gas station, even though its mortgage does not extend to Bob's interest in the station.

Let's take a close look at **C** and **D**, which are alike in that both say the bank can foreclose on some property interest. Under **D** the bank's foreclosure will transfer Susan's possessory right (more precisely, her undivided one-half interest). Under **C** the foreclosure will transfer this possessory right plus Susan's survivorship right. This will not work. The joint tenancy will be severed no later than the time of completion of the foreclosure sale. Bob and the foreclosure purchaser will become tenants in common. **D** is our answer.

As an aside, you may have learned that there is a split of authority as to whether a joint tenant's grant of a mortgage severs the joint tenancy at the time the mortgage is made. A number of courts have held that a severance occurs if the state follows the title theory of mortgages (that is, the idea that a mortgage grants title, rather than a lien, to the mortgagee). To answer this question, it is not necessary for you to decide which competing rule to apply. If the joint tenancy was not severed when Susan granted the mortgage on the gas station, it definitely will be severed when foreclosure is completed.

B.   Death

At English common law, one spouse never inherited from his or her mate. Only blood relatives qualified as heirs. Thus, if a husband made a will that did not devise property to his wife, that choice did not harm her. Instead of protecting a spouse as an heir, English common law awarded surviving spouses a share of the land through what was known as *legal life estates*. The wife's estate was known as dower and the husband's estate as curtesy. Dower and curtesy attached to all of the freehold estates owned by the decedent spouse at any time during the marriage, provided the estate was inheritable by children of the marriage. These estates have had a major impact on land titles because they applied to land owned at any time during the marriage, even though conveyed by the owner prior to death. When the husband had sole title, the wife had to join in execution of the deed to release dower (and vice versa for land titled in the wife). Failure to join meant the grantee was subject to dower should the wife become a widow.

Dower and curtesy were not symmetrical estates. There are two key distinctions. First, for the husband to have curtesy, the couple must have had a child, but birth of a child was not required for dower. Second, curtesy applied to all of the wife's freehold estates, but the wife's dower applied to one-third of the husband's freehold estates.

Most American states have abolished dower and curtesy, concluding that this form of spousal protection has become anachronistic. Today dower is recognized in only four states: Arkansas, Kentucky, Michigan, and Ohio, where it extends to husbands as well as wives on an equal footing.

Most states have replaced dower and curtesy with a forced share or elective share, specified by statute. The survivor is entitled to a percentage of the deceased spouse's estate, typically one-third or one-half. If the decedent's will is less generous to the survivor, that spouse has the right to disaffirm the will and take the mandated share. The forced share treats real property and personal property alike and doesn't give the survivor rights in property conveyed by the spouse before death.

One weakness of the traditional forced share statute is that it operates independently of assets transferred by the decedent outside of probate. Many decedents leave behind significant non-probate assets, including life insurance proceeds, retirement benefits, and joint tenancy property. Depending upon whether such assets go to the surviving spouse or to other persons, the forced share may give the survivor too much or too little property. The Uniform Probate Code (UPC) resolves this problem by defining an "augmented estate," which includes non-probate assets. Under the UPC, the survivor is guaranteed a percentage of the augmented estate, which increases based upon the length of the marriage. UPC §2-202. For marriages of at least 15 years, the survivor takes 50 percent. UPC §2-203. Prenuptial agreements may allow spouses to "contract out" of forced share rules, subject to limitations of the laws of particular states.

QUESTION 3. Dower and the husband's three properties. Randolph has just died after having been married to Mary for the past 24 years. Seven years ago he purchased an apartment building for $300,000. Randolph took title in his name alone. Three years ago he sold the apartment building to a buyer for $420,000. Mary did not agree to this sale or sign any documents in connection with the sale. Randolph's will devised all of his property to the couple's two children, Bob and Babe. In addition to the apartment building, the only other real property that Randolph had owned during his lifetime was (1) his residence, where his family lived, and (2) a leasehold (Randolph owned and ran a bookstore, which he rented under a term of years for 15 years). At his death, he still owned the residence and the leasehold for the bookstore. After Randolph's death, at traditional English common law, which of the following is true?

A. Mary has property rights in the apartment building, but not the residence or the bookstore.

B. Mary has property rights in the residence, but not the apartment building or the bookstore.

C. Mary has property rights in the apartment building and the residence, but not the bookstore.

D. Mary has property rights in all three properties.

E. None of the above.

ANALYSIS. First, let's consider the apartment building. At traditional English common law, Mary as widow has a right to dower with respect to all *freehold estates* owned at any time during the marriage. From the facts, we should assume that Randolph owned the apartment building and the house in fee simple. A fee simple is a freehold, and Mary has dower with respect to both of these properties. This is true for the apartment building even though Randolph sold it before he died. The purchaser should have bargained for Mary to release her dower.

A leasehold, by definition, is not a freehold estate. Mary has no dower rights with respect to the leasehold. Thus, our right answer is **C**.

Let's take the same facts involving Randolph and Mary and transport them to a modern state that has abolished dower and curtesy.

QUESTION 4.   The husband's three properties under modern law. With our facts from Question 3, assume that Randolph and Mary had lived in a state that recognizes common law property rights (that is, the state does not follow community property) and has abolished dower and curtesy. After Randolph's death, which of the following is true?

A. Mary has property rights in the apartment building, but not the residence or the bookstore.
B. Mary has property rights in the residence, but not the apartment building or the bookstore.
C. Mary has property rights in the apartment building and the residence, but not the bookstore.
D. Mary has property rights in all three properties.
E. None of the above.

ANALYSIS. Turning to the apartment building first, because Randolph sold it before he died, it is water under the bridge. In the absence of dower, Mary has no property right or other type of claim to that property. With this information, we can eliminate choices **A**, **C**, and **D** because we know Mary has no rights in the apartment building.

So do we pick **B** or **E**? Randolph died owning the residence and the bookstore leasehold. If his will is valid, both of these estates go to his two children, Bob and Babe. Because Randolph's will left Mary nothing, in most states she can disaffirm the will, claiming a forced share of the property that passed into Randolph's estate. The leasehold is traditionally classified as personal property, but Mary's forced share applies to both real property and personal property. Thus, we should conclude that there is no basis for treating a claim by Mary differently with respect to the residence and the bookstore. Either she presently has property rights in both properties because she has the right to disaffirm the will, or she presently has property rights in neither (because she has not yet acted to disaffirm the will). **B** is a poor answer because it discriminates between the residence and the bookstore. We have to take **E**.

C. Divorce

Divorce law has changed greatly in the United States during the past half century. The two major reforms are no-fault divorce and the equitable division of property. Both represent a drastic change from prior law. Under traditional divorce law, a husband or wife who sought a divorce had to bring judicial action to establish "grounds" for divorce. What grounds were sufficient varied considerably from state to state. Usually the plaintiff spouse had to prove major wrongdoing by the defendant, such as adultery, bigamy, desertion, or physical abuse. Beginning in the 1960s, state legislatures reformed their divorce statutes to eliminate the need to establish grounds for a divorce. Courts are now authorized to grant divorces without identifying fault or grounds by making a general finding such as "irreconcilable differences" or "marital discord." Judicial action is still required — it's still easier to get married than to get divorced. But a consequence of the reform is that if one spouse wants a divorce and files an action, that action will succeed even if the other spouse (the defendant) wants the marriage to continue. In effect, this has led to a system in which any spouse has a "legal right" to a divorce.

The second major divorce reform was the legislative adoption of the concept of *equitable division* of property. This modified a prior system of splitting property at divorce based upon *separate title*. Under the separate title system, property was divided by the relatively simple process of deciding who owned what and confirming that ownership. For assets for which there was documentary evidence of title, such as land, automobiles, and stocks, this was relatively easy. For assets typically lacking such evidence, such as household furniture and other goods, conflicting claims were harder to resolve. The court divided the assets into three groups: first, things owned solely by husband; second, things owned solely by wife; and third, things they owned together (as cotenants in so-called common law property states or community property in those states recognizing that concept — we'll study community property later in this chapter). Assets in the third category were divided, with each spouse keeping whatever share they already owned and with provision for partition or sale when appropriate.

When the separate title system produced results that were thought to be inequitable, the court awarded *alimony*. If a poorer spouse (usually the wife) needed economic support after divorce, the court set an amount of alimony, payable periodically. Alimony is conceptualized not as a claim on the wealthier spouse's property but as a personal obligation of that spouse. The justification for alimony is the recipient's need; it is not that the recipient "owns" a right to collect money because the payor left the marriage with greater wealth or earning potential. In many states today, the term "maintenance" has replaced "alimony," with no change in the underlying concept.

The equitable division system replaced the separate title system as the method of dividing property at divorce in common law (i.e., not community property) states. Under an equitable division statute, all property owned by either spouse is classified as "separate property" or "marital property." Separate property consists of property acquired by a spouse prior to the marriage and gifts (including inheritances and devises) made specifically to that spouse during the marriage. Everything else, including income earned by either spouse during the marriage, is marital property. In most states, the divorce court must give each spouse all of that person's separate property, although in a few states the divorce court has the power to divide even separate property between the parties. The court, conversely, has discretion as to how to allocate the marital property, based upon a number of factors, including need.

In order for a court to recognize a spouse's claim as "marital property," the claim must first be considered to be "property." Equitable division statutes do not contain a definition of "property." One context that has expanded the realm of property involves spousal claims that a professional license or human capital constitutes divisible marital property. In the leading case of *O'Brien v. O'Brien*, 489 N.E.2d 712 (N.Y. 1985), the court classified a husband's medical license as marital property when the wife made significant contributions that supported the husband's acquisition of the license. Those contributions included the wife's use of her income from her job as a teacher to pay household expenses while her husband attended medical school. The court granted the wife an award equal to 40 percent of the present value of the husband's medical license. In 2016, however, the New York legislature enacted a statute that rejects *O'Brien*, N.Y. Dom. Rel. Law §236(5)(d)(7), and in other states, most of the courts to consider the issue have rejected *O'Brien*, holding that marital property does not include a license or enhanced earning potential.

> **QUESTION 5. Putting the wife through law school.** Frank and Jean were married five years ago. The next year Jean enrolled in law school. She graduated on time, three years later, and passed the bar exam on her first attempt during the summer after graduation. Jean has just filed an action against Frank for divorce on the grounds of incompatibility. Throughout their marriage, Frank worked full-time as an auto mechanic, providing the financial resources for most of the couple's living expenses. Jean received a scholarship that paid the full costs of her tuition, fees, and books for all three years. In the divorce action, Frank claims that he should receive a monetary award from Jean due to Jean's future earning capacity. Jean's best defense to Frank's claim is that
>
> A. Marital property rights are for the protection of women.
> B. Frank did not materially contribute toward her career advancement.
> C. Frank did not suffer any opportunity costs due to Jean's decision to study law.
> D. Jean never expressly gave Frank an interest in her professional degree.
> E. Frank's statutory right to a forced share or elective share constitutes adequate protection.

ANALYSIS.   Let's start with **A.** Equitable division statutes are gender neutral. If a state chooses to recognize a law degree or a license to practice law as marital property, it will not discriminate based on the sex of the lawyer. Although *O'Brien* granted a wife a share of her husband's medical license, gender of the parties had nothing to do with the court's reasoning.

E is also a highly flawed answer. Frank's state probably gives him a statutory right to a forced share or elective share, but this only protects Frank if the couple remains married and Jean dies before Frank. This won't happen; they're getting divorced.

D is an argument Jean is likely to make. She will say that she, and she alone, owns her degree and that she did not grant Frank any interest in that degree. But this argument misperceives the nature of marital property. At divorce one spouse is entitled to a share of marital property earned by the other spouse simply because the equitable division statute says so — not because the earning spouse granted an interest or agreed to that result.

We're left with **B** and **C** as the remaining contenders. **C** may be factually accurate. There's no evidence that Frank would have behaved differently in making choices with respect to occupation or anything else had Jean not gone to law school. We don't know either way. It is plausible to argue that one reason we may protect a spouse by labeling a professional license marital property is that the working spouse often has forgone opportunities to support the spouse who is in school. **B** states that Frank did not materially contribute toward Jean's earning of her law degree. This restates the rationale of *O'Brien*, which rested on the wife's contributions to the marital unit. There is some factual support for **B** because Jean obtained a generous scholarship. On the other hand, Frank paid the couple's entire living expenses from his earnings. This may be a close call, but **B** is the stronger pick.

D.   Community Property

Nine states, the largest being California and Texas, do not have common law marital property rights. Instead they follow the institution of community property. The common law system starts from the premise of *separate title*. In contrast, community property starts from the premise that the marriage is an economic partnership. All income earned during marriage belongs to both partners equally, regardless of which spouse does the work or receives the income.

In all community property states, spouses are allowed to own *separate property*, which consists of:

- All premarital property (property owned by husband or wife at the time they married)
- Gifts (inter vivos and testamentary) made to one spouse, and
- Inheritances

There is a strong presumption that all property owned by either spouse is community property. A person who claims a particular asset is separate property has the burden of proof. Moreover, *proceeds* of community property are community property. This means that when one spouse buys something using money that is community property, the item purchased is also community property. The manner in which the couple holds title to property doesn't matter. It makes no difference if one spouse alone holds record title to an asset, such as an automobile or a bank account.

> **QUESTION 6.   The mountain resort property.** Wendy works as a computer consultant, and her husband Hank is a real estate broker. They are residents of a community property state. They each deposit their earnings in separate bank accounts. Wendy uses some of her earnings to buy a vacant lot at a mountain resort, taking title in her name only. The resort is located in a neighboring state that does not have a community property system. Instead, that neighboring state recognizes common law marital property rights. Three years later Wendy dies intestate, leaving Hank and their daughter Diane as her only surviving relatives. Who owns the lot at the resort?
>
> **A.**   Hank owns the entire interest in the lot.
> **B.**   Diane inherits the entire lot, subject to Hank's right to curtesy.
> **C.**   Hank and Diane inherit the entire interest in the lot, the proportions depending upon the state law of inheritance.
> **D.**   Hank owns an undivided one-half of the lot, with the other half passing to Hank and Diane as heirs.
> **E.**   The state where the lot is located takes the lot by escheat because Wendy failed to make an effective will.

ANALYSIS.   Let's dispose of the last choice, **E**, at the outset. Escheat of a fee simple estate takes place if the owner dies without a will *and* has no ascertainable heirs. Escheat cannot happen because Hank and Diane are Wendy's heirs.

The key to this question is to decide whether the resort lot is community property or is Wendy's separate property. All income earned by Wendy from her employment while the couple is married is community property. The proceeds of her income (i.e., what she buys with her income) also are community property. The facts that she kept her income in a separate bank account and took title to the resort lot only in her name are not relevant. Wendy and Hank may have been able to enter into an agreement that the lot was to be Wendy's separate property, but there is no evidence of such an agreement in our facts.

Because the lot is community property, Hank owned an undivided one-half interest while both spouses were alive. He continues to own that one-half share after Wendy dies. Wendy's one-half will go to her heirs, who are Hank and Diane. So **D** is the right choice.

E.   The Closer: Treatment of Real Property Held by Both Spouses at Divorce

One of the tricky points about marital property is that sometimes the form in which a couple chooses to hold title to a certain property is ignored. In a community property state, an asset held by one spouse is community property if it was purchased using community property. In common law states, earnings of a spouse are marital property for purposes of equitable division at divorce. Yet sometimes the form of title selected by one or both spouses matters. It can serve as evidence that one spouse made a gift to another. There may be a presumption that the form of holding title reflects the underlying reality of ownership.

QUESTION 7.   Who gets the family home? Henry and Wilma managed to save enough money during the first four years of their marriage for a down payment on a small "starter" home. The deed to the property named "Henry and Wilma" as grantees, without any further indication of the nature of their interests. They lived together happily for the next 14 years, during which time the mortgage loan was paid solely from Wilma's salary as a computer technician. Henry was employed full-time as a high school teacher, and he paid other household expenses out of his salary.

Unfortunately, troubles then developed and Henry filed for divorce. At this time, Henry and Wilma have two children, Mary (age 12) and Brian (age 10). What is the court likely to decree with respect to ownership of the residence?

A. Under an equitable division statute, ownership of the residence will go to the spouse who is awarded custody of the children.
B. The court will grant Wilma a greater share of the residence due to her sole payment of the mortgage loan.
C. If Henry and Wilma live in a community property state, the residence will go to Wilma as her separate property.
D. The court will divide the residence equally because the deed granted Henry and Wilma equal rights as joint tenants.
E. None of the above.

ANALYSIS.   The first step is to label the residence. Notice the facts do not tell us whether Henry and Wilma live in a community property or a common law marital property state. This hole is intentional. As you read the choices, consider both alternatives. In a community property state, the residence is community property for two reasons. Wilma has used her income to pay the mortgage, and Henry and Wilma are both named as grantees on the deed. In a common law state, the house is marital property for the same reasons.

This lets us dispose of choices **B** and **C**. B fails because the residence is either community property or marital property. In either case, Wilma's payment of the mortgage does not give her a greater claim than Henry. **C** likewise fails; the residence is community property, not Wilma's separate property.

Choice **A** tells us we're in a common law state due to the reference to an equitable division statute. There may be some connection between the court's decision on custody of the two minor children and its ruling on the residence. The court might conclude that the best outcome is for the spouse with custody to occupy the residence. But the court is not required by the statute to award the family house to the spouse with custody. Moreover, it could grant the custodial spouse the right to possess the house without granting full ownership to that spouse. **A** is false.

Turning to **D**, this choice is flawed by the last words "joint tenants." There's a strong chance that the court will divide the residence equally between Henry and Wilma (and order partition by sale or some other appropriate financial arrangement) but not because the deed created a joint tenancy. In a common law state, the deed created either a tenancy by the entirety or a tenancy in common. In a community property state, the deed granted the house to Henry and Wilma as community property. All four statements are false. **E**'s the right answer.

 ## Smith's Picks

1. Mortgaging the station	**B**
2. Mortgaging a joint tenancy property	**D**
3. Dower and the husband's three properties	**C**
4. The husband's three properties under modern law	**E**
5. Putting the wife through law school	**B**
6. The mountain resort property	**D**
7. Who gets the family home?	**E**

16

Leasehold Estates

"When I was kidnapped, my parents snapped into action.
They rented out my room."
Woody Allen, *Standup Comic* (Rhino Records, 1999)

CHAPTER OVERVIEW
A. Nature of Leasehold Estates
B. Tenancy for Years
C. Periodic Tenancy
D. Tenancy at Will
E. Tenancy at Sufferance
F. The Closer: Keeping Straight the Leasehold Estates
⬥ Smith's Picks

This chapter, together with the following three chapters, addresses most of the issues concerning landlord-tenant relationships covered in the typical property course. Many property teachers make the law of landlord and tenant a major unit in their course. This body of law is highly important because leases are extensively used in many transactions, and they are employed in a wide variety of commercial and residential settings. Countless numbers of people enter into leases in the United States and in other countries. Leases are popular and valuable for three reasons. First, they enable a person to bargain for the right to possess and enjoy land and improvements to land. Second, they serve as a type of financing, allowing a person to gain possessory rights by paying periodic rent, without having to pay the purchase price for the property. Finally, they are a reliable way for owners to place land use controls on their real property. This is true because leasehold covenants run with the parties' respective estates.

At the outset, it's important that you learn the basic vocabulary of landlord and tenant law. You have to have this down before you attempt to handle any exam questions. The term *leasehold* refers to the tenant's interest or estate in the property. The word *lease* is sometimes used as a synonym for leasehold (referring to the tenant's estate), but other times *lease* has different meanings. It can refer to the transaction entered into by the two parties. Leases can be written or oral, and when the parties sign a document, *lease* may refer to that writing. As a verb, *lease* is what either party does in entering into the transaction. The tenant leases the property from the landlord, or the landlord leases the property to the tenant.

Each lease has two parties. The landowner who transfers possession pursuant to the lease is the landlord or lessor. The possessor is the tenant or lessee. Under modern law and practice, no distinction is made between the terms landlord/tenant and lessor/lessee. In the landlord-tenant chapters, we'll use the terms "landlord" and "tenant." But don't be surprised if you spot "lessor" and "lessee" on your exam — just be sure to read carefully. Students (and lawyers) who aren't reading or proofreading carefully enough sometimes get these terms switched, writing lessee when they mean lessor, or vice versa.

A. Nature of Leasehold Estates

In our system of estates in land, the fee simple, the life estate, and the fee tail (where recognized) are called *freehold estates*. For reasons of history, a lease is classified as a *non-freehold* estate. The owners of the "higher" freehold estates had *seisin*, a term that roughly correlates to the modern conception of "title to property." In feudal England, the position of a freeholder (an owner of a freehold estate) had a higher status than a tenant who owned a leasehold.

Modern law recognizes four types of leasehold estates:

- **Tenancy for years or term of years.** Possession is for a fixed period of time agreed upon by the parties.
- **Periodic tenancy.** Possession is for a fixed period of time, which repeats unless a party terminates the lease by giving notice.
- **Tenancy at will.** Possession is for no definite length of time, and either party can terminate the lease at any time.
- **Tenancy at sufferance.** This tenancy only results when a tenant under another type of lease holds over. Possession is for no definite length of time.

The four leasehold estates are alike in that the tenant has the *exclusive right of possession* of the leased premises. They are distinguished by the duration of the tenant's right to possession. Later sections of this chapter discuss the differences among the four leasehold estates in more detail. For now, our focus is upon their similarities. The key similarity is that the tenant, and not the landlord, has possession of the premises (or the right to possession) while the lease continues. The landlord still has an ownership interest, which is known as a *reversion*.

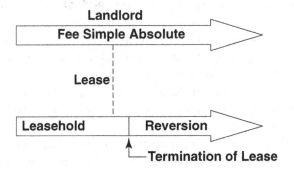

It is possible for a person to occupy or use real property owned by another person without being in possession of that real property. If the owner has sufficient dominion and control over the property, the owner is said to have retained possession. Such a transaction is called a *license*. The owner is the *licensor*, and the user is the *licensee*.

QUESTION 1.   A motel stay. "Stay a day, a week, or a lifetime," says the banner over the roof of Steve's Suite Motel. Each motel unit has two rooms, including a small kitchen area. Most of Steve's clientele consists of business travelers, whose average stay is five to seven days. One occupant, Lucy, paid $400 in advance for one week. Lucy took possession of Unit 201 on Monday. No writing (except for Lucy's check for $400) reflects the parties' agreement. On Friday, Lucy told Steve that she wanted to extend for one more week. They agreed that Lucy would pay an additional $400 for the second week next Monday. Next Monday Lucy failed to pay, and she remained in occupancy of Unit 201. Steve confronted her, demanding that she pay up or leave immediately, but she refused. Which of the following facts would make it more probable that the rental of Unit 201 is a lease rather than a license?

A. Steve's Suite Motel provides maid service on a daily basis.
B. Steve's Suite Motel does not have an express right to move an occupant to another unit once a room assignment is made.
C. Steve's retains a pass key, which can open any unit.
D. The parties expressly refer to the occupant's consideration as "rental."
E. The parties have not signed a writing that sets forth the terms of their agreement.

ANALYSIS. This question tests your understanding of the distinction between a lease and a license. The most important point to keep in mind as you analyze the possible factors is that the more dominion and control the owner has over the premises and the user's behavior while on the premises, the more likely it is that the user has only a license. A and C are similar in that they show Steve's Suite Motel has retained a degree of control. These answers are incorrect because they point in the wrong direction. Providing maid service and keeping a pass key make it more likely that there is a *license* of Unit 201.

E is wrong because oral leases are permissible, provided they do not exceed the period specified by the Statute of Frauds, which in most states is one year. Lucy may have a tenancy for years for a term of one week, even though there is no writing.

D contends that the parties' use of the term "rental" counts in favor of finding a lease. This is plausible in that the term "rental" (or "rent") is customarily used in leasehold transactions. For a license, it's possible for the parties to refer to the agreed-upon price as "rental," but typically they would instead call it a fee or charge (or just price). Because Steve's Suite Motel and Lucy used the word "rental," they may have been thinking they were entering into a landlord-tenant transaction.

B indicates that Steve's Suite Motel does not have an express right to relocate an occupant to another motel room. That points toward Lucy having more dominion and control over Unit 201 and Steve's Suite Motel having less. This is a better answer than D because it focuses not on the parties' labels or their subjective thinking about their transaction, but instead on actual dominion and control.

B.   Tenancy for Years

The tenancy for years, also sometimes called an *estate for years* or a *term of years*, is the most important of the four leasehold estates. The basic idea is that the parties have agreed to a fixed duration for the lease, expressed in units of time such as days, weeks, months, or years. At common law, the parties are allowed to pick any length of time. The name of the tenancy ("years") might mislead you into thinking that at least one year is necessary. This is not correct. Tenancies for less than a full year are permissible and are commonly created. It is possible to create a lease for a period as short as one day, although this would probably not be in the landlord's best interest compared to the alternative of giving the occupant a license.

Traditionally, it's required that the tenancy for years have a *term certain*. This means that the term must have a definite, fixed ending date, which is ascertainable no later than the time the tenant takes possession of the premises. If the duration is uncertain, there is no tenancy for years. Uncertainty as to duration may stem from two causes. First, the parties may have poorly expressed their agreement in fact as to the term. This is more common for oral leases but also can result from written leases that employ imprecise or conflicting language. When there is uncertainty of this type, the court or fact finder will decide whether there is a tenancy for years based upon standard principles of contract interpretation.

Second, uncertainty arises when the parties pick a length for their lease by referring to an event that cannot be assigned a calendar date at the commencement of the term. Uncertainty as to the event may have several facets. The event may be certain to occur (the next snowfall in Minnesota) or uncertain to occur (the Cleveland Guardians, formerly known as the Indians, win the World Series). It may be within or not within the control of one or both parties.

Some courts are stricter on the definitional requirements for a tenancy for years than others. Traditional courts do not allow the parties to have a tenancy for years when they detect uncertainty as to duration, regardless of the reason for uncertainty or the parties' apparent intent that they wanted to create a tenancy for years. When a court refuses to allow a tenancy for years, it must label the parties' relationship as something else. Rather than call the occupant a trespasser or a licensee, usually the court will pick another type of possessory estate, such as a periodic tenancy, a tenancy at will, a life estate, or a defeasible fee simple.

A number of modern courts have relaxed the traditional requirement of certainty for a tenancy for years. Typically, this happens when the parties clearly expressed an intent to enter into a tenancy for years but introduced an element of uncertainty by directly providing for lease termination upon the occurrence of a future event. Notwithstanding the uncertainty, these courts have upheld a tenancy for years on the basis that assigning a different classification to the transaction would frustrate the parties' professed intent.

Sometimes parties enter into an agreement for a lease with a fixed term that is to commence at a time in the future. Sometimes the commencement date is not determinable at the outset when the agreement is reached. The commencement date will depend upon a future event. Although such a transaction appears to violate the rule that a tenancy for years must be for a "term certain," courts uniformly uphold such transactions. These arrangements are useful, and once the tenant takes possession there is certainty as to how long the leasehold will continue.

QUESTION 2.   Lease for a cellular tower. Global Communications has negotiated a lease of a small parcel where it plans to install a cellular transmission tower. The landlord and Global Communications have agreed to an annual rent of $2,000. The parties' written lease provides:

> The term of this lease is five (5) years from the date hereof and so long thereafter as the Tenant uses the leased premises in connection with its cellular communications business.

Global Communications promptly installed a cellular transmission tower and timely paid the rents for the original five-year term. After that five-year term expired, Global Communications informed the landlord that it wanted to continue the lease. The landlord, however, wants to terminate the lease. Does Global Communications have the right to continue the lease for subsequent years?

A. No, because the lease does not have a definite ending date.

B. No, because the event that terminates the lease is within the tenant's sole control.

C. Yes, because there is no uncertainty as to when the term of the lease will expire.

D. Yes, because the parties' agreement created a tenancy from year to year.

E. The outcome depends upon the relationship between the $2,000 annual rent and the fair rental value of the premises after the expiration of the five-year term.

ANALYSIS. This is a hard question. Some courts would hold for the landlord, and others would hold for the tenant. The outcome will turn on how seriously the court applies the requirement that a tenancy for years must have a fixed expiration date. There is no clear majority rule. Let's first look at E, which is the only contextual choice. Unfortunately, it fails. The parties have bargained for a fixed rent, which appears substantial and appears to reflect their perceptions of value at the time they made their agreement. The court is highly unlikely to terminate the lease on the ground that subsequently the rent has become too low.

First, let's look at the "yes" answers (Global and the tenant may continue the lease). C is factually wrong. Objectively there is uncertainty as to when the lease will expire. We can't tell how long Global Communications may decide to continue to use the premises for cellular communications purposes.

D may be slightly better. If a court decides that the agreement did not create a tenancy for years due to an uncertain duration, it might label the transaction as a tenancy from year to year (periodic tenancy), at least for the time period after the original five-year term. But the problem is that then either party, including the landlord, could terminate by giving proper advance notice to the other party. The question asks whether Global has the right to continue "for subsequent years," and if there is a periodic tenancy it would not, due to the landlord's right to terminate.

So now we're left with A and B, the "no" answers (landlord may terminate). B is plausible. There is a line of authority holding that if one party has the express right to terminate a lease, that right is mutual and the parties have a tenancy at will. This line of authority, however, is thin and most of it is old. More recent cases tend to allow one party to have a termination right without extending that right to the other party.

A directly expresses a better reason for holding that the parties have a tenancy at will. Because we cannot tell how long Global Communications will use the property for the permitted purpose, there is no "term certain" and thus no tenancy for years.

C.   Periodic Tenancy

The periodic tenancy continues from period to period until one party terminates by giving notice to the other party. The period depends upon the parties' express or implied agreement. They can select any period, but monthly and annual tenancies are the most common. Weekly tenancies are sometimes encountered. The parties can expressly create a periodic tenancy, but this form of leasehold is often created by implication. When the parties don't discuss the duration of their lease, but the tenant pays rent, they have a periodic tenancy.

A periodic tenancy ends when one party (either landlord or tenant) gives a valid notice of termination to the other party. In addition, the parties may mutually agree to a termination. In the absence of such a notice or agreement, the periodic tenancy continues automatically. This gives rise to successive new periods.

Notices to terminate periodic tenancies can be tricky. There are two key rules concerning timing that you should know.

- **Minimum advance notice.** First, the notice must precede the date of termination by a minimum amount of time. Usually the notice must be given one period in advance, but for a tenancy from year-to-year, the common law requires only six months advance notice, not an entire year. In many states a statute modifies the time requirements for notices.
- **Effective date of termination.** Second, termination must coincide with the end of one of the regular periods. Neither party has the right to terminate during the middle of any period.

QUESTION 3.   A tenant who won't sign up. On July 26, Franklin, the owner of Blackacre, and Drago agreed to a five-year lease of Blackacre, for which Drago was to pay a rent of $1,000 per month. They agreed that the term would commence on August 1. Franklin prepared a written draft for a lease document, which he submitted to Drago. With Franklin's permission, before signing the lease Drago took possession on August 1 and paid the first month's rent. Drago subsequently refused to sign. He requested a number of changes, which Franklin considered unacceptable. In most jurisdictions, Drago's status after taking possession of Blackacre is best described as:

A. Trespasser.
B. Tenant at will.

C. Periodic tenant.
D. Tenant for a term of one year.
E. Tenant for a term of five years.

ANALYSIS. Franklin and Drago plainly agreed to a term of years (tenancy for years) for a period of five years, but there's a problem. The parties' agreement is oral, and in all states the Statute of Frauds prohibits long-term oral leases (usually an oral lease for a term of one year or less is allowed as an exception to the statute). So **E** is incorrect. Drago must have another type of interest in Blackacre.

A is wrong. Drago should not be classified as a trespasser because he is in possession of Blackacre with Franklin's permission.

This leaves our choices as **B**, **C**, and **D**, all of which classify Drago as a tenant with a leasehold estate. All three choices have some plausibility. Most states broadly apply a rule that says that if a tenant takes possession and pays rent and there is no other enforceable agreement as to the term, by implication the parties have created a periodic tenancy. So **C** is the best answer. **B** (tenancy at will) is less likely because either party could terminate the lease immediately, and this is not what Franklin and Drago apparently intended. **D** (term of one year) has the virtue of giving the parties the longest guaranteed duration that is possible with an oral lease, but most courts prefer the periodic tenancy.

Notice that the question does not require you to decide whether the periodic tenancy is month-to-month or year-to-year. Under our facts, month-to-month is probable because there is no evidence that the parties bargained on the basis of a stated annual rent for Blackacre. Had they bargained for an annual rent of $12,000 payable in monthly installments, some courts would find a tenancy from year-to-year.

QUESTION 4.   Notice to quit. On January 5, a landlord and tenant orally agreed to the rental of single-family house for a term of six months at a rent of $2,000 per month. The tenant paid the first month's rent before moving in, and paid the same amount to the landlord for the next five months on February 1, March 4, April 1, May 5, and June 1. The tenant did not move out, and instead sent payment for $2,000 to the landlord, which the landlord accepted on July 1. On July 20, the landlord notified the tenant that the lease would expire on September 1 and that the tenant must vacate the property by that date. Will the lease terminate on or before September 1?

A. Yes, because the notice is valid.
B. Yes, although no notice was necessary.
C. No, because landlord does not have good cause to terminate.
D. No, because the notice is not sufficient.
E. No, because this type of tenancy cannot be terminated by notice.

ANALYSIS.   Clearly the parties have entered into a lease, but what type of lease? At first, they had a tenancy for years, but this expired on July 5.

When the tenant offered payment of an additional $2,000 on July 1, which the landlord then accepted, obviously the tenant was offering to stay for at least one more month. The landlord immediately accepted this payment, so the tenant did not become a trespasser or a tenant at sufferance. Do these facts create a new tenancy for years for an additional one month or a periodic tenancy from month-to-month? Either outcome is plausible, and the distinction is important in this context.

The periodic tenancy is more likely because the parties never discussed how long their relationship would continue. Thus, the landlord needs to give proper notice to terminate the tenancy. So Choices **B** and **E** are wrong. Likewise, Choice **C** is wrong. The landlord does not have to have "good cause" or a good reason to terminate; it's sufficient that the landlord simply does not want the lease to continue.

This leaves us with Choices **A** and **D**. Notice that the original lease began on January 5, and each succeeding rent period began on the fifth day of the month. Although most periodic tenancies run for calendar months (the first of the month to the first of the next month), this one does not. Thus, by specifying a termination date of September 1, the landlord picked an improper date of termination — four days too early. Choice **D** is the right answer.

D.   Tenancy at Will

The tenancy at will, true to its name, lasts as long as both parties will that it shall last. The duration depends upon the mutual will of landlord and tenant.

The tenancy at will has no set duration. Either party can terminate the lease at any time by giving notice to the other party. The notice is effective immediately upon receipt unless the notice states a future date for termination. For many leases, it is not practical for a tenant to vacate possession immediately upon receipt of the landlord's notice. For this reason, the tenant is given a reasonable period of time to vacate and to remove her personal property. The tenant, however, must commence efforts to vacate immediately.

The parties can expressly agree to enter into a tenancy at will. This does not commonly happen, however, in a negotiated transaction in which the tenant pays a market rent. Occasionally a lease for a tenancy for years will provide that a tenant who holds over after expiration of the term will become a tenant at will.

Usually the tenancy at will is created by implication. The tenancy at will serves as the "default tenancy" for the entire law of estates. Thus, whenever a court cannot or will not decide that a transfer of the right to possession of land fits within another classification, it calls the transfer a "tenancy at will."

This preference, however, does not mean that whenever a conveyance has ambiguous language the court will find a tenancy at will. Other presumptions may come into play. Under modern law, there is a presumption that a written grant conveys the grantor's entire estate unless the writing has language expressly pointing to a lesser estate. Thus, an ambiguous conveyance may give the grantee a fee simple estate rather than a leasehold. The tenancy at will is the default tenancy in this sense: whenever the transfer, oral or written, does not create another estate under the applicable interpretational standards, including presumptions, a tenancy at will arises.

QUESTION 5. **A speedy checkout.** Herman rents a residential condominium unit from Lorena under a tenancy at will. He pays monthly rent of $600, in advance, on the first day of each month. In early August, Herman decides that he wants to move to another state and that he will leave the condominium by the end of the month. He does not tell Lorena his plans at this time. On August 31, Herman moves out, packing all of his belongings in his Chevy Suburban. At 9 PM, just before Herman leaves the condominium, he telephones Lorena's cell phone. Lorena doesn't answer so Herman leaves a message on her voicemail, informing her that he no longer wants to rent the property and that he has already moved out. He gives Lorena an address where he'd like her to send his $600 security deposit. Lorena first hears the message the next time she checks her voicemail, at 10:21 AM on September 1. Lorena refuses to refund the security deposit, claiming she is entitled to keep it because Herman owes rent for September. Herman brings an action to recover his security deposit. Who should prevail?

A. Lorena may keep all of the security deposit because legally it constitutes prepaid rent.

B. Lorena may keep all of the security deposit because Herman could have given her notice in early August when he decided that he would move.

C. Lorena may keep at least part of the security deposit because Herman did not give her sufficient advance notice of termination.

D. Herman is entitled to a refund of all of the security deposit because he did not damage the leased premises.

E. Herman is entitled to a refund of all of the security deposit because he notified Lorena of lease termination before he became obligated to pay any rent for September.

ANALYSIS. We have four "all or nothing" answers (Lorena keeps the entire security deposit or Herman gets it all back) and one "split the difference" answer, which is C. When in doubt, it's often good advice to pick the "nuanced" choice like C, but that's a strategy to use only if you can't determine the best answer with any degree of certainty.

The facts stipulate that Herman has a tenancy at will, and the only issues to consider are whether Herman properly terminated that estate, and if so, what is the effective date of termination. First let's look at the "Lorena keeps it all" choices. **A** misperceives the nature of a security deposit. Legally a security deposit is not prepaid rent, even though the landlord may apply the security deposit to unpaid rent if the tenant defaults. **B** addresses the key issue—was Herman's notice timely or too late—but it asserts that the time when the tenant must notify the landlord depends upon when the tenant has subjectively made a decision to terminate. This is not the law. After Herman decided to move, he had the right to keep his mouth shut and to change his mind.

Now let's study the "Herman gets it all back" choices. **D** also misperceives the purpose for a security deposit. It secures not only the tenant's obligation not to damage the leased premises but also the tenant's rent obligation.

Now we're down to **C** and **E**, both of which focus on the key issue of whether Herman's 9 PM phone call validly terminated the tenancy at will. A number of students will pick **C** for two reasons that may appear plausible. Although a tenant at will may terminate at any time, if Herman did not terminate until the morning of September 1, he owes some additional rent (probably one day's rent—that would be $20, calculated as one-thirtieth of the monthly rent of $600). First, Herman did not give a written notice of termination. Although a written notice is advisable, the common law allows an oral notice, and the facts do not indicate that either a state statute or the parties' agreement required a written notice. Second, Lorena will claim that she did not receive the notice until September 1, when she retrieved her voicemail. A court should reject this argument because Herman entered the message on her voicemail on August 31, and at that point he had no control over when Lorena might choose to listen to the message. For written mail, receipt generally takes place when a mailed item is delivered to the address or mailbox of the addressee, not the later time when the addressee chooses to retrieve the item or open the envelope and read it. So **E** is the best answer. Herman gave a valid notice of termination on August 31.

E.   Tenancy at Sufferance

The tenancy at sufferance arises when a tenant who has one of the other three types of leaseholds holds over after expiration of the lease. The tenant at sufferance is also known as a *holdover tenant.*[1]

---

1. Our focus in this chapter is the tenant who stays after termination of a lease, but the tenancy at sufferance also applies to other possessors whose original entry was rightful. For example, a life tenant who remains after the life estate terminates becomes a tenant at sufferance, as does a buyer of real property whose contract of purchase terminates after the buyer has taken possession of the property.

The tenancy at sufferance is created by implication, rather than by the parties' express agreement. This happens by operation of law. A tenant who remains in possession after her lease terminates automatically becomes a tenant at sufferance. This retention of possession is wrongful because the landlord has not consented to the holding over.

If the landlord consents to the holding over, then there is no tenancy at sufferance. Instead, the holdover tenant becomes a tenant at will, a periodic tenant, or a tenant for years—which one depends upon the content of the consent and any other relevant facts. Likewise, if the landlord objects to the holding over in an appropriate manner, the holdover tenant who refuses to leave will become a trespasser. Under modern law, the main purpose of the tenancy at sufferance is to recognize that the holdover tenant has an uncertain status. The tenant at sufferance is in a "holding pattern" with a change in the parties' relationship likely to occur fairly quickly. The parties may resolve their relationship at least four different ways:

- The tenant may voluntarily relinquish possession of the leased premises.
- The landlord may choose to treat the tenant as a trespasser and then force the tenant to leave by using eviction procedures.
- The parties may expressly negotiate a new tenancy.
- The landlord may elect to hold the tenant to a new lease, even though the tenant objects to that outcome.

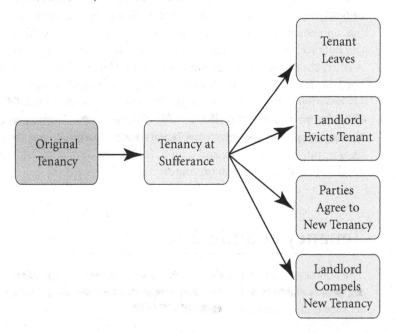

QUESTION 6.   A bit late in getting out. Travis rents a single-family home to Julie for a term of one year from August 1 through July 31. On July 28, Julie mails a note to Travis, telling him that she does not want to

extend or renew her lease, but that she will not be able to vacate the unit until the afternoon of August 1, when her big brother is going to be able to come by with his big pickup truck to assist her in moving out. Travis receives the note on July 30 and does not reply to it. On August 1, big brother arrives at the home at 1:30 PM, and he and Julie begin loading up the truck. At this moment, before they finish moving out, what is Julie's status with respect to the property?

A. Periodic tenant.
B. Tenant under a term of years.
C. Tenant at sufferance.
D. Tenant at will.
E. Trespasser.

ANALYSIS. Our choices are straightforward. We can pick any one of the four types of leasehold estates for Julie's present status, or we can call her a trespasser. Prior to August 1, Julie clearly had a term of years, but this changed when that term expired. Her note to Travis implicitly asked his permission for her to stay one more day. Travis's silence, however, was not consent. Thus, **B** is wrong. They did not agree to extend the term of years for one additional day.

For the same reason, **D** is incorrect. After July 31, Julie and Travis would have a tenancy at will only if they both agreed to a lease extension for an indefinite period of time.

Likewise, Julie cannot be a periodic tenant. She was not one at the outset, and the parties had no agreement for her to pay periodic rent after July 31.

We're down to **C** (tenant at sufferance) or **E** (trespasser). Travis's silence means Julie is not a trespasser. He must affirmatively ask her to leave before she, as a holdover tenant, becomes a trespasser. **C** is the right answer.

F.   The Closer: Keeping Straight the Leasehold Estates

Pay careful attention to the distinguishing characteristics of the four types of leasehold estates. To do well on the exam, it's highly likely that you will need to be able to attach the proper label to a fact pattern.

QUESTION 7.   A place to live until finals are over. Tracy, a first-year law student, needs a place to live for the rest of the spring semester. She drives past an apartment complex that advertises "rentals by the week or month." On January 6, she visits the apartment manager's office and

> speaks with Sonny. Tracy tells him that she needs a quiet, comfortable apartment "for a couple of months." Sonny shows Tracy a spacious one-bedroom unit that's open, which she agrees to take. They agree to a weekly rental of $200, and she moves in the next morning. Tracy and Sonny do not sign any writing or document. What sort of leasehold does Tracy have?
>
> A. Tenancy for years.
> B. Periodic tenancy.
> C. Tenancy at will.
> D. Tenancy at sufferance.

ANALYSIS. As Closers go, this question is fairly straightforward, but there's enough here in this short fact pattern to test how well you understand the four types of leasehold estates. Let's dispose of **D** first because it's obviously wrong. Tracy can have a tenancy at sufferance only if she at first became a tenant for years, a periodic tenant, or a tenant at will, and stayed in possession as a hold-over tenant after her lease expired. There's nothing at all in the facts to indicate that her lease has expired or that Sonny is claiming that her possession is no longer rightful. So I hope you didn't pick **D**.

A may look attractive. Tracy has a certain time period in mind for which she wants the apartment. After the semester ends (when finals end), presumably she plans to go somewhere else. Moreover, she told Sonny she wanted the apartment for a "couple of months." Thus, the parties might have bargained for a tenancy for years, with the lease to end on a particular date. However, they didn't actually pick an ending date—a "couple of months" from January 6 is very imprecise. Thus, they did not enter into a tenancy for years because they failed to pick a certain ending date for the term.

C is the "second-best" answer, but it's nevertheless wrong. Sometimes courts imply a tenancy at will when the parties fail to specify another type of leasehold. That will not apply here, however, because the parties said that Tracy would pay rent weekly. That is sufficient to make the transaction a periodic tenancy. Courts prefer periodic tenancies to tenancies at will because the relationship is more stable. With a tenancy at will, either Sonny or Tracy could terminate immediately, resulting in surprise to the other person. In contrast, with a periodic tenancy, each party will know at least one week ahead of time that they need to make alternate plans.

B is the best choice. They expressly agreed that Tracy would pay a es courts imply a tenancy at will when the parties fail to specify another type of lease-hold. That will not apply here, howeveacts and circumstances. This fact pattern shows the prototypical situation for implying a periodic tenancy—the parties have not expressly picked one of the leasehold estates, but they have agreed on the frequency of payment of rent. Thus, Tracy has a tenancy from week-to-week. Either Sonny or Tracy may terminate the tenancy by giving the other person one week's advance notice.

 ## Smith's Picks

1. A motel stay   **B**
2. Lease for a cellular tower   **A**
3. A tenant who won't sign up   **C**
4. Notice to quit   **D**
5. A speedy checkout   **E**
6. A bit late in getting out   **C**
7. A place to live until finals are over   **B**

17

Quiet Enjoyment and Condition of Leased Premises

~

"Honk if you love peace and quiet."
American bumper sticker

~

CHAPTER OVERVIEW
A. Creation of Covenant of Quiet Enjoyment
B. Identity of Wrongdoer
C. Actual Eviction
D. Constructive Eviction
E. Condition of Premises: Caveat Emptor
F. Implied Warranty of Habitability
G. The Closer: Review of the Tenant's Options
 Smith's Picks

In landlord-tenant law, the covenant of quiet enjoyment serves to protect the tenant's right to possess and to use the leased property. If the landlord or a person for whom the landlord is responsible interferes with the tenant's rights, then the tenant is entitled to contract remedies for breach of the covenant. The covenant of quiet enjoyment may be breached by conduct that amounts to an actual eviction or by conduct that amounts to a constructive eviction.

The covenant of quiet enjoyment may affect the tenant's rights with respect to the physical condition of the leased premises, although the covenant by itself generally does not assure the tenant of a particular level of quality. Traditionally, the tenant's rights as to condition turned on the express terms of the lease. In the absence of an express provision that protected the tenant, the landlord had no obligations with respect to condition. Today in most states, residential tenants have the benefit of an implied warranty of habitability due to judicial decision or statute.

A.   Creation of Covenant of Quiet Enjoyment

Most leases today include a covenant of quiet enjoyment. Often the covenant is often expressly stated in the lease. No particular words are required for an express covenant. The following short clause is typical:

> Landlord covenants and agrees that Tenant may peaceably and quietly enjoy the leased premises.

When the covenant is not expressly stated, in most states the covenant of quiet enjoyment is implied for all types of leases. This development began long ago. In the late nineteenth century state courts began to imply the covenant. Prior to this reform, an express covenant was necessary for a tenant to have the right to quiet enjoyment. This older rule treated leases the same as other conveyances of estates in land. In deeds of conveyance, the common law recognizes no implied covenants. All covenants must be express, although today in many states a statute implies certain covenants if a grantor uses a particular deed form or particular language in the deed.

In the landlord-tenant context, a few states still follow the old rule, refusing to imply the covenant of quiet enjoyment for some or all leases.

QUESTION 1.   Presence of the covenant. Responding to a Web real estate advertisement, Looser visited a two-story row house, which Trudy had offered to rent. The row house has common walls with adjoining units on both sides. Looser is leaving an apartment complex, where he found noise easily traveled through the walls and disturbed him. Looser told Trudy that he wanted a quiet place to live. He asked Trudy how well insulated the common walls were for noise, and Trudy replied, "No problem. This development is only three years old, and they put in premium multiplex R-45 insulation plus deluxe sound baffling." Looser had no idea what this insulation factor or "deluxe sound baffling" meant, but he nevertheless found Trudy's answer to be reassuring. Looser and Trudy orally agreed to a periodic tenancy for a monthly rental of $900. Looser took possession on the first day of the next month. The parties have not signed a written lease. Which of the following statements is correct?

A. Looser has the benefit of an express covenant of quiet enjoyment.

B. Looser has the benefit of an implied covenant of quiet enjoyment.

C. Looser has no covenant of quiet enjoyment because the parties did not discuss "quiet enjoyment."

D. Looser has no covenant of quiet enjoyment because Trudy may terminate the tenancy by giving Looser a proper notice of termination.

E. Looser has no covenant of quiet enjoyment because oral leases cannot include such a covenant.

ANALYSIS. We'll begin by taking a look at the "no covenant" answers. Choice **C** assumes that a lease may have a covenant of quiet enjoyment only if it is an express covenant. **C** is incorrect because the covenant is commonly implied.

D confuses the duration of the tenancy from the issue at hand. The parties have a tenancy from month-to-month, but such a lease may have a covenant of quiet enjoyment, which will be operative unless and until one party gives a notice that properly terminates the lease.

E is wrong for two reasons. First, it ignores the possibility that the parties to an oral lease could expressly agree that the tenant has the right to quiet enjoyment. Second, it ignores the widely followed rule that the covenant is implied in leases; this includes oral as well as written leases.

We're down to a pick between **A** and **B**. We have to decide whether the parties' conversation about quietness and the walls' insulation factor amounts to a covenant of quiet enjoyment. This may be a trick question but one that I think is nonetheless fair. Literally, Trudy made a representation that the premises were "quiet," but this is not a covenant of quiet enjoyment. Trudy's representation is not a promise by Trudy that she will not interfere with Looser's quiet enjoyment of the premises. Instead it is a representation of fact, on which Looser may have reasonably relied. If that representation turns out to be untrue, Looser may have protection but not because of a breach of a covenant of quiet enjoyment. Thus, because there is no express covenant, Looser has an implied covenant. **B** is our answer.

B. Identity of Wrongdoer

The covenant of quiet enjoyment is not an ironclad guarantee that nothing is going to happen that will disturb the tenant in her quiet enjoyment of the property. It is a covenant *by the landlord* not to disturb the tenant. The scope of the covenant, however, is broader than it might first appear. Not only is the landlord responsible for her own conduct, but the landlord is held responsible for the conduct of persons claiming under or through the landlord and any paramount titleholders:

- **The landlord.** Wrongful action by the landlord that interferes with the tenant's possession breaches the covenant of quiet enjoyment.
- **Persons claiming under or through the landlord** (landlord's "**successors**"). Interference by a person who gets title or other rights from the

landlord breaches the covenant. "Successors" includes the landlord's agents. It may include an independent contractor when the landlord has authorized work that is certain or likely to interfere with the tenant's enjoyment.

- **Paramount titleholders.** Interference by a person having better title to the premises than the landlord breaches the covenant.

The common link across the three categories is the landlord's fault. When a landlord's successor interferes with quiet enjoyment, the landlord has either authorized the harm or has taken action, in assigning rights to another person, that allowed the harm to be inflicted. When a paramount titleholder interferes with quiet enjoyment, the landlord is at fault in the sense that her lack of good title led to the harm. Except for these categories, a landlord is not generally liable when other third persons ("strangers") cause interference with the tenant's use and possession.

QUESTION 2.   Neighbor moves a fence. Doris rents a house and yard from Lorie for a <u>term of one year</u>. At the time of the lease, a wooden fence separates the side yard from the property of a neighbor, Woodrow. From appearances, it looks like the fence is located on the boundary line. Four months after the lease begins, Woodrow demolishes the fence, erecting a new fence along a different line, lying five feet closer to the house Doris is renting. Doris complains about the loss of part of the side yard. Woodrow asserts that he has a survey that shows the new fence is on the boundary line, and the original fence was within his lot and not on the line. Which of the following facts would support a conclusion that <u>Lorie has breached</u> the covenant of quiet enjoyment?

A. The prior owner of Lorie's property built the fence 15 years ago.
B. The prior owner of Woodrow's property built the fence 15 years ago.
C. Woodrow is Lorie's twin brother and they see each other every week.
D. Woodrow's survey is accurate.
E. Woodrow's survey is erroneous.

ANALYSIS.   C is a red herring, but some students have bit on it. Whether the neighbors are relatives, friends, or strangers does not matter. If Lorie explicitly authorized Woodrow to move the fence, then Lorie may have liability for breach of the covenant of quiet enjoyment. That might make Woodrow her agent, or Woodrow could be said to be acting or claiming under her. She would be liable because she authorized the wrong, not because her brother committed the wrong.

Choices **A** and **B** both deal with the history of the fence, in particular, who built the fence years ago. This does not matter. If the fence was built in the wrong location by Lorie's predecessor, that fault would not be attributed to Lorie because (1) the event occurred before Doris rented the property and (2) the predecessor is not Lorie's successor or a paramount titleholder.

We're left with **D** and **E**. If Woodrow's survey is accurate, then he was justified in moving the fence (the facts do not give sufficient information to conclude that Lorie has acquired title to the five-foot strip by adverse possession). This means Woodrow has paramount title to the strip, and thus Lorie has breached the covenant of quiet enjoyment. Conversely, if Woodrow's survey is erroneous, he lacks paramount title and Lorie is not legally responsible for his actions. So it's **D**.

C. Actual Eviction

Actual eviction is just what you think it is. This is conduct that physically excludes the tenant from all of the leased premises (total eviction) or from part of the leased premises (partial eviction). It is conduct that, if we were applying the law of torts, would amount to a trespass. Just as for a trespass, the eviction or exclusion may be accomplished by human agency (a person evicts the tenants) or by an object that intrudes or invades the leased premises.

An actual eviction may be total (the tenant is evicted from all of the leased premises), or it may be partial (the tenant is evicted from part of the premises and remains in possession of the remainder). For either type, the landlord has breached the covenant of quiet enjoyment. The tenant may terminate the lease or sue for damages. In addition, for a partial actual eviction, the common law rule, still followed in many states today, allows the tenant to suspend the payment of rent while the eviction continues, provided that the eviction is not by a paramount titleholder. If a paramount titleholder evicts the tenant from part of the premises, the tenant is entitled to only partial relief from rent payment. The rent is allocated according to the respective values of the part subject to eviction and the part remaining.

> **QUESTION 3. Obnoxious colors.** Colorblind rents her house to Fanatic under a tenancy for years with a three-year term. The parties' written lease has an express covenant of quiet enjoyment. Fanatic is a rabid fan of a sports team called the Bay City Bombers. The Bombers' arch rivals are the River City Racketeers. The Racketeers' colors are purple and gold. At the time of the lease, the house is painted a sedate tan. One year into the lease term, Colorblind discovers that the rent provided for in the lease is way below the market rent for her property. Knowing Fanatic's allegiance, Colorblind decides that if she paints the exterior of the house Racketeers' colors, she may induce Fanatic to leave. While Fanatic is out of town for the weekend, attending a Bay City Bombers' away game, Colorblind has

a crew repaint the house purple and gold. After a Bombers' win, Fanatic is euphoric, but his euphoria turns to horror when he sees his home. Fanatic is incensed. Has Colorblind's conduct breached the covenant of quiet enjoyment?

A. Yes, because the painting crew physically entered the premises without permission.
B. Yes, because the paint is a physical object which, after applied, occupies space.
C. No, because a coat of paint is very thin.
D. No, because a landlord has the legal right to repaint a rented house.
E. The outcome depends upon whether the jurisdiction has adopted the doctrine of retaliatory eviction.

ANALYSIS. This is a toughie. I may be going out on a limb, but I'll attempt to rank the answers worst to best. I'm picking **D** as worst. It sounds plausible, but unless the lease reserves to the landlord the right to enter the premises to make improvements, changes, or repairs, the landlord has no right. The tenant is entitled to exclusive possession for the entire lease term. The warranty of habitability may modify this to some extent, but there is no evidence that the house needed repainting (i.e., that it was not habitable unless repainted).

The next worst answer is **E**. The doctrine of retaliatory eviction protects the tenant from conduct engaged in by the landlord for the purpose of forcing or persuading the tenant to leave as retaliation for the tenant having engaged in some protected conduct. An example is a landlord's notice for a periodic tenant to vacate given after the tenant has complained about a defect in the premises that impairs habitability. Colorblind is not seeking to evict because Fanatic has done something—Colorblind wants to evict only so she can charge more rent to someone else.

We'll tackle **B** next. It's factually true that a coat of paint occupies space, but this is de minimis. At a level that is close to microscopic, the siding is now thicker and thus the yard is smaller, but no one can plausibly argue that this makes the yard less useful to the tenant. The colors may be obnoxious, but that downside does not dispossess the tenant.

A and **C** remain. **A** seems attractive. For the reason discussed above, the painting crew's entry was wrongful. However, they left before Fanatic returned home and objected. Although the entry was a trespass, it probably did not continue long enough to amount to a dispossession of Fanatic.

Only **C** is left standing. Although it doesn't sound like a right answer ("a coat of paint is very thin"), with simple language it expresses my criticism, given above, of choice **B**. There is no actual eviction (no breach of quiet enjoyment) because the object added to the premises without the tenant's consent has too little mass to make a practical difference for use and enjoyment.

D.   Constructive Eviction

The covenant of quiet enjoyment is breached if the tenant is actually evicted or constructively evicted. A constructive eviction results from wrongful conduct, other than an actual physical eviction, that deprives the tenant of use and enjoyment of the premises. Four elements are commonly required for there to be a constructive eviction:

- The landlord's conduct has interfered with the tenant's possession.
- The interference is substantial.
- The tenant has given notice to the landlord of the condition (or the landlord already knows of the condition so that notice is unnecessary).
- The tenant abandons possession of the premises.

A constructive eviction may stem from action or inaction. When the landlord or a person for whom the landlord is responsible has taken action that causes the offending condition, this may constitute a constructive eviction.

A landlord's failure to act may also constitute a constructive eviction. This is a harder case than affirmative action for the tenant to establish. Every failure to act that impairs the tenant's possession and use is not a constructive eviction. The landlord must have a *legal duty* to act, which the landlord has ignored. There are two possible sources for the legal duty. It may be contractual, based upon an express or implied covenant in the lease by which the landlord is obligated to do something. Second, the legal duty may be imposed by law. For example, a statute or a regulation may require that the landlord maintain the premises a certain way or install a particular item, such as a fire alarm.

Contractual duty merits special emphasis. A traditional rule of landlord-tenant law, still followed in many states today, states that lease covenants are *independent*. When a covenant is independent, this means that a breach does not relieve the injured party of that party's duty to perform. This ancient rule of landlord-tenant law is contrary to the modern contract rule that allows a party to withhold performance upon a material breach by the other party.

The doctrine of constructive eviction is an exception to the doctrine of independent covenants. Generally when the landlord breaches a covenant, the tenant does not have the right to cancel the lease or to withhold the payment of rent. If, however, the landlord's breach of covenant meets the general requirements for the doctrine of constructive eviction, then the tenant has the ability to cancel or rescind the lease and possibly to get other relief as well, such as damages.

QUESTION 4.   Broken furnace. Tommy rents the first floor of a three-story building from Lucinda, which once was a grand house, to use as Tommy's dental office. They agree to a one-year term, with rent payable monthly. The remainder of the building is also used for commercial purposes. Six months later, in the dead of winter, the furnace breaks on a Monday morning.

The furnace is located in the basement of the house. Tommy immediately notifies Lucinda of the need to make repairs, but she refuses to arrange for repairs. She tells him that if he wants heat, he better get the furnace fixed. By early afternoon on Monday, Tommy's office is too cold to keep open. He closes down and calls Lucinda again, pleading with her to call someone to get the furnace fixed. She refuses to do so. On Wednesday, Tommy vacates possession and sends Lucinda a certified letter, which states that he has chosen to terminate the lease due to her failure to repair. The next month, Tommy does not tender payment of rent. Lucinda promptly sues him for nonpayment. If Lucinda prevails, the probable reason is:

A. The lack of heat has not substantially interfered with Tommy's use of the premises.
B. Tommy did not give Lucinda an adequate amount of time to arrange for repair of the furnace.
C. The state does not have an implied warranty of habitability.
D. The lease does not expressly require Lucinda to provide heat to the premises.
E. The state follows the doctrine of independent covenants.

ANALYSIS. This question tests the basic requirements for the doctrine of constructive eviction even though that term does not appear in the question or in any of the five choices. **A** focuses on a primary requirement — the condition must substantially interfere with the tenant's use and enjoyment — but the claim that the lack of heat is less than substantial is not credible, given our facts. Tommy can satisfy this element.

Choice **B** also focuses on an important consideration. Tommy cannot use the doctrine of constructive eviction unless Lucinda has notice of the problem and is given an opportunity to fix it. Given Lucinda's response — she was not going to try to hire anyone — she cannot complain that Tommy should have waited beyond Wednesday. Maybe Lucinda could not have found a repairman who was able to come on Monday, but due to her unequivocal refusal to act we do not need to decide what is a reasonable time period for making this repair.

C turns away from the core elements of constructive eviction. Because this is a commercial lease, it does not matter if the state has recognized (like almost all states have) a warranty of habitability. The warranty of habitability applies to residential leases, and this is a commercial lease, notwithstanding the fact that the building once was used as a house. A few states have a similar implied warranty of fitness or suitability for commercial leases, but this is a different animal.

E refers to the doctrine of independent covenants. It may help Lucinda if her state continues to follow this old doctrine, but it is only significant if Lucinda was legally obligated to repair the furnace. The source of such an obligation would be an express covenant (promise) or an implied covenant (promise). If Lucinda had such an obligation, she might then argue that her obligation was independent of Tommy's obligation to pay rent. This argument, however, seems to be a loser because Tommy would be able to establish all the required elements of constructive eviction, thereby trumping the doctrine of independent covenants.

We're left with **D**, our best answer. As indicated in the preceding paragraph, it's highly unlikely that Lucinda can prevail if the lease expressly required her to furnish heat or to repair the furnace.

E.   Condition of Premises: Caveat Emptor

Traditional landlord-tenant law followed the concept of *caveat emptor*. The landlord generally had no duty to repair or maintain the leased premises. If there was a defect in the premises when the parties made their lease, or if a defect arose later after the tenant took possession, the landlord was not responsible, assuming that the landlord had made no express covenants or representations concerning the subject matter.

Caveat emptor is often described as putting a burden on the tenant to make a careful inspection of the premises. The tenant is supposed to rent the property only if she decides, based upon the inspection and consideration of possible risks and given the length of the term and other factors, that she is willing to undertake such risks. Alternatively, the doctrine of caveat emptor puts the burden on the tenant of negotiating lease terms that shift the risk of defects to the landlord if the tenant is unwilling to shoulder those risks. When the landlord makes an express covenant, courts usually enforce such covenants in accordance with their terms.[1]

QUESTION 5.   Stolen television. Trisha rents a one-bedroom dwelling unit in a large apartment complex, signing a lease for 16 months. While Trisha is away during the day at work, a thief breaks into her unit through the front door and steals her plasma television set. The front door lacks a dead-bolt lock, which Trisha believes made it easier for the thief to gain access. If Trisha brings an action against the landlord for the value of the television, she is more likely to prevail if:

A. The jurisdiction generally treats residential leases like contracts.
B. The jurisdiction generally treats residential leases like conveyances.
C. The jurisdiction follows caveat emptor.
D. The neighborhood where the apartments are located basically is crime free.
E. Trisha's lease contains a covenant of quiet enjoyment.

---

1. In this regard, one should consider the doctrine of independent covenants, discussed in Section A of chapter 18.

ANALYSIS.   A line of cases addresses the ability of a tenant to recover damages from the landlord when a third party injures the tenant or her property by committing a criminal act on the leased premises or in a common area. Most of the cases that allow recovery do so on the basis of negligence. A few cases do so on the basis of implied covenant, reasoning that the landlord has an implied duty to provide reasonably safe premises. The negligence cases that favor the tenant reason that a landlord should have the same liability as most other actors, being under a duty to exercise reasonable care under all the facts and circumstances. Such cases reject the older view, which applied caveat emptor broadly, including this situation involving safety from crime. Thus, **C** is incorrect. Trisha is *not* likely to recover if the jurisdiction broadly follows caveat emptor.

Under negligence analysis, the fact mentioned in Choice **D** hurts Trisha's case. In a safe neighborhood, with no prior history of break-ins like the one Trisha suffered, it is more likely to be reasonable for a landlord not to install more secure dead-bolt locks.

The covenant of quiet enjoyment referred to in Choice **E** is not relevant. The purpose of the covenant is to give the tenant a contract remedy if the landlord, or someone for whom the landlord is responsible, interferes with the tenant's use and enjoyment or possession. The covenant does not create an independent obligation on the landlord's part to provide safe or crime-free premises.

We're left with **A** and **B**. The contract approach, compared to the conveyance approach, is the more modern and usually is employed to confer greater rights on the tenant. Although the contract approach has nothing directly to do with tort liability for negligence, it would support recovery on the implied covenant theory. So **A** is the best answer.

F.   Implied Warranty of Habitability

Beginning in the 1960s, courts developed the implied warranty of habitability. The warranty places an obligation upon a residential landlord to keep the premises in a habitable condition throughout the term of the lease. The warranty covers defects in the premises that are present when the lease commences and any defects that subsequently arise.

Almost all states presently have a warranty of habitability. In many states, the warranty is set forth in a state statute, which may have the effect of codifying, supplementing, or replacing a judicially declared warranty.

The warranty of habitability is based on contract law. The courts who developed the concept announced that they were applying the "contract theory" of leases rather than the older "conveyance theory." An implied contract warranty is generally thought to depend upon the parties' actual or probable intent. Thus, normally an implied warranty can be modified or waived if the parties so agree. In most states, however, a waiver or modification of the implied warranty of habitability is not permitted. Courts that developed the warranty feared that landlords would routinely obtain waivers in the form leases that they drafted, thereby leaving residential tenants without needed protection. One consequence of the "no waiver" rule is that the warranty covers not only latent defects in the premises but also obvious defects that are visible to the tenant at the time the parties enter into the lease.

The warranty does not guarantee the tenant premises that are perfect or totally free of defects or problems. A defect or condition violates the warranty if it makes the premises unhealthy or unsafe. In many states, the warranty also covers defects that make the premises "unlivable" to a person of ordinary sensibilities, even if the problem does not directly appear to present a health or safety risk.

> **QUESTION 6.   Too much radon gas.** Lamar is a college professor who owns a single-family house. While he is away for the year on sabbatical, he rents his home to a graduate student, Judy, with the lease beginning on September 1 and running for nine months. Judy, who is pursuing a master's degree in environmental science, decides to conduct a radon test in the basement of the house. In October, she finds radon levels significantly exceeding recommended levels. Two weeks later she retests the basement, with the same results. She asks Lamar to install a radon abatement system at his expense, which he refuses to do. Judy's strongest argument that Lamar is obligated to install such a system would be:
>
> **A.** Doctrine of independent covenants.
> **B.** Warranty of habitability.
> **C.** Doctrine of waste.
> **D.** Implied covenant of quiet enjoyment.
> **E.** Housing code requirement.

ANALYSIS.   This is a straightforward question designed to test recognition of the basic type of fact pattern where the warranty of habitability applies. Most students will get this question right.

The doctrine of independent covenants (generally but not always pro-landlord in application), referred to in **A**, is not relevant for two reasons. First, the doctrine is not a source of covenants or duties. It deals only with remedial choices. Second, this question does not tell us what remedy Judy is seeking. If Lamar has a duty to install a radon abatement system, Judy's remedial options are maximized if Lamar's duty is treated as a *dependent covenant*.

The doctrine of waste, referred to in **C**, puts duties on tenants to maintain or repair the leased premises, when it applies. It cannot help Judy.

The covenant of quiet enjoyment, referred to in **D**, is also a remedial tool. Judy may assert that the excessive radon level impairs her quiet enjoyment of the premises, amounting to a constructive eviction if she chooses to vacate the premises. But we don't know if she wants to vacate, and there's a better answer.

E, a housing code requirement, is a decent answer, and we'd be all right taking it if we spotted nothing better. If a housing code requires that residences not have excessive radon levels, Judy may well prevail. She needs to convince the court that she has the right to compel the landlord to comply with the code. In many states this is a winning argument.

B directly points to the warranty of habitability, our best answer. If Judy wins this case (which is not a sure thing), in most states the reason would be the warranty of habitability. In a number of states that give tenants a private right to enforce the housing code, the reason is that the warranty of habitability incorporates the housing code into the parties' lease.

G.   The Closer: Review of the Tenant's Options

This question provides you with the opportunity to review some of the basic rules relating to the tenant's right to quiet enjoyment and the parties' rights and obligations with respect to the condition of the premises.

> **QUESTION 7.   Garage storage space.** Larue rented a two-story house with detached garage to Teresa on a <u>month-to-month basis</u>, with rent payable on the first day of every month. The parties' <u>written lease said nothing about quiet enjoyment or the condition of the premises</u>. The garage, an A-frame structure with a steep roof, has a spacious storage loft, which was empty at the time the lease began. Seven months after Teresa took possession of the property, Larue bought a large load of lumber. He was not ready to use the lumber, and he needed a place to store it. Thinking that Teresa had no need for the storage loft, he drove his truck to the house on Saturday morning. He planned to ask Teresa if he could use the loft, but she was not at home. The garage door was open, so Larue placed the lumber in the storage loft. When Teresa returned home the next day she observed the lumber and complained, asking Larue to remove the lumber promptly. He refused, stating, "It's my garage. You don't need that space." If Teresa brings an action against Larue, the most likely outcome would be:
>
> **A.** Larue will prevail because the premises comply with the warranty of habitability even with the lumber in the garage.
> **B.** Larue will prevail because Teresa had no plans to use the garage loft at the time Larue stored his lumber.

C. Larue will prevail, provided that the jurisdiction follows the doctrine of caveat emptor in the field of landlord-tenant law.

D. Teresa may vacate possession of the house and assert rights under the doctrine of constructive eviction.

E. Teresa may withhold all of the rent until Larue removes the lumber from the garage.

ANALYSIS.   Starting at the beginning, Choice **A** invites us to think about possible application of the warranty of habitability. Almost all states imply this warranty, but there is no evidence that the lumber storage is dangerous or otherwise impairs Teresa's use of the premises as a habitation. Thus, we'll pick **A** unless we find a better answer.

Choice **B** also stipulates that Larue should win, this time because Larue's storage of lumber did not interfere with Teresa's actual use of the property. This is a weak answer. Normally we protect an owner of property from another person's interference, regardless of whether the owner presently is using or needs her property.

Choice **C** implicates the caveat emptor doctrine. When it applies, it protects a landlord who has failed to act, either by not making repairs or not disclosing an unfavorable condition to the tenant. Here Teresa's complaint is not Larue's inaction—rather, she is complaining that he has entered the leased premises and had done something he had no right to do.

The first clause of **D** is correct (Teresa has the right to vacate possession of the house and assert her rights) but not because of constructive eviction. Larue has *actually* evicted Teresa from part of the premises. This breaches the covenant of quiet enjoyment, which is implied because the lease does not contain an express covenant. For this breach, Teresa may remain in possession of the house and the rest of the premises and withhold rent for so long as Larue keeps his lumber in the garage. **E** is the right answer.

 # Smith's Picks

1.	Presence of the covenant	**B**
2.	Neighbor moves a fence	**D**
3.	Obnoxious colors	**C**
4.	Broken furnace	**D**
5.	Stolen television	**A**
6.	Too much radon gas	**B**
7.	Garage storage space	**E**

18

Landlord's Remedies

"You're outta here!"
Baseball umpire's traditional exclamation
when ejecting a player who contests the umpire's call

CHAPTER OVERVIEW
A. Tenant's Default
B. Tenant's Abandonment
C. Collection of Rent
D. Mitigation of Damages
E. Eviction Procedures
F. The Closer: Destruction of Improvements by Casualty
 Smith's Picks

The previous chapter, which focuses on the covenant of quiet enjoyment and the implied warranty of habitability, addresses the tenant's remedies for certain types of breaches by the landlord. This chapter considers the opposite situation: what remedies are available to the landlord when the tenant commits a breach of the lease agreement?

A. Tenant's Default

Landlord's remedies for default by the tenant is an area of landlord-tenant law where the influences of the competing property (conveyancing) and contract theories are prominent. Student understanding of these theories can be tested not only through the use of essay-type questions but also through the use of multiple-choice questions.

221

Before a landlord has a right to any remedy, the landlord must be able to prove that the tenant has committed a default. What constitutes a default depends upon the party's lease agreement. At a minimum, the tenant's failure to pay rent when due is a default, but modern leases usually contain many other promises by the tenant, for which a failure to perform constitutes a default.

Traditional landlord-tenant law views promises by landlord and tenant as independent. Under the doctrine of independent covenants, a breach by one party, even if material, does not excuse performance by the other party. This doctrine is contrary to modern contract law, and for this reason a number of states have rejected it, either for landlord-tenant law generally or with respect to particular applications within landlord-tenant law.

Parties are allowed to contract around the independent covenants doctrine, where it still applies. Here is a sample of a broadly worded lease provision that protects the landlord from the independent covenants doctrine:

> Failure by Tenant to make any rental payment within ten (10) days after the same shall become due, or to do any other act or perform any duty of Tenant hereunder, shall be considered a default. In the event of such a default, Landlord may serve Tenant with written notice of such default, and, if such default shall then continue without being wholly remedied for a period of ten (10) days after the service of such notice, then Landlord may, at its option and without further notice, immediately reenter and repossess the Premises, with or without process of law, and Tenant does, in such event, waive any demand for possession of the Premises and shall surrender and deliver up the Premises and property peaceably to Landlord.

Moreover, many states have a statute that authorizes a landlord to terminate the lease upon the tenant's failure to pay rent.

QUESTION 1.   Failing to pay taxes. Luann, the owner in fee simple of an office building, leased the same to Timothy for a six-year period. The written lease obligated Timothy to pay monthly rent of $3,000 and to pay the annual real estate taxes on the property, which were due each year on October 1. During the second year of the term, Timothy failed to pay the taxes. After this failure came to Luann's attention on October 16, she demanded that Timothy pay the taxes to the proper governmental entity. Timothy refused. On October 25 Luann paid the taxes. The lease says nothing about the consequences of Timothy's failure to pay the taxes. Luann brought an action to terminate the lease and to recover damages. The probable outcome of the action is that:

A. If the jurisdiction views lease covenants as **independent**, the court will award damages and order termination of the lease.

B. If the jurisdiction views lease covenants as **dependent**, the court will award damages and order termination of the lease.

C. If the jurisdiction views lease covenants as **independent,** the court will order termination of the lease but will not award damages.

D. If the jurisdiction views lease covenants as **dependent,** the court will order termination of the lease but will not award damages.

E. The court will not award damages or order termination of the lease because the lease does not expressly provide for either remedy.

ANALYSIS.   This question tests the student's understanding of the traditional concept that leasehold covenants are independent. Let's look at Choice **E** first, which is the only response that does not incorporate the distinction between independent and dependent covenants. **E** states that Luann will obtain neither remedy. This is highly unlikely because Timothy's breach was both material (taxes generally are a significant amount and nonpayment can create a serious problem) and, at least after Luann asked him to pay, intentional. Nothing in the facts suggests Timothy has an affirmative defense.

Let's consider whether Luann should be able to recover damages. She paid the taxes that Timothy promised to pay, and thus she has the right to recover this amount from him. This is true whether or not the jurisdiction views leasehold covenants as independent. If Timothy's right to possess the premises is *independent* of his obligation to pay taxes, then Luann does not have the right to terminate the lease. Her only right, once she has elected to pay the taxes herself, is to recover damages from Timothy.

Conversely, if the jurisdiction follows modern contract law, viewing leasehold covenants as dependent, then Timothy's right to possess the premises is dependent upon his obligation to pay taxes. This means that Luann has the right to terminate the lease. The right answer is **B.**

B.   Tenant's Abandonment

Most leases do not expressly require that the tenant take possession of the premises and remain in possession. By entering into the lease, the tenant acquires the right to possession, just as a person who accepts a conveyance of a present fee simple estate acquires the right to possession. In landlord-tenant law, the term "abandonment" has a special meaning. It refers to a tenant who not only relinquishes possession of the premises but also defaults in the payment of rent. Thus, a tenant who abandons is in breach of the lease.

An estate for years may terminate before the scheduled expiration date by mutual agreement between landlord and tenant. This type of premature termination is called a *surrender*. It is viewed as a conveyance by the tenant to the landlord of the unexpired portion of the term. A surrender may take place by the party's express agreement, and it may also take place by implication based on the party's conduct.

Abandonment by the tenant is usually considered to be an offer of surrender. The tenant is proposing an early termination. The landlord may accept the offer by express assent. Alternatively, the landlord may accept the offer by conduct alone, with no verbal expression. Litigation often results when the landlord attempts to collect future rents from an abandoning tenant, who claims rental immunity based upon surrender. Frequently the outcome turns on a question of fact.

QUESTION 2. Leaving the apartment. Karen signed a one-year lease for an apartment with Deluxe Properties, obligating herself to pay monthly rent. Two months into the term she failed to pay the rent, which was due on the first of every calendar month. On the sixth day of the month, she moved herself and all of her belongings out of the apartment and did not return. She stopped by the apartment manager's office. Finding the office open but the manager gone, she left her apartment keys on the manager's desk, along with a note that she signed that stated, "I no longer can afford the apartment." The apartment manager reentered the apartment and arranged for its cleaning and reletting to another tenant. Deluxe Properties then brought an action against Karen to recover unpaid rent until the time when the replacement tenant took possession. If Karen successfully defends this action, the most likely reason will be:

A. The landlord's reentry breaches the covenant of quiet enjoyment.
B. The landlord is estopped to recover additional rent.
C. Karen's default is not material.
D. The landlord has successfully mitigated its damages.
E. The landlord has accepted a surrender.

ANALYSIS. Let's start at the top. **A** is wrong. Deluxe Properties's reentry into the apartment was lawful, even if (as we should assume — never assume unstated facts) the lease did not expressly reserve a right to reenter under these circumstances. Karen had abandoned possession by leaving her apartment with no intention of returning. Deluxe Properties knew this when it reentered. Thus, Deluxe did not breach the covenant of quiet enjoyment or commit any other wrong when it reentered.

Choice **C**, which argues that Karen's failure to pay rent is not material, is bad for two reasons. First, a tenant's failure to pay an entire month's rent goes to the core of the bargain and plainly is material. Second, it does not matter whether Karen's default is material because Deluxe Properties is not seeking to avoid a duty to perform. Rather it is suing for damages, which are collectable whether the default is material or nonmaterial.

Likewise, mitigation of damages, the subject of Choice **D**, is not on point. The landlord did mitigate its damages by obtaining a replacement tenant, but it is seeking damages for the time period before the replacement tenant took possession. Karen could use the landlord's mitigation as a defense were the landlord seeking to collect rent for a period of time after rental to the replacement, but this is not the case here.

We're down to Choices **B** and **E**. The doctrine of estoppel, the subject of Choice **B**, has some plausibility as a possible defense for Karen. The claim would be that Deluxe Properties's failure to notify Karen that it intended to relet the premises and to hold her liable for the rental deficiency has caused a change in her position to her detriment. But there are two weaknesses. First, Deluxe Properties has not taken any action that has misled Karen. On occasion, a person's silence or inaction can give rise to an estoppel, but this is rare. Second, it is not clear how Deluxe's inaction has prejudiced Karen. So we're left with **E** as the best answer. Karen argues that her vacation of possession, along with leaving behind the keys and an explanatory note, constitutes an offer of surrender. Deluxe Properties arguably accepted the surrender by taking possession of the premises without a protest, followed by the reletting.

C.   Collection of Rent

Upon a tenant's abandonment of the premises, the landlord does not have to accept the tenant's offer of surrender. Instead, the landlord has the right to do nothing and insist upon the tenant's continued payment of rent until the end of the term. This follows from the conveyance theory of landlord-tenant law. The tenant is the full owner of the unexpired term and has no right to force the landlord to acquire that property interest.

> **QUESTION 3.   Closing the warehouse.** Oldtown leased a warehouse building to Brewster for a term of seven years with an annual rent of $30,000 payable in quarterly installments of $7,500. Halfway through the lease term, at a time when Brewster was in full compliance with all of his obligations under the lease, Brewster encountered several business setbacks, one of which was occasioned by an employee's commission of embezzlement. The setbacks quickly necessitated a close in Brewster's business. Brewster promptly notified Oldtown of his difficulties, asking Oldtown to seek another tenant for the warehouse. Oldtown refused to do so. Brewster then offered Oldtown $25,000 in exchange for a release of liability for all future rents. Oldtown rejected this offer, and Brewster vacated possession and ceased making quarterly rent payments. At this point in time, the annual fair rental value for the warehouse was $27,000. The warehouse sat vacant for the next 14 months, when Oldtown filed an action against Brewster to collect unpaid rents. If Oldtown prevails, the most probable reason is that

A. The original term of the lease exceeded five years.
B. The annual rent of $30,000 exceeded the fair rental value of the warehouse at the time Brewster abandoned possession.
C. Brewster is the owner of the unexpired portion of the seven-year term.
D. The abandonment stemmed from Brewster's own negligence in monitoring his employee's behavior.
E. Brewster's request that Oldfield seek a replacement tenant was not in writing.

ANALYSIS. In most jurisdictions today, Oldtown's success in recovering rents from Brewster will depend upon the application of mitigation-of-damage rules. This question, however, avoids that path by asking about a rationale for victory by Oldtown and by providing no keys that invoke mitigation principles.

A is incorrect. Neither the original length of the term (seven years) nor the remaining length at the time Brewster abandoned (approximately three and one-half years) will affect Oldtown's chances at prevailing.

B focuses on the relationship between the contract rents and the market rents at the time of abandonment. This isn't relevant. The relationship between these two numbers would affect the measure of damages were Oldtown suing for expectation damages, but instead Oldtown is suing to collect all of the rents.

The tenant's negligence, or fault, raised by Choice **D**, also has no bearing on Oldtown's action. Brewster's liability for breach of his promise to pay rents is the same, whether his breach is willful, or due to negligence, or solely due to factors beyond his control.

Choice **E** is a red herring. True, the facts don't tell us whether Brewster's notice and request were written or oral, but it does not matter. Oldfield's theory is not that Brewster gave a defective or inadequate notice of his intentions. Rather the theory is simply that Brewster promised to pay rents and has not done so.

We're down to **C**, which asserts that Brewster owns the unexpired lease term. This is pretty conclusory, but all of the other answers are demonstrably wrong. The assertion has some value in that it points to the conveyance theory of the nature of a lease and thus points away from a contract-law-based mitigation duty. In essence, Oldfield claims Brewster owes rent because he has purchased property (the leasehold), which he still owns and for which he has not yet fully paid.

D.   Mitigation of Damages

In terms of contract law, the landlord's prerogative to sit back and collect rent is expressed in terms of there being no duty for the landlord to mitigate damages. During the past decades most states have changed this rule by common law judicial action or by statute. In some states the landlord's duty to mitigate damages applies to all leases, and in others it applies only to residential leases.

QUESTION 4.   Closing the warehouse reprise. Under the facts of Question 3 above, if Brewster successfully defends Oldtown's action to collect rents, the most probable reason is that

A.   Oldtown did not seek to obtain a replacement tenant for the warehouse.

B.   Brewster notified Oldfield of his intention to vacate possession before he committed a default.

C.   Brewster's business failure has made his performance impracticable.

D.   Oldtown's rejection of Brewster's offer to pay $25,000 for a release was not made in good faith.

E.   The decline in fair rental value of the warehouse makes collection of the original rent inequitable.

ANALYSIS.   This question tests basic understanding of the landlord's duty to mitigate damages after a tenant's abandonment. Neither the question nor the keys use the term "mitigate" or "mitigation," so it's necessary for the student to understand the underlying concepts, not just pick the magic word or phrase.

B does not really help Brewster. In a loose sense it may be to Brewster's credit that he contacted Oldtown before he abandoned and ceased paying rent, but this will not provide Brewster with a substantial defense. Giving advance notice to another party to a lease (or any other contract) of the intention to default is no excuse for the default.

Brewster might try to use his business setbacks to fashion an impracticability (or impossibility) of performance defense, but this is a long shot. No facts point to a business failure caused by events that are extraordinarily unusual. We'll hold **C** in reserve, selecting it only if the other remaining choices are unequivocally wrong.

D fails—good faith is a nonissue. It does not matter whether Brewster's offer to surrender the lease in exchange for payment to Oldtown of $25,000 was fair or even generous. Oldtown has the right to insist upon the original lease (contract), with whatever set of remedies the law provides thereunder.

Likewise, the decline in rental value referred to in **E** does not provide the basis for a defense for Brewster. There is always the possibility that rental value will increase or decrease after a lease is entered into. Both parties undertake risk here. This risk was foreseeable and should not excuse Brewster from paying the contract rent.

Now let's look at Choice **A**. If Oldtown has a duty to mitigate damages upon Brewster's abandonment (as would be the case in most states today), this means that Oldtown has to make some efforts to find a replacement tenant. Because Oldfield did nothing at all, the court may preclude Oldfield from recovering against Brewster. Alternatively, the court may reduce the award. So **A** is our strongest answer.

E.   Eviction Procedures

Landlords often seek to evict a tenant, prior to the expiration of the term of the lease, when the tenant has failed to pay rent or has committed another serious breach under the provisions of the lease. This can raise a number of different legal issues. In a beginning course in property, the issue most often discussed is whether the landlord must resort to judicial process when the defaulting tenant has remained in possession of the leased premises. If judicial process is not required, then the landlord may legally retake possession by *self-help*.

Two competing rules are followed by courts today, both of which may be considered more enlightened than an earlier common law rule, stemming from English law. The old, now obsolete rule allowed a landlord to retake possession by self-help, using no more force than was reasonably necessary. Today's pro-landlord rule still sanctions self-help repossession but only if the landlord is able to accomplish repossession in a peaceable manner. This means that the landlord must not commit a "breach of the peace" in retaking possession. The "breach of the peace" standard is highly flexible, so much so that it is often indeterminate. At a minimum it means that the landlord may not commit violent acts or intimidate the tenant into leaving by threatening violence. Courts, however, have often found breaches of the peace for a landlord's conduct that is more innocuous. Such courts will find the repossession nonpeaceable by speculating that the landlord's method might have led to violence or a confrontation under other circumstances (for example, had the tenant been present at the time the landlord accomplished the repossession).

A number of states, but not a majority, bar self-help repossession as a general matter. In some of these states self-help repossession is unlawful for all leases, regardless of the provisions of the lease agreement. With such a rule, if a landlord retakes possession without filing an action in court, the landlord's only hope is to demonstrate that the tenant abandoned possession prior to the landlord's entry. If this claim fails, the landlord is liable for an unlawful eviction, for which the tenant may recover damages and might also be restored to possession.

Some states take what may be viewed as an intermediate position, barring self-help repossession for some but not all leases. The principal variations turn on the type of the lease and the content of the lease agreement. Self-help repossession may be prohibited for residential leases but not other leases. Also, some states prohibit self-help repossession generally but allow the parties to contract for self-help repossession. The consequence is that the lease may contain a clause allowing the landlord to retake possession peaceably.

QUESTION 5.   **Molly's Morsels.** Lewis rented a restaurant to Molly for a term of four years, where Molly opened a restaurant named Molly's Morsels. Three months ago Molly defaulted in paying monthly rent, and despite Lewis's repeated demands, Molly refused to make payment. She became angry, insisting that Lewis leave her alone, claiming she would make up the past-due rent when business improved. Molly's Morsels regularly opened seven days a week at 11:00 AM and closed at midnight. Lewis sent Molly a letter stating that he was terminating her lease, effective at the close of business on November 30, for nonpayment of rent. The letter demanded that she vacate possession by that time. Molly failed to do so, and on December 1, and on the next day, she opened Molly's Morsels for business as usual. On the night of December 2, Lewis hired a locksmith. Lewis still had a key to the building, but he thought Molly might have changed the locks. Lewis and the locksmith sat in a parked car across the street from Molly's Morsels, which closed as usual at midnight. At 12:55 AM Lewis noticed Molly and one of her employees leave, locking the building and departing from the restaurant's parking lot in their cars. No other cars remained in the parking lot. Before going in, Lewis called the sheriff, who drove over to observe the proceedings. With the locksmith's help, Lewis entered the building and changed the locks. On December 3, Molly was unable to enter the restaurant building. When she learned the reason why, she became highly upset. After seeing an attorney, Molly brought an action against Lewis for unlawful eviction. Which of the following facts make it <u>more likely</u> that <u>Lewis</u> will <u>successfully defend</u> the action?

A. Lewis hired a professional locksmith rather than use his own key.
B. Lewis contacted the sheriff and arranged for the sheriff to be present.
C. Molly became angry when Lewis attempted to collect past-due rents.
D. Lewis accomplished the repossession during the night.
E. Lewis accomplished the repossession after the restaurant closed for business.

ANALYSIS.   If the jurisdiction bars self-help repossession as a general matter for leases including commercial leases such as this restaurant lease, then Lewis cannot successfully defend the action. It is clear that Molly did not abandon possession and that she had no intention of doing so. Thus, the question implicitly asks the student to consider the "breach of the peace" standard—in particular, what factors make it more likely that Lewis has repossessed peaceably, without committing a breach.

The fact in Choice **A**, use of locksmith compared to the landlord's own key, is neutral. Forcibly breaking a lock may be viewed as bad (tending toward a breach), but this is not what happened.

As for Choice **B**, one might think that contacting and involving the sheriff, a law enforcement officer, is a positive, making a breach of the peace less likely. However, a number of cases hold this against the landlord on the theory that if the tenant is present, the officer's presence may intimidate the tenant, preventing the tenant from making a protest. The idea is that a tenant who is present should have the right to protest, forcing the landlord to back off.

Choice **C** also cuts the wrong way. Molly's prior anger may be unreasonable, but it makes it more likely that, had Molly been present at the time of repossession (or had she returned to the restaurant that night for some reason while Lewis was entering), a confrontation and possible violence may have ensued.

Repossession at night, rather than day, is not necessarily safer or riskier. Thus, **D** is not a good answer. **E** is preferable to **D** because **E** focuses not on nighttime, but the fact that the business was closed late at night. The absence of customers, employees, and the owner makes a breach of the peace less likely, so **E** is the best answer.

F.   The Closer: Destruction of Improvements by Casualty

When the leased property has improvements, the tenant expects to be able to use and enjoy those improvements for the duration of the lease term. Similarly, the landlord expects that when the lease expires, those improvements along with the underlying land will be returned to the landlord in good shape, subject to a normal amount of depreciation (reasonable wear and tear).

The landlord's expectations are protected by the doctrine of waste. Under the doctrine of waste, the tenant has twin duties: (1) the duty not to commit *affirmative waste* by intentionally removing or injuring improvements, and (2) the duty not to commit *permissive waste*. The latter duty means that the tenant must make reasonable repairs to the improvements. The extent of the repair duty depends upon all the facts and circumstances, including the length of and nature of the lease. Because the standard is amorphous, a well-written lease will specifically describe the tenant's duty and the landlord's corresponding duties.

A casualty, such as fire or flood, that affects the leased premises may have a drastic impact on the parties. The traditional common law rule allocates the risk of casualty according to fault. If the negligence of either party caused the casualty, that party has the obligation to repair or rebuild and is entitled to no relief under the lease. If neither party is at fault then the loss is shared—the tenant has the choice of doing without the improvements (or using them in their impaired state) until the lease expires or repairing or rebuilding. If the tenant picks the former choice, when the lease ends the property will revert to the landlord in its casualty-impaired state. A number of states have modified the common law rules by statute or judicial decision. Usually the **new rule** calls for termination at the tenant's option if a casualty that is not the tenant's fault causes the substantial destruction of improvements.

These are the default rules. In a well-structured transaction, if the improvements are valuable, the lease will obligate one of the parties to get and maintain casualty insurance. The lease will also provide guidelines for repair or termination in the event of casualty damage to improvements.

QUESTION 6. Fire in the hair salon. Larry, the owner of a two-story building in fee simple, rented the first floor to Tammy for her to use as a hair salon. The parties signed a three-year lease, with Tammy promising to pay rent of $1,800 per month. Larry retained possession of the second floor, where he lived. One evening after Tammy's salon had closed for the day, a fire erupted, causing major damage to both floors. The next month Tammy refused to pay rent because she could no longer use the first floor for her business. Larry demanded that she both pay rent and make repairs to the damaged parts of the leased premises. When she refused, Larry brought an action to recover rent and damages attributable to her failure to make repairs. At the trial, evidence showed that the <u>fire originated in one of the rooms of Tammy's salon</u> because she had <u>improperly stored</u> combustible hair products near a coffee pot, which overheated after Tammy closed the salon because <u>she forgot to turn it off</u>. The jurisdiction has no statute that alters the <u>common law</u> of landlord-tenant relations. Judgment should be for

A. Tammy on both claims.
B. Larry on the rent claim but for Tammy on the repair claim.
C. Tammy on the rent claim but for Larry on the repair claim.
D. Larry on both claims.

ANALYSIS. At common law Tammy is responsible for continuing to pay rent, regardless of destruction of improvements by casualty, unless the landlord negligently caused the destruction. Tammy is liable to repair the leased premises only if she caused the destruction (intentionally or negligently). Here the evidence plainly points to negligence on her part. Thus, **D** is the correct answer.

QUESTION 7. Fire of undetermined origin. Assume all the facts stated in Question 6 above, with one exception. The fire marshal who investigated the <u>fire was unable to determine the fire's origin</u>, and based on the evidence submitted at trial the jury was likewise unable to determine where the fire started and whether either Larry or Tammy was responsible. The jurisdiction has no statute that alters the <u>common law</u> of landlord-tenant relations. Judgment should be for:

A. Tammy on both claims.
B. Larry on the rent claim but for Tammy on the repair claim.
C. Tammy on the rent claim but for Larry on the repair claim.
D. Larry on both claims.

ANALYSIS. Tammy is responsible for paying rent after the fire because she cannot show that the fire was due to Larry's negligence. However, she is not responsible for repairing the fire damage to the leased premises because Larry cannot show that the fire was her fault. Thus, **B** is the correct answer.

 ## Smith's Picks

1.	Failing to pay taxes	**B**
2.	Leaving the apartment	**E**
3.	Closing the warehouse	**C**
4.	Closing the warehouse reprise	**A**
5.	Molly's Morsels	**E**
6.	Fire in the hair salon	**D**
7.	Fire of undetermined origin	**B**

19

Subleases and Assignments

~

"There's a new kid in town
I don't want to hear it"
Eagles, *New Kid in Town*, on *Hotel California*
(Elektra Entertainment, 1976)

~

CHAPTER OVERVIEW
A. Nature of Sublease
B. Nature of Assignment
C. Distinction between Sublease and Assignment
D. Lease Restrictions
E. The Closer: Rent Liability after Multiple Assignments
◈ Smith's Picks

A. Nature of Sublease

There may be more than one valid lease on a parcel of land at the same time. This results from subleasing. A is created when a tenant under an existing lease transfers her right to possession under a new lease to a new tenant. The original tenant, known as the sublandlord or sublessor, enters into a lease with a new tenant, who is known as the subtenant or sublessee. The original lease is often called the prime lease or the main lease.

The sublease creates a landlord-tenant relationship between the sublandlord and the subtenant. The sublease leaves intact and undisturbed the landlord-tenant relationship between the prime landlord and the sublandlord (original tenant). Normally, the subtenant pays rent (sometimes called subrent) to the sublandlord as provided for by the sublease, and the sublandlord pays rent to the prime landlord as provided for by the original lease.

The ability to make a sublease is often valuable for two reasons. First, it allows the original tenant to transfer possession for less than all of the remaining term, enabling the original tenant to regain possession after the subtenant vacates. Second, a sublease can allow the original tenant to profit from transferring possession. A profit results if the original tenant charges subrent that is higher than the rent under the prime lease.

A single tract of land may have multiple subleases. For example, *A* may lease Blackacre to *B* for a term of 20 years. *B* then subleases Blackacre to *C* for a term of ten years, and *C* sub-subleases Blackacre to *D* for a term of five years.

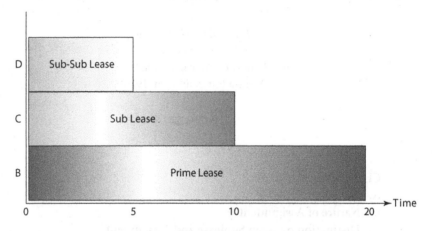

QUESTION 1.   **Painting the garage.** Abigail, the owner of a single-family house in fee simple, enters into a written lease with Frank for one year. Monthly rent is $1,200, and Frank has an option to renew the lease for an additional one-year term plus an option to purchase the property. Four months into the original term, Frank subleases the property to Polly, the painter, for a term of six months. At the time of the sublease, Frank has noticed that the garage exterior is badly in need of a new paint job. Frank bargains for Polly to paint the garage, and in the sublease Polly promises to pay $1,200 in monthly rent and to paint the garage no later than three months after commencement of the sublease. Abigail learns about the sublease, and she is pleased that Frank has arranged for painting the garage. Polly fails to paint the garage within the time specified, and Abigail brings an action against her for damages or injunctive relief. The court should hold for

A. Abigail, because Polly has failed to perform a bargained-for promise.
B. Abigail, because performance of Polly's promise would improve Abigail's property.
C. Polly, because her promise does not run with the land.
D. Polly, because only Frank is the beneficiary of Polly's promise.
E. Polly, but only if she has the benefit of a warranty of habitability.

ANALYSIS.   This question focuses on the relationship between the original landlord, Abigail, and the subtenant, Polly. Although both Abigail and Polly own estates in the same land, the key is to understand that neither one owes direct obligations to the other person. Abigail is not Polly's landlord. Only Frank is Polly's landlord, and Polly's obligations as tenant run only to him.

The first two choices state that Abigail should win. The reason given in **A**—Polly has breached a bargained-for promise—is factually true but does not support relief for Abigail because Frank, not Abigail, bargained for the promise. The reason given in **B**—painting would benefit Abigail by improving or maintaining her property—is also true but does not support Abigail because she has not bargained for this benefit.

Choice **E**, the only nuanced answer, asserts that the outcome should turn on whether Polly has the benefit of a warranty of habitability. Arguably, if Frank is obligated on a warranty of habitability and repainting the garage is necessary for him to comply with the warranty, Frank should be precluded from suing Polly on her promise. This follows from the widely followed rule that a warranty of habitability cannot be waived. However, **E** is weak, first because it's unlikely that a garage that's badly in need of painting makes the property nonhabitable, and second because Polly should win regardless of the presence of a warranty.

Which of the "Polly should win" choices (**C** or **D**) is better? Whether Polly's promise "runs with the land" is not the issue because Abigail is not a successor to Frank. Had Frank assigned his interest in the property to another person, then it would be important to determine whether the benefit of Polly's promise runs to a successor.

We're left with **D** as our best answer. Polly's promise was intended only to benefit Frank. This reflects the basic idea of a sublease, which creates an independent landlord-tenant relationship between the sublandlord and the subtenant. A good student who has studied third-party beneficiary rules in contract law would consider whether Abigail qualifies as a third-party beneficiary of Polly's promise. This is unlikely because Frank has an independent interest in wanting to have the garage painted. When the sublease expires, he will benefit by resuming possession with a more attractive and better maintained garage. Moreover, if Frank were to exercise his option to purchase the property, he would retain the entire benefit of Polly's performance.

B.   Nature of Assignment

Either the landlord or the tenant may assign its interest in the lease to a third party. When the tenant makes an assignment, the assignee becomes the new owner of the leasehold.

The conveyance theory and the contract theory of landlord-tenant relations are discernible in vocabulary used to describe the nature and source of the parties' mutual obligations to perform their covenants. Each party is obligated by virtue of his status. This is called "privity of estate." Each party is also obligated on the basis of promise. This is called "privity of contract." When the original parties have a dispute concerning a covenant and become litigants, the source does not matter. For example, when the landlord sues the tenant for unpaid rent, the landlord does not have to specify "privity of estate" or "privity of contract" as the basis for the claim.

This archaic sounding vocabulary becomes relevant after an assignment. The assignee of the tenant or landlord becomes liable on the *real covenants*[1] based upon privity of estate. This happens automatically. The provisions of the assignment make no difference. Upon the assignment, the assignor relinquishes privity of estate. The assignment, however, does not relieve the assignor from liability on the real covenants. The assignor's liability to the landlord continues based upon privity of contract. Relief from liability takes place only if the landlord expressly agrees to a release from liability.

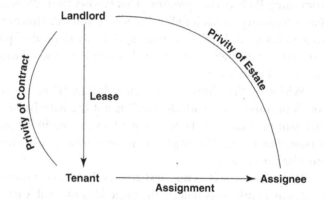

There are two types of assignments. In the first type, discussed in the previous paragraph, the assignee accepts the assignment and does nothing more. In the second type, the assignee makes a promise to the assignor. The assignee *assumes* the obligations of the assignor. This means that the assignee promises to perform the covenants set forth in the lease. An assuming assignee becomes liable based on privity of contract. Thus, the assuming assignee puts himself in the same position as the original party—liability based on the dual prongs of privity of estate and privity of contract.

---

1. Real covenants are those that meet the requirements to "run with the land." Examples are the tenant's covenant to pay rent and the landlord's covenant to repair the premises. Some covenants set forth in a written lease may not qualify as real covenants. They are called *personal covenants*. For discussion of real covenants, see chapter 24.

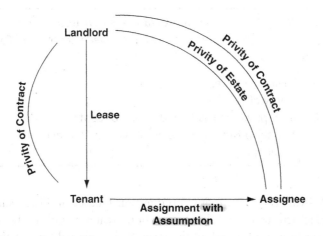

QUESTION 2. **Two tenant transfers.** Lorena and Tobias entered into a written four-year lease of Blackacre. One year later Tobias assigned the lease to Elsie, who paid for the assignment by giving Tobias $500 in cash and a promissory note for $1,000. Two months later Elsie entered into a separate written one-year lease of Blackacre, pursuant to which Elsie as lessor rented the property to Fanta as lessee. The relationship between Lorena and Elsie can best be described as:

A. Privity of estate.
B. Privity of contract.
C. Both privity of estate and privity of contract.
D. Neither privity of estate nor privity of contract.
E. Cotenants.

ANALYSIS. This question is a straightforward testing of the terms "privity of estate" and "privity of contract." Choice E, which takes us to another ballpark, is completely off base. A landlord and a tenant cannot be cotenants. By definition, cotenants must have simultaneous rights to possession. A tenant has the present right to possession, and a landlord owns a future interest (a future right to possession).

Back to the ballpark that we belong in. When Elsie took the assignment of lease from Tobias, this created privity of estate between Lorena, the landlord, and Elsie. The next step is to ask whether Elsie also became obligated under the privity of contract concept. The description of the assignment says nothing about Elsie "assuming" the lease or promising to perform any of the covenants. Her payment of consideration is totally distinct from the question of assumption or nonassumption of obligations. Thus, Elsie is a nonassuming assignee. **A** is the right answer.

QUESTION 3.   Two tenant transfers revisited. Under the facts of Question 2 above, the relationship between Lorena and Fanta can best be described as:

A. Privity of estate.
B. Privity of contract.
C. Both privity of estate and privity of contract.
D. Neither privity of estate nor privity of contract.
E. Cotenants.

ANALYSIS.   This follow-up question focuses on Elsie's subsequent lease of Blackacre to Fanta. This transaction creates a sublease because Fanta's one-year term expires before the term of the original lease. This sublease creates relationships of privity of estate and privity of contract between Elsie and Fanta, but creates no such relationship between Lorena and Fanta. Thus our answer is **D**.

C.   Distinction between Sublease and Assignment

Any consensual transfer of possession by a tenant must be either a sublease or an assignment. At traditional common law, if the tenant transfers the right of possession for the entire remainder of the term, then the transfer is an assignment. Conversely, if the transfer covers less than the entire term, it is a sublease.

The idea can be restated by asking whether the tenant has retained a reversion. When the entire term is transferred, there is no reversion. The assignor has no remaining property interest in the leased premises. When less than the entire term is transferred, the sublessor has a reversion. It does not matter how short a reversion the parties create. If the original tenant keeps a month, a week, or even a day at the end of the term, the parties have a sublease. The common law rule looks to the substance of the parties' transaction. If the parties attach an incorrect label to their transaction or use other inappropriate terminology, a court applying traditional rules overrides their language.

Judicial overriding of the parties' labels sometimes has the effect of defeating the parties' probable intentions. For this reason some courts have departed from the traditional common law distinction. Two approaches have emerged. First, in some states courts strain to find that a purported sublessor has retained a reversion, even though the purported sublessee has the right to possession for the remainder of the original term. The prime example is when the sublessor has reserved an express right of entry if the sublessee defaults under the sublease.

The second approach is broader, substituting a new test that looks to the parties' intention based on all the facts and circumstances. The presence of a reversion or a right of entry is one fact to consider, along with the parties' terminology and any other relevant evidence. The best known case is *Jaber v. Miller*, 239 S.W.2d 760 (Ark. 1951), which held that a transfer denominated as an "assignment," pursuant to which the assignee executed a series of promissory notes as consideration, legally was an assignment.

QUESTION 4.   An office lease. Carlos rented space in his office building to Silvia at a monthly rent of $2,000 with the term scheduled to expire on June 30, 2008. After Silvia had taken possession, she decided to move her business to another location. She had a friend, Medici, who was willing to pay $2,400 per month for the office space. They entered into an agreement, denominated a "Sublease," pursuant to which Medici was to take possession and pay Silvia $2,400 per month through June 30, 2008. Medici took possession and timely paid the agreed-to rent to Silvia for all succeeding months of the term. Silvia, however, stopped paying rent to Carlos five months before expiration of the term. Carlos brought an action to recover five months of rent ($10,000) against both Silvia and Medici. Which of the following statements best supports an argument that Carlos should obtain judgment against Medici?

A. Medici agreed to pay a higher rent than Silvia was obligated to pay to Carlos.

B. Silvia did not retain a reversion when she leased the space to Medici.

C. Carlos is a third-party beneficiary of Medici's promise to pay rent to Silvia.

D. Medici became obligated to pay rent to Carlos by privity of contract.

E. Medici expressly assumed Silvia's obligation to pay rent to Carlos.

ANALYSIS.   The key fact here is that the "Sublease" agreement between Silvia and Medici runs until June 30, 2008, just the same as the original lease between Carlos and Silvia. Under the traditional test for distinguishing subleases and assignments, Silvia and Medici have an assignment. Some modern courts, however, have replaced the traditional test with an "intent of the parties" test. Under the "intent test," a court might allow Silvia and Medici to have a sublease with all of its legal characteristics. Carlos wants the Silvia-Medici transfer recast as an assignment. Then Medici, as an assignee, would be Carlos's new tenant, obligated to pay rent to Carlos based on privity of estate.

Choice **A** refers to the increased rent provided for by the "Sublease," compared to the prime lease. This does not help Carlos argue that the Silvia-Medici transfer is really an assignment. If anything, it points in the opposite direction if the court applies an "intent of the parties" test because in the real world tenants commonly utilize subleases to make a profit when the leased premises have risen in value.

Choice **C** may prove attractive to students who seek to integrate their contract law learning with landlord-tenant law. But third-party beneficiary theory simply cannot apply here. Silvia did not bargain for Medici to render performance to a third party, such as Carlos. Silvia bargained for Medici to pay rent to Silvia.

Choices **D** and **E** are alternate expressions of the same idea. Medici, in entering into the "Sublease" with Silvia, could have promised Silvia that he would pay rent (or perhaps guarantee the payment of rent) to Carlos. **D** expresses this idea as privity of contract, and **E** expresses it as an assumption of the obligation. But there is no indication in our facts that Medici agreed to anything like this. Had Medici done so in a coherently structured transaction, Medici would have agreed to pay $2,000 directly to Carlos each month and to pay Silvia only the remaining $400 each month.

This takes us to **B**, which observes that Silvia failed to keep a reversion in the "Sublease" to Medici. This conclusion lies at the heart of the traditional sublease-assignment distinction and is what Carlos would argue to persuade the court that Medici is liable to him under privity of estate.

D.   Lease Restrictions

Many leases contain provisions that prohibit or restrict subleases and assignments. Such provisions are valid restraints on alienation, although courts tend to construe them strictly, resolving any ambiguities in favor of the tenant. In the absence of express restrictions, the tenant has the right to make an assignment or a sublease without notifying the landlord or obtaining the landlord's consent. A few states have modified this rule by statute, requiring the landlord's consent for certain types of transfers by tenants.

Often a lease restriction on transfers is written as a consent clause. For example, a simple lease clause may provide

> Tenant shall not have the right to sublet the Premises or any part thereof, or to assign this lease to any third party, without the prior written consent of Landlord.

Such clauses do not expressly indicate what standard the landlord will apply when evaluating a tenant request to sublet or assign. Most courts have refused to intervene when tenants challenge landlord refusals to consent, holding that the landlord may arbitrarily withhold consent. A growing minority of states, however, have imposed the requirement that the landlord have reasonable grounds for blocking the transfer. A leading case is *Kendall v. Ernest Pestana Inc.*, 709 P.2d 837 (Cal. 1985), holding that a landlord's desire to bargain for extra rent or other consideration from the tenant or the transferee is unreasonable.

> **QUESTION 5.   Renting to a deadbeat.** Vanna rents her single-family house to Koby at a monthly rent of $1,400 for a term of one year, beginning and ending on January 1. The written lease provides: "No transfers without Landlord's consent. Tenant shall not assign this lease to any person without the prior written consent of Landlord." In June, Koby decides to move to another city. He asks Vanna to release him from his obligations under the lease, but she refuses. Koby then asks his friends and relatives whether any of them would like to take over his lease. His cousin, Deadbeat, is willing. He went through bankruptcy two years ago but now has a steady job and is willing to pay the contract rent of $1,400 per month. Koby and Deadbeat enter into a "sublease agreement," which has a term beginning on July 1 and ending on December 30. Deadbeat goes into possession. In August, Vanna learns of Deadbeat's presence and the sublease. She brings an action against Koby to terminate the lease and for damages. Judgment should be for
>
> A. Vanna, because Koby made a transfer without obtaining her consent.
> B. Vanna, because Koby has not acted in good faith.
> C. Vanna, because Deadbeat's bankruptcy indicates he is not creditworthy.
> D. Koby, because there is no evidence that Deadbeat is an unsuitable tenant.
> E. Koby, because he did not violate the lease restriction on transfers.

ANALYSIS.   Choices **C** through **D** present opposite conclusions as to whether it is reasonable for a landlord such as Vanna to object to Deadbeat as a new tenant taking possession of the leased premises. The question might be a close one if we must answer it to solve the problem. Deadbeat now is employed and apparently can afford to pay the rent, but a recent bankruptcy is viewed as a black mark on a person's credit rating (and perhaps Deadbeat's name should be held against him).

Choice **B**, which asks about Koby's good faith, is a red herring. Either he had a legal right to "sublease" to Deadbeat or he did not. If he had the right, the fact that Vanna is aggrieved and arguably harmed does not impugn his good faith. If he lacked the right, then he has breached the lease and judgment should be for Vanna, regardless of whether one might characterize his breach as a "good faith breach" or a "bad faith breach."

The key to this question is to decide whether Koby's transfer to Deadbeat violates the quoted lease provision. The provision expressly prohibits an assignment without the landlord's consent but says nothing about a sublease. Koby's transfer to Deadbeat is a sublease because he retained a reversion for one day (December 31). Courts strictly construe anti-transfer provisions in leases. Judgment probably will be for Koby. Vanna will argue that (1) the reversion is so short that in substance Koby has assigned the lease and (2) the caption preceding the sentence ("*No transfers without Landlord's consent.*") indicates a broader scope because a sublease is one type of transfer, but she is unlikely to prevail. Most leases clearly restrict both assignments and subleases, and for whatever reason this one does not. **E** is the best answer.

E.   The Closer: Rent Liability after Multiple Assignments

A leasehold is sometimes assigned more than once. This is especially likely to happen for leases that have long terms. The concepts of privity of estate and privity of contract, introduced above in Section B of this chapter, determine the liability of successive assignees for rent and for other tenant obligations. The same is true when the landlord has transferred its property rights to another person, who becomes the new landlord.

> **QUESTION 6.   Multiple transfers.** Lomar Inc., the owner of Blackacre in fee simple, entered into a written sixty-year ground lease with Trane Corp. The lease obligated the tenant to pay quarterly rent of $50,000. Ten years later Trane Corp. assigned the lease to Uvalde Corp., who assumed all the obligations of the tenant under the ground lease. Two years later Lomar Inc. assigned the lease and sold the reversion to Mick Inc. Five years later Uvalde Corp. assigned the lease to Viva Corp. This instrument of assignment contained no language indicating an assumption of obligations by the assignee. Eight years later Viva Corp. assigned the lease to Wawa Corp. This instrument of assignment also lacked language of assumption. One year after this assignment, Wawa Corp. stopped paying quarterly rent and abandoned possession of the leased premises. Lomar Inc. may collect unpaid rent from:
>
> A.   Trane Corp. only.
> B.   Trane Corp. or Uvalde Corp.
> C.   Trane Corp., Uvalde Corp., or Wawa Corp.
> D.   Trane Corp., Uvalde Corp., Viva. Corp., or Wawa Corp.
> E.   No one.

ANALYSIS. Twelve years after entering into the ground lease, Lomar Inc. assigned the lease and sold its reversion to Mick Inc. The assignment of the lease necessarily includes all rights to collect rents that accrue after the date of the assignment. Lomar no longer owns an interest in the property or the rents and thus can collect rent from no one. It is true that the original ground lease created a privity of contract relationship between the original parties (Lomar

Inc. and Trane Corp.), which is still intact. But the only consequence of this continuing relationship from Lomar's point of view is to make Lomar potentially liable to the current tenant if the current landlord (Mick Inc.) breaches a real covenant set forth in the lease. **E** is the right answer.

QUESTION 7. Multiple transfers revisited. Under the facts of Question 6 above, assume that Mick Inc., the assignee of Lomar Inc., brings an action for unpaid rent. Mick Inc. may collect unpaid rent from:

A. Trane Corp. only.
B. Trane Corp. or Uvalde Corp.
C. Trane Corp., Uvalde Corp., or Wawa Corp.
D. Trane Corp., Uvalde Corp., Viva Corp., or Wawa Corp.
E. No one.

ANALYSIS.   There are plenty of assignments to track here, but the rule to apply is straightforward. The present owner of the leasehold, Wawa Corp., is liable for unpaid rent based on privity of estate. This follows because the tenant's covenant to pay rent is a real covenant that runs with the leasehold estate. Wawa Corp.'s decision to abandon possession of the premises does not eliminate this liability.

Prior tenants are also liable for the unpaid rent if they became liable based on privity of contract. Trane Corp. remains liable based on privity of contract, even though its assignee, Uvalde, agreed to assume the lease obligations. A release takes place only if the landlord (then Lomar) agrees to release the original tenant from liability. There's no indication in the facts of an express release given by Lomar, or any other conduct by Lomar that might amount to an implied release.

Uvalde Corp. became liable when it assumed the lease. The next assignee, Viva Corp., did not assume the lease. It was liable for the rent only while it owned the leasehold based on privity of estate. That liability was extinguished when it made the assignment to Wawa Corp. Thus **C** is the right answer.

 # Smith's Picks

1. Painting the garage   **D**
2. Two tenant transfers   **A**
3. Two tenant transfers revisited   **D**
4. An office lease   **B**
5. Renting to a deadbeat   **E**
6. Multiple transfers   **E**
7. Multiple transfers revisited   **C**

20

Real Estate Contracts of Sale

"Real estate cannot be lost or stolen, nor can it be carried away.
Purchased with common sense, paid for in full, and managed with reasonable care,
it is about the safest investment in the world."
Franklin D. Roosevelt

CHAPTER OVERVIEW
A. Statute of Frauds
B. Part Performance and Equitable Estoppel
C. Equitable Conversion and Risk of Loss
D. Property Quality and Seller's Duty to Disclose Defects
E. Marketable Title
F. The Closer: Contract to Sell Adversely Possessed Land
♦ Smith's Picks

M ost property casebooks have some material on the law governing contracts for the sale of real property. How much emphasis this material receives—and whether it makes it onto the professor's syllabus at all—varies widely. Traditionally, contracts for the sale of personal property (now codified in Uniform Commercial Code article 2) was taught in the contracts law course, and contracts for the sale of real property was taught in the property course, although there is no pedagogical reason justifying that split (at least, no reason apparent to me). In law schools in which real estate contracts receive little emphasis in the introductory property course, the topic is usually covered in the upper-level curriculum, often in a real estate transactions course. Whether or not you are studying real estate contracts in your property course, the subject of the first two sections of the chapter—the statute of frauds and its exceptions, as applied to real property—are usually taught in the beginning course on contracts law.

Real estate contracts are functionally different from the typical contract for the sale of personal property in several respects. When real property is sold, almost always there is a significant period of time between formation of the contract and performance by the parties, which takes place at what is known as the *closing* or *settlement*. The time period between formation and closing is known as the *executory period*. The executory contract period allows the parties to make plans and take a number of actions that usually are not practicable to take before entering into a binding contract. Usually the parties must plan for a change in possession of the property. For a residential sale, the seller must find somewhere else to live, while the buyer must make plans to move, which may involve cancelling an apartment lease or selling an existing residence. Most buyers need financing, so time is needed for shopping for a mortgage loan and the loan application process. Title to the property needs to be investigated, with plans for the buyer and the mortgage lender to receive some type of title assurance in connection with closing—today, usually a title insurance policy. The closing puts an end to the executory contract stage. Although the number and length of documents exchanged and signed at a modern closing can be daunting, the main point is that the seller conveys title to the buyer by execution and delivery of a deed, in exchange for the buyer's payment of the price, which may be facilitated by mortgage financing.[1]

A.   Statute of Frauds

The statute of frauds requires a writing to enforce a contract for the sale of real property. In most states, the modern statute of frauds follows the formulation of the original English statute of frauds from 1677, which requires a "memorandum" signed by "the party to be charged." Laypersons, including some real estate brokers, sometimes believe that this means that the parties must sign a formal, complete contract, but this is not the law. Only a memorandum is required, stating the essential terms, which are:

- **Names of parties**. The writing must identify the parties.
- **Description of real property**. The writing must identify the land. From the description one must be able to locate all the boundaries of the tract.
- **Intent to sell and buy**. The writing must manifest an intent for the seller to sell, and the buyer to buy, the property.
- **Price**. States are divided as to whether price or consideration is an essential term. One position requires a sufficient written statement of price in all cases. Another view allows the memorandum to be silent as to price when the parties have not agreed upon a price, with the law implying a reasonable price. A few states have statutes providing that

---

1. Deeds and mortgages are discussed in chapters 21 and 22, respectively.

the memorandum does not have to state the consideration, which are interpreted to allow proof or an oral price agreement.

Because the memorandum need express only essential terms, it may contain less than the parties' complete agreement. The parties may have understandings that are not clarified or expressed in the writing. Either party may seek to prove other, nonessential terms and conditions that are oral or are set forth in collateral writings. That attempt, however, will not succeed if the court applies the *parol evidence rule* based on a finding that the parties intended the memorandum to serve as a full and complete statement of their agreement.

The traditional statute of frauds does not require mutuality—that both parties sign the memorandum. The party seeking to enforce need not sign; only a signature by the party to be charged is required. This is a point that sometimes confuses students. Before it is determined which person wants to go forward, and which person wants to avoid the contract, the non-signing person in effect has an option. However, when the non-signing person seeks to enforce the deal, manifesting that intent in litigation, that person then becomes bound.

Multiple writings construed together may satisfy the statute of frauds. A single writing signed by the party to be charged is not required. The easiest case is when each of the several writings are signed by the party to be charged. It is generally accepted that signed and unsigned writings may be linked together, when adequate evidence exists that they relate to the same transaction.

The modern statute of frauds no longer requires a paper writing and a traditional signature. The Electronic Signatures in Global and National Commerce Act, 15 U.S.C. §§7001 to 7031 (enacted in 2000 and sometimes called the "E-sign Act"), validates electronic signatures in any transaction in or affecting interstate or foreign commerce, including contracts, sales, leases, or other dispositions of personal and real property. Thus, email, voice mail, and web-based signatures are valid. The signature requirement is flexible, but to be enforceable, the court must find that the person executed or adopted the electronic record "with the intent to sign the record." 15 U.S.C. §7006(5).

QUESTION 1. Agreeing to sell the family farm. Adriana, the elderly owner of an 80-acre farm where she has lived for the past 60 years, no longer has sufficient income to attend to her needs. She meets with her nephew Brock, in her living room. They orally agree that Brock will pay Adriana $180,000, with the understanding that she will be allowed to keep possession of the farmhouse and farm for the rest of her life. Brock writes out a check to her "to seal the deal" for $1,000, adding to the notation field, "purchase of farm." Adriana endorses the check and deposits it into her bank account. Three days later Brock has his lawyer

draft a warranty deed, which purports to convey a present fee simple
from Adriana to Brock and expressly reserves a life estate for Adriana.
The deed describes the land, using the previous description contained
in all the prior deeds in the chain of title since the land was conveyed
by a patent from the United States in 1868. Brock meets Adriana and
asks her to sign the deed in exchange for his payment of the remaining
$179,000. She refuses. Six months later Brock brings an action for
specific performance. Adriana's answer pleads a statute of frauds
defense. Which of the following is likely to become the most important
issue with respect to compliance with the statute of frauds?

A. Identification of the parties.
B. Intent to sell and buy.
C. Description of the property.
D. Description of the price.

ANALYSIS.   Adriana is the "party to be charged," so we must ask whether
she has signed anything. At first blush, maybe not—but her endorsement
of Brock's check is her signature on the back of the check, which acknowl-
edges her receipt of the $1,000 down payment, and the face of the check says,
"purchase of farm." She may claim that her endorsement does not manifest
an intent to be bound by the terms stated on the check, but she isn't likely
to prevail on this point. Moreover, if the check does not count as a memorandum signed by Adriana, then because she has signed nothing else, Brock
cannot establish compliance with any of the elements listed in Choices **A**
through **D**, so there would be no basis for saying one is more of a problem
than the others.

Let's tackle the list in order, assuming she has signed the check for purposes of the statute of frauds. She has not signed the warranty deed, but multiple writings can be considered together when there is evidence that they relate
to the same transaction. Here the notation of the check would satisfy many
courts. Choice **A** asks whether the two writings, read together, adequately
identify the parties. No reason to believe there's a problem here.[2] What about
B, an intent to sell and buy? Together, the two writings point to the intent of
Adriana to sell and Brock to buy her farm. Likewise, there is no major issue
with **C**—the deed amplifies the vague description on the check ("the farm")
by giving a proper legal description of the land and Adriana's retained life
estate. That leaves **D**, the price, as the hardest nut to crack. The check is for

---

2. This multiple-choice question follows the often-followed norm that law school exams refer to parties by first names only. You should presume Adriana and Brock have surnames, shown both on the
check and the deed.

$1,000, with no indication of the total price ($180,000) or how much remains to be paid ($179,000). So **D** is the best answer.[3]

B.   Part Performance and Equitable Estoppel

Relatively few legal rules have no exceptions. The statute of frauds is not one of them. The statute's purpose is to prevent the fraud of a false assertion that an owner had agreed to sell her land, when in fact she had manifested no such intent. After enactment of the statute, the opportunity for fraud in the opposite direction, through invocation of the statute, quickly became apparent. Buyers were sometimes misled into thinking they had a contractual right to property, only to have the alleged seller raise the absence of a writing as a defense to enforcement. Hardship was heightened when the buyer made substantial improvements to the land in reliance on an oral promise to sell.

Courts responded to the occasional harsh consequences of strict enforcement of the statute of frauds by developing the doctrine of part performance, sometimes identified by the alternative label equitable estoppel. There are different views as to what constitutes part performance for the purpose of avoiding the bar of the statute of frauds. Most states require both that the buyer has taken possession under the oral contract and additional acts of the buyer that show a change of position, such as repairing or improving the property or paying all or part of the purchase price. Two separate theories have emerged to justify part performance. First, that the acts serve an evidentiary function, substituting for a writing alternative solid proof that the contract exists and is not the buyer's fabrication. The second theory is the prevention of hardship; the buyer will suffer irreparable injury unless the court intervenes to enforce the oral agreement. Most states have not firmly adopted either the evidentiary theory or the hardship theory; instead, case law has elements supporting both perspectives.

Although most states apply a single doctrine for the enforcement of oral contracts for the sale of real property, the terms *equitable estoppel* and *part performance* have different nuances. Under part performance, as indicated above, courts focus on the actions of the parties, which either provide firm evidence of an oral contract or result in hardship if the alleged contract is not enforced. Conversely, under equitable estoppel, the courts generally focus on the actions of the alleged seller, which may have misled the buyer into spending time and other resources on improving the property.

---

3. This analysis should make you a bit uncomfortable, as it implies that Brock's case becomes much stronger if his attorney had drafted the deed to include a recital of the actual consideration (price). Should an enforcing party be able to "manufacture" statute of frauds compliance by preparing a writing containing an essential term, which is not signed by the party to be charged but is linked to a signed writing through extrinsic evidence? This appears to the author to be a weakness in the standard rule followed in most states that allows multiple writings to be linked together by extrinsic evidence.

> **QUESTION 2. Agreeing to sell the family farm revisited.** Under
> the facts of Question 1 above, suppose that one week after Adriana
> refuses to sign the warranty deed presented to her by Brock, she dies
> of a heart attack. Two weeks later Brock takes possession of Adriana's
> farm and demolishes the farmhouse, a small dilapidated structure. He
> hires an architect to draw up plans for his dream house, and then hires a
> contractor who begins construction work. Four months later an executor
> is appointed for Adriana's estate. Brock meets with the executor, explains
> the agreement he had reached with Adriana for the purchase of her farm,
> and seeks to pay the remaining $179,000 in exchange for the executor's
> conveyance of the property to him. The executor refuses. Brock promptly
> brings an action for specific performance. The executor's answer pleads
> a statute of frauds defense. The court rules that under the law of the
> jurisdiction, the warranty deed prepared by Brock's attorney may not
> be combined with the check for purposes of establishing compliance
> with the statute of frauds. What is Brock's best argument that <u>he should
> prevail,</u> notwithstanding that ruling?
>
> **A.** The check by itself establishes the essential terms of the alleged
>   contract.
> **B.** Brock's actions in paying $1,000, taking possession, demolishing the
>   farmhouse, and beginning construction of a new house demonstrate
>   the existence of a contract.
> **C.** Adriana and the executor are estopped from denying the existence of
>   a contract because they allowed Brock to take possession, demolish
>   the house, and begin construction of a new house.
> **D.** The statute of frauds does not provide a defense to a third party of
>   the alleged contract.

ANALYSIS. The analysis of Question 1 above should have convinced you
that the check alone cannot satisfy the statute of frauds—at best, it identifies the parties and loosely reflects an intent to sell and buy some undefined
"farm." So strike Choice **A**.

  D might seem plausible. Sometimes third parties aren't allowed to gain
benefits or raise claims related to contracts entered into by other people. But
this isn't the case for the statute of frauds. The risk of fraud or perjury is not
diminished when a contracting party dies and a contract is alleged against the
decedent's estate. Indeed, the risk seems greater because the decedent is no
longer able to testify to the falsity of the plaintiff's assertions.

  That leaves us with **B** and **C**. They refer, respectively, to the part performance and equitable estoppel exceptions to the statute of frauds. The language
of **B**, arguing that Brock's actions "demonstrate the existence of a contract,"
invokes the evidentiary theory of part performance. The language of **C**, arguing estoppel, focuses on the conduct of first Adriana, and later the executor,

in allowing Brock to rely on the alleged oral contract to his detriment. This is weak factually. Brock took possession after Adriana died, so plainly she did nothing to mislead or encourage him beyond cashing his down payment check. Brock did not meet with the executor until after he began construction of his house, and there is no evidence that the executor knew he was in possession of the farm before that meeting. So **B** is the better answer.

This is not to say that Brock would necessarily win this case, or even that it's probable that he would win. The question asks you to select his best argument. The court well might conclude that at best there was an oral agreement that was not completed before Adriana's death, and there is no sufficient reason to compel a conveyance after her death.

C.   Equitable Conversion and Risk of Loss

Laypersons often view a contract as having no effect on the seller's ownership of the property prior to closing, with the buyer equivalently acquiring no property rights prior to closing. This straightforward view, however, contravenes the doctrine of equitable conversion. The doctrine of equitable conversion splits title between the seller and the buyer. The moment the contract is formed, the buyer is said to acquire equitable title, or equitable ownership, and the seller is said to retain legal title. At closing, when the contract is fully performed (executed), the seller conveys legal title to the buyer by signing and delivering a deed. That reunites the separate equitable and legal titles, giving the buyer complete title.

Equitable conversion, as the name implies, is a rule of equity. It rests upon the equitable remedy of specific performance. More particularly, it applies only when the court finds that the alleged agreement is binding and is specifically enforceable at the point in time that is relevant, based on the dispute in question.

The splitting of the title by way of the doctrine of equitable conversion has a number of consequences. First, under equitable conversion both parties have property rights while the contract is executory. They may transfer all or part of their property rights to third parties, unless the contract imposes express restrictions on transfer. For example, either party may assign, mortgage, or devise her interest.

Second, the buyer's equitable title is treated as real property, but the seller's legal title is treated as personal property, the reasoning being that the seller has bargained for a price, to be paid in money (money, like chattels, is personal property). The seller holds legal title as security for the buyer's obligation to pay the price. Notwithstanding the buyer's equitable ownership, the seller retains the right to possession until closing, unless the contract otherwise provides.

A third important consequence of equitable conversion has to do with risk of loss. The buyer's equitable title is conceived as the real, beneficial ownership of the property, and thus the buyer has both the advantage of any increase in value that may occur, and the risk of loss that may occur, during the executory period. Common situations involve casualty—the destruction of improvements or damage to the land by fire, hurricane, or similar natural disasters. The traditional view of equitable conversion allocates risk of loss to the buyer, unless the contract has an express term providing for a different risk allocation. Many states have departed from the traditional risk of loss rule, at least in some circumstances. Some of the departures are based on statute, others are judge-made law. The most prominent statute is the Uniform Vendor and Purchaser Risk Act, adopted by 12 states, which allocates the risk to the vendor if the purchaser has not taken possession and "all or a material part [of the property] is destroyed without fault of the purchaser or is taken by eminent domain." Judicial softening of equitable conversion sometimes has followed the uniform act's approach. Other alternatives include consideration of which party is in a better situation to prevent or reduce the loss, and the application of contract doctrines of impossibility of performance, frustration of purpose, and failure of consideration.

QUESTION 3.   Ice storm ravages orange grove. Savannah enters into a written contract to sell a 44-acre orange grove to Bruce for $400,000. Bruce pays Savannah $40,000 in earnest money. During the executory contract period, while Savannah is still in possession, an ice storm damages all the orange trees upon the real estate, which reduces the fair market value of the real estate by $150,000. The contract has no provision that covers this problem, and neither party has any insurance that covers the loss. Bruce tells Savannah that he is rescinding the contract and he wants his earnest money back. Savannah refuses and brings an action against Bruce for specific performance. If Savannah prevails, the most likely reason will be:

A. The failure of Bruce to insure his interest as the purchaser precludes any relief for him.

B. Bruce did not take adequate precautions to reduce the risk of damage from the storm.

C. After the parties entered into the contract Savannah's interest in the orange grove is personal property and Bruce's interest is real property.

D. Equity treats Bruce as the real owner of the orange grove after the parties entered into the contract.

E. The risk of damage from an ice storm was reasonably foreseeable when the parties entered into the contract.

ANALYSIS. This question tests understanding of the doctrine of equitable conversion. In many states today, Savannah might not succeed in her action of specific performance, but the question in essence stipulates that she will win, and asks you to select the best explanation or rationale for that outcome.

Choice **A** is incorrect because the doctrine of equitable conversion applies regardless of whether seller or buyer has insurance. If Bruce had obtained insurance, he would still bear the risk of loss of the ice storm. Insurance would have eliminated or reduced his economic loss stemming from having to go forward with the contract, but it would not immunize him from Savannah's specific performance action.

Choices **B** and **E** are similar. Both are nuanced responses that may initially sound plausible, but do not withstand scrutiny. Nothing in the facts suggests anything Bruce could have done to protect the orange trees from the ice storm, but this is beside the point. Equitable conversion transfers the risk of loss to the buyer, whether or not the buyer's exercise of reasonable care (or extraordinary care) would prevent the loss. Similarly, it does not matter whether the ice storm is seen as reasonably foreseeable, or an astonishing meteorological event.

Both **C** and **D** have the virtue of correctly stating elements of the doctrine of equitable conversion. **D** is the better answer. **C** accurately indicates that equitable conversion treats the seller as owning personal property (the right to collect the price) and the buyer as owning real property, but characterization is not the issue raised by this question. By referring to Bruce as "the real owner of the orange grove" **D** implies that he bears the risk of loss (and has the benefit of any possible increase in value) — this is the core of the equitable conversion doctrine.

D. Property Quality and Seller's Duty to Disclose Defects

Traditionally, the doctrine of caveat emptor governs the buyer's right with respect to quality and condition of the property being purchased. Commonly translated as "buyer beware," the buyer is expected to inspect the property and draw her own conclusions as to its condition and suitability for her purposes. Concomitantly, the seller is not liable for defects existing at the time of sale, and has no duty to disclose defects to the buyer, even when known to the seller.

Substantial erosion to the caveat emptor doctrine has taken place, beginning more than a century ago. Many jurisdictions retain some version of caveat emptor, modified by exceptions, the most typical ones being (a) a seller duty to disclose defects that present a risk of personal injury to possessors or users, (b) a seller duty not to take affirmative measures to conceal defects, and (c) a seller duty to disclose latent defects (those that are not discoverable by a buyer's reasonable inspection). Some jurisdictions (e.g., California) impose a duty on the seller to disclose all material defects known to the seller.

The baseline rules on property quality and disclosure rules are generally subject to modification in the contract of sale. Many contracts have express provisions on point. The contract may contain express representations and warranties by the seller; alternatively, many contracts provide that the buyer will take the property "as is" with the buyer waiving any claims with respect to defects. Often the contract provides for the buyer to inspect the property prior to closing, setting out procedures and the buyer's rights if the inspection discloses problems.

Until the middle part of the twentieth century, sales of new homes by builders and developers were subject to the normal baseline of caveat emptor, modified by any express representations and warranties given by the seller. Most states have departed from this framework, treating the sale of new homes much like the sale of goods. Courts developed an implied warranty of habitability, similar to the Uniform Commercial Code implied warranty of merchantability for the sale of goods (UCC §2-314). Merchantability means the house must be reasonably fit to live in according to the community standards for housing of the type involved. As is common for the sale of goods, most sellers of new homes use contracts that disclaim all implied warranties and in its place substitute an express warranty. Many builders offer their own express warranties to buyers of new homes, but more significant are standardized warranties given or guaranteed by third parties. Also, many real estate brokerage companies offer insurance on used homes to help relieve buyers' fear of unknown problems with respect to the property they are purchasing.

> **QUESTION 4:   A house infested with bats.** Tucker contracted to sell a 12-year-old single-family house to Donatella for $380,000, pursuant to a contract providing that the purchaser would take the property in an "as is" condition. Prior to closing, Donatella arranged for a termite inspection and an inspection of the central heating and cooling system, which revealed no problems. Donatella and her family took possession immediately after closing. Two weeks later, they started to hear noises in the walls of the house at night. The noises were not heard during the day. Donatella hired a pest-control company, which found that there were bats living in the walls, entering through several small holes near the roof line. Donatella learned that it would cost $4,000 to remove the bat colony that is living in the walls. Tucker had lived in the house immediately prior to the sale, <u>heard the sounds</u> of bats at night, and <u>said nothing</u> about the noise to Donatella. She brings an action against Tucker for damages. The most probable result is:
>
> **A.** The action will fail because the "as is" clause immunizes Tucker from liability.
> **B.** The action will fail because the bats are a patent defect.

C. The action will succeed because Tucker actively concealed the presence of the bats in the house.

D. The action will succeed because the bats violate the implied warranty of habitability.

ANALYSIS. The fact pattern presents a close case, with the outcome difficult to predict and likely to turn on the particular rules followed by the state whose law governs. If these facts were presented in an essay question, you would need to develop the arguments for both parties. These facts are based upon *Donnelly v. Taylor*, 786 N.E.2d 119 (Ohio Ct. Common Pleas 2002), which held in favor of the seller based on Ohio's retention of caveat emptor, subject to exceptions that include the seller's active misrepresentation of the condition of the property or active concealment of a defect. Because you cannot tell who is likely to prevail, your task is to evaluate the strength of the four rationales set forth in the answers.

Choice **A** is plausible, in that the "as is" clause is a plus factor for the seller in many states. Its weakness is its bluntness. No qualifications are expressed. No state will treat an "as is" as airtight, to insulate the seller from all liability, no matter how egregious the facts.

Choice **B** says the bats are a patent defect. True, if the court finds that the bats are a patent defect, that conclusion means Tucker will not be liable, but the facts point the other way. The bats only make noise at night, and presumably Donatella did not visit the house then. It's highly likely the bats are a latent defect. **C**, like **B**, is flawed because it's contrary to the facts. There's no evidence that Tucker did anything that would amount to concealment of the defect, such as removing bat droppings from visible areas or covering holes in the structure used by the bats for access.

Choice **D** says the bats violate the implied warranty of habitability. This might be a good answer if there is one, although the facts do not indicate whether the noise is a sufficiently major problem so as to render the home uninhabitable, or not reasonably habitable. Perhaps the noise is just an annoyance. But even if the noise is severe enough to make the home not inhabitable, this transaction is the sale of a used house by an individual. The implied warranty applies to the sale of new housing (or sometimes almost new housing) by builders or developers. We must circle back to **A** as the best answer. It's the only one without a major flaw.

E.   Marketable Title

Under the contract of sale, the buyer has the right to marketable title (a synonymous term is merchantable title). A marketable title is one that is good in fact, not subject to any encumbrances or encroachments, and free from reasonable doubt.

Marketable title is both an implied promise and an implied condition. As a promise, the buyer has the right to collect damages if the seller's title turns out not to be marketable. As a condition, if title is not marketable, the buyer has the right to rescind, ending her obligation to pay the price and close the purchase.

Issues of timing sometimes arise. The seller's title must be marketable only at the closing, not earlier. This means that when the buyer identifies a title defect, the seller is entitled to a reasonable time to cure that defect; and if the defect is a lien, the seller is entitled to use the purchase price to pay off the lien as part of the closing process.

Marketable title is an implied term, which the parties' contract may elaborate, expand, or limit. For example, sellers commonly include a provision that makes the title subject to easements and building restrictions. This means that the buyer is waiving her right to complain about the impact of those encumbrances.

QUESTION 5.   Judgment lien stops closing. Terrance enters into a written agreement to sell his house and lot to Hayley for $450,000. The agreement says nothing about the quality of the title that Terrance must provide, or the procedure by which Hayley may raise a title objection. At the place and time designated for the closing, Terrance tenders an appropriate warranty deed, but Hayley refuses to accept the deed and to pay the price. She explains that her title search has revealed a judgment lien on the property, filed against Luther, a prior owner of the property, securing a judgment for $800. Terrance denies that he is responsible for the lien. He brings an action against Hayley for specific performance. The probable outcome is:

A.   The court will deny specific performance.
B.   The court will grant specific performance because the amount of the lien is de minimis compared to the purchase price.
C.   The court will grant specific performance because Terrance is not responsible for the failure of a third party to pay his debt.
D.   The court will grant specific performance because Hayley should have made her title objection before the date of closing.

ANALYSIS.   The key to this question is understanding the scope of the seller's obligation to provide a marketable title. The answers follow a pattern that I use with some regularity. You must decide which party is likely to prevail—will Terrance succeed in his action for specific performance? If so, then you must choose among **B, C,** and **D** for the best explanation of why the court should grant relief. If not, **A** is the right answer, even though it gives no explanation whatsoever of the law that supports that conclusion.

Here **A** is correct. Title is not marketable if it is subject to any encumbrance that is not permitted by the parties' contract. All liens, including judgment liens, are encumbrances. Because the contract is silent as the standard for title, Hayley has the implied right to marketable title, free of all encumbrances.

Choices **B**, **C**, and **D** are wrong because they reach the wrong conclusion as to the merits of the action. Moreover, none of the rationales hold up. As for **B**, the amount of the lien makes no difference. The smaller it is compared to the price, the more likely it is that the seller will agree to discharge it at his expense, rather than risk losing the sale—but that isn't what Terrance did here. As for **C**, the facts imply that the judgment lien is valid. Terrance's culpability for the title defect is not material. The buyer is guaranteed marketable title, regardless of the seller's fault. As for **D**, the contract imposes no time limit on the buyer's right to object to title. If Hayley makes an objection at closing, she has to give Terrance a reasonable period of time to cure the problem, if he agrees to seek a cure—but he did not do so; instead, he disclaimed his obligation.

F.   The Closer: Contract to Sell Adversely Possessed Land

As we saw in the last section, a contract of sale obligates the seller to provide a marketable title. Title examination is complicated and is typically done by a specialist, either a real estate attorney or another professionally trained person, such as a title abstractor or title insurance employee. There is a split of authority on whether the seller's title must be provable based solely on the public land records. Record title requires proof of the status of title, gathered solely from deeds and other instruments that are recorded in the public records for recording interests in real property.[4] This means that the seller's title cannot depend on an unrecorded instrument, such as a deed that hasn't been recorded or a will that hasn't been probated. Some states (e.g., California) hold that marketable title must be based on the records. If the seller is relying on evidence that is not on the records, the seller must cure the problem by recording sufficient documentation. Other states (e.g., New York) allow the seller to establish marketable title by producing adequate unrecorded evidence that establishes title or resolves a particular problem.

One area addressed by the competing rules involves the problem of adverse possession. If the seller relies on the doctrine of adverse possession to establish title to all or a part of the land under contract, the seller lacks record

---

4. For discussion of recordation and its legal significance, see chapter 23.

marketable title unless the seller has sued the true record owner and obtained judgment.[5] The record-marketable-title rule allocates the cost and risk of litigation to the seller, allowing the seller to transfer that risk to the buyer only by an express contract term. Conversely, the rule allowing marketable title to be proven by off-record evidence allocates the litigation risk to the buyer, based on the idea that the seller's evidence is strong enough that either there never will be litigation, or if there is, the buyer will easily win. In a state following this rule, the buyer may include a term in the contract requiring that the seller have a record marketable title.

QUESTION 6.   Fence encroaches on ranch. Sejal contracts to sell 120 acres of ranch land to Jared for $9,000 per acre. The tract of land is rectangular in shape, with fences running along all boundaries. The written contract attached a survey obtained by Sejal when she bought the ranch 18 years ago, which certified the acreage. The contract allowed Jared to obtain a new survey prior to closing and to raise an objection to title if the survey or a title search revealed any defect that made title unmarketable. Jared orders a survey, which shows that the fence running along the western boundary line encroaches upon the record title of the adjoining tract to the west of Sejal's property. Jared objects to Sejal's lack of record title to that area, which constitutes six acres in size. Sejal responds that she has title to that area by adverse possession, and that such title is marketable for purposes of her contract with Jared. But Jared seeks to rescind the contract, and brings an action against Sejal for the recovery of the earnest money that he had paid into escrow. Which of the following makes it most likely that the court will deny the relief required by Jared?

A.   Sejal tenders affidavits from persons attesting that the fence has been in its present location for the past 40 years, with no objection raised by the record owner.

B.   Sejal tenders proof that she had paid real estate taxes on the disputed six-acre parcel every year since she purchased the ranch.

C.   Sejal tenders a quitclaim deed, in recordable form, signed by the record owner of six-acre parcel, releasing and relinquishing all of his right and claim to that property.

D.   Sejal tenders an agreement, signed by the record owner of six-acre parcel, consenting to the fence remaining in its present location.

---

5. The judicial decree in favor of the seller would be recorded in the land records.

ANALYSIS.   The contract of sale guarantees Jared marketable title, but does not provide that Sejal must produce a clear title of record. Many states hold that title resting in adverse possession, if clearly established, is marketable. The affidavits referred to in choice **A** may meet that standard, although the content of the affidavits are not described in sufficient detail to be sure.

Choice **B**, Sejal's long-term payment of taxes, may support her adverse possession claim in some jurisdictions, but by itself, it is not sufficient for her to gain title by adverse possession. It is a much weaker answer than **A**.

Choices **C** and **D** share a strength: both consist of submission of a writing signed by the owner of the record title that, hopefully, would have the effect of precluding a future claim of title by that person. The quitclaim deed, a conveyance, is much stronger than the agreement described in **D**. The agreement, couched in terms of consent, does not bear on any of the essential elements of adverse possession.[6] Indeed, depending upon its exact wording, it could work *against* an adverse possession claim by indicating that Sejal's possession is (and was) with the consent of the true owner, with that consent being revocable (a license). At best, the agreement grants an easement that allows the continued use of the land between the fence and the record boundary line. It does not transfer title. The quitclaim deed, on the other hand, conveys title to Sejal, which she can pass to Jared, regardless of the merits of Sejal's adverse possession claim. So **C** is the best answer.

✦ Smith's Picks

1. Agreeing to sell the family farm	D
2. Agreeing to sell the family farm revisited	B
3. Ice storm ravages orange grove	D
4. A house infested with bats	A
5. Judgment lien stops closing	A
6. Fence encroaches on ranch	C

---

6. For discussion of adverse possession of real property, see chapter 6.

Deeds

"Our deeds determine us, as much as we determine our deeds."
George Eliot,[1] Adam Bede ch. XXIX (1859)

CHAPTER OVERVIEW
A. Covenants of Title
B. Quitclaim Deeds
C. Delivery
D. Land Descriptions
E. Defects in Deeds
F. The Closer: Estoppel by Deed
 Smith's Picks

Many property courses include an introduction to deeds, covering the requirements for a deed to be legally effective, the types of deeds and deed warranties, the parts of the standard deed, and some focus on the rules governing interpretation and construction of deeds. In other beginning property courses, especially single-semester courses, the law of deeds receives little or no coverage. With the latter approach, study of this subject is deferred until the upper-level curriculum, where it is included in a course such as real estate transactions. This chapter lays out the basic concepts that you are likely to encounter if your property course includes deeds in its subject matter. It is worth noting that even if your course does not include a specific unit on deeds, learning some of the basics will help further your understanding of related subject matters such as estates, future interests, covenants, and servitudes. Many of your assigned cases refer to deeds, and fact patterns on law school property exams often refer to deeds. Even when those cases and exams are not focused on a problem related to the deed, it improves

---

1. Pseudonym of Mary Ann Evans.

your overall understanding of the material if you have a general sense of the various types of deeds and the sorts of issues involving deeds that often arise.

A deed is an instrument that conveys an interest in land. Although other types of instruments may function to convey interests in land, a deed is by far the most common instrument of conveyance used in the United States. Oral transfers of title to land are prohibited by the statute of frauds, which imposes the following requirements:

- **Parties.** The writing must identify the parties.
- **Land.** The writing must identify the land. The part of the deed that does this is often called the *legal description*.
- **Intent to convey.** The writing must manifest an intent to convey an estate or other property interest.

The parties to a deed are usually identified as *grantor* and *grantee*, whether the deed consummates a sale of the land or a gift of the land. The deed plays the crucial role of effecting and documenting, in final form, the transfer of title from the grantor to the grantee. Deeds tend to be standardized forms, but the forms vary substantially from state to state. In many states, a statute specifies a deed form that may be used, with many printed forms and software-generated forms following the statutory guidelines. Such a *statutory-form deed* is optional. Parties may use other forms that also satisfy the legal requirements for deeds, but in many states statutory-form deeds are widely used.

A.   Covenants of Title

Deeds have different allocations of title risk between the parties. The allocation is often bargained over in transactions involving the sale of land. With a quitclaim deed, the buyer bears all the risk of title defects, and seller has no risk.[2] Every deed that is not a quitclaim deed has one or more covenants of title.

Historically, all title covenants had to be expressly written in the deed. There were no implied title covenants at common law. A deed with no express covenants was a quitclaim deed as a matter of law. In most states today, however, the use of a certain phrase or a statutory deed form creates implied title covenants. These statutes vary widely from state to state. This means that every deed of conveyance must be construed in light of the state statutes that govern deeds.

There are six different covenants of title in standard use in the United States. Three of the six are considered to be *present covenants*. Any breach of a present covenant occurs at the time of delivery of the deed. This is when the statute of limitations begins to run. Present covenants do not run with

---

2. Quitclaims deeds are further discussed in Section B of this chapter.

the land. This means that a grantee may sue only her immediate grantor on a present covenant. If the grantee has conveyed the property to another person, that subsequent grantee does not acquire the cause of action. The three present covenants are:

- **Covenant of seisin.** The grantor promises that she is seized of the estate the deed purports to convey. The concept of seisin implies that the grantor is in possession of the land being conveyed. If the grantor is not in actual possession at the time of the conveyance, the immediate right to possession suffices. Today most courts view the covenant of seisin as a promise of good title to the estate, although historically a person could be in wrongful possession of land and still have seisin if she claimed ownership of an estate.
- **Covenant of right to convey.** The grantor promises that she has the legal right to convey the estate the deed purports to convey. This covenant overlaps with the covenant of seisin, but not completely. Normally, an owner who is in possession of a fee simple estate has an unqualified right of transfer. A trustee, however, may have a power of sale but may not have seisin (the right to present possession). Such a trustee may include a covenant of the right to convey in a deed but would not want to include a covenant of seisin. Conversely, an owner in possession may have seisin but may lack the right to convey because there is an outstanding interest that limits transfer, such as a restraint on alienation or a right of first refusal.
- **Covenant against encumbrances.** The grantor promises that there are no encumbrances on the land. An encumbrance is a nonpossessory right or interest in the property held by a third party that reduces the value of the property, restricts its use, or imposes an obligation on the property owner. Encumbrances include easements, real covenants, equitable servitudes, marital property rights, mortgage liens, tax liens, and other liens and charges.

The other three covenants of title are considered to be *future covenants*. A future covenant looks to the future in that it protects the grantee from certain specified events that may occur after the deed is delivered, that is, in the future. A future covenant may be breached at the time of delivery, and a breach also may take place at any time later. Future covenants run with the land provided they have not been breached at the time of the transfer of title to the subsequent grantee. "Running with the land" means that the present owner may sue a former owner of the land, in the chain of title past the owner's immediate grantor, who conveyed by a deed containing a future covenant. The three future covenants are

- **Covenant of quiet enjoyment.** The grantor promises that the grantee may possess and quietly enjoy the land.[3] The covenant of quiet enjoyment

---

3. This covenant is much like its namesake in landlord tenant law, in which the landlord covenants that the tenant may quietly enjoy the leased premises. See chapter 17. The only significant difference is that the covenant is usually implied in leases but at common law all covenants in deeds must be express.

is breached if the grantee is evicted from all or part of the land by the grantor, by someone claiming under the grantor, or by someone with paramount title. The eviction may be actual or constructive. An *actual eviction* occurs when the grantee physically loses possession of some or all of the property. A *constructive eviction* occurs when the grantee still has physical possession, but an event related to title substantially limits the grantee's ability to make full use of the property. Compare *Brown v. Lober*, 389 N.E.2d 1188 (Ill. 1979) (no constructive eviction when grantee cannot sell coal rights due to outstanding two-thirds interest in mineral rights), with *Booker T. Washington Construction & Design Co. v. Huntington Urban Renewal Authority*, 383 S.E.2d 41 (W. Va. 1989) (when grantor warrants a fee simple but has only a life estate and grantee has contracted to resell the property, constructive eviction occurs when grantee is sued for lack of marketable title).

- **Covenant of warranty.** The grantor warrants the title to the grantee. The typical language of this covenant is that the grantor will "warrant and forever defend" title to the conveyed land. In most states, this covenant has the same scope as the covenant of quiet enjoyment: a breach results from an actual or constructive eviction of the grantee. In many states, there is a remedial distinction between the covenant of quiet enjoyment and the covenant of warranty. Both covenants allow the grantee to recover damages based on the loss of possession. The covenant of warranty provides additional protection. Due to the promise to defend title, the grantor must pay the grantee's costs of defending title against third parties, including reasonable attorneys' fees.

- **Covenant of further assurances.** The grantor promises to give whatever "further assurances" may be required in the future to vest the grantee with the title the deed purports to convey. If the deed is defective in some respect, this covenant obligates the grantor to execute a new, corrected deed. Often, this covenant also obligates the grantor to take reasonable measures to cure title. For example, the grantor may have to obtain the release of a lien or another interest held by a third party. For the other five covenants described above, the remedy for breach is damages. In appropriate cases, if the grantor breaches by refusing to give further assurances, the court will allow the remedy of specific performance.

A covenant of title can take one of two forms. The form used has a major impact on the allocation of risk of title defects between the grantor and the grantee. Most deeds used in the United States are *general warranty deeds*. With this type of deed, the covenant protects the grantee against any and all defects that may have arisen anytime during the entire chain of title up to the time of delivery. In contrast, a *special warranty deed* or *limited warranty deed* protects the grantee only against defects arising while the grantor owned the property. Defects that arose prior to the grantor's acquisition of title are not covered by the title covenant.

> **QUESTION 1.   A missing share of Blackacre.** In 2009 Abigail, the owner of Blackacre, dies intestate. Title passes to five heirs, who take equal interests as tenants in common. In 2010, four of the heirs join in a general warranty deed to Bruno that purports to convey the entire estate. This warranty deed contains all six of the standard covenants of title. In 2014 Bruno conveys Blackacre to Claire, using a special warranty deed that contains all six of the standard covenants of title. In 2015, the missing heir appears and informs Claire that he owns an undivided one-fifth interest in Blackacre. Does Claire have a cause of action against Bruno under the 2014 warranty deed?
>
> **A.** Yes, because the missing heir's interest breaches the covenant of seisin.
> **B.** Yes, because the missing heir's interest breaches the covenant against encumbrances.
> **C.** No, because Claire has not been evicted from all or part of Blackacre.
> **D.** No, because the title Bruno conveyed to Claire had the same quality as the title he received in 2010.

ANALYSIS.   Let's go down the list in order. Claire certainly has not obtained what she expected because she owns only 80 percent of Blackacre. The missing heir owns an undivided one-fifth interest. Of the three present covenants (covenant of seisin, covenant of right to convey, and covenant against encumbrances), which one might apply? The first two are cited in answers **A** and **B**. At the time of conveyance in 2014, Bruno did not have good title to the entire estate, so this could breach the covenant of seisin. Bruno did have the right to convey all that he owns, so there is no breach of the covenant of right to convey. Whether there might be a breach of the covenant against encumbrances depends on whether the missing heir's interest is an encumbrance. There are many types of encumbrances, but they are all non-possessory rights to real property. The missing heir, as cotenant, has a right to shared possession. That outstanding interest, although a title defect, is not an encumbrance. Thus, **B** is incorrect.

Answer **C** appears plausible. It is related to the covenant of quiet enjoyment and covenant of warranty, both of which require the grantee to prove an eviction to establish a breach by the grantor. The facts do not indicate that the missing heir has entered Blackacre, so clearly there is no actual eviction. Many states recognize a constructive eviction as sufficient for a grantee to obtain relief. If the heir has threatened Claire that he will take possession, or if he is otherwise interfering with Claire's use and enjoyment, that might constitute a constructive eviction. We don't have enough facts here to tell.

Let's study **D**. The proposition stated there is true. Bruno received four-fifths of Blackacre by the deed from the four heirs in 2010, and he passed this precise interest to Claire by deed in 2014. Why might this matter? The critical fact is that Bruno conveyed to Claire by special warranty deed. This type of deed provides the grantee with limited protection. Bruno is covenanting only that he didn't create any title defects—that he didn't mess up the title. Here the defect, a missing one-fifth fee interest, predated his acquisition of title, and therefore he isn't liable under a special warranty deed. **D** is the best answer. **A** would be correct if Bruno had conveyed by general warranty deed, but he did not. **C** is weak for two reasons. As indicated above, the missing heir's "informing" Claire of his share might be a constructive eviction. More important, Bruno cannot be held liable for breach of the covenant of quiet enjoyment or covenant of warranty because his special warranty deed promises only that Claire will not be evicted due to a title defect he created or suffered.

B.   Quitclaim Deeds

A quitclaim deed has no covenants of title expressly stated in the instrument or implied by statute because the deed uses certain language. A warranty deed gives the grantee some types of protection with respect to title defects, but with a quitclaim deed the grantee bears all the title risk. If it turns out that the property is subject to liens, encumbrances, or other title defects, the grantor is not liable. A quitclaim deed, however, is completely effective in transferring to the grantee whatever title the grantor actually has.

Quitclaim deeds are rarely used in the sale of real estate when the buyer agrees to pay a market value price. Such buyers almost always insist on a warranty deed. People regularly use quitclaim deeds in either of two scenarios. In a gift of real property, the donor may choose a quitclaim deed to make it clear that the donor will not be liable if the donee discovers title problems. Quitclaim deeds are also often used to resolve title disputes or to clear up questions about titles. The present owner will attempt to persuade the holder of a potential claim to the property to execute a quitclaim deed to relinquish that claim. The owner, of course, would prefer not to have to pay the quitclaim grantor but may decide to offer a modest payment to "buy off" a debatable outstanding claim.

QUESTION 2.   Unpaid property taxes on a run-down house.
Cassandra owns a small lot that has a small, dilapidated house that has stood vacant for the past eight years. She is approached by a community land trust that seeks to acquire such properties to rehabilitate the structures and sell them as affordable housing to first-time homeowners. Cassandra decides that this is a great use for this property, which she no longer wants. She agrees to donate the property to the land trust, planning to reduce her income taxes by taking a charitable deduction.

Cassandra conveys the lot to the land trust using a quitclaim deed. At the time of conveyance, it turns out that Cassandra is two years delinquent in paying local real property taxes on the lot. Under state law, the local government holds a tax lien on the lot, which arose prior to Cassandra's conveyance to the land trust. When the community land trust learns about the unpaid taxes, it brings an action against Cassandra to compel her to pay the back taxes or to pay damages. What result?

A. Cassandra prevails because the land trust assumed the risk of a tax lien.

B. Cassandra prevails because the local government has not yet sought to foreclose its tax lien.

C. The land trust prevails because the tax lien is an encumbrance.

D. The land trust prevails because Cassandra breached an implied duty to disclose the fact that she was delinquent in paying taxes.

ANALYSIS. The key here is to focus on Cassandra's use of a quitclaim deed to convey to the land trust. The idea is that she is making no promises whatsoever with respect to the quality of title to the property. Therefore, even before you begin reading the answer choices, you should expect that Cassandra will prevail by reason of the quitclaim deed. Although none of the answers uses the term "quitclaim deed," right off the bat **A** expresses the core idea. By accepting a quitclaim deed, the land trust assumed the risk of all title defects, which, of course, includes the tax lien. **A** is the right answer.

Now let's check off the remaining choices. **B** is weak because Cassandra should win because of the quitclaim deed even if the local government is actively pursuing foreclosure or has already foreclosed. **C** is wrong: although the tax lien is an encumbrance and thus would breach a covenant against encumbrances, by definition the quitclaim deed contains no such covenant against encumbrances.

D asserts that Cassandra breached an implied duty to tell the land trust that the property she was donating was subject to delinquent property taxes, which she was planning not to pay. There's a good chance that Cassandra knew she was delinquent in paying the taxes at the time she agreed to make the donation and conveyed to the land trust, although the facts are silent on this point. I rank **D** as the second-best answer, as it recognizes that if the land trust is to prevail, it must allege a claim that is not based on the quitclaim deed. I can conceive of the land trust winning on an implied duty theory in some court, but it would be very much an uphill battle. Cassandra made no express representation as to the payment of taxes. Although sellers of real estate are sometimes held liable for failing to disclose material defects to buyers, the facts here don't match the typical cases for liability. First, Cassandra is a donor, not a seller. Second, the unpaid taxes are a matter of public record, so the land trust could have checked into this before accepting the deed. Third, when Cassandra tendered a quitclaim deed, this put the land trust on notice that there could be title defects for which Cassandra was eschewing responsibility.

C.   Delivery

A deed must be signed by the grantor (this is called *execution*), but this is not sufficient for the deed to be valid. Delivery to the grantee is essential. Physical transport of the instrument to the grantee is the normal method of delivery. Such a transfer of possession of the deed, called *manual delivery*, transfers title at that moment, provided the grantor intended the conveyance to be effective then. When land is sold, delivery is rarely called into question because the buyer had possession of the deed after closing. Manual delivery has taken place.

The law does not always require manual delivery of the deed. Delivery is more broadly defined as any objective manifestation that the grantor intends the deed to be presently operative and intends to transfer ownership. In dona-tive transfers, unlike sales transactions, delivery is frequently contested, giving rise to an appreciable volume of litigation. Delivery may be called into question when the grantor never physically delivers the signed deed to the grantee but stores it under circumstances indicating she may have intended it to be legally effective. See *Wiggill v. Cheney*, 597 P.2d 1351 (Utah 1979), finding there was no delivery when the grantor put a deed in her safety deposit box, instructing her co-depositor to give the deed to the grantee at the grantor's death.

Disputes over delivery often arise when the grantor hands or transfers the deed to a third person. Courts sometimes resolve the question by resort to agency principles. If the holder is the grantee's agent, physical transfer of pos-session of the deed to the agent is as effective as manual delivery to the grantee personally. But if the holder is the grantor's agent, there is no delivery because the grantor has the power and the right to recall the deed.

QUESTION 3.   **Deed held by attorney when grantor dies.** Virginia, the owner of Blackacre, had three children: Carol, Susan, and James. Carol had severe medical problems and needed surgery but had no health insurance coverage. Carol and Susan were expecting to inherit Blackacre someday. They approached Virginia, asking her to convey Blackacre to them as an "early inheritance." They planned to obtain a $100,000 mortgage loan on Blackacre, using the funds to pay for Carol's medical expenses. After Virginia orally agreed to the plan, Carol and Susan visited Frank, who was Virginia's lawyer and had represented Virginia in the past on a number of matters. Carol and Susan asked Frank to prepare a deed. Frank prepared a warranty deed to Blackacre. Three days later, on Friday, June 1, Virginia came to Frank's office, where she signed the deed. Her signature was notarized by Frank's paralegal. Carol and Susan were not present at this meeting. Frank retained the deed, telling Virginia that he would record it in the public record next week. On Sunday, June 3, Virginia died in an auto accident. She had no will at the time of her death. Frank did not record the deed. Carol and Susan claim that the deed is valid and that they own Blackacre as cotenants. James claims the deed is invalid and thus he and his sisters each own a one-third share of Blackacre as heirs. Which is true?

A. The deed is valid because Virginia voluntarily signed it.
B. The deed is valid because Virginia transferred possession of the deed to her agent before she died.
C. The deed is invalid because there was no delivery before Virginia died.
D. The deed is invalid because it was not recorded before Virginia died.

ANALYSIS. Recognize that the crucial issue here is the delivery of Virginia's deed to Carol and Susan. The facts are not sufficiently detailed to enable us to predict the outcome with confidence. The key question is whether Virginia, when she left the deed with Frank on Friday, gave up control of the deed, with no right to recall it. In other words, did she intend a present transfer of title to her daughters then, or at some later point, such as the time of recording? Frank's testimony as to his conversation with Virginia on Friday will be highly important. The facts of this question are based on *Caruso v. Parkos*, 637 N.W.2d 351 (Neb. 2002), finding delivery after careful examination of evidence presented by both sides.

A is incorrect. Not only does it omit the key issue of delivery, but it implies that a grantor's signature of a deed (execution) itself is sufficient to transfer ownership to the grantees. Similarly, **D** is wrong as it implies that a deed must be recorded in order for title to be transferred to the grantees.[4]

Choices **B** and **C** both speak of delivery, the point of this question. Which is better? **B** assumes a valid delivery based on Virginia's allowing Frank to retain the deed, after she signed it, for the purpose of recording. **C** states there was no delivery, with no explanation of why not. If we could spot no additional information in either response, we would essentially have a coin flip. But read **B** again carefully. It describes Frank as Virginia's agent. An attorney normally serves as the agent of the client and an agent has a duty to follow the principal's reasonable instructions. The wording in **B** implies that if Virginia asked Frank to return the deed to her before recording, he would have obeyed. Thus, **B** is weak. **B** would be much stronger if it said, "Virginia transferred possession of the deed to *a third party* before she died" or "Virginia transferred possession of the deed to *an agent of both parties* before she died." Therefore, **C** is the best answer because it's the only one left standing. **C** is certainly not ideal because it's a conclusion with no reference to the underlying reasoning, although it

---

4. For discussion of recordation and its legal significance, see chapter 23.

qualifies under the common multiple-choice exam instruction "Pick the best answer among the choices given, not the best possible answer."

D. Land Descriptions

Descriptions of land, sometimes called *legal descriptions*, are pervasive in real estate documents. The statute of frauds requires an adequate description of the land for every deed of conveyance. This is also true of other instruments that affect real property, such as leases, mortgages, easements, and covenants.

The goal of the land description is to describe one and only one tract of land. In order to do this, the written description must provide a means of locating all the boundary lines of the tract.

The three main types of land descriptions are:

- **Metes and bounds**, which describe every boundary line by its length and compass direction.
- **Subdivision plats**, which describe a tract by reference by a plat or map recorded in the public land records.
- **Government survey system**, which describes a tract (usually rural land) using a system developed by the federal government.

Most modern courts, when possible, strive to discern the parties' intent and uphold a land description even if it has flaws and is less than perfect. Courts, however, tend to be stricter concerning the quality of the land descriptions in deeds than they are for contracts of sale, leases, and other instruments that are typically not recorded in the public land records. Deeds become part of the chain of title for the property, to be retrieved and evaluated for many decades. For this reason, successive owners come to rely on the descriptions in the chain of title, and they generally lack access to extrinsic evidence as to the original parties' actual intent.

QUESTION 4. Street address. Maja, the owner of a single-family house in Lake County, contracts to sell her property to Bond. Their written contract describes the property only as 295 Barnett Shoals Road, Lake County, State of Confusion USA. At closing, Bond pays the purchase price and Maja signs and delivers a warranty deed that describes the property as "295 Barnett Shoals Road, Lake County, State of Confusion, more particularly described in Exhibit A attached thereto." Due to a mistake, no Exhibit A with a legal description of the land was attached to the deed. The attorney who prepared the closing documents should have prepared an Exhibit A containing a metes and bounds description of the property. The deed is recorded in the public land records before the mistake is noticed. At this point in time, is the deed effective to convey title to Bond?

A. No, because the missing exhibit makes it uncertain as to how much land surrounding the house is to be conveyed to Bond.
B. No, because Bond was negligent when he accepted the deed without noticing the missing exhibit.
C. Yes, because recording the deed cured the mistake of failing to attach the exhibit.
D. Yes, because Bond is entitled to reformation of the deed to add the missing exhibit.

ANALYSIS.   In transactional law practice, missing exhibits in fact patterns like this question happen a lot. Many cases have held that describing real property only by street address in a deed, mortgage, or other recorded instrument is insufficient. The courts in these cases reject attempts by a party (usually the buyer) to overcome the lack of a legal description by introducing extrinsic evidence of the parties' intent. A few cases come out the other way, upholding a description by street address when a party offers to introduce parol evidence that the seller owns a tract of land at the given address with a particular area (such as 2.45 acres) and that the parties intended that the deed convey all of this acreage. But this lenient approach is exceptional. This means that Choice **A** is the best answer.

Choice **B** also reflects the correct probable outcome that at this point in time the deed conveys nothing to Bond, but the reasoning is flawed. Whether Bond, the purchaser, was careless or negligent is not relevant. At closing many parties rely on the closing attorney with respect to the adequacy of the closing documents, but again, it doesn't matter whether Bond was reasonable in not checking the deed.

Choice **C** is wrong because in U.S. practice, recording the deed does not fix any problems with the deed, including not only problems with the land description but also problems such as lack of delivery, fraud, or the grantor's lack of capacity. Recording the deed only serves to make the deed part of the public land records.

Choice **D** properly points out that Bond may be able to fix the missing exhibit problem by seeking the equitable remedy of reformation. He would allege mutual mistake: that both parties intended to attach an exhibit with a proper legal description, a mistake sometimes called scrivener's error. If Maja does not voluntarily cooperate to fix the problem, a court probably will order reformation, but until this happens, Maja still owns the property.

E.   Defects in Deeds

Deeds may contain defects or flaws that make them void or voidable. Although these two words may sound similar, they have different legal meanings.

A deed that is *void* has no legal effect at all. The grantee named in the deed has acquired no property right; title remains fully in the named grantor. A deed not signed by the grantor is void. So is a forged deed, which appears to be signed but was in fact signed by an imposter rather than the true present owner of the real property.

Nondelivery of a deed also renders the deed void. A deed is not valid, even if signed by the proper person, until it is delivered. Nondelivery of a deed, like forgery, often represents a hidden defect. Although it is easy to see if a deed has not been signed by anyone, a forged deed or a nondelivered deed may look perfectly regular and normal in the chain of title. Yet because it is void, a person who reasonably relies on the apparent genuineness of such an instrument in attempting to purchase the property does not acquire title.

Other types of defects are considered less serious, making the deed voidable rather than void. If a deed is *voidable*, this means that the grantor has the right to rescind the transfer. Sometimes the right to rescind is described as a right to *avoid* the transfer (note the similarity between the words "voidable" and "avoid"). The grantee has title to the property until the grantor rescinds, which might never happen. A grantee who exerts undue influence upon the grantor obtains a voidable deed. Similarly, a grantee who induces a grantor to sign and deliver a deed by making a fraudulent misrepresentation gets a voidable deed. In both cases, the grantor has the right to rescind the transfer. The law, however, imposes some limitations on this right. There may be a time limit based on a statute of limitations or the doctrine of laches. If the grantor has received a benefit from the grantee, the grantor may have to make restitution. The defects that render a deed voidable are usually hidden from the viewpoint of third parties. A person who buys the property from the grantee without knowledge of the defect is often protected as a bona fide purchaser (BFP).

QUESTION 5.   **Finding a lucky deed.** Although Taylor was 33 years old, he still lived at home with Mom and Dad, never having met with enough success to get a place of his own. His father owned a vacation home in the mountains, where Taylor regularly stayed when not in the city at his parents' house. He had no idea what his father intended to do with the vacation house. One day he saw an envelope lying on the floor under his father's desk. Taylor opened it and found a warranty deed, signed by his father and notarized, conveying the vacation home to him. Without telling anyone, he recorded the deed in the land records. Two months later he applied for a $160,000 mortgage loan. The lender approved and funded the loan, taking a mortgage on the vacation home to secure Taylor's promise to repay the loan. Taylor used the money to move out of his parents' house and rent an apartment. After he had spent all of the money, he defaulted on the mortgage. The lender has now brought an action to foreclose. Dad has learned about the unhappy events, and he is now a party to the action, claiming that the lender's mortgage is not valid. Which is true?

A. The mortgage is invalid because the deed to Taylor is voidable.
B. The mortgage is invalid because the deed to Taylor is void.
C. The mortgage is valid because there was constructive delivery of the deed to Taylor.
D. The mortgage is valid because a recorded deed is presumed delivered.
E. The mortgage is valid because the lender reasonably relied on the recorded deed, which appeared genuine.

ANALYSIS. This question is pretty straightforward. It is necessary only to apply the void/voidable distinction to a deed where nondelivery is obvious. Deed defects that are considered highly serious—such as forgery and nondelivery—render the deed totally ineffective. We call such an instrument *void*. The point here is that Taylor's father never manifested any intent that the deed be made effective. He may have arranged for its drafting and signed it, thinking that he might at some point in the future make a gift of the property to his son, so **B** is the right answer.

Choices **C**, **D**, and **E** are all wrong because the father wins this case when he proves the facts that show nondelivery. With **C**, the mortgage would be valid if there was a constructive delivery to Taylor, but the facts give us no evidence pointing in this direction. At a minimum, we need some conduct by the father indicating a present intent that the deed transfer ownership to Taylor. However, the facts don't indicate that he ever told Taylor or anyone else about the deed or gave the deed to another person to hold.

As for **D**, it's true that courts often say that when a deed is recorded there is a presumption of delivery. Like other presumptions, though, this one is rebuttable, and our facts clearly demonstrate nondelivery.

As for **E**, it does not matter if the lender reasonably relied on the deed in making the loan. The lender may look like a BFP, as it has parted with value and has reasonably relied upon record title, but nondelivery is one of the inherent risks in our title assurance system. This is one reason prudent mortgage lenders obtain title insurance, which protects against such risks.

F.   The Closer: Estoppel by Deed

On occasion, a person signs a deed that purports to convey an interest she does not own or that purports to convey an interest larger than she owns. That person might be dishonest, but the person may believe she has title but is mistaken. If the person conveys by warranty deed, the doctrine of estoppel by deed may come into play. Any title subsequently acquired by such a grantor passes directly to the grantee by virtue of the warranty. An explanation often given by courts is that, without estoppel, the grantor would have breached his deed warranties of title. The estoppel by deed rule prevents this breach by passing the appropriate title to the grantee. For this reason, a number of courts have refused to apply estoppel by deed in transactions involving quit-claim deeds, but some modern cases have extended the doctrine to quitclaim deeds if the deed represents that the grantor has title. Estoppel by deed is also often called the *doctrine of after-acquired title.*

QUESTION 6.   Dad's deed to one daughter. Blackacre was an 80-acre tract of unoccupied rural land. Amos, the elderly owner in fee simple absolute of Blackacre, decided he wanted his daughter Nicole to own Blackacre when he died. He signed a deed naming Nicole as grantee and properly describing Blackacre as the conveyed premises. He handed the deed to Nicole, telling her, "You've always been so good to me. Here's a deed to Blackacre, which makes it yours after I'm gone." Nicole accepted the deed and stored it in her desk with her other valuable papers. Six months later, Nicole sold Blackacre to Tammy for $240,000, signing a deed wherein she covenanted "to warrant and defend title to said land against the whole world." One year later Amos died, intestate, survived only by Nicole and her sister, Kristin. Who owns what interest in Blackacre?

A. Nicole owns Blackacre in fee simple absolute.
B. Kristin owns Blackacre in fee simple absolute.
C. Tammy owns Blackacre in fee simple absolute.
D. Nicole and Kristin each own an undivided one-half interest in Blackacre in fee simple absolute.
E. Nicole and Tammy own an undivided one-half interest in Blackacre in fee simple absolute.
F. Kristin and Tammy each own an undivided one-half interest in Blackacre in fee simple absolute.

ANALYSIS.   Like so many property problems, this one is best approached by going through the transactions chronologically. The first step is to analyze the deed from Amos to his daughter Nicole. Everything with respect to the deed appears fine. It might seem that the delivery requirement is satisfied with the manual delivery. Amos handed the deed to Nicole, and she still has physical possession of the deed. But the words Amos spoke demonstrate that he did not intend a present transfer of ownership. His intent was testamentary. Therefore, the deed was void.

This takes us to the second step, Nicole's purported conveyance to Tammy. Because Nicole had acquired no ownership interest in Blackacre, through Nicole's deed Tammy obtained nothing.

The third step is Amos's death. When Amos died intestate, Nicole and Kristin, being his closest relatives, inherited Blackacre in equal shares. Estoppel by deed applies because Nicole covenanted "to warrant and defend title." This is a covenant of warranty, which makes the deed a warranty deed, not a quit-claim deed. Estoppel by deed automatically passes to Tammy the undivided one-half interest Nicole inherited from her father. Tammy does not acquire the other half, which Kristin inherited. There is no basis for applying estoppel against Kristin because she did not sign the deed to Tammy or engage in any other conduct that may have misled Tammy. This leads us directly to the right answer. Nicole no longer owns any share of Blackacre due to estoppel. Kristin and Tammy each have an undivided one-half interest, so **F** is right.

Some students may end up picking **C** or maybe even **E** based on Amos's expressed intent that Nicole get all of Blackacre, with none of the property going to Kristin. The only way to arrive at this outcome, however, is to treat the Amos-to-Nicole deed as a will. Depending on the particulars of this deed, including witnesses who signed the deed if any, and the will formalities required in the jurisdiction, it may be possible to probate the deed as a will. But the facts exclude this possibility, as you can see if you look closely enough, by stating that Amos died intestate. If the deed can legally function as a will, then he didn't die intestate.

 ## Smith's Picks

1.	A missing share of Blackacre	D
2.	Unpaid property taxes on a run-down house	A
3.	Deed held by attorney when grantor dies	C
4.	Street address	A
5.	Finding a lucky deed	B
6.	Dad's deed to one daughter	F

22

Mortgages

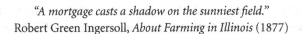

"A mortgage casts a shadow on the sunniest field."
Robert Green Ingersoll, *About Farming in Illinois* (1877)

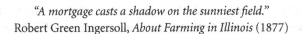

CHAPTER OVERVIEW
A. The Nature of the Mortgage
B. Mortgage Theories: Does the Lender Have Title or a Lien?
C. Waste by the Borrower
D. Deficiency or Surplus after Foreclosure
E. The Closer: Borrower's Transfer of Mortgaged Property
   Smith's Picks

Some property courses include a brief introduction to the law of mortgages. Usually the subject is addressed in more detail in an upper-level course, such as real estate finance or real estate transactions. This chapter provides the basics that you are likely to encounter if your course includes mortgages as a discrete topic. Even if your course does not emphasize mortgages, you will benefit from reading this chapter. Mortgages are very widely used, and for this reason many of your assigned cases and other materials will refer to mortgages on real property even though the focus is on other points. You'll have a better understanding of the materials if you understand why parties enter into mortgages and how a mortgage generally affects the ownership interest.

A. The Nature of the Mortgage

A mortgage is a voluntary transfer of an interest in real property to secure the payment or performance of an obligation. Usually the obligation is a debt of the property owner, although a person may grant a mortgage on his land to secure an obligation owed by another person. Most often the debt arises from a loan transaction. A bank or other lender makes a loan and requests collateral; the property owner grants a mortgage to the lender to secure the repayment of the loan.

The real property owner who grants the mortgage is called the *mortgagor*. The holder of the obligation who has the benefit of the mortgage is called the *mortgagee*. The mortgage functions to make the property serve as *collateral* to secure payment or performance of the obligation. This means that if there is a default in performance, the mortgagee has the right to resort to the collateral to satisfy all or part of the obligation.

A mortgage must comply with the statute of frauds. In this respect, it is treated the same as a deed of conveyance. Therefore, the mortgage must be in writing, must identify the parties, must contain a valid description of the real property, and must demonstrate an intent that the property secure an obligation. Most mortgage instruments have many additional clauses and are recorded in the public real property records, the same as warranty deeds and other instruments that bear on title to land.

QUESTION 1.   When is a mortgage useful? In which of the following transactions may the parties find it useful to enter into a mortgage?

A. Alice plans to buy an automobile from Car Dealer on credit, making monthly loan payments to Car Dealer, with the automobile serving as collateral to secure the loan.

B. Brian buys a retail store, with one physical location, on credit, agreeing to pay the price in installments to the seller, with the store assets serving as collateral to secure the loan.

C. Carlos, the owner of a house subject to a bank mortgage, was the losing defendant in tort litigation, with the plaintiff willing to forbear collection efforts on the condition that Carlos's house serve as collateral to secure payment of the judgment.

D. None of the above.

E. A only.

F. B only.

G. C only.

H. A and B.

I. A and C.

J. B and C.

ANALYSIS.   Whew, a lot of choices here! But notice, all that's required is to examine **A, B,** and **C** and to make a decision in each case as to whether a mortgage might help the parties achieve their apparent objectives.

A should not trip you up. Alice is planning to get a standard automobile loan. Although the plan is to have the automobile serve as collateral to secure her obligation to repay the loan, the automobile is plainly not real property. A mortgage is appropriate only when real property serves as the collateral.[1] The automobile is goods. Alice and Car Dealer will accomplish their objective not with a mortgage but with a security agreement covered by Article 9 of the Uniform Commercial Code. Under Article 9, Car Dealer will hold a "security interest," not a mortgage, in the automobile.

You might strike **B** for the same reason, thinking that the store assets are all personal property, but we need to take a harder look. The facts state that the store has one physical location, so this is not a virtual (online) store. Many of the store assets will be personal property: the store inventory is goods; contracts, licenses, the trade name, and the like are intangible personal property. All of this will be made collateral by an Article 9 security agreement. However, the store location is real property, with respect to which the seller undoubtedly has some recognized legal right. If the seller owns the premises, it has an estate in land. If the seller is a tenant, it owns a leasehold estate. Both forms are real property for which the seller will want Brian to execute a mortgage to secure the price for the sale of the store assets. So a mortgage is useful here. This illustrates that a mortgage may cover not only a fee simple estate, but other types of real property as well, including a leasehold. Such a mortgage is called a *leasehold mortgage*.

C raises two additional issues related to potential uses of mortgages. First, unlike Alice and Brian, Carlos is not voluntarily entering into a loan transaction or incurring a debt in order to buy property. He already owes the tort plaintiff money, and not because of a loan between the parties or another type of voluntary transaction. A mortgage, however, can secure any obligation, at least if the obligation is sufficiently defined that it can be quantified in monetary terms. Because the tort plaintiff's claim has been reduced to a judgment, it is a stated dollar amount, as reflected by the court's order of judgment. Carlos may grant a mortgage to secure his obligation to pay the judgment creditor. Second, the facts state that Carlos already has one mortgage on his home, held by a bank. This does not prevent Carlos from granting a mortgage to his creditor. An owner may grant multiple mortgages on a single property. The judgment creditor's mortgage will become a "second mortgage," meaning it is second in rank or priority to the bank's mortgage. In practical terms, this means that the mortgage has value to the judgment creditor only if Carlos has "equity" in his home, meaning that its market value is greater than the amount he owes on the bank mortgage. But whether or not Carlos has equity, a second mortgage granted to his creditor will have legal effect.

---

1. Old cases and other authorities often referred to *chattel mortgages*, which made chattels (e.g., goods, movable personal property) serve as collateral to secure an obligation. The term chattel mortgage is now obsolete in U.S. law, replaced by the UCC Article 9 security interest during the 20th century.

So having gone down the **A-B-C** tree, we see that the final choice, **J**, is the correct one.

B.   Mortgage Theories: Does the Lender Have Title or a Lien?

The mortgage theories address whether the mortgagor or the mortgagee has title to the real property between the signing of the mortgage and the time of foreclosure. These theories are the starting point for analyzing the competing possessory claims of mortgagor and mortgagee. Under the title theory, the signing of the mortgage transfers title to the real estate from the borrower to the lender, who retains title for the duration of the mortgage. This theory comes from traditional English common law, where a mortgage was a conveyance of title from the mortgagor to the mortgagee. The mortgagee had a freehold estate, typically in fee simple. The mortgagee's estate could be defeasible or indefeasible. If the latter, the mortgagee had the obligation to reconvey the mortgaged property to the mortgagor upon payment of the obligation in full. In U.S. practice, states originally adopted the English title theory of mortgages as part of their common law. A number of eastern states have retained the title theory.

Most states follow the lien theory of mortgages, rejecting the title theory. Under the lien theory, the mortgagee prior to foreclosure has only a lien. The mortgagor keeps legal and equitable title to the estate after signing the mortgage, and the mortgagee's property rights are limited to the right to foreclose after default. The rationale of the lien theory is that the mortgagee does not need title to protect its legitimate interests. The purpose of the mortgage is to secure payment of the debt, and a lien is sufficient to protect the lender's interest in security. Under the lien theory, the language used in the mortgage instrument is irrelevant. The lien theory rejects the parties' freedom to contract for the passage of title. The parties' title rights are defined by their status rather than by their agreement in fact.

QUESTION 2.   A mortgage granted by one joint tenant. A will devised a fee simple absolute estate in Blackacre "to my daughter Rebecca and my son Isaac as joint tenants with the right of survivorship." Isaac needed money, and he approached his friend Travis, asking for a loan of $20,000. He said he would be able to pay back the money within a year and offered to pay 8 percent interest. Travis was unwilling to lend such a large amount without security. Isaac mentioned that he recently acquired a one-half interest in Blackacre when his mother died, and he offered that interest as collateral. Travis made the loan. Isaac signed a promissory note describing his obligation and a mortgage covering "my entire right, title, and interest" in Blackacre. Eight months later, before repaying any part of his loan, Isaac died from acute pneumonia, survived by his wife, Grace. Rebecca brings an action to quiet title to Blackacre against Grace and Travis. What result is probable if the jurisdiction applies the lien theory of mortgages?

A. Rebecca owns the entire fee simple subject to no mortgage.
B. Rebecca owns the entire fee simple subject to the mortgage granted to Travis.
C. Rebecca owns an undivided one-half and Grace owns an undivided one-half subject to no mortgage.
D. Rebecca owns an undivided one-half and Grace owns an undivided one-half with Grace's share subject to the mortgage granted to Travis.

ANALYSIS. The will created a joint tenancy, not a tenancy in common, between Rebecca and Isaac.[2] Certain events can terminate a joint tenancy, converting it into a tenancy in common, before the death of either joint tenant. Such an event causes "severance" of the joint tenancy. The first issue raised in this question is whether Isaac's mortgage severed the joint tenancy. If so, Rebecca and Isaac became tenants in common, with the consequence that upon Isaac's death his share went to Grace rather than to Rebecca. Most courts have held that a conveyance of title by one joint tenant to a third person severs the joint tenancy and that this rule also applies when the conveyance of title is pursuant to mortgage. Conversely, the creation of a lien on the interest of one joint tenant is not a severance. The facts state that the jurisdiction applies the lien theory of mortgages. Therefore, Rebecca's survivorship right was still intact when Isaac died. So **C** and **D** are incorrect.

The second issue raised in this question is whether Travis's mortgage survives Isaac's death. This is the distinction between answers **A** and **B**. Although there is some contrary authority, the generally accepted rule is that a mortgage does not survive the death of the mortgaging joint tenant. See *Harms v. Sprague*, 473 N.E.2d 930 (Ill. 1984) (joint tenancy not severed because newer Illinois case law adopted lien theory; surviving joint tenant does not acquire share from deceased joint tenant but takes by virtue of original conveyance that created the joint tenancy). Thus, **A** is the best answer.

C.   Waste by the Borrower

The common-law doctrine of waste applies whenever the borrower is in possession of the collateral, protecting the lender against unreasonable or

---

2. These two forms of cotenancy are discussed in chapter 14.

improper conduct that reduces or threatens to reduce the value of the collateral. Waste applies in many different settings when multiple persons own interests in the same property. Before answering the next question, you may want to review the discussion in chapter 10 (pages XXX-XXX) of the doctrine of waste as applied to life tenants; the principles are much the same.

QUESTION 3.   Selling stuff from a house. Three years ago, Hank bought his lake home in the north woods for $400,000, financed with a mortgage loan for $360,000 from Big Bank. Presently, the loan has a principal balance of $345,792. Last month, near the end of March, Hank had a garage sale. He sold the home central air conditioning system (compressor and fan) for $8,000. Hank decided the air conditioning cost too much to run and that he'll do just fine opening the windows next summer and using the house's existing ceiling fans. He also sold the wall-to-wall carpeting in two rooms for $2,000. The carpeting was only four years old and had been fastened to the floor the usual way with tackless strips. Under the carpeting are the house's original hardwood floors, which need refinishing. Hank plans to refinish them next year. Big Bank discovered what Hank did and sued him for waste. The most probable result is:

A. Big Bank prevails because Hank acted in bad faith by not telling Big Bank of his plans to sell the air conditioner and the carpeting.
B. Big Bank prevails because Hank's conduct has reduced the value of the collateral precipitously, compared to the outstanding loan balance.
C. Hank prevails because his conduct is reasonable measured by community standards for normal behavior.
D. Hank prevails because the air conditioner and carpeting are Hank's personal property and are not part of Big Bank's collateral.

ANALYSIS. This question is challenging because it's not clear whether Hank's conduct is wrongful under the doctrine of waste. It's a close question. Mortgage instruments usually are long and complicated documents, with the borrower making many express representations and promises in addition to repaying the loan. With this fact pattern and a typical mortgage, Big Bank usually would have the right to object to Hank's conduct without the need to argue that Hank has violated an obligation implied by the law of waste.

Logically, the first issue to address is whether Hank has sold mortgaged property. Hank wants to argue that he has the right to sell contents of the house, like furniture and televisions, without telling Big Bank and getting its permission. But this argument fails. The air conditioning system and carpeting are sufficiently attached to the real estate to make them qualify as fixtures, which are covered by the mortgage, just like the land and the building. So Choice **D** is wrong.

Let's look at Choice **A.** This response assumes that Hank is liable for waste only if he acted in bad faith. Waste, like most other tort causes of action, has an intent element, but not a requirement that the tortfeasor has intentionally harmed another person or acted in bad faith (for example, a trespass consists of an unauthorized entry upon another person's land; good faith or ignorance is no defense). Thus, Choice **A** is wrong.

This leaves us with Choices **B** and **C**, both of which are plausible. As **B** reflects, Big Bank will say that Hank's sale of the air conditioner and carpeting (without refinishing the wood floors) should be considered waste because the collateral is now less valuable. If Hank defaults in paying back the loan and foreclosure results, a buyer at foreclosure will likely bid less because of the removal of these items.

Choice **C** does not focus on the impact on market value directly, but instead reflects Hank's defense that he has behaved reasonably, like a normal homeowner who wants to make modifications to his home. This comes down to a judgment call. I think **C** is the better answer for two reasons. First, Big Bank's argument that the home value has declined too much is not well supported by the facts. Assuming that Hank's conduct has reduced the value of the property by approximately the $10,000 he received, through monthly payments he has paid down the original loan balance more than this amount, and there's no evidence that home values have dropped in the community during the past three years since he paid $400,000 for the house. Second, Choice **C**, by asserting that Hank has acted reasonably, tracks the modern general rule that waste operates flexibly to balance the competing claims of parties to reach a reasonable outcome, protecting both the possessor and the other owner.

D.   Deficiency or Surplus after Foreclosure

A foreclosure in the United States almost always results in a public sale of the mortgaged property by auction.[3] The point of foreclosure is to extinguish the mortgagor's ownership interest, which is known as her *equity of redemption*. Foreclosure may be by judicial process. With *judicial foreclosure*, the mortgagee brings an action or bill in equity. Alternatively, many states allow *non-judicial foreclosure*, also called power of sale foreclosure, which proceeds without court involvement.

If the value of the property is less than the debt, foreclosure will result in a *deficiency*. Often the mortgagee will seek to collect the deficiency. If the proceeding is a judicial foreclosure, the mortgagee may seek a judgment equal to

---

3. England historically used strict foreclosure, in which the lender could retain or acquire ownership in satisfaction of the debt. Strict foreclosure became part of early U.S. law, but in almost all states today strict foreclosure is no longer allowed as the primary method of foreclosure. It is reserved for solving specialized problems.

the shortfall in that proceeding. The outcome is called a deficiency judgment. If the proceeding is a non-judicial foreclosure, after the sale the mortgagee will have to initiate an action on the debt in order to get a deficiency judgment.

Most mortgage foreclosures result in a sales price that yields a deficiency, or a price that equals the outstanding debt. But on occasion the net foreclosure sales price exceeds the outstanding debt that is being foreclosed. The excess is called *surplus*. The surplus belongs to the mortgagor and is paid to the mortgagor if no other party has a better claim to it. Any other parties owning property rights that are terminated by the foreclosure are entitled to compensation before the mortgagor is paid. If there are multiple parties, their entitlements are ranked according to their priority under recording system principles.

QUESTION 4.   Foreclosure on a home equity mortgage. Ava owns a large, expensive home subject to two mortgages. The first mortgage, which Ava obtained when she bought the home, is held by Big Bank. This mortgage now has a balance due of $200,000. Several years ago, she took out a home equity loan, granting a second mortgage to Lemon Lender. That home equity mortgage has a present balance of $50,000. Ava has made all required monthly payments on the first mortgage but has defaulted by failing to make payments on the second mortgage. Lemon Lender properly takes all of the necessary steps to foreclose its home equity mortgage. Ava's home is sold at foreclosure by auction, with the high bid accepted. The price paid by the foreclosure purchaser results in net proceeds of $160,000 after the payment of foreclosure expenses. The foreclosure purchaser pays the agreed-upon price in exchange for a foreclosure deed to Ava's home. How should the foreclosure proceeds be distributed?

A. $160,000 to Big Bank and nothing to Lemon Lender.
B. Nothing to Big Bank and $160,000 to Lemon Lender.
C. $110,000 to Big Bank and $50,000 to Lemon Lender.
D. Nothing to Big Bank, $50,000 to Lemon Lender, and $110,000 to Ava.
E. Nothing to Big Bank, nothing to Lemon Lender, and $160,000 to Ava.

ANALYSIS.   A, B, and **E** are alike in that they award the entire pot of foreclosure proceeds to one of the three possible claimants, leaving the other two completely out in the cold. The latter two are the easiest to strike. **B** is wrong because a mortgagee's claim is limited to the amount of its obligation. If the property sells for more than the total outstanding debt of the foreclosing lender, that excess has to go somewhere else. Lemon Lender is made whole when it collects all it is due, $50,000. It would be an unjustifiable windfall to

Lemon Lender if it were allowed to keep the additional $110,000. This excess is surplus and must go elsewhere.

E is also an easy strike. Were Ava to sell her home outside of foreclosure in a voluntary sale, she would get to keep the entire payment. But foreclosure is very different. The whole point of foreclosure is to hold a forced sale for the purpose of paying all or part of the owner's mortgage obligation. **E** is wrong.

A has more plausibility but likewise falls short. Paying the entire $160,000 to Big Bank would not be a windfall; it would not overcompensate Big Bank because Ava owes $200,000 to that lender. Also, Big Bank made its loan to Ava before Lemon Lender made its loan, so it has first priority and thus an expectation of being paid before Lemon. But this isn't how it works. You have to focus on which lender, or lenders, are foreclosing. Ava has defaulted only on Lemon Lender's (the second) mortgage; Lemon is foreclosing and Big Bank is not. As a consequence, Big Bank's (the first) mortgage will survive the foreclosure sale. The foreclosure purchaser takes title subject to that outstanding $200,000 obligation. (This means that, in effect, the foreclosure purchaser agreed to pay $360,000 for the home, the sum of the outstanding first mortgage obligation and the bid price.) Thus, Big Bank should get nothing, as its mortgage is not impaired by Lemon Lender's foreclosure sale.

Because Big Bank is to get nothing, **C** is also a bad choice. That leaves **D** as our answer. The entire surplus of $110,000 goes to Ava.

E.   The Closer: Borrower's Transfer of Mortgaged Property

When mortgaged property is sold or transferred, either the mortgage is retired or it continues. When it is retired, typically someone pays the full amount of the mortgage obligation to the holder of that obligation. In a sales transaction, usually the seller uses part of the purchase price to pay off the mortgage as one element of the closing process. Then the mortgagee signs a release of mortgage or a similar instrument so that the mortgage no longer affects title.

When the existing debt and mortgage continue after the sale or transfer, the buyer or grantee may agree to become responsible for that debt in one of two ways. She may assume the mortgage debt, or she may take title subject to that debt. *Assumption* is a promise the buyer makes to the seller to pay all of the debt in accordance with the seller's terms. Usually an assumption agreement is contained in the deed that conveys title from seller to buyer. An assumption results in a set of rights and obligations involving three parties: the seller, the assuming buyer, and the mortgagee. The following triangle encapsulates the parties' positions.

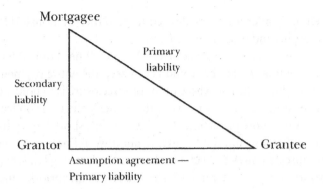

The grantee becomes personally liable for the debt by agreeing to "assume" that debt. The mortgagee may sue the buyer for failing to pay. When, as is often the case, the grantee makes the assumption promise only to the grantor, the enforcement right of the mortgagee is justified on the ground that the mortgagee is a third-party beneficiary.

The grantor becomes a surety. This is a type of secondary liability. The grantor remains liable as the maker of the promissory note, but because the grantee is primarily liable, the grantor's liability is secondary.

When the seller is personally liable for the mortgage debt, the seller can avoid continuing liability as a surety only if the lender agrees. An express *release* of liability accomplishes this objective. Courts will not find an implied release or waiver or estoppel solely from the lender's knowledge of and consent to the transfer and assumption. In that situation, the lender is entitled to rely on the normal principle that the seller is becoming a surety.

Taking property subject to existing debt means that the buyer has no personal liability if he fails to pay the debt. This is a form of nonrecourse financing. The buyer who takes "subject to" usually pays the debt because if he does not pay, he risks losing the property to the mortgagee, who may choose to foreclose.

QUESTION 5.   A sale and a quick resale. Two years ago Brittany signed a promissory note payable to the order of Lancelot to secure her debt to him. The note is secured by a mortgage on Blackacre. The loan is payable in monthly installments of principal and interest over an extended time period. In March, when the principal due to Lancelot is $300,000, Brittany sells Blackacre to Chandler for $350,000, with Chandler paying Brittany $50,000 in cash at closing and assuming the mortgage debt owed to Lancelot. In October of the same year, when the mortgage balance owed to Lancelot is $298,000, Chandler sells Blackacre to Dimples for $370,000. Dimples meets this price by (1) paying Chandler $12,000 in cash at closing, (2) signing a promissory note for $60,000 payable to the order of Chandler and secured by a second mortgage on Blackacre, and (3) taking subject to the prior mortgage. The warranty deed from Chandler to Dimples states, "Grantee takes subject to, and does not assume, that certain mortgage debt [owed to Lancelot]." Several months later, Dimples defaults on the first mortgage by failing to make monthly payments to Lancelot. Lancelot responds by bringing an action on the debt against Brittany, Chandler, and Dimples. Which parties are personally liable for the mortgage debt?

A. Brittany only.
B. Chandler only.
C. Dimples only.
D. All of the above.
E. Brittany and Chandler.
F. Brittany and Dimples.
G. Chandler and Dimples.
H. None of the parties.

ANALYSIS.   Let's analyze the positions of the successive owners of Blackacre in order. Because Brittany signed the promissory note, she is personally liable for the amount owed to Lancelot in the absence of an express term that limits her liability to the collateral. When she sold Blackacre to Chandler, that personal liability continued. There are no facts pointing to an agreement by Lancelot to release Brittany from personal liability.

Chandler became personally liable for the outstanding debt by agreeing to "assume" that obligation. The word "assumption" is a term of art in real property law, meaning the person agrees to perform another person's obligation and to bear personal liability if she fails so to perform.

Dimples struck a different bargain from that of Chandler by taking subject to the existing first mortgage. Like assumption, "taking subject to" is a term of art meaning that the person is not undertaking personal liability. This can be confusing because Dimples, by taking subject to, is agreeing that Chandler will no longer be making payments to Lancelot and that Dimples is undertaking the risk of losing Blackacre by foreclosure if she fails to make the mortgage payments.

So the right answer is **E**. Only Brittany and Chandler are personally liable on the debt. Between them, Brittany is surety and Chandler is the primary obligor.

 ## Smith's Picks

1. When is a mortgage useful?   J
2. A mortgage granted by one joint tenant   A
3. Selling stuff from a house   C
4. Foreclosure on a home equity mortgage D
5. A sale and a quick resale   E

23

Recording System

*"Not to know what happened before we were born is to remain perpetually a child.
For what is the worth of human life unless it is woven into the life of our ancestors
by the records of history?"*
Cicero

CHAPTER OVERVIEW
A. How Recording Acts Modify the Common Law
B. Types of Recording Acts
C. The Meaning of Notice
D. Unrecorded Interests Noticeable from Inspection of Land
E. Payment of Value
F. The Closer: Chain of Title Problems
⊕ Smith's Picks

Many property courses introduce students to the public land records system. The law provides for the public recording of deeds, mortgages, and other instruments that affect title to land. The recording system provides methods for determining who owns a tract of land and for ranking the priority of various interests. The basic idea is giving notice to third parties. When the parties record their deed or other instrument, that instrument becomes part of the public record and can be found by anyone who conducts a title search for the tract of land in question. Each state has its own recording act or recording statute, which establishes the system for that state. There is no uniform recording act, and the statutes vary widely in scope and content. This chapter focuses on the basic principles, those that most states follow.

Some property courses cover this subject extensively, although in many schools detailed treatment is left to an upper-level elective course, such as real estate transactions. If your instructor emphasizes the recording system, you should study it carefully, of course. If your course doesn't emphasize recording act principles, it is still highly useful to learn the basics. Many cases that deal with other real property subjects mention that a deed or other instrument was recorded in a particular office on a certain date, and to fully understand the case it helps if you understand the significance of recording and why it often affects the legal rights of property claimants.

A. How Recording Acts Modify the Common Law

Recording acts only partially replace the common law. Prior to the adoption of recording acts by U.S. states, the common law resolved most disputes by applying the rule of "first in time, first in right." This is still the baseline rule today. It means that when there are conflicting grantees all holding under an executed (signed) instrument that was delivered, one must ascertain which instrument was delivered first. Normally, the instrument that was executed first will also be the first one to be delivered, but that isn't always the case.

Recording acts require the acknowledgment of a deed or other instrument as a condition to recordation. Most instruments are acknowledged before notary publics ("notarized"), but other public officials such as judges also may acknowledge a person's signature of an instrument. It is important to distinguish the legal issue of the validity of the instrument from its recordation. A deed is valid and passes title as long as it complies with the statute of frauds and meets the common-law requirements of delivery and acceptance by the grantee. From that moment on, the grantee owns the estate described therein, whether or not the deed is recorded or even is recordable. A deed that is not acknowledged or is defectively acknowledged is perfectly valid between the parties but is not entitled to be recorded.

The basic purpose of a recording act is to protect third persons from unrecorded claims to the property. Recording acts modify the common-law "first in time, first in right" rule by defining which third persons qualify as bona fide purchasers (BFPs). The third person must acquire an interest in the property after the holder of an unrecorded interest in order to become a BFP. The BFP takes free of a prior interest that is unrecorded. This means that the grantee, who held her interest under an unrecorded instrument—which was sufficient under the statute of frauds and under the common law—loses her ownership interest. In the next section, we'll discuss what the third person must establish in order to qualify as a BFP.

> **QUESTION 1.   A deed to the family condominium.** Sabrina owns an oceanfront condominium, which her family has enjoyed as a vacation home for the past 22 years. In connection with her estate planning, she

has decided to convey the condominium to her sons, Ricardo and Rafael. She has her attorney draft a deed of gift, which names them as grantees, contains a sufficient legal description of the condominium, and otherwise complies with the statute of frauds. Sabrina goes to the attorney's office, where she signs the deed, with her signature acknowledged by one of the law firm's notaries. Sabrina, Ricardo, and Rafael are together on Christmas Eve at Sabrina's home. She explains that the condominium is their Christmas present and hands them the deed. They thank their mother profusely. When they leave the next day, they hand the deed back to Sabrina, asking her to store it in her home lockbox for them. In January Sabrina is visited by her daughter, Tonya, who insists that her siblings are financially irresponsible, as demonstrated by their recent spending sprees on luxury items when they were vacationing in Europe. Tonya persuades Sabrina that her gift was improvident. Sabrina has possession of the deed, which has not been recorded as provided for by the state recording act. Sabrina writes a letter to Ricardo and Rafael, telling them that she has changed her mind and will retain ownership of the condominium for the time being. What results if Ricardo and Rafael insist that they own the condominium?

A. Sabrina owns the condominium because Ricardo and Rafael have not paid value.

B. Sabrina owns the condominium because title has not yet passed to Ricardo and Rafael.

C. Ricardo and Rafael own the condominium because they have the right to obtain possession of the deed and record it.

D. Ricardo and Rafael own the condominium because title passed to them on Christmas Eve.

E. Ricardo and Rafael own the condominium, but Sabrina has the right to rescind the conveyance based on the information she received from Tonya.

ANALYSIS. The main point is to recognize that Sabrina has made a completed gift of the condominium to her sons. **D** is the right answer. The parties have not complied with the recording act, but the deed is still valid as between the parties. Ricardo and Rafael obtained title when manual delivery of the deed took place on Christmas Eve. Delivery and the passage of title are not impaired by their decision on Christmas Day to let their mother hold the deed. They have title because the disposition of the deed complies with both the common-law requirements for conveyances and the statute of frauds.

The recording act does not change the analysis. The failure to record the deed means that Ricardo and Rafael's ownership is at risk if a third person enters the scene and qualifies as a BFP. Although Tonya is a third person, she cannot be a BFP because Sabrina has not conveyed an interest in the condominium to her.

Two of the other answers, **C** and **E**, also correctly affirm that Ricardo and Rafael presently own the condominium, but they have flaws. With respect to **C**, it is true that they have a right to obtain possession of the deed and record the deed. A court would order Sabrina to turn over possession to them. However, their ownership is not a consequence of their right to get possession of the deed. It's the other way around: because they own the property, they have a right to the deed. Stated another way, if the deed became lost or destroyed before they obtained possession of the deed, they would still own the condominium. With respect to **E**, there may be situations in which a gift can be rescinded due to misconduct of the donees (for example, if the donees induced the gift through undue influence or by making fraudulent misrepresentation), but there's no evidence of such conduct by Ricardo or Rafael. Wasting their own money without telling Mom isn't nearly enough.

B.   Types of Recording Acts

Recording acts protect grantees by allowing them to record their deeds or other instruments and thereby provide public ownership of their rights. Moreover, the acts penalize grantees who fail to use the system to provide notice. A subsequent taker of an interest who qualifies as a BFP is afforded priority over earlier unrecorded interests. This priority often means that the earlier interest terminates, but in some contexts priority may allow the earlier interest to continue but become subordinate to the BFP's interest.

There are three basic types of recording acts, which differ according to when the subsequent taker qualifies as a BFP so as to trump the holder of the earlier interest:

- **Race statute.** Under a race statute (sometimes called a "pure race" statute), the first person to record her instrument wins. There is a split of authority as to whether the subsequent grantee must pay value to the grantor in order to qualify as a BFP and thereby cut off an earlier, unrecorded interest. This depends on the statutory language.
- **Notice statute.** Under a notice statute, a subsequent purchaser who takes without notice of the earlier, unrecorded interest wins. To be a "purchaser" the grantee must pay value to the grantor.
- **Race-notice statute.** A race-notice statute is a hybrid of the race and notice types of recording acts. To be a "purchaser" the grantee must pay value to the grantor. The subsequent purchaser must both record first (as under a race statute) and take without notice of the earlier interest (as under a notice statute). Thus, of the three statutes, the race-notice statute makes it hardest for BFPs to prevail.

Only three states — Delaware, Louisiana, and North Carolina — have a race statute as their general recording act. Of the other states, roughly half have notice acts and half have race-notice acts.

QUESTION 2.   A lender's delay in recording the mortgage. Kevin borrowed $10,000 from Alice. To secure his obligation to pay the loan, he executed and delivered to Alice a mortgage covering a tract of land that he owned in fee simple. Alice did not record her mortgage. Three months later, Kevin sold the land to Brenda for $120,000, executing and delivering a warranty deed to the property. Brenda purchased with knowledge of Alice's prior, unrecorded mortgage. Brenda promptly and properly recorded her deed. Four months later, Brenda sold the land to Carlos for $140,000, executing and delivering a warranty deed to the property. Carlos purchased without knowledge of Alice's prior, unrecorded mortgage. One week later Alice properly recorded her mortgage, and four days after that Carlos properly recorded his deed. Carlos brings a quiet title action against Alice, claiming that he has title free and clear of her mortgage. In a jurisdiction subject to a notice recording act, what's the probable result?

A. Alice prevails because Brenda had notice of Alice's mortgage and Carlos can get no better title than Brenda had.
B. Alice prevails because Alice recorded before Carlos.
C. Carlos prevails because Alice had not recorded at the time Carlos purchased.
D. Carlos prevails because Brenda would prevail against Alice by recording first.

ANALYSIS.   Alice is "first in time," having taken a valid mortgage before Brenda and Carlos came on the scene. This means that under the common law, her mortgage is valid and takes priority over Carlos's interest unless the notice recording act modifies this outcome by making Brenda or Carlos a BFP.

Both Brenda and Carlos paid value, so they meet that requirement for qualifying as BFPs. The issue is whether either had no notice of Alice's mortgage. The facts state that Brenda purchased with knowledge of the mortgage, so she had notice. Thus, **D** is incorrect: Brenda would not prevail against Alice in a BFP contest if Brenda still owned the property because Brenda had notice.

Let's examine **A** and **B**, the two answers in which Alice prevails. **A** starts out correctly by noting that Brenda had notice of Alice's mortgage but then fails with the proposition "Carlos can get no better title than Brenda had." In fact, Carlos seeks to establish that he is a BFP entitled to take free of the prior unrecorded mortgage, and if he succeeds in his proof, he will acquire a better title than Brenda had.

B is also incorrect. Although it's true that Alice recorded before Carlos, a notice act does not require that the BFP record before the prior interest holder records. All that Carlos need do is pay value in exchange for his interest without notice of the prior (then unrecorded) interest. Carlos has done this, so **C** is the right answer.

C.   The Meaning of Notice

The purpose of every state recording act is to require persons owning interests in real property to give notice of those interests to others. Determining whether people have notice is critical for resolving most recording act disputes. There are three types of notice:

- **Actual notice.** A purchaser who has actual knowledge of a conflicting prior interest in the property is said to have actual notice. This is a state-of-mind test.
- **Constructive notice.** A purchaser is charged with notice of all conflicting prior interests that are shown on properly recorded instruments. This notice is based on the idea that the purchaser should search the public records before buying and that the search will reveal relevant information about prior interests. Sometimes authorities call this type of notice "record notice."
- **Inquiry notice.** A purchaser who knows facts suggesting that someone might have an unrecorded interest has a duty to inquire further. The purchaser is charged with whatever information that inquiry would have revealed.

Under both notice and race-notice statutes, it is critical to determine when a person has "actual notice" or "inquiry notice" of an earlier, unrecorded claim. Such notice disqualifies the subsequent purchaser from being a BFP. A race statute follows a narrower view of notice: only "constructive notice" ("record notice") disqualifies the subsequent purchaser.

Notice is evaluated at the time the grantee pays value. It does not impair the grantee's status as BFP if she obtains any of the three types of notice of the earlier interest in the property after she has parted with value. Conversely, this means that a buyer who enters into a contract of purchase and who receives notice of an unrecorded interest before closing cannot proceed to closing and pay the price with an expectation of getting a title that is superior to the unrecorded interest.[1]

---

1. This assumes that any down payment made by the buyer when entering into the contract is not sufficient "value" to qualify the buyer as a BFP. For discussion of payment of value, see Section E of this chapter.

QUESTION 3.   **Buying a condominium that excludes cats.** Natasha was interested in buying a condominium, so she contacted Brandon, a real estate broker, to show her properties. Brandon showed her several units on the market, including a two-bedroom condominium unit at Northlake Village. Natasha turned in an offer to buy for $205,000, which the seller accepted. Prior to the time of her contract, the condominium developer had properly recorded a Declaration of Condominium that prohibited all residents from having pets of any type. Brandon knew that Natasha had two cats; to try to get an idea of what size and type of condominium unit might appeal to her, he earlier asked if she had family, and she answered, "No, just me and my cats, Tulip and Topsy." Yet Brandon did not tell Natasha about the pet restriction, or even that Northlake Village had a recorded Declaration of Condominium that she should read. Natasha closed on her purchase without learning about the pet prohibition. The warranty deed conveying the condominium unit to Natasha said nothing about the pet restriction and made no reference to the recorded Declaration of Condominium. Three weeks after Natasha moved in with Tulip and Topsy, the condominium unit owners association learned of the cats. The association demanded that Natasha remove her cats. After she refused, the association brought an action seeking an order that she remove them from the property. What's the probable result?

A. The association prevails because the Declaration of Condominium was properly recorded before Natasha contracted to buy the condominium unit.
B. The association prevails because Natasha had actual notice of the pet restriction.
C. Natasha prevails because Brandon had an obligation to inform her about the pet restriction.
D. Natasha prevails because her warranty deed failed to mention the pet restriction or the Declaration of Condominium.

ANALYSIS.   Many students will recognize that the facts are closely based on a famous case often included in property casebooks, Nahrstedt v. Lakeside Village Condominium Association, 878 P.2d 1275 (Cal. 1994). Although the buyer in that case claimed she was ignorant of the pet restriction before she moved in, the primary issue addressed by the court was whether the association could enforce the restriction in the absence of proof that Nahrstedt's cats were annoying neighbors or causing any other problems in the community. The court held for the association, allowing enforcement regardless of her cats' behavior. Here the question has a different focus. It assumes that the pet prohibition is generally enforceable against condominium residents but asks whether Natasha has a viable defense based on the state's recording act.

Natasha paid value (presumably full market value) for the condominium, so she can qualify as a BFP if she had no notice of the pet restriction. The restriction meets the requirements for a real covenant or equitable servitude, so it will run with the land to bind subsequent purchasers like Natasha who have notice. Natasha is considered to have notice and thus to be bound by the pet restriction if she has actual notice, constructive notice, or inquiry notice. She lacks actual notice, which requires that she actually know about the pet restriction. So **B** is incorrect.

Likewise, **C** is incorrect. Brandon may have had an obligation to tell Natasha about the pet restrictions and perhaps about the Declaration more generally, and he may have breached that obligation, thereby opening himself up to liability if she sues him. However, that does not mean that she actually knew of the restriction.

That leaves **A** and **D**. The latter is incorrect because a purchaser takes subject to the contents of all recorded instruments that affect the property, not just those created by or referred to in the deed to the purchaser. Natasha had constructive notice of all instruments relating to the condominium that are properly recorded. This is an important point about the chain of title to a property. Interests held by third parties can be created anywhere in the chain of title, which stretches back from the present owner to the sovereign. In connection with Natasha's purchase, it is possible that the failure of the warranty deed to refer to restrictions in the Declaration of Condominium makes the seller liable for breach of a covenant of title in the deed. But that possibility, like Brandon's possible liability to Natasha, does not negate constructive notice.

So **A** is the right answer. Choice **A** does not give itself away as the right answer by stating that Natasha has constructive notice of the Declaration of Condominium, but it correctly states that the association prevails because the Declaration was of record before she contracted to buy her unit.

D.   Unrecorded Interests Noticeable from Inspection of Land

Inquiry notice is relevant for subsequent purchasers in states with notice or race-notice recording acts. The most important aspect of inquiry notice is a duty to inspect the land. The purchaser generally takes subject to the rights of parties in possession who have unrecorded interests. The purchaser also takes subject to unrecorded rights that are not considered to be possessory, provided there is visible evidence of those rights that should be noticed with adequate inspection of the land. Most often, such "visible rights" consist of an easement that is being used by the holder in an open, above-ground fashion. Even though possessors and other holders of visible rights could have recorded but failed to do so, they are protected by the concept of inquiry notice.

The doctrine holds that possession by someone other than the seller gives rise to a duty of inquiry. The rule envisions a dialogue between the purchaser and the possessor. The purchaser is bound by whatever rights would have been uncovered by diligent inquiry of the possessor. Usually this means asking questions. If you are a purchaser and you see someone on the property other than the seller, you are supposed to ask that possessor why she is there and if she claims any ownership or other rights in the property.

There is one general exception to the duty to inquire of possessors. When possession is consistent with record title, there is no duty of inquiry. Thus, when there is a recorded lease, there is no duty to ask the tenant why he is there. The purchaser may assume that the tenant's rights do not exceed those stated in the recorded lease. Similarly, when record title is held by cotenants and only one cotenant is in possession, there generally is no duty to check with the possessing cotenant when buying an interest from a nonpossessing cotenant. For property held in cotenancy, any cotenant is entitled to possess all of the property—and this is not wrongful or unusual, provided the possessor has not ousted his cotenants. In many states, there is also an exception to inquiry notice for possession by a grantor who recently deeded the property to the seller. The rationale is that it is not unusual for a grantee to let the seller remain in possession for a reasonable period of time after the conveyance.

QUESTION 4.   An empty mobile home. Rufus responds to an advertisement posted by Jim Bob, which offers a rural lot for sale. The lot is described as two acres with trees, suitable for building a country home. Rufus contacts Jim Bob, obtains the address, and drives to the property by himself. The lot looks ideal, but Rufus immediately notices a mobile home on the lot, near the county highway. The mobile home is still on wheels and a carriage, but it is hooked up to an overhead electrical line running from a pole next to the highway. No car is present near the mobile home. Rufus knocks on the door to the home, thinking Jim Bob might be present, but no one answers. Rufus leaves, and the next day he phones Jim Bob, telling him that he'll pay Jim Bob's asking price of $32,000. Rufus and Jim Bob meet. Before they sign a contract, Rufus asks Jim Bob about the mobile home. Jim Bob says, "That's my cousin, Melba. I'm letting her stay there temporarily, since she had nowhere else to go after she left her no-good husband. Melba knows I'm trying to sell the lot. She'll leave next month and move her home to a trailer park a few miles closer to town." Rufus accepts Jim Bob's explanation, and two weeks later they close the transaction. Rufus pays cash in exchange for a warranty deed, which he properly records the next day. Four days after closing, Rufus drives to the lot. He notices that the mobile home is still there and there's a pickup truck parked near the home. Rufus rings the doorbell and introduces himself. A woman answers, who admits to being Melba. However, she says that she will not be moving her home off the lot because she has a

written lease signed by Jim Bob, which also gives her the option to buy
the lot at the end of the lease term. Two months later, after unsuccessfully
trying to get Jim Bob to solve his problem, Rufus sues Melba to quiet
title to the lot. A title search conducted two days prior to the filing of
the complaint reveals that Jim Bob has record title to the lot, subject to
no encumbrances or other outstanding interests. Thus, Melba's lease
is unrecorded. The state has a race-notice recording act. What results
and why?

A. Rufus prevails because Melba could have recorded her lease and
    failed to do so.
B. Rufus prevails because Melba was not in possession of the mobile
    home on the day he inspected the property.
C. Rufus prevails because he reasonably relied on Jim Bob's statement
    that Melba was staying on the lot temporarily and would move soon.
D. Rufus prevails because Melba's possession is consistent with record
    title.
E. Melba prevails because Rufus has inquiry notice of her rights.

ANALYSIS.   Let's go down the list. Notice that the first four choices say that
Rufus wins, and only the last item picks Melba as the victor in this litigation.
Does this suggest that Rufus's odds of victory are 80 percent?

Answer **A** is wrong. This is a race-notice jurisdiction, meaning that Rufus
is on inquiry notice of unrecorded interests of persons in possession of the lot.
The inquiry notice doctrine is intended to protect a person like Melba, who
could have recorded and is arguably subject to criticism for failing to record.
A race recording act reflects a different judgment as to public policy. Answer **A**
would be correct under a race recording act.

Answer **B** is better than **A**. It forces you to ask what it means for a person
to be in possession of real estate for purposes of the inquiry notice doctrine.
A court conceivably could say that Melba's possession was discontinuous: she
was in possession whenever she was in the mobile home or outside on the
lot and out of possession when she was elsewhere. A court might say this
if it believed that Rufus made a diligent inspection by noticing the mobile
home and checking to see if anyone was then present. But **B** is weak because
possession of land as a general matter is seen as continuous when a person is
frequently present physically and that person's improvements remain on the
land at all times. For example, in another context, if Melba were making an
adverse possession claim to this lot, no court would require her to prove that
she was on the land 24/7 for the statutory number of years. The court would
find her possession to be open and continuous even though she left the property to go to work, shop, visit friends, and so forth, provided her absences
were similar to the conduct of other homeowners in leaving and returning
to their homes.

C is incorrect. If, in fact, Melba was in possession on the day Rufus visited the lot, any assurances given by the seller will not excuse the duty of inquiry. There's a good chance Rufus can prove that Jim Bob's statement amounted to fraudulent misrepresentation. If he succeeds, that's a cause of action Rufus may assert against Jim Bob; it doesn't affect Melba's rights vis-à-vis Rufus.

Answer **D** is also wrong. Record title is in Jim Bob, and Melba's lease is not recorded. If Melba's lease were recorded, record title and possession would be consistent. In this event, Rufus would have actual or constructive notice of the lease and thus no duty to inquire whether Melba had unrecorded rights in addition to or different from her rights in the recorded lease.

I expect you can see where this is headed. Melba wins this case so long as we conclude that living in a mobile home counts as possession, which I think it plainly does. **E** is the best answer.

E. Payment of Value

A grantee must pay value for the property interest in order to qualify as a BFP in notice statute jurisdictions, in race-notice statute jurisdictions, and in at least some race statute jurisdictions. The statutes often describe this requirement as payment of "valuable consideration."

One issue concerning value is measurement of the amount. How much consideration is needed? The value requirement is intended to disqualify a donee who receives a gift, either by deed or as heir or devisee. The idea is that a donee, heir, or devisee does not rely on the public record when acquiring her interest in the land, and thus there is no need to protect such a person by terminating a valid earlier property right.

In the real world it isn't always easy to distinguish purchasers and donees. Standard deed forms often state that the grantee has paid "ten dollars and other good and valuable consideration," and such forms are often used for gifts. Nominal consideration, however, does not suffice to make a donee a BFP. The famous "peppercorn theory" of contract law does not apply here. Many courts treat a deed recital of the payment of consideration with some respect, saying it gives rise to a presumption that valuable consideration was given. Like other presumptions, such a recital can be rebutted by evidence as to the actual amount, if any, paid. The value paid has to be substantial, but it doesn't have to rise to the level of full market value.

A second issue concerning value is the timing of payment. Generally the purchaser is not a BFP before she actually pays the bargained-for price to the seller. This means that a binding promise to pay, although it may be consideration in the general contract law sense, is not enough for the recording act. For example, when a purchaser signs an executory contract, paying the seller a normal amount of down payment or earnest money, the purchaser is not yet a BFP. Only at closing, when she pays the remainder of the purchase price, does she become a BFP. Some courts have modified the traditional rule that the purchaser must pay all or most of the price in the context of installment land contracts, in which the purchaser goes into possession and pays the price to the seller in installments over a number of years. Applying the traditional rule here puts the purchaser in a very difficult position. To avoid the risk of potential loss to third parties, the buyer would have to do a new title search prior to making each payment, clearly an unreasonable burden. For this reason some courts have ruled that an installment land buyer may qualify as a BFP after having made significant payments, even if such payments constitute a relatively low percentage of the total contract price.

QUESTION 5.   Swapping real estate. Lana and Mike sign an agreement involving an exchange of their real properties. Both expect to get substantial income tax benefits by structuring their transaction as a like-kind exchange of real property. Lana owns a 60-acre farm worth $900,000, and Mike owns an apartment building worth $1.2 million. To make up the difference, the agreement provides for Lana to give Mike a promissory note for $300,000, secured by a mortgage on the apartment building. Lana's attorney searches title and finds that Mike has record marketable title. Lana and her attorney do not know, however, that two years ago Mike conveyed a one-fourth fee interest in the apartment property to Natalie by deed, which is unrecorded. In the exchange agreement, each party promises it has marketable title to the respective property, but the agreement says nothing about who is responsible for curing title defects. A week before the scheduled closing of the exchange, Natalie learns of Mike's plan to sell the apartment building. Natalie calls Lana's attorney and says that the exchange cannot take place without her. Natalie is willing, however, to convey her interest to Lana for $350,000. As of the time of Natalie's call to Lana's attorney, Lana has spent $1,000 on the title search, $2,200 for an engineer's inspection of the apartment building, and $3,800 in legal fees. She has also spent many hours and several thousands of dollars to remove her equipment and other personal property from the farm. Lana wants to go forward with the exchange. Both parties decide to close as soon as possible, without handling Natalie's interest ahead of time. They close, with the two parties specifying by warranty deed the intent to convey entire ownership of their respective properties. The day after closing, Natalie records her deed. Two days later Lana's attorney records the warranty deed conveying the apartment building from Mike to Lana. Natalie brings an action to quiet title against Lana, claiming she owns an undivided one-fourth of the apartment building. The state has a notice recording act. Natalie's best argument is:

A. Lana does not qualify as a bona fide purchaser because she learned of Natalie's rights before conveying her farm to Mike.

B. Lana does not qualify as a bona fide purchaser because Natalie recorded her deed before Lana paid value.

C. Lana does not qualify as a bona fide purchaser because Natalie recorded her deed before Lana recorded her deed.

D. Lana does not qualify as a bona fide purchaser because she learned of Natalie's rights before she entered into a binding agreement to exchange her farm for Mike's apartment building.

ANALYSIS. All four answers directly focus on Lana's possible BFP status, making it clear that this is the question's sole focal point. The state has a notice recording act, which means that Lana must pay value at a time when she lacks notice of Natalie's claim. Under a race-notice recording act, Lana would have to satisfy the additional requirement of recording before Natalie. But with a notice act, this is not required, so **C** is wrong.

Answer **B**, like **C**, compares the time Natalie recorded her deed to another event. The problem with **B** is that Lana paid full value at closing, the day before Natalie recorded. So **B** is wrong. Had Natalie recorded before Lana paid value, Natalie would win because Lana would have constructive notice of her deed, but the facts are contrary.

Answer **D** is also incorrect chronologically. Lana and Mike entered into their exchange agreement before Lana learned of Natalie's interest, and there are no facts suggesting that the agreement does not bind Lana. Even though Mike may have breached the contract because he lacked marketable title, Lana had the right to refuse to close until Mike solved the problem of Natalie's outstanding interest. This may affect the BFP analysis; a court may hold that Lana should have refrained from paying additional value to Natalie in the absence of Mike's solving the title problem. But the phrasing of **B** does not support such a conclusion. Even if Lana had the right to withhold performance, she still had entered into a binding contract.

This leaves **A** as the best answer. Lana had actual notice of Natalie's claim before closing. The issue is whether she paid sufficient value before the moment she acquired actual notice. This is debatable. Lana will claim that she has already given substantial consideration by promising to convey her farm. She may point out that under the doctrine of equitable conversion, Mike had equitable title before she learned about Natalie. By analogy, she can rely on decisions in some states protecting purchasers under installment land contracts. But she may lose. Natalie will point out that Lana's out-of-pocket expenses amount to only several thousand dollars, clearly not unusually high for earnest money or a down payment on a major property purchase. Natalie will rely on cases holding that the payment of typical earnest money is not sufficient to make a buyer a BFP prior to closing, while the contract is executory.

F.   The Closer: Chain of Title Problems

Some interests in land, even though recorded, are difficult or impossible to locate during a title search of the public record due to inherent limitations of the records system. Purchasers take subject to such an interest, provided the jurisdiction considers that the instrument creating that interest is in fact legally recorded.

A limitation of all public records is the index system used. Most states have name indexes in which deeds and other instruments are indexed by the names of the parties. Traditionally, indexes were printed and bound or compiled separately for each calendar year or for some other time period. Today many recording offices have the name index on a computer system, but sometimes the index does not include the older records. In a few states the public land records use a tract index, either as an alternative to a name index or as an additional indexing system. A tract index organizes deeds and other instruments according to the parcel or parcels they affect.

Under either type of index system, a person searching title seeks to discover and examine the chain of title for the property in question, going back to the sovereign or covering a shorter period of time. A name index system sometimes presents special problems with finding relevant instruments. Examples include the late recorded deed and the early recorded deed. A deed or other instrument is late recorded when there is a substantial gap in time between delivery and recordation, during which the record owner transferred ownership to someone else, who promptly recorded. The difficulty is that the searcher will stop looking in the grantor name index for adverse transfers after the time the record owner transferred ownership to the second person.

The early recorded deed is the flip side of this: a person transfers an interest in land he does not own and subsequently acquires an estate in that land. States are about evenly split on whether or not late recorded deeds and early recorded deeds are treated as validly recorded. If such a deed is considered to be validly recorded, it imparts constructive notice to subsequent purchasers. Late and early recorded deeds can be found by checking the indexes for the years before and after the dates each record owner acquired and parted with title. The policy issue is one of efficiency: which person can overcome the problems associated with such deeds at the lowest cost? The searcher can solve the problem by using an expanded search technique. The late recorder or early recorder, who put his deed on record out of sequence, could have avoided the problem either by recording promptly (the late recorder) or by doing a careful search and finding that the grantor lacked record title (the early recorder).

QUESTION 6.   **An easement dispute.** Alice and Bernie are neighboring owners of undeveloped tracts of land. Alice's tract, Blackacre, fronts a county highway, but Bernie's tract does not. In 2000 Alice granted a right-of-way easement across Blackacre to Bernie to allow him access to the highway. Bernie did not record his easement until 2009. In the meantime, Alice decided to make a gift of Blackacre to her niece, Claire. In 2006 she conveyed Blackacre to Claire by warranty deed, without telling her about Bernie's easement across the property. Claire immediately recorded her deed. In 2011 Claire needed money and decided to sell Blackacre. Claire sold Blackacre to Dimitri, who paid fair market value for the property in exchange for a warranty deed executed by Claire. Prior to closing his purchase, Dimitri ordered a title search for Blackacre, which failed to disclose Bernie's easement. The parcels are located in a state with a race-notice recording act that organizes its records by name index. Is Bernie's easement valid?

It is now six months after the closing, and Bernie decides to develop his parcel. He wants to improve the easement area by clearing trees and other vegetation and by installing an asphalt driveway. Dimitri objects. What is his best argument that Blackacre is not subject to the easement claimed by Bernie?

A. Bernie cannot qualify as a bona fide purchaser because there is no evidence that he paid value for his easement.

B. Bernie's delay in recording his easement impairs the ability of a title searcher to find the instrument.

C. Bernie's easement was extinguished when Claire recorded her deed because Bernie's easement was not then recorded.

D. Bernie's easement is an early recorded instrument and therefore is outside of the chain of title.

ANALYSIS. We can strike **D** first. An early recorded instrument is one that is recorded before the grantor has acquired the estate or interest that is necessary to make the instrument effective. We might have an early recorded easement problem if Alice did not own Blackacre in 2000 but nevertheless granted Bernie an easement in 2000 and later acquired a fee simple estate in Blackacre. Instead we have a late recorded easement: Bernie obtained a valid easement in 2000 and waited nine years to record, and in the meantime Alice conveyed the servient estate (part of Blackacre) to Claire.

B is the best answer. It reflects the concern that some courts have over late recorded instruments. Dimitri's title searcher probably found the Alice-Claire deed, executed and recorded in 2006, and concluded that there was no reason to look for adverse transfers by Alice in the name indexes after 2006.

A is incorrect because it reverses the BFP analysis. It doesn't matter whether Bernie paid value or whether Alice gave him the easement. Bernie's interest is first in time. To defeat that interest, Dimitri must establish that he or Claire qualifies as a BFP. Bernie's easement will fail if it's considered to be outside the chain of title because it's late recorded; it will succeed if the state considers a late recorded instrument to be within the chain of title.

C also hints at BFP analysis, but founders also. When aunt Alice conveyed to Claire, Claire lacked actual notice of Bernie's easement; no facts point toward inquiry notice, and there was no constructive notice because Bernie had not yet recorded. But this was a gift. Because Claire did not pay value, she cannot qualify as a BFP to cut off Bernie's easement, even though she acquired her interest without notice and recorded before Bernie.

 Smith's Picks

1. A deed to the family condominium   D
2. A lender's delay in recording the mortgage C
3. Buying a condominium that excludes cats   A
4. An empty mobile home   E
5. Swapping real estate   A
6. An easement dispute   B

24

Easements: Creation

*"In geometry it holds true that a straight line is the shortest way between
two points; in practical psychology it is mostly not true."*
Hugo Munsterberg, *The World Language*
28 *McClure's Magazine* 102, 104 (1907)

CHAPTER OVERVIEW
A. Appurtenant Easements and Easements in Gross
B. Affirmative Easements, Negative Easements, and Profits
C. Granting an Easement to a Third Party
D. Easements Implied from Prior Use
E. Easements by Necessity
F. Prescriptive Easements
G. The Closer: Planning for Access When Subdividing a Parcel
◈ Smith's Picks

asements are widely used to define the legal relationships of landowners. An easement is a right to make a specific limited use of land that is
possessed by another person. It is a *servitude*, which means it is a non-
possessory interest in land. The easement has much in common with other
servitudes: real covenants, equitable servitudes, and licenses. The similarities
have led analysts to propose unification into a single integrated interest. For
example, Restatement (Third) of Property: Servitudes §1.1 cmt. a (2000) (servitude "is the generic term that describes legal devices private parties can use
to create rights and obligations"). Most courts, however, continue to use the
traditional separate terminology.

Easements are created either expressly or by implication. An express easement means that there is language in a deed or in another writing that explicitly grants or provides for the easement. Express easements are of two types:

- **Grants.** The grantor conveys an easement to the grantee. For a grant of an easement, the instrument's only purpose may be the conveyance of an easement, or the grant may be tied to the conveyance of an estate from the grantor to the grantee.
- **Reservations.** An easement is reserved if a grantor conveys an estate and wishes to make some use of the conveyed property after delivery of the deed. The grantor reserves an easement over the conveyed property.

A. Appurtenant Easements and Easements in Gross

Most easements are *appurtenant*. The land subject to an easement is called the *servient estate*. An easement is appurtenant when its purpose is to enhance the value of land that adjoins the servient estate or is near the servient estate. That benefited land is called the *dominant estate*. The significance of calling an easement "appurtenant" is that ownership of the easement is tied to ownership of the dominant estate. The easement is not viewed as owned by an individual in her personal capacity. Instead, the easement is one of the rights and privileges of owning the dominant estate.

In contrast to an appurtenant easement, an *easement in gross* is owned by an individual person. There is no dominant estate to which ownership of the easement is linked. For an easement in gross, the only relevant parcel of land is the servient estate where the easement is located and where its owner exercises her rights.

A written easement should indicate expressly whether it is appurtenant or in gross. If the former, the document should precisely identify the dominant estate, as well as the servient estate. Often, however, the parties fail to state the type of easement that they intend, or they use ambiguous language. Then courts must interpret the parties' intent based on the facts and circumstances. The court will conclude that the easement is appurtenant if it appears that the purpose of the easement is to benefit the easement holder in connection with her ownership of particular land, which can be identified as the dominant estate.

QUESTION 1. Shortcut to the golf course. David and Lucy are next-door neighbors. David's lot borders a public golf course. David grants to Lucy an easement to walk across David's backyard to the golf course. The grant says nothing about whether Lucy's easement is appurtenant or in gross. Should a court hold the easement in appurtenant or in gross?

A. In gross, because if an instrument that creates an easement is ambiguous, then an easement in gross is presumed.

> **B.** In gross, because this allows Lucy to include family members and friends as permitted users of the easement.
> **C.** Appurtenant, because an easement is in gross only if the instrument uses the term "in gross" or a synonym.
> **D.** Appurtenant, because use of the easement by a person who lives somewhere other than Lucy's property is unlikely.

ANALYSIS.   Lucy's easement to walk to the public golf course clearly has to be interpreted as appurtenant. It would be of no value to anyone except the owner of Lucy's lot. If Lucy sells her residence and moves, would she want to return to exercise the right to walk across David's backyard to the golf course? Of course not. If Lucy still plays golf at that course, she will travel there by another way. Therefore, **A** and **B** are incorrect.

Choice **C** is also incorrect. An easement may be in gross even if the instrument does not use the words "in gross" or contain other language pointing toward an easement in gross.

This leaves **D** as the right answer. Lucy's easement is appurtenant because the purpose of the easement is to allow Lucy, as next-door neighbor, to get to the golf course by taking a shortcut across David's backyard.

B.   Affirmative Easements, Negative Easements, and Profits

A second type of classification for easements distinguishes between affirmative easements and negative easements. An *affirmative easement* confers upon the holder the right to make a physical entry upon the servient estate. The entry may be at ground level, subsurface, or in the airspace. The easement may permit the entry of people or it may authorize the installation of equipment or other tangible property, such as an electric power line. An affirmative easement functions as a privilege to enter the land of another. But for the easement, the entry would be a trespass, entitling the landowner to an appropriate remedy such as damages or an injunction.

A *negative easement* allows the holder to restrict the use of the servient estate. The owner of a negative easement has no privilege to enter the servient estate. The right is limited to insisting that the possessor of the servient estate not engage in the forbidden conduct. Negative easements are much less common than affirmative easements. Historically the law has considered negative easements to be a closed set. The traditionally recognized negative easements are an easement for light, an easement for air, an easement of view, an easement for support, and an easement for water in a defined channel (e.g., a stream or pipe). The *conservation easement*, a newer type of negative easement first used in the 1960s, prohibits or limits development of the servient estate or other changes thereto, such as the demolition of an historic building.

A negative easement closely resembles a covenant. Both of these servitudes can accomplish the same end. The distinction between the two devices is traditional and formal, not functional, and turns upon the method of their creation. A writing that creates a negative easement uses conveyancing language and easement vocabulary. In contrast, a covenant is expressed in promissory language, typically accompanied by words signifying that the covenant is intended to run with the land.

A *profit*, more fully called a *profit à prendre*, is a right to take something of value from another person's land, such as deer or gravel. A profit may be in gross or appurtenant. Under modern law, profits are often viewed as a subcategory of affirmative easements, with the same rules applying to both interests.

QUESTION 2.   "I like to look at Indian Lake." Garth owns a lot that fronts on the pristine waters of Indian Lake. His neighbor, Francine, owns an adjoining uphill lot. Presently Francine enjoys an unobstructed view of Indian Lake from her house, and she wants assurance that Garth's lot will not be used in a fashion that interferes with her view. In exchange for $1,000, Garth signs a writing that grants to Francine "the right to an unobstructed view of the waters of Indian Lake." The writing provides that Francine has the right "to trim and top trees and other vegetation" on designated parts of Garth's land with the limitation that this "shall not be done more than once per calendar year." This writing may plausibly be interpreted as creating

A.   An affirmative easement.
B.   A negative easement.
C.   Both A and B are plausible interpretations.
D.   A profit à prendre.
E.   A, B, and D are all plausible interpretations.
F.   A license.

ANALYSIS.   Let's start at the bottom. A license allows a person to enter land owned by another, but it is revocable by the landowner. Francine has bargained for greater rights than a license, so **F** is not plausible.

Francine might have a profit à prendre because she is authorized to enter Garth's land and cut vegetation. After cutting, can she remove the tree branches, leaves, and so on, from Garth's lot and take them to her property? Possibly the writing allows this, but these things are of no apparent value to her. Likely they're only yard waste. The point of the transaction is to protect her view of Indian Lake. A court should not call this a profit, so let's strike **D** (this means we also strike **E**).

We're left with the two easement choices. Many easements of view are negative easements because the owner of the servient estate (Garth) has the duty to maintain his property so as not to interfere with the easement owner's sight lines. We should call this a negative easement only if the writing does *not* grant Francine the right to enter Garth's lot. Garth is not obligated to cut his vegetation. Francine is expressly authorized to enter, no more than once a year, to cut vegetation to preserve her lake view. Thus, she has an affirmative easement. Choice **A** is the best answer.

C.   Granting an Easement to a Third Party

A traditional common law rule prohibits the reservation of an easement in a stranger (i.e., a third party). This means that a deed conveying an estate from **A** to **B** cannot grant to, or reserve an easement for, **C** even though **C** may own land that neighbors the conveyed estate. Some states still follow the traditional prohibition, but other states have abandoned the restriction, now allowing the creation of an easement in a third party if the intent to do so is clearly expressed.

QUESTION 3.   Trying to help the neighboring church. Wanda owns a vacant lot next to the church she attends. She lets members of the congregation park on part of her lot during church services because there isn't enough parking on the church premises. She wants to sell the vacant lot but would like to make sure that church parking on the lot can continue after the sale. Wanda realizes that she may get a smaller sales price if she insists on this condition. You are Wanda's attorney. She would like your advice on how best to accomplish her objective. Suppose you research the law of the state where the property is located, and you find no relevant modern authority dealing with the reservation of an easement in a third party. Which of the following alternatives do you think best serves your client's interests?

A. Prior to the sale of the lot, prepare and record a grant of a parking easement to the church.

B. In the sale of the lot, make the deed conveying the lot to the buyer subject to a parking easement for the benefit of the church.

C. In the contract of sale require that the buyer grant a parking easement to the church after delivery of the deed to the buyer.

D. When a buyer of the lot is identified, convey the lot to the church, with the church then conveying title to the buyer and reserving a parking easement.

ANALYSIS.   Any of the four choices might work. Your task is to decide which one is best in terms of minimizing risk and cost for the client. It is most important to pick an alternative that is safe. If more than one alternative is workable and low risk, you then want to pick the alternative that is simpler and presumably less expensive.

Choice **A** envisions a two-step transaction. Wanda first will grant the church an easement and then sell the property to a buyer subject to the easement. Here there is no attempt to reserve an easement in a stranger or a third party, so the lack of authority as to whether this is permissible in the state does not matter. Grants of easements like this one are valid in all states.

Choice **B** attempts to reserve an easement for the church, a third party. In some states this is allowed, but others follow the traditional rule and invalidate such an attempted reservation. This fact pattern is based on *Willard v. First Church of Christ*, 498 P.2d 987 (Cal. 1972), which changed California law to uphold the reservation. Here we do not know if our state will follow *Willard*, so there is substantial risk for Wanda and the church.

Choice **C** may work if the contract obligation placed on the buyer is clearly drafted and made to survive the closing of the sale. Even if the drafting is done properly, there is the risk that the buyer may fail to sign the grant of easement. Wanda would then have to sue the buyer, hoping to get specific performance.

Choice **D** may also work. Here Wanda would be trusting the church, rather than the buyer. Although this may be better than choice **C**, it is still a complicated transaction. Choice **A** is the best choice.

D.   Easements Implied from Prior Use

An easement implied from prior use may arise when land is subdivided into two or more parcels. The purpose of the implied easement is to protect pre-existing beneficial uses. The easement claimant must prove a use that is open, apparent, continuous, and necessary. There are different views as to the degree of necessity required. Traditionally, many courts required *strict necessity*, but today in most states it is enough if the prior use is *reasonably necessary* for the enjoyment of the dominant estate.

> **QUESTION 4.   Water and sewer lines.** Brian owned Whiteacre, a four-acre parcel of land fronting on Lingam Road. Brian lived in a house on Whiteacre, which was located near the parcel's rear boundary line. Brian wanted a larger, newer house, so he contracted to sell the house along with the back half of Whiteacre (two acres) to Cecelia. The parties closed the sale, with Brian conveying that two-acre parcel to Cecelia. In the deed Brian granted Cecelia an easement to use the existing driveway for access to Lingam Road. The house is connected to the city's water and

sewer system through underground pipes that run from Lingam Road to the house. The deed is silent as to any rights Cecelia might have with respect to the water and sewer lines, and the parties never discussed the issue. Brian is planning to build a new house on the front two-acre parcel, and he has discovered that the water and sewer lines will interfere with his plans for the basement for the house. He asserts he has the right to remove the lines. Cecelia insists that they must remain in place. Who will most likely prevail?

A. Brian, because Cecelia should have bargained for a water and sewer line easement.

B. Brian, because the water and sewer lines were underground and he did not know where they were located when he sold the house to Cecelia.

C. Cecelia, because the water and sewer lines are necessary to the enjoyment of her property.

D. Cecelia, because Brian had a duty to disclose the location of the water and sewer lines when he contracted to sell his house to Cecelia.

E. The court will order rescission of the contract, requiring Cecelia to reconvey the back two-acre parcel to Brian in exchange for his refund of the purchase price.

ANALYSIS.   Here's a sketch of what the facts look like.

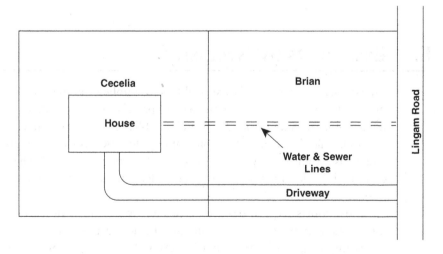

The main issue is whether Cecelia has an implied easement based on prior use. Such an easement arises when, at the time a tract is subdivided, part of the property is being used for the benefit of another part. The use must be open and obvious, and it must be necessary for the enjoyment of the benefited part.

The argument in **A** (that Cecelia should have bargained for an express easement) is a rational position, but the law has not accepted it. The law recognizes implied easements and thus relieves a person from the onus of obtaining an express easement when the elements of an easement implied from prior use are present.

Choice **D** confuses duties of disclosure in the sale of real property with implied easements. Brian as a seller may have a duty to disclose under certain circumstances—for example, if he knew of a material defect in the water or sewer system. But here there is no defect for him to disclose, and his failure to inform Cecelia about facts with respect to the house's water and sewer service has nothing to do with the question of whether an easement ought to be implied.

Choice **E** is not a good answer. The facts do not suggest that either Brian or Cecelia has asked for rescission, and even if one party did ask, that outcome is unlikely in the absence of fraud, of which there is no evidence here.

Now let's turn to choices **B** and **C**. Both are plausible responses, and both focus on the core elements of easements implied from prior use. Choice **B** indicates that Brian should win because the water and sewer lines are not open and obvious. Choice **C** indicates that Cecelia should win because the necessity requirement is satisfied. In making the choice, you must consider which argument you believe is stronger. Choice **B** has a significant weakness. Brian lived in the house and certainly would know that it was connected to city water and sewer—undoubtedly he received bills he had to pay. He should have assumed that the underground lines went directly through his property to the street. Choice **C**, the right answer, has no similar weakness. Most people today would consider running water in a house to be a necessity, not a mere convenience or luxury.

E.   Easements by Necessity

An easement by necessity is a special type of implied easement for which no preexisting use is required. It arises when a parcel of land is subdivided, resulting in a subparcel that has no access to a public road. The subparcel, which is said to be "landlocked," is the dominant estate. The owner of the dominant estate has a right-of-way easement to travel to the public road. The servient estate and the dominant estate must be under common ownership at the time of the subdivision.

Most courts require strict necessity for an easement by necessity. This means that extreme cost or difficulty in using legally available access does not justify implying an easement by necessity. Other courts follow the view that reasonable necessity is enough. Under this view, a landowner obtains an easement by necessity when her parcel is not literally landlocked, but the construction of usable access to a public road is very expensive compared to a modest expense through the servient estate.

An easement by necessity continues only so long as the necessity persists. If the owner of the dominant estate acquires another method of legal access, the easement by necessity terminates.

QUESTION 5.   Stuck in the middle. Iggy owned a 60-acre tract of land bounded by North Street on the north and South Street on the south. Iggy made a gift of the north 20 acres ("Tract 1") to Hilda, conveying by deed of gift. Two years later Iggy sold the south 20 acres ("Tract 2") to Gabriel, conveying by warranty deed. This resulted in Iggy retaining the middle 20 acres ("Tract 3"). Tract 3 has no access to any street or road, nor are there any existing driveways or paths that connect Tract 3 to North Street or South Street. The deeds to Tract 1 and Tract 2 have no provisions that bear on access for Tract 3. Does Iggy have an easement that allows him access to Tract 3?

A. No, because Iggy caused the problem by failing to reserve an easement when he conveyed Tract 1 and Tract 2.

B. No, because the statute of frauds requires that easements be written.

C. Yes, because the conveyance of Tract 1 created an easement for Iggy to cross Tract 1 to North Street.

D. Yes, because the conveyance of Tract 2 created an easement for Iggy to cross Tract 2 to South Street.

E. Yes, because both conveyances created an easement and Iggy may pick between Tract 1 and Tract 2 for access to a street.

ANALYSIS.   Here is a map.

North Street		
Tract 1	Iggy ⟶	Hilda
Tract 3	Iggy	
Tract 2	Iggy ⟶	Gabriel
South Street		

Iggy's two conveyances have caused Tract 3 to become landlocked. Because there is no access to Tract 3, there should be an easement by necessity to allow ingress and egress. An easement by necessity arises when a parcel of land is subdivided, with one part cut off from access to a public road. Therefore, **A** is incorrect even though it is true that Iggy has caused the problem by failing to create an express right-of-way easement. In this situation, the law gives Iggy relief even though he could have protected himself.

Choice **B** is incorrect because Iggy has an easement by necessity. The statute of frauds applies to grants of easements, but this does not prevent the creation of an easement by necessity. The easement by necessity is not created by the parties' oral words. The deed that causes the tract to become landlocked is written, and this satisfies the statute of frauds.

Choices **C**, **D**, and **E** require that we determine where the easement by necessity should be located. We have to determine when Tract 3 became landlocked. The easement by necessity must be across land that was in common ownership at the time of the severance of ownership. The conveyance of Tract 1 to Hilda did not make Tract 3 landlocked. Immediately after that conveyance, Iggy owned both Tract 3 and Tract 2 and thus had access from Tract 3 across Tract 2 to South Street. At this point in time there is no easement by necessity. Choice **C** is wrong. For the same reason, **E** is wrong. Iggy does not have a choice as to which tract is subject to the easement by necessity.

Choice **D** is the correct answer. The second conveyance (Tract 2 to Gabriel) made Tract 3 landlocked. Thus, Iggy's easement by necessity is across Tract 2 to South Street.

QUESTION 6.   **Stuck in the middle revisited.** Let's return to the facts of Question 7 above. Assume we have more conveyances to consider. Four years after the conveyance of Tract 2 to Gabriel, Iggy sells Tract 3 to his neighbor to the east, Natalie, who owns Tract 4, a 30-acre tract that has frontage on North Street. Five years later, Natalie dies, devising Tract 3 to her nephew Nasty and Tract 4 to her niece Natasha. Here's a map.

North Street		
Tract 1 Iggy → Hilda		Tract 4
Tract 3 Iggy → Natalie → Nasty		Natalie → Natasha
Tract 2 Iggy → Gabriel		
South Street		

Over all of these years no one has put in a driveway or path to connect Tract 3 to any road. Does Nasty have an easement that allows him access to Tract 3?

A. No, because Iggy's conveyance of Tract 3 to Natalie eliminated the easement by necessity.
B. No, because Nasty can seek Natasha's permission to cross Tract 4.
C. Yes, because Natalie's will created an easement for Nasty to cross Tract 4 to North Street.
D. Yes, because Iggy's easement by necessity to cross Tract 2 is appurtenant and is now owned by Nasty.

> E. Yes, because both the conveyance of Tract 2 and Natalie's will created easements by necessity, and Nasty may pick which one he prefers to use.

ANALYSIS.   An easement by necessity is different from an express easement in that it continues only for so long as the necessity continues. Here Iggy's easement by necessity to cross Tract 3 to reach South Street terminated when he sold Tract 3 to his neighbor, Natalie. She did not need an easement by necessity to reach Tract 3 because she could get to that tract through Tract 4.

Choice **A**, however, is not correct because a subsequent event, Natalie's will, created a new easement by necessity. When Natalie divided ownership of her two tracts between Nasty and Natasha, she made Tract 3 landlocked once again.

Choice **B** is wrong. An easement by necessity is a property right, and Nasty does not need Natasha's permission to cross Tract 4 for ingress and egress to Tract 3.

Choice **D** is wrong, although it is true that an easement by necessity is appurtenant and transferable to a new owner of the dominant estate. That did not happen here because Iggy's conveyance to Natalie terminated the easement by ending the necessity.

Choice **E** is incorrect because the owner of an easement by necessity can never pick between neighboring tracts of land for the location of access. The easement must be over the tract that was in common ownership at the time of the severance that gave rise to the necessity.

Choice **C** is the right answer: Nasty will have an easement by necessity across Tract 4, which the will devised to Natasha.

F.   Prescriptive Easements

Express easements and implied easements are founded on an actual or presumed agreement of the parties. In contrast, prescriptive easements are nonconsensual, deriving their existence from long-standing adverse use.

The rules for prescriptive easements closely resemble those applicable to adverse possession. An easement by prescription is established only if the claimant's use was adverse or hostile. If the use is with the owner's permission, the claimant has a license and there can be no prescriptive easement. To determine whether a use is adverse or permissive, most states apply the same standards used for adverse possession.

There are two key distinctions between prescriptive easements and adverse possession. First, to gain title by adverse possession the claimant must show exclusive possession of the land in question. For a prescriptive easement, the claimant only needs to show regular use. This is an easier standard to meet. Use of the land in question by other people, including the fee owner, does not prevent the creation of a prescriptive easement.

Second, traditionally the law of prescriptive easements has required that the true owner acquiesce to the prescriptive use. Acquiescence is not necessary for title by adverse possession. It is commonly said that part of acquiescence is notice to the true owner coupled with the true owner's failure to object to the adverse use. Notice need not be a direct communication that the claimant is making an adverse use. It can be proven circumstantially based on the nature and frequency of the use.

QUESTION 7.   Picnic in the park. Over a period of twelve years, Kendrick and his family frequently walked across the field owned by his neighbor, Crystal, to reach a public park. Crystal never gave Kendrick or members of his family permission to enter her property, and she never forbade them to enter either. Which of the following facts would help Kendrick to establish an easement across Crystal's property?

A. The Kendricks were aware that they were trespassing on Crystal's property.

B. The Kendricks could have walked to the public park on public sidewalks, and the shortcut through Crystal's field saved them only five minutes per trip.

C. The Kendricks were careful not to cause any damage to plants or other objects on Crystal's property.

D. Six years ago Crystal built a new barn over part of the path the Kendricks used to cross her property, and this caused them to modify their route.

E. Crystal was aware that the Kendricks were crossing her field.

ANALYSIS.   This question tests the basic requirements of prescriptive easements. If Kendrick owns an easement, he has acquired it by prescription. **A** is incorrect. The state of mind of a claimant of a prescriptive easement is not relevant. Although some states require subjective good faith for an adverse possessor to gain limitation title, this good faith requirement is not replicated for prescriptive easements.

Choice **B** is wrong because there is no necessity requirement for a prescriptive easement. It does not matter how valuable the prescriptive easement is to the claimant. If the claimant can prove the elements, it is established.

Choice **C** is wrong. Physical damage or the lack thereof to the servient estate does not matter to the creation of a prescriptive easement.

Choice **D** incorporates a relevant fact, but it cuts the other way, *against* a finding of prescriptive easement. A prescriptive easement, like other easements, has to have a defined location. A change in location is prejudicial to Kendrick, the claimant.

A common requirement for a prescriptive easement is that the landowner had notice of the adverse claim and acquiesced to the adverse use. Thus, it will help Kendrick if he can prove that Crystal knew that he and his family repeatedly crossed her field to go to the park and she failed to object. Choice E is the right answer because it incorporates the idea of notice.

G. The Closer: Planning for Access When Subdividing a Parcel

Easements, like the other types of property rights that you're studying, are tools used by persons to accomplish certain objectives. Often a person will have choices as to which tools to employ. Transactional lawyers assist their clients by selecting the proper interest and documenting the transaction by preparing appropriate instruments. Easements are highly flexible, but they are not always the best choice. Recall that there are many types of easements with differing characteristics. When creation of an easement is desirable, the transactional lawyer has to consider what type of easement to use and how it should be documented.

QUESTION 8.   Selling part of the land. Rufus owns a five-acre parcel of land that has frontage on a rural road. He wants to sell the part of his property, consisting of two acres, that fronts the road. He will then continue to own the back three acres. Rufus wants to have access to the road for his three-acre parcel after he sells the two-acre parcel. The best way for him to accomplish this objective would be, when he sells the two-acre parcel,

A. To have the county government use its power of eminent domain to condemn a right-of-way easement.
B. To obtain a license to cross the two-acre parcel.
C. To have the buyer of the two-acre parcel grant Rufus an easement across the two-acre parcel.
D. To reserve an easement across the two-acre parcel.
E. To obtain an easement by necessity.

ANALYSIS. Rufus ought to obtain a right-of-way easement that allows access from the three-acre parcel to the road. He should bargain for this right when he sells the property. If he fails to do so, it is unlikely that the county government will solve his problem using eminent domain, but even if it would do so, this is an expensive and time-consuming solution. **A** is not a wise choice.

The buyer of Rufus's two-acre parcel might grant Rufus a license for access to the road, but this is not a good solution because a license is generally revocable by the licensor and nontransferable. Rufus would probably lose his right of access if the buyer at any time in the future told him that he should no longer cross the land.

Rufus should plan to obtain an express easement when he negotiates a sale of the front two-acre parcel. If the contract of sale and the deed are silent as to an easement for Rufus, there is a good chance that he would obtain an implied easement by necessity. The facts do not indicate whether his retained three-acre parcel will be landlocked. If it will be, he probably will have an easement by necessity to cross the two-acre parcel. But litigation may be necessary to establish an easement by necessity. Therefore, **E** is not his best alternative.

Both **C** and **D** involve the creation of an express right-of-way easement across the two-acre parcel. With Choice **D**, Rufus accomplishes this directly by reservation of an easement. The deed that conveys fee simple title to the two-acre parcel to a buyer will also reserve for Rufus an easement across that parcel. Choice **C** reaches the same functional end but by a more cumbersome two-step process. Instead of reserving the easement, Rufus is relying on the buyer to execute a separate instrument that grants the easement to him. Thus, **D** is the best answer.

Smith's Picks

1.	Shortcut to the golf course	**D**
2.	"I like to look at Indian Lake"	**A**
3.	Trying to help the neighboring church	**A**
4.	Water and sewer lines	**C**
5.	Stuck in the middle	**D**
6.	Stuck in the middle revisited	**C**
7.	Picnic in the park	**E**
8.	Selling part of the land	**D**

25

Easements: Scope and Termination

"What is or is not a reasonable use of a way does not become crystallized at any particular moment of time. Changing needs of either owner may operate to make unreasonable a use of the way previously reasonable, or to make reasonable a use previously unreasonable. There is an element of time as well as of space in this question of reasonableness. In the absence of contract on the subject, the owner of the dominant estate is not limited in his use of the way to such vehicles only as were known at the time the way was created, but he may use the way for any vehicle which his reasonable needs may require in the development of his estate."

Justice Peter Woodbury
Sakansky v. Wein, 169 A. 1, 3 (N.H. 1933)

CHAPTER OVERVIEW
A. The Scope of Easements
B. Transfers of Easements
C. Duration of Easements
D. The Closer: Easement Rights of New Owners
 Smith's Picks

Easements are valuable property rights because they are relatively permanent. Their long-term nature has had important impacts on the development of legal rules to govern easement relationships. For express easements, interpretation of the parties' rights begins with standard rules of contract interpretation. But evolving methods of interpreting easements go beyond typical contract interpretation. Interpretation of easement agreements assumes the parties realized that circumstances would change and therefore easement terms would change as well. Common examples illustrating this concept are easements granted prior to significant technological changes the parties were incapable of predicting, such as the automobile.

In addition to the need for easement law to accommodate changing circumstances over time, it is important to bear in mind that the original parties to the easement often depart the scene. The rights of use and enjoyment reflected by an easement generally survive transfer of the servient parcel that is subject to the easement. Easement rights themselves are also often transferable. Thus, new owners acquire rights and take on responsibilities, and should be able to ascertain those rights and responsibilities with a reasonable degree of certainty.

A. The Scope of Easements

By definition, an easement allows a person to make a limited use of another person's land. The nature and extent of the permitted uses can vary considerably. In other words, the scope may be narrow or broad. For example, a right-of-way easement may allow vehicular traffic only, foot traffic only, or both vehicular and foot traffic.

For an express easement, the scope of the rights of the easement owner depends upon the intent of the parties. The language of the easement instrument is of paramount importance. Courts ascertain intent by using standard rules of contract interpretation, including the admission of extrinsic evidence when the instrument is found to be ambiguous.

The same issues of scope come up with nonexpress easements—implied and prescriptive easements. Although the court has no language to examine, results tend to be similar, with the focus on discerning the reasonable expectations of the parties at the time of the easement's creation.

The easement owner has the right to make reasonable use of the servient estate, including the installation of improvements that are reasonably necessary for the enjoyment of the easement. The servient owner must not interfere with the use of the easement. However, the servient owner has the right to use the servient estate, provided that such use does not interfere with use of the easement. The scope of reasonable use of an easement is not frozen at the time of creation of the easement. The scope may change over time to keep up with the changing needs of the owners and changing circumstances in the neighborhood.

QUESTION 1. **"I want my cable TV."** In 1945, Rocky granted a ten-foot wide power easement to Big Sky Power Company across his 40,000-acre ranch. The easement authorized Big Sky to construct and maintain "an electric transmission or distribution line or system." This year Cantankerous Cable Company (CCC) is establishing a cable television network in the community where Rocky's ranch is located. CCC contacted Big Sky and bargained for an assignment of nonexclusive rights to install cable lines on Big Sky's easement. Rocky's heir, Rosette, complains that CCC's installation of cable lines will infringe upon her property rights. If Rosette prevails, the most likely reason would be:

A. The easement is not binding against Rosette because she did not have notice of the easement when she acquired the ranch.

B. The purpose of the easement contemplated by the parties to the 1945 grant did not extend to the transmission of information or communication.

C. The parties to the 1945 grant of easement could not have intended to allow the installation of cable lines because cable television did not then exist.

D. There is a public policy in favor of extending cable-television service to the entire community.

E. Installation of the cable lines would decrease the market value of the servient estate.

ANALYSIS. The primary purpose of this question is to focus on the rules used to determine the scope of an express easement. Choice **A** goes off on a tangent. Rocky granted the easement in 1945, but he is no longer the owner of the servient estate. An easement always binds a new owner of the servient estate unless the new owner qualifies as a bona fide purchaser. Here it's not possible for Rosette to be a bona fide purchaser. As Rocky's heir, she did not pay consideration for the ranch. Thus **A** is wrong.

For an express easement, the scope of the rights of the easement owner depends upon the intent of the parties. The language of the easement instrument is of paramount importance. Here the grant limits CCC and its assigns to use of the easement "for an electric transmission or distribution line or system." Easements are allowed to accommodate new technology that is developed after creation of the easement. For example, a right-of-way easement created in the nineteenth century generally can be used by automobiles even though they did not exist when the easement was given. For this reason **C** is not a good answer. There were no cable-television systems anywhere in the United States in 1945, but that is not sufficient to hold for Rosette.

Choice **D** is incorrect because the proper focus is on the intent of the parties who created the easement, not a public policy that makes judgments as to the importance of the activity that the easement holder wishes to pursue. It may be true that the extension of cable systems is in the public interest, but this does not justify a biased interpretation of an easement grant that takes a right away from the servient owner and awards it to the easement holder.

In other contexts, **E** might be a good answer. Putting an easement to a new use might have a significant negative impact on the servient estate, and when that is the case, it is plausible to conclude that the original parties to the easement would not have intended to allow the new use. Here, however, there is no evidence that CCC's installation of cable lines would interfere with Rosette's use of the ranch. It's not likely to have an appreciable impact.

The critical issue raised by this question is whether a cable television distribution system can reasonably be described as a new species of an "electric transmission or distribution line or system." Perhaps it might be; television signals are electric. Choice **B** puts the finger on the real issue. Does the easement extend to the electrical transmission of information or communication? Or is it limited to the transmission of electricity for its sale and use as power?

B.   Transfers of Easements

Easements are valuable property rights because they are relatively permanent. The rights of use and enjoyment reflected by easements generally survive transfers of the lands that are subject to the easements (servient estates).

Easement rights themselves are also often transferable. When considering transfers of easements, it is essential to distinguish between appurtenant easements and easements in gross. Thus the first step for analysis is to determine which type of easement is present. By definition, ownership of an appurtenant easement must coincide with ownership of the dominant estate. The only way to convey ownership of an appurtenant easement is to convey all or part of the dominant estate. The deed that conveys the dominant estate does not have to refer to the appurtenant easement. The easement passes by implication to the new owner of the dominant estate.

Transfers of easements in gross are treated differently. For an easement in gross, there is no dominant estate to which ownership of the easement can be linked. Early American common law generally treated easements in gross as personal to the original grantee. Thus, they were neither assignable nor inheritable. During the twentieth century most states recognized major exceptions to the rule of nonassignability. They allowed transfers of easements when the instrument creating the easement expressly authorized transfer or when it was reasonable to imply the power to transfer.

When applying these rules courts often distinguished *commercial easements in gross* and *personal easements in gross*. With a commercial easement, the grantee uses the easement in connection with a trade or business or a profit-seeking activity. With a personal easement, the grantee uses the easement for pleasure or personal purposes. Courts have treated the commercial easement in gross as assignable but often have retained the rule of nontransferability for the personal easement in gross.

QUESTION 2.   Fishing rights. Paul, the owner of a lot on Lake Garrulous, a public lake, is approached by his neighbor Eros, whose lot had no lake frontage. Eros asked for permission to walk across Paul's lot so he could fish at the lakefront. Paul said he would consider it and would let him know soon. The next week, Paul sent Eros an email, which stated in pertinent part: "I've decided that you may walk across my land to fish at the lake. Just make sure that you don't leave any litter on my property." Two years later, Eros sold his lot to Fernanda. Fernanda now wants to cross Paul's lot to fish at the lake. She will succeed if:

A. Eros had an easement in gross.
B. Eros had an appurtenant easement.
C. Eros had a license.
D. Eros had a fee simple estate.
E. Eros had a profit à prendre.

ANALYSIS. This question tests your understanding of the basic types of easements. Choice **A** is incorrect. Although the transaction may have created an easement in gross, this characterization would not help Fernanda in asserting a right to cross the lot and to fish. An easement in gross is often nontransferable, and even if it is capable of being transferred, a transfer would not be accomplished by a deed conveying a fee simple estate owned by Eros, the easement owner.

Choice **C** is incorrect even though it might be the case that Eros had a license, rather than an easement. If Eros had a license to cross Paul's lot to fish, Fernanda will not succeed to this right. A license is personal to the holder and is generally considered nontransferable.

Choice **D** fails because the facts do not support a claim that Paul transferred fee title to any of his property to Eros.

Choice **E** is incorrect, even though the story is about fishing rights and Fernanda, like Eros, wants to catch fish. The fish are not on the servient estate, Paul's lot. They are in Lake Garrulous, which is on the other side of Paul's lot. Eros sought permission to walk across Paul's property, not to take fish from a body of water located on his property.

The right answer is **B**. If Eros obtained an appurtenant easement from Paul, Eros's conveyance to Fernanda transferred his rights to cross Paul's lot and to fish at Paul's lakefront to Fernanda. This happened automatically, even if the contract of sale and deed between Eros and Fernanda were silent as to these rights. This is what it means to say that an easement is appurtenant to property. Eros's lot is known as the dominant estate. Ownership of the easement is intrinsically tied to ownership of the dominant estate. Note that the easement is also affirmative, rather than negative. Eros had the right to enter Paul's lot for the purpose of walking to the lake.

C.   Duration of Easements

Most easements are perpetual, but the parties can agree to a shorter term, such as an easement for ten years. Easements may be expressly made defeasible, with the instrument describing an event of termination.

An easement, unlike an estate in land, may terminate by abandonment. *Abandonment* takes place when the easement owner ceases to use the easement, intending to relinquish ownership. To establish abandonment, the servient owner must point to acts of the owner from which the intent to abandon can be inferred. Those acts must be something other than the fact of non-use, even when the period of non-use is lengthy.

Merger may also terminate an easement. Merger occurs when the same person acquires ownership of the servient estate and the dominant estate (or the easement itself when there is an easement in gross). Merger destroys the easement, which is seen as "merging" into the servient estate.

An easement may terminate by adverse possession on the part of the servient owner. This happens when acts of the servient owner prevent the easement owner from exercising her easement rights for a period longer than the state statute of limitations for standard cases of adverse possession. Normally the acts consist of the servient owner's installation of a fence or other barrier or the removal or alteration of improvements made by the easement owner.

QUESTION 3.   Access to the river. O owned four contiguous parcels of pine woods identified as Lots 1, 2, 3, and 4 below.

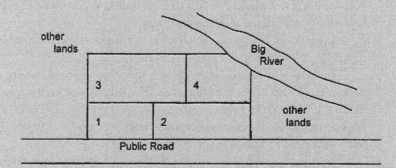

The following transactions take place, each one month apart.

1. O deeds Lot 4 in fee simple to A, reserving the right of access to Big River.
2. O deeds Lot 2 in fee simple to B.
3. O deeds Lot 3 in fee simple to A, reserving the right of access to Big River.
4. A leases Lot 3 for a term of 50 years to C.
5. B leases Lot 2 for a term of 99 years to D.

> After the fifth transfer, which parties own easements over which parcels?
>
> **A.** O, B, C, and D.
> **B.** O, C, and D.
> **C.** C and D.
> **D.** O and C.
> **E.** O and D.
> **F.** None of the above.

ANALYSIS. This one is tricky. The best way to approach this is to analyze the situation step-by-step, after each transfer. After the first transfer, O owns an access easement over Lot 4 for the benefit of all three of the lots that he has retained. Lots 1-3 are the dominant estate.

After the second transfer, B owns an easement appurtenant to Lot 2. O still has an easement appurtenant to Lots 1 and 3.

The third transfer conveys Lot 3 (a dominant estate) to A, the owner of Lot 4 (the servient estate). By merger, the easement appurtenant to Lot 3 terminates. O now has an easement appurtenant only to Lot 1. B still owns an easement appurtenant to Lot 2.

The fourth transfer, a lease of Lot 3 to C, has no effect on easement rights. Due to merger that happened earlier, C does not acquire an easement for access to Big River.

The fifth transfer, a lease of Lot 2 to D, transfers the easement appurtenant to Lot 2 to D for the duration of the lease. O still has an easement appurtenant to Lot 1.

So after the smoke clears, O and D have easements appurtenant for the benefit of Lots 1 and 2, respectively. Choice **E** is the right answer.

D.   The Closer: Easement Rights of New Owners

> **QUESTION 4.   A flagstone footpath.** Priscilla owned Blackacre, which had substantial frontage on Big River, a navigable river. Priscilla's neighbor Trudeau owned land with no river frontage. In 2000, Priscilla granted an easement to walk across Blackacre to Big River "to Trudeau, his heirs and assigns." Trudeau recorded the grant of easement in the county real property records. He promptly cleared a path across Blackacre to Big River, paving it with flagstones. Trudeau used the path frequently, but in 2004 he died. His will devised his land to Tipsy. Tipsy moved onto the property but had no interest in going to the river. She did not maintain the path, and soon it became overgrown with vegetation. In 2009,

Priscilla sold Blackacre to Peter. Peter did not do a title search, and he was not aware of the easement when he bought Blackacre. In 2013, Peter in turn sold Blackacre to Princess, who also did not search title or learn of the easement. Shortly after this sale, Princess cleared part of Blackacre of brush and weeds, and she found the flagstone path. She asked Peter why it was there, and he told her that a prior owner of Blackacre had installed the stones and that she could remove them if she wished. But Princess let the stones remain in place. In 2016, Tipsy sold her land to Tommy. He spotted the flagstone path and immediately began using it to walk to Big River, where he then hiked along a public footpath along the river. Princess brought a trespass action against Tommy. Who should prevail and why?

A. Princess because the doctrine of estoppel bars Tommy from claiming easement rights.

B. Princess because the easement granted to Trudeau has terminated.

C. Tommy because the period of non-use did not result in abandonment of the easement.

D. Tommy because the easement cannot terminate so long as passage along the path is not physically obstructed.

ANALYSIS. The trespass action will fail if Tommy presently owns the 2000 easement. The key, therefore, is to determine whether Tommy owns it. When considering the duration of an express easement, the first step is to study the language of the document that created the easement. Here the 2000 easement was granted "to Trudeau, his heirs and assigns," with no other language bearing on duration. The reference to "heirs and assigns" reflects the parties' intent that Trudeau's rights should be assignable. There is no other indication as to how long the easement should last. Thus, the easement may be perpetual. It should continue so long as its purpose can be achieved; in other words, so long as the owner of Trudeau's land may consider it useful or enjoyable to walk to Big River. However, an earlier termination can result from conduct by the easement owner or the owner of the servient estate. This question explores several possibilities for early termination.

Actions by Tommy or prior owners of the easement might result in loss of the easement by estoppel. Those actions would have to mislead the owner of the servient estate. Tommy and his predecessors have done nothing that might qualify. Peter's statement to Princess was incorrect and misleading, but this is not attributable to Tommy. Choice **A** is wrong.

Choice **D** posits that this easement cannot terminate so long as the path isn't physically obstructed (presumably by a fence, a building, or another object). This is incorrect. An obstruction by the servient owner may terminate an easement under a rule akin to adverse possession, but this is not the only method of termination. The easement owner may abandon the easement.

We're left with **B** and **C** as plausible choices. **B** concludes that the easement has terminated without giving an explanation why. Choice **C** asserts that there has been no abandonment of the easement. There is no credible theory of termination under these facts other than abandonment. The owners of the easement did not use it from 2004 to 2016. They let the path become overgrown with weeds and vegetation. But abandonment requires more than non-use, even if the period of non-use is lengthy. Here there is no evidence of the easement owner's intent to abandon in addition to non-use. Therefore, **C** is the best answer.

 ## Smith's Picks

1. "I want my cable TV"   **B**
2. Fishing rights   **B**
3. Access to the river   **E**
4. A flagstone footpath   **C**

Covenants: Creation

"Promises are the uniquely human way of ordering the future, making it predictable and reliable to the extent that this is humanly possible."
Hannah Arendt, *Crises of the Republic* 92-93 (1972)

CHAPTER OVERVIEW

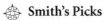asements, studied in the last two chapters, and covenants are the two pillars of the law of servitudes. There are two key distinctions between easements and covenants. First, the nature of the interest usually is different. Most easements (called *affirmative easements*) entitle the owner to enter land possessed by someone else for a specific limited purpose. A covenant does not allow the person benefited by the covenant (the covenantee) to enter the covenantor's land.

The second key distinction turns on how easements and covenants arise (the body of law that creates them). An easement, when it arises consensually, is considered to be a conveyance of an interest in land. With an easement, there is a grantor and a grantee, and the instrument used to create and document the easement is either a deed or a writing that resembles a deed. In contrast, a covenant is an agreement between neighboring landowners that is not a conveyance. Due to the statute of frauds, the covenant must be in writing.

Normal contract law principles have much to do with the creation, interpretation, enforcement, and termination of covenants. But a covenant is more than a mere contract because under certain circumstances it becomes legally tied to one or more parcels of land. This tie or linkage imparts a substantial degree of stability to covenants. They may remain in place and enforceable after their creation even though sales or other transfers of the affected parcels of land have taken place. Covenants serve as primary tools for land use planning in the neighborhood context. They are seen as the private law analogue to zoning, which regulates land use through the public law vehicle of zoning ordinances enacted by cities and other units of local government.

A. Traditional Real Covenant

The basic concept of a *real covenant,* or its twin the *equitable servitude* discussed later in this chapter, is that successors to the original contracting parties are bound by the covenant or may enforce the covenant. In the quaint, old-fashioned language of real property law, the covenant is said to *run with the land.*

At the time this concept developed in feudal England, this was a novel idea. Prior to the development of a mercantile economy, which gave rise to modern contract law, contract rights were generally nonassignable. It was extremely rare for courts to find a contractual promise to be binding on a person other than its maker. Property law developed the concept of the real covenant, running with the land, prior to the advent of modern contract law. For this reason, the legal terms used to define covenants and servitudes sound archaic. Modern contract law has evolved a different vocabulary to handle the involvement of third parties in contract relationships.

Early English courts imposed the following requirement for a covenant or a promise[1] to qualify as a real covenant:

- **Intent.** The original parties to the covenant intended, when they made the covenant, that the covenant would run with the land.
- **Privity of estate.** When the covenant was made, the original parties to the covenant had a relationship that qualified as "privity of estate" (this is commonly called horizontal privity).
- **Touch and concern.** The subject matter of the covenant is found to "touch and concern" the land.

Subsequent sections of this chapter analyze these three requirements. Two of the three elements for real covenants — intent, and touch and concern — also

---

1. A covenant is historically defined as a promise under seal. Under modern American law a seal has lost almost all of its legal significance. For analysis under the modern law of covenants and servitudes, it no longer matters whether a landowner's promise is set forth in a document that has a seal.

apply to equitable servitudes. Horizontal privity of estate is necessary for a real covenant but not for an equitable servitude.

QUESTION 1. Two lots and their transfers. Walter owns two adjoining lots (Lots 1 and 2) in a subdivision. Walter conveys Lot 2 to Brian, the deed to Brian stating in pertinent part: "The grantee shall not use the land for any commercial purpose." Imagine the following four different scenarios that could arise with respect to performance of the covenant made by Brian:

1. The next year Brian opens a store on Lot 2. Walter brings an action against Brian to enforce the covenant.
2. The next year Brian dies, devising Lot 2 to Bunny. Bunny then opens a store on Lot 2. Walter brings an action against Bunny to enforce the covenant.
3. The next year Walter conveys Lot 1 to Willie. Brian, who still owns Lot 2, opens a store on Lot 2. Willie brings an action against Brian to enforce the covenant.
4. The next year Brian dies, devising Lot 2 to Bunny. One month later Walter conveys Lot 1 to Willie. Bunny then opens a store on Lot 2. Willie brings an action against Bunny to enforce the covenant.

In which of the above fact patterns will it be important for the plaintiff to demonstrate that the covenant made by Brian meets the legal requirements for a real covenant?

A. None of the above fact patterns.
B. All of the above fact patterns.
C. 4 only.
D. 2 and 4.
E. 2, 3, and 4.

ANALYSIS. Let's go down the list to look at each variation. In 1, the original covenantee, Walter, is suing the original covenantor. No successor landowner for either lot is involved. Ordinary contract law will determine whether Walter is entitled to enforce the promise made by Brian. It does not matter whether the covenant is a real covenant capable of running with the land.

In 2, we have the original covenantee, Walter, suing a successor to the original covenantor, Brian. The issue is whether the *burden of the covenant* runs with the land. For this to happen, the covenant must be a real covenant (or an equitable servitude — but that comes later in this chapter).

In 3, we have a successor to the original covenantee, Walter, suing the original covenantor. The issue is whether the *benefit of the covenant* runs with the land. For either the burden or the benefit to run with the land, we have to have a real covenant (or an equitable servitude).

In 4 all we've done is to cumulate fact patterns 2 and 3. Now a successor to the original covenantee is suing a successor to the original covenantor. Of course, it's still essential that we have a real covenant (or an equitable servitude) for the action to succeed. Putting it all together, our answer is **E**.

B.   Horizontal Privity of Estate

Horizontal privity of estate refers to the relationship between the original parties to the covenant at the time they made the covenant. What constitutes horizontal privity of estate? The answer varies state by state, but there are three principal alternatives:

- **Tenure (landlord-tenant).** The strictest position is the original English rule, which required the parties to be in a tenurial relationship. As English land law developed throughout the Middle Ages, tenure gradually but constantly faded away as an organizing principle. With the elimination of many forms of English tenure and diminished significance for remaining forms, this strict view of horizontal privity confined real covenants to leases. There is tenure between a landlord and tenant, and the English law of real covenants developed primarily as a branch of landlord-tenant law.
- **Ownership of simultaneous interests.** Courts in the United States accept tenure as creating horizontal privity, but they have expanded its scope. The second test finds horizontal privity when the parties own simultaneous interests in the same property. If one party owns an easement over the other party's land, the parties may make an agreement concerning some aspect of the easement. Similarly, cotenants own simultaneous interests in the same property. Horizontal privity exists when cotenants enter into an agreement to define or modify their rights with respect to the cotenancy property.
- **Deed privity.** The most commonly followed American position expands privity by extending it to covenants set forth in deeds of conveyance. Every state except Massachusetts follows this expansion. When an estate of land is sold or when there is a gift of land by deed, a covenant agreed to as part of the transaction can qualify as a real covenant.

Under all three views of horizontal privity, a mere agreement by parties who own land does not qualify. For a long time, a number of commentators have soundly criticized the concept of horizontal privity. The Restatement eliminates the requirement completely. Restatement (Third) of Property: Servitudes § 2.4 (2000) ("No privity relationship between the parties is necessary to create a servitude").

QUESTION 2.   Pond and a tennis court.   Lucinda bought Lot 12, containing a single-family residence, from a developer, who executed a deed conveying Lot 12 to her. Three months later Jerry bought a neighboring residential property, Lot 13, from the same developer, who gave Jerry a deed to his lot. The rear part of Lot 12 (but not Lot 13) borders a pond. Jerry would like access to the pond. He asked Lucinda if he could have access to the pond by walking across her backyard. She signed a writing granting him that right for the next five years. At the same time, Lucinda was concerned that Jerry had a tennis court on his property, located near their common boundary, with bright lights mounted on poles to allow nighttime play. When turned on, the lights hit several of her windows. Lucinda asked Jerry to promise not to leave the lights on after 11 PM, and he signed a writing so promising. Is there horizontal privity with respect to the "lights off" covenant?

A.   Yes, because there was tenure between Jerry and Lucinda when the covenant was made.
B.   Yes, because the covenant was made at the same time Lucinda granted an easement to Jerry.
C.   Yes, because there was deed privity between the parties.
D.   No, but there would have been horizontal privity if the tennis court were located on Lucinda's property and she had made the "lights off" covenant in the same document that granted the easement to Jerry.
E.   There is no horizontal privity under the original facts and under the facts as modified in Choice D.

ANALYSIS.   This question provides an opportunity to test your understanding of the three main views of horizontal privity, which can qualify a covenant as a real covenant. Choice **A** asks about privity based on tenure. Jerry and Lucinda are next-door neighbors. They never have been landlord and tenant, nor have they had any other type of relationship that could qualify as tenure.

Choice **C** is also relatively easy to handle. Don't let the fact that both Lucinda and Jerry have deeds from the same grantor confuse you. The "lights-off" covenant was negotiated between the neighbors after they purchased from the developer. There would be deed privity if we were concerned with a promise between the developer and Lucinda or Jerry, set forth in one or both of their deeds, but that's not what we have here. The harder issue in this question deals with the "simultaneous interest" view of horizontal privity. We need to sort this out to pick among our remaining choices **B**, **D**, and **E**. Lucinda and Jerry have simultaneous interests in the part of Lucinda's backyard where Jerry has an easement to walk to the pond. That will establish horizontal privity for an agreement between them, but the content of the agreement has to have some relationship to the easement. Here the tennis court and Lucinda's concern about the lights late at night, has nothing to do with the rights of either party with respect to Jerry's easement. It does not matter whether Jerry's promise was consideration given in exchange for Lucinda's grant of the easement.

As for **D**, moving the tennis court to Lucinda's property and making her, rather than Jerry, the covenantor, does not change our analysis. The content of the covenant is still functionally unrelated to the easement. **E**'s our best answer.

C. Rise of the Equitable Servitude

Prior to the famous English case of *Tulk v. Moxhay*, 41 Eng. Rep. 1143 (Ct. Ch. 1848), the only covenants that ran with estates in land were real covenants. In *Tulk*, a landowner sold a garden in fee, retaining adjoining residential apartments, with the purchaser covenanting not to build upon the garden and to maintain the garden. These covenants clearly were unenforceable at law due to the English requirement of privity in the form of tenure. However, the Court of Chancery decided that such covenants between owners of fee estates could nonetheless run "in equity" when the covenantor's successor had notice of the covenant.

Tulk proved extremely influential, leading to the recognition of a new type of covenant: the equitable servitude. Horizontal privity of estate between the contracting parties is not required for an equitable servitude. Any covenant that fails to satisfy the real covenant technicalities of privity can be labeled as an equitable servitude, whereupon it will have the same legal effect as if it had been a real covenant.

In the United States, the initiation of recording systems for land records heightened the significance of the case. In *Tulk*, the covenantor's successor had actual notice of the covenant, and American courts extended the ruling to bind successors who had *constructive notice* of the covenant. As long as the document creating the equitable servitude is properly recorded, successors of the covenantor will have sufficient notice to allow enforcement against them.

More than a century ago, the distinction between a real covenant and an equitable servitude had remedial consequences because courts of equity did not award damages and courts of law did not issue injunctions. In modern American law, the distinction between real covenants and equitable servitudes virtually never matters. The procedural integration of law and equity has eviscerated remedial distinctions, and notice to the successors of the covenantor is required for real covenants in most situations, just as it is for equitable servitudes, due to the recording acts. Commentators have long proposed collapsing the categories, and the Restatement agrees. Restatement (Third) of Property: Servitudes §8.2, cmt. a (covenants "may be enforced by any appropriate remedy, whether the remedy is traditionally classified as legal or equitable"). A number of cases also support this convergence.[2]

QUESTION 3.   Sharing satellite TV.   Miranda, a technological whiz, just bought a new satellite television dish. She has figured out a way to split the signals without loss of quality. She agrees to furnish television signals to her next-door neighbor, Duval, through coaxial cable. In exchange, Duval has agreed to pay her $30 per month. Their agreement has a term of three years and is reflected by a writing, signed by both Miranda and Duval. One year after reaching this agreement, Miranda sells her house to Mary. As part of the sale, Miranda agreed not to remove the satellite dish and related equipment. Mary now uses the dish, entering into her own contract with the satellite service provider. One month after Mary bought Miranda's house, Duval sold his house to Dick. Dick has offered to pay Mary the monthly fee in exchange for the continued use of the television signals, but Mary wants to discontinue the arrangement. Dick has brought an action against Mary to obtain a decree requiring that she provide the signals for the remainder of the three-year term. What must be true in order for Dick to prevail?

A.   Privity of estate between Miranda and Duval must be satisfied.
B.   The satellite dish agreement must be properly recorded in the public land records.
C.   Mary must have had notice of the satellite dish agreement when she bought her house.
D.   Dick must have had notice of the satellite dish agreement when he bought his house.
E.   The satellite dish agreement must be a real covenant.

ANALYSIS.   This question tests some of the key requirements for an equitable servitude. Choice **A** is a bit fuzzy because it says "privity of estate," rather than "horizontal privity of estate." Because **A** refers to the original parties, Miranda and Duval, and not their successors, from context it's clear that horizontal privity is meant.[3] Dick may prevail without horizontal privity if he establishes that he has the benefit of an equitable servitude that runs with the land. For the same reason, **E** is wrong.

---

2. For these reasons, your professor may allow you to analyze all covenants issues under the equitable servitude requirements. Of course, you should determine the extent to which you're responsible for the more complex requirements of real covenants, including but not limited to the requirement of horizontal privity.

3. Dick has to establish that "vertical privity" is satisfied, even if he proceeds on the equitable servitude theory. Vertical privity is discussed later in Section G of this chapter.

For an equitable servitude to arise, notice is required, but notice to whom? What we care about is notice to the covenantor's successor. The burden of the covenant will not run in equity unless the covenantor's successor knew (or should have known—constructive notice) of the covenant when that successor acquired the burdened property. Mary is resisting performance, so notice to her is relevant. This knocks out **D**, but isn't **B** plausible? True, Mary would have constructive notice of the satellite dish agreement if it was recorded before she bought her house, but that is not the only type of notice that is sufficient. Dick can prevail if the agreement is not recorded if he can prove Mary had actual notice of that agreement. Choice **C** is a better answer than **B**.

D.   Intent that Covenant Runs

A covenant is firmly a creature of contract law, and thus the contractual intent of the original parties plays a predominant role in defining the rights and obligations of third parties, that is, successors in interest to the parties. This means that if the original parties did not intend that their agreement burden or bind successors, a court should not allow it to do so. Well-drafted formal covenants include an express statement of intent to bind and benefit successive landowners. No particular language is necessary, but it is common to use phrases stating that the interests and obligations shall "run with the land" or that they "bind" or "inure" to the benefit of "heirs and assigns" or "successors" of the parties.

Parties do not always include a clear expression of intent. From a very early date, courts have been willing to infer an intent that a real covenant or equitable servitude should run with the land in appropriate cases. The Restatement tersely explains:

> *Intent To Create A Servitude.* The intent to create a servitude may be express or implied. No particular form of expression is required.

Restatement (Third) of Property: Servitudes §2.2 (2000). The Restatement text provides no guidance at all as to when courts should find an implied intent that a covenant runs with the land to benefit and burden successive owners. It depends upon all of the facts and circumstances. Although generalization is hazardous, usually intent is implied if the covenant is of a type (1) that legally can run with the land (i.e., it "touches and concerns" the land[4]) and (2) that is expressly made to run with the land in a large number of similar transactions.

---

4. The touch and concern requirement is addressed in Section F of this chapter.

> **QUESTION 4.   Building height limit.**   Ferguson and Giselle own adjoining five-acre parcels of land in a zoning district that allows medium-density commercial uses. Their parcels are both undeveloped. Ferguson and Giselle agree that Ferguson will not erect a building on Ferguson's parcel taller than four stories for a period of 50 years. In exchange for this agreement, Giselle grants Ferguson a right-of-way easement across her property. This easement allows Ferguson access to a highway that does not border Ferguson's parcel. Nothing is stated in the building height agreement (or in any other document) about what should happen if either party sells or otherwise transfers an interest in their parcels. Should the building height agreement run with the land?
>
> A.   Yes.
> B.   Yes, because the right-of-way easement, as an appurtenant easement, runs with the land.
> C.   Yes, but only if the four-story limit is not significantly shorter than the covenants that bind similar parcels in the community.
> D.   No.
> E.   The outcome should depend upon whether Giselle gave fair consideration for the building height agreement.

ANALYSIS.   The answer set is unusual in its pairing of yes/no choices with three longer choices. It is often recommended to drafters of multiple-choice questions that all answers be reasonably similar in length to avoid "tipping off" students as to what they should do. This is a drafting norm that I violate on occasion (my thinking being that the students who really know the material can get the right answer and that they shouldn't be guessing by excluding responses that appear overly short or overly long).

The issue here is fairly obvious. A well-drafted covenant that limits the height of buildings should expressly state whether it is binding on Ferguson's successors and whether the benefit may be enforced by Giselle's successors. Let's look at the longer choices that give reasons. Choice **B** says we should imply an intent that the height limit covenant runs with the land because the right-of-way easement will run with the land. Almost certainly the right-of-way easement will run with the land, but does this persuasively tell us what Ferguson and Giselle intended for the height limit? It's possible they intended the easement should run, but the height limit should not run. It would seem if they had that disparate intent, Giselle was getting a bad bargain, but bear in mind we have no idea as to the relative values of the easement and the agreement.

Choice **C** gives us a qualified yes. The height limit covenant should run if it's not too onerous on Ferguson, compared to restrictions that apply to similar properties in the community. It may be that the more burdensome the covenant is, the more reluctant the court should be to infer the intent to run.

But we have the same problem we did before for **B**—we don't know the value of the easement that Giselle has given in exchange for the covenant.

Choice **E**, which calls for an explicit measure of the values of the easement and the height limit covenant, is in some respects a variation of **B** and **C**. You should rule out **E** not only for what you may have learned in studying property, but because it runs counter to a basic principle of modern contract law—courts will not evaluate the adequacy of consideration if it is bargained for by apparently competent parties and there are no other special facts (such as fraud or a fiduciary relationship between the parties).

So we're left with our short choices, **A** and **D**, where you must supply the reason for whichever one you pick. Counting in favor of implication are two facts. The term is long—50 years—and even if Ferguson and Giselle are presently young adults, it's not likely that they assumed that they would both own the property for that lengthy period. Second, Giselle did give consideration that has some value (the easement) in exchange for the covenant. If Ferguson can sell the property tomorrow, with the buyer constructing a ten-story building, she certainly struck a bad bargain. On balance, a court is likely to hold that the parties intended the covenant to run. Choice **A** is the better answer.

E. Negative and Affirmative Covenants

One classification for covenants distinguishes between negative covenants and affirmative covenants. A *negative covenant*, often called a restrictive covenant, is a promise by the owner not to execute or permit specified uses or activities on her land. An *affirmative covenant* is one in which the covenantor promises to take some action or actions on her land. This distinction is often confusing to students because the law of easements uses parallel vocabulary, but with a meaning that is not quite the same. A negative easement prevents the owner of the burdened land from using her property in a certain way, whereas an affirmative easement allows the easement owner to enter the burdened land for some purpose.[5] The following chart may help you to discern the different usages.

	Affirmative	*Negative*
Easement	Easement holder may enter Servient Estate to do X	Servient owner restricted from doing X on Servient Estate
Covenant	Promise to do X on Servient Estate	Promise not to do X on Servient Estate

---

5. For further discussion, see Section B of chapter 24.

From the chart you should notice the functional identity between the negative easement and the negative covenant. Both restrict the owner of the servient estate from doing some act on her land. When we compare the affirmative easement and the affirmative covenant, the same cannot be said. A covenant cannot allow an outsider to enter the covenantor's land and do something on the land; such a purpose can be accomplished only with an affirmative easement. Similarly, an easement cannot require the servient owner to perform an affirmative act on her land; such a purpose can be accomplished only with an affirmative covenant. One occasionally sees authorities use the term *spurious easement* to refer to an easement that obligates the burdened owner to do something on her land, such as maintain a boundary line fence separating her land from the neighbor's land. The word "spurious" means false, so the term "spurious easement" means it's really not an easement, but a disguised affirmative covenant.

QUESTION 5.   **Two neighbors plan to install a green fence.**   Trudy and Julio own neighboring homes. Presently, their side and back yards have grass lawns, with no fence or other barrier separating their properties. Although they and their families are good friends, they both would prefer defining their yards with a nice hedge. They agree on English privet. At first, they consider planting the privet right on their common boundary, but Trudy's house is located much closer to the boundary than Julio's house. Thus a boundary hedge would give Trudy a very small side yard. After discussing the matter, they agree to plant the hedge on Julio's lot, five feet in from the boundary line. The deal they have worked out is that Trudy will buy and install all the plants, in exchange for which Julio will handle all subsequent care of the hedge, including watering, fertilizing, and pruning. They want to document their agreement in writing, which will be recorded in the public land records so that it will benefit and bind subsequent owners of their homes. With respect to Julio's agreement to maintain the hedge after planting, which type of servitude is most appropriate?

A. Negative covenant.
B. Affirmative covenant.
C. Negative easement.
D. Affirmative easement.
E. Spurious easement.

ANALYSIS.   To decide which type of servitude works best, we must pay close attention to the nature of the agreement. At first Trudy is to enter Julio's land to plant the hedge. Because Julio is permitting this entry, Trudy obviously will not be a trespasser. Her right to enter is either a license or an affirmative easement. The question, however, does not ask about labeling this aspect of the parties' agreement. Rather, the issue is how to classify Julio's obligation to care for and maintain the hedge once it's in place. Choice **A** is not appropriate. A negative covenant in this context would be Julio's promise not to remove, or perhaps even touch, the hedge. He is promising to do something affirmatively, so the right answer is **B**. Julio is making an affirmative covenant.

None of the three easement choices — **C, D,** and **E** — work for this agreement. A negative easement fails for the same logical reason a negative covenant fails: Julio is promising to do something, not refrain from doing something. There is no affirmative easement because neither neighbor will be entering the other's land. (Trudy is permitted to enter Julio's yard to install the hedge, but the question concerns maintenance of the hedge after planting.) Finally, a spurious easement means that the burdened owner is supposed to perform an affirmative act, so this might work. But **E** is a poor choice. Recall that "spurious" means false. No one should ever draft a document that expressly attempts to create a "spurious easement," that is, a falsehood. Instead, call the interest you're trying to create by its recognized legal name.

F.   Touch and Concern Requirement

A covenant must "touch and concern" the land in order that it may "run with the land." Of the several primary elements required for a valid covenant, the touch and concern test is the only one that has substance, rather than mere form. Intent, privity, and, for equitable servitudes, notice, are formalistic in the sense that no matter what the content of the covenant happens to be, each can be satisfied by proper structuring of the method of creation of the covenant.

When discussing "touches and concerns," we must consider two sides of the equation. For any particular covenant, it is necessary to distinguish the running of the burden and the running of the benefit. In any given case, the question of whether a covenant runs with the land depends upon the answer to one or both of the following inquiries:

- Does the burden run with the land? This is necessary if the original covenantee seeks to enforce the covenant against a successor in ownership to the covenantor's land. The burden can run only if it touches and concerns the covenantor's land.
- Does the benefit run with the land? This is necessary if a successor in ownership to the covenantee's land seeks to enforce the covenant against the original covenantor. The benefit can run only if it touches and concerns the covenantee's land.
- When there are successors on both sides of the equation, both the burden and the benefit must run in order for the covenant to remain alive.

The separate examination of the running of burdens and benefits has an analogue in modern contract law. There is no single principle "transferring" a contract to successor parties. Rather, different doctrines apply to delegations of contract duties (burden transfers) and assignments of contract rights (benefit transfers).

A covenant touches and concerns a parcel of land if its performance is logically connected to the use and enjoyment of that parcel. If the nexus between the covenant and the land is substantial, the covenant is said to touch and concern the land. Sometimes the inquiry is framed by asking whether the parties entered into the covenant in their status as landowners, rather than as parties who acted independently of their property interests. This test, however, is circular. If the court holds that the covenant runs, then it is in effect saying that they contracted as landowners. Conversely, if the court does not let the covenant run, then they contracted as individuals apart from their property holdings.

Under traditional English law, only *negative covenants* qualified as touching and concerning the burdened land. The benefit of a negative covenant touches and concerns land when the covenantee's land is made more valuable or enjoyable by observance of the covenant. Usually the benefited land will adjoin or be near the burdened land.

Affirmative covenants could not touch and concern the covenantor's land under traditional English law. Thus, successors to the covenantor were not bound to observe affirmative covenants. Courts in the United States have rejected this strict view. Following the famous case of *Neponsit Property Owners Assn. v. Emigrant Industrial Savings Bank*, 15 N.E.2d 793 (N.Y. 1938), they allow certain affirmative covenants to run. The *Neponsit* court enforced a promise by purchasers of lots in a residential subdivision to pay annual assessments for the maintenance of common areas within the subdivision, including roads, parks, and sewers. The *Neponsit* test asks whether the affirmative covenant substantially affects the legal relationships associated with the ownership of land. The "substantial effects" test, although widely utilized in many states, provides very little guidance for resolving hard cases.

Traditionally, the touch and concern requirement has not applied symmetrically to the two halves of burden and benefit of a covenant. When the issue is the running of the burden (because the covenantor has transferred her estate), the traditional view requires that the burden touch the land of the covenantor's successor *and that the benefit touch the land of the covenantee*. In other words, for the burden to run, *both* the burden and the benefit must touch the land. Many states have moved to a more liberal view, however, permitting a burden to run as long as the burden touches and concerns the covenantor's land. This recognizes as a valid covenant what is called a *covenant in gross*, which traditional doctrine prohibited. Under the newer view, a covenant in gross is sometimes allowed to bind the successor to the covenantor's land. The new Restatement adopts this position. Restatement (Third) of Property: Servitudes §§ 2.6, 8.1 (2000).

When the issue is the running of the benefit, traditional and modern law looks only to the benefit side of the equation. For the benefit to run, only the benefit need touch the covenantee's land. It is irrelevant whether the burden

touches and concerns the covenantor's land. The differential treatment is justified on the basis that, when only a benefit is running, there is no inhibition or
restraint on the alienability or usefulness of land. The only reason for requiring "touching" on the benefit side is to ascertain the intent of the parties to the
transfer. If the original covenantee did not expressly assign the benefit when
conveying her estate, it is reasonable to infer an intent to assign only if the
benefit touches and concerns the transferred estate. The following chart sum-
marizes the touch and concern burden/benefit rules.

	Does the Burden Run?	*Does the Benefit Run?*
Does the Covenant touch and concern the burdened land?	Required	Not Required
Does the Covenant touch and concern the benefited land?	Required *If* State Prohibits Covenant in Gross	Required

The Restatement calls for replacement of the "touch and concern" requirement with a more generalized inquiry as to whether the servitude complies
with or violates public policy. Restatement (Third) of Property: Servitudes
§§ 3.1, 3.2 (2000).

QUESTION 6.   Not another convenience store.   David owns two
neighboring lots (Lots 6 and 7) located at two of the corners of an
intersection of busy city streets. On Lot 6 David operates a convenience
store. Lot 7 is a parking lot. David sells Lot 7 to Emily, with the deed
stipulating in pertinent part: "Said grantee hereby agrees not to open or
operate a convenience store, gas station, or any similar retail outlet on
the property at any time during the next ten years. This covenant shall
run with the land and shall bind said grantee's heirs, successors, and
assigns." One year later Emily sells Lot 7 to Hannah, who promptly begins
construction of a convenience store. David brings an action against
Hannah for injunctive relief. Hannah's best defense would be:

A. David has the benefit of a real covenant, and therefore he could bring
    an action for damages but not for injunctive relief.
B. There was no privity of estate between the original parties to the
    covenant, David and Emily.
C. The burden of the covenant does not touch and concern Lot 7.
D. The benefit of the covenant does not touch and concern Lot 6.
E. David's purpose in bringing the action is to restrain a competitor, and
    this violates public policy.

ANALYSIS.   Let's label the interest created by David's deed to Emily. Notice that the parties have clearly expressed their intent that the covenant should run with the land. It is a negative covenant, not an affirmative covenant, because Emily has promised not to do something on the conveyed parcel. There is horizontal privity of estate under the widely accepted "deed privity" rule. This makes the covenant a real covenant, rather than an equitable servitude. Thus **B** is wrong.

Choice **A** starts off correctly—David has a real covenant—but then asserts that he should not obtain an injunction, presumably because he does not have an equitable servitude. This is wrong. Courts regularly enjoin the violation of covenants, regardless of whether the particular covenant is a real covenant or an equitable servitude.

Let's turn to **E.** Courts rarely invalidate covenants on public policy grounds. In this context, a court is not likely to deny relief to David because his purpose is anti-competitive. A seller is generally allowed to bargain for a promise by the buyer not to use the conveyed property to compete with the seller's business. Here the time limit (ten years) makes the covenant more reasonable than one of unlimited or indefinite duration.

That leaves us with **C** and **D**, both of which deal with the touch and concern requirement. Negative covenants, such as this one, almost always are considered to touch and concern the promisor's land. If the court rules in favor of Hannah, it will be on the basis that the benefit of the covenant must touch and concern David's land in order for him to enforce it against Emily's successor (Hannah). Arguably the covenant does not touch and concern David's land (Lot 6) because it does not make his real property more valuable. Rather, it benefits his business, which at the present time he happens to be conducting on Lot 6. Under this analysis, David has bargained for a *covenant in gross*, which traditionally and in many states today is not allowed to run with the land. **D** is correct.

G.   Vertical Privity of Estate

The law of covenants includes a second type of privity, in addition to horizontal privity of estate, which is called vertical privity of estate. Vertical privity is used to identify the proper parties to sue or to be sued on a covenant that runs with the land. It describes the relationship between the original parties and their successors. When a successor is said to be in vertical privity with an original party, then that successor is an appropriate plaintiff or defendant.

The proper parties to an action on a covenant ordinarily are the present owners of the estates held by the original covenanting parties. Therefore, when successors to the original parties have acquired the entire interests of their transferors, vertical privity is established. The strict view of vertical privity confines the litigation to successors who have the entire estate. At law, for a real covenant only a successor to the covenantor's entire estate is bound by the covenant. Similarly, for the running of the benefit only a successor with the covenantee's entire estate can enforce the covenant.

Under modern American law, vertical privity has diminished in importance, both for the running of burdens and for the running of benefits. Equity has intervened in both situations. First, successors who acquire lesser interests in the burdened land are often charged with performance of the covenant provided the successor had notice of the covenant upon acquisition of her interest. Second, successors of limited interests in the benefited land are permitted to enforce covenants when such enforcement is consistent with the terms of the instrument by which the successor acquired her interest.

Relatively few cases address the involvement of an original party in covenant litigation after that party has transferred her entire estate to a successor. There is consensus for denying standing to the original covenantee because that person no longer owns benefited land. That person lacks a legitimate interest to justify an award of damages or injunctive relief. When the original covenantor has transferred her entire estate, there is some authority for the proposition that the covenantor cannot be held liable for breach of the covenant.

Often a property owners' association will seek to enforce real covenants. If the association owns real property within the development that is benefited by the covenant, such as recreational facilities, standing is no problem. Vertical privity is clearly satisfied. However, when the property owners' association itself does not have title to benefited land, a challenge to its standing is possible. Standing can only be justified if the court recognizes that there is an agency relationship, viewing the association not as an entity but as an alter ego of its members. Although cases have split on this issue, most courts follow the leading case of *Neponsit Property Owners Assn. v. Emigrant Industrial Savings Bank*, 15 N.E.2d 793 (N.Y. 1938), which allowed standing for the plaintiff association based on the agency rationale.

QUESTION 7.   Shovel your snow. A covenant in a residential subdivision with 80 lots requires that each homeowner remove snow and ice from the sidewalk in front of each residence. The covenants, which are properly recorded in the county land records, authorize the property owners' association to remove snow and ice if an owner fails to do so within 48 hours after conclusion of the storm. If the association removes snow or ice, the covenant requires the owner pay the association $30 per incident. All of the covenants are stated to "run with the land; and all said covenants shall bind and benefit heirs, successors, and assigns of said parties." Larry has leased his residence to Tanya for one year. Following a winter storm, neither Larry nor Tanya timely removed snow from their sidewalk. In an appropriate action, the property owners association should be able to collect the $30 fine from:

A. Larry or Tanya.
B. Larry only.
C. Tanya only.
D. Neither person, because the property owners' association does not own benefited land.
E. Neither person, because the covenant is an affirmative covenant without a substantial nexus to the burdened lot.

ANALYSIS.   First, let's dispose of the last two choices, which assert that the property owners' association should not be able to collect the fine from anyone. The facts do not mention that the association owns any real property (remember the operating rule—never assume facts that are not given), so **D** is on solid ground on this point. But should this disqualify the association as plaintiff? Neighbors of Larry in the subdivision clearly own benefited lots, and *Neponsit* authorizes a property owners' association to sue as their agent. Most courts would agree.

As for **E**, this is an affirmative covenant (both to remove snow and ice and to pay a fine upon the failure to do so), and sometimes affirmative covenants do not run with the land. This one, however, is a covenant to do an act on the covenantor's land. It satisfies the requirement that there be a substantial connection or nexus between the covenant and the burdened land.

Should Larry be liable for the fine? We're not told the details of his lease with Tanya, but even if the lease obligated Tanya to remove snow and ice, Larry should not be off the hook. He is a landlord and still owns the fee simple estate. The value of covenants would be impaired if owners could escape liability whenever they rent their property. Often it would be difficult for a property owners' association to track down a tenant and compel performance from the tenant. Thus, **C** is a weak answer.

The harder question is Tanya's liability, which we must resolve to pick between **A** and **B**. It is hard because the facts say nothing about Tanya's actual notice of the snow removal covenant. If she had actual notice (or the lease obligated her to remove snow and ice, which would be tantamount to actual notice), then she should have liability. Constructive notice may suffice. It may not be reasonable to charge Tanya with the burden if the covenant in question related to an obligation usually performed only by landlords and not tenants (such as a covenant to repair the roof of the residence), but snow removal is the sort of chore that tenants are often expected to perform. So I conclude that **A** is the better answer, but this is a close question, and I'm not entirely confident of my decision.

H.   The Closer: Reciprocal Negative Easement

Generally, covenants must be expressly created and set forth in a writing. The one exception is the *reciprocal negative easement*, also known in some jurisdictions as the *implied equitable servitude*. When a landowner subdivides her property and begins selling lots, expressly imposing each lot with the same restrictive covenant pursuant to a *common plan* for the neighborhood, the seller's retained lots become similarly restricted by implication. The servitude becomes mutual. Typically, the covenant at issue restricts the property to residential use only. The rule becomes important if the subdivider transfers one or more of the later lots without expressly imposing the covenant. The reciprocal negative easement not only binds the subdivider, but like other covenants it runs with the land, binding successors who can be said to have notice of its contents. States that recognize the doctrine of reciprocal negative easements protect the early buyers by implying a servitude on the subsequent lots. Usually these courts reject a subsequent buyer's claim to bona fide purchaser (BFP) status, reasoning that the purchaser either has inquiry notice because the neighborhood lots are only used for residences or has record notice because the purchaser could have found and read the deeds to the neighboring lots, spotting the express restrictions in those deeds.

Not all states recognize the doctrine of reciprocal negative easements. Many states, such as California and Massachusetts, reject the doctrine of reciprocal negative easements, holding that the statute of frauds always requires a writing for a valid restriction.

QUESTION 8.   Restricting lots by implication.   Potter, the owner of 70 acres of undeveloped land, prepares and records a subdivision plan called Pottersville. The plan showed 60 one-acre lots, plus a system of streets. Potter sells the first 45 lots to individual purchasers, inserting in each deed a covenant limiting use of the conveyed lot to "residential use only." Then Potter sells the next lot to Barrymore, with no restrictions or covenants mentioned in the deed. Barrymore begins using his lot as a branch office for his bank, and one of the earlier purchasers, George Bailey, sues Barrymore to enjoin this business use. The court will probably enjoin Barrymore if:

A.   The jurisdiction recognizes the doctrine of reciprocal negative easements and the court finds a common plan or general scheme of development.

B.   The jurisdiction takes a strict view of the Statute of Frauds, requiring all servitudes to be in writing.

C.   The jurisdiction takes an expansive view of third-party beneficiaries.

D.   The jurisdiction has eliminated the requirement of horizontal privity for the creation of real covenants.

E.   The jurisdiction allows a covenant in gross to run with the land.

ANALYSIS.   The reciprocal negative easement is a tough critter and thus fitting for the closer. This question is about as straightforward as one can be, given the subject.

Let's examine the choices after **A**. Choice **B** heads in the wrong direction. A jurisdiction taking a strict view of the Statute of Frauds is likely to reject the doctrine of reciprocal negative easement completely. A jurisdiction taking a relaxed view would make the injunction more probable.

Choice **C** does not matter. George Bailey doesn't need third-party beneficiary theory as part of his case. If the reciprocal negative easement arose, George Bailey's lot became benefited (and restricted) at the time Potter first began selling lots in Pottersville.

As for **D**, if the jurisdiction no longer requires horizontal privity, we can call the implied servitude a "real covenant." But this would not affect the outcome. If there is a reciprocal negative easement, an injunction is proper regardless of whether the covenant is labeled a real covenant at law, or an equitable servitude in equity.

Choice **E** also is irrelevant. If George Bailey prevails, it is because he owns land benefited by a reciprocal negative easement. He does not own a covenant in gross.

Choice **A** is the best answer. The insertion of the "residential use only" covenant in the first 45 deeds, with no omissions, is powerful evidence that Potter, at the outset, had a common plan or general scheme for Pottersville. The same uniformity means a court probably will decide that Barrymore had notice of the common plan so that it is appropriate to enjoin his business use.

 # Smith's Picks

1. Two lots and their transfers	E
2. Pond and a tennis court	E
3. Sharing satellite TV	C
4. Building height limit	A
5. Two neighbors plan to install a green fence	B
6. Not another convenience store	D
7. Shovel your snow	A
8. Restricting lots by implication	A

27

Covenants: Scope and Termination

*"As soon as one promises not to do something, it becomes the one thing
above all others that one most wishes to do"*
Georgette Heyer, *Venetia* (1958)

CHAPTER OVERVIEW
A. Interpretation of Covenants
B. Residential Use Restrictions
C. Change of Circumstances and Abandonment
D. The Closer: Single-Family Use
✦ Smith's Picks

This chapter continues the subject of covenants, building on the material in the previous chapter. I recommend that you study chapter 26 before this one. Here our focus is on two topics, interpretation of covenants and their duration. Interpretation often involves determining the *scope* of a covenant. One party will claim that an activity or condition is regulated by a covenant (within its scope), whereas the other party will claim that the covenant is not applicable (the activity or condition is outside its scope).

The duration of covenants, just as for property rights generally, is an important consideration. Many covenants are drafted with a fixed duration, such as 40 years. Some are drafted with a fixed term, but with an express term that provides for renewal periods, usually based on the preference of a majority or a super-majority of the property owners who are subject to the covenants. And many covenants have no express termination provision, and thus are perpetual—or at least potentially perpetual.

A.   Interpretation of Covenants

The traditional method of interpreting covenants is to construe language strictly, refusing to extend the scope of restricted behavior by reasonable implication. The goal of this approach is to safeguard the fee simple property rights of the owner of the burdened estate. Another judicial method to rein in covenants is to require language that is precise and specific. Ambiguous or unclear language is deemed vague, thus invalidating the covenant either as a general matter or as applied to a particular situation.

A more modern approach interprets covenants according to their ordinary meaning, seeking to effectuate the parties' intent in an evenhanded manner. This is consistent with modern contract law. This interpretive style recognizes that restrictive covenants often add substantial value to neighborhoods. A number of states have eschewed traditional strict construction in favor of this approach.

> **QUESTION 1.   Cellular tower next to the waterworks.** Dolly established a subdivision with 50 lots, restricting almost all of the lots for "residential use only." However, Dolly conveyed one large lot to a water company, which planned to supply water to the residences in the subdivision and to other nearby property. Dolly's deed to the water company had the following restriction: "Said premises and the structures and improvements erected and maintained thereon shall be used for water supply purposes or purposes incidental or accessory thereto." The water company improved most of the lot for use in its water supply business and has continually used the lot for this purpose. Just last month the water company leased a small part of the property to a wireless telecommunications provider, who plans to construct a cellular tower. Several residents in the subdivision, who purchased their properties from Dolly years ago, have brought an action against the water company and the telecommunications provider. What outcome is more probable?
>
> **A.** The court will enforce the covenant because the language of the covenant is clear and unambiguous.
> **B.** The court will enforce the covenant because a strict construction of covenants is necessary to protect property rights.
> **C.** The court will refuse to enforce the covenant because the benefit of the covenant does not touch and concern the lots owned by the plaintiffs.
> **D.** The court will refuse to enforce the covenant because Dolly has not joined the litigation.
> **E.** The court will refuse to enforce the covenant because the deed does not express an intent that the covenant run with the land.

ANALYSIS.   We have two choices concluding the plaintiffs should prevail (**A** and **B**) and three going the other way (**C** through **E**). Let's examine the "no enforcement" answers first. The residents bought into a residential neighborhood with lots restricted to residential use. The restriction on the water company's lot was imposed, at least in part, to make sure that a commercial use injurious to the residential properties was not located on that lot. It is plausible for the residents to argue that a tall, unsightly cellular tower may diminish the value of their properties and detract from their enjoyment. A court would conclude that the touch and concern requirement is satisfied. (It is also satisfied on the other side—this is a negative covenant, so the burden touches and concerns the water company's lot.)

Choice **D** is wrong. Because the benefit touches and concerns the residential lots, Dolly need not join the action as a plaintiff. Indeed, if Dolly no longer owns any lots, she is not qualified to be a plaintiff as she has no interest that merits protection.

As for **E**, it's true that the facts do not say that the deed expressed the intent that the covenant should bind the water company's successors (and, *remember*—we should not assume facts not stated). But a court would find that intent to be implied from the nature of the covenant and the transaction that gave rise to the covenant.

So we should enforce the covenant, picking **A** or **B**. The logic of **B** is reversed. The defendants will argue for the rule of strict construction, claiming it's not completely clear that the parties intended to ban a cellular tower, especially if the large majority of the lot continues to be used for water company purposes. So **A** is our answer. It's plausible for the court to rule for the plaintiffs on the ground that the covenant is unambiguous. This question is closely based on *Morgenbesser v. Aquarion Water Co.*, 888 A.2d 1078 (Conn. 2006), which so concluded.

B.   Residential Use Restrictions

In residential subdivisions and in attached housing, such as condominiums, it is extremely common that covenants restrict each lot for "residential use only." Business and commercial uses are prohibited. Usually the covenants contain no specific information as to what constitutes a forbidden business use. Courts differ as to where to set the threshold for proscribed business activities. For example, no court is going to enjoin ordinary babysitting, but at some level a child care provider runs the risk of violating the covenant.

> **QUESTION 2.   Turning a house into apartments.** Serena owned two neighboring lots on Victoria Street, both improved with three-story Victorian houses on half-acre lots. She lived in one home, and rented

the other home to Pablo. Serena sold the rental unit to Pablo, inserting in the deed a covenant stating that the property could be used only for "residential purposes." At the time of the sale, both homes as well as all other homes situated on Victoria Street contained a single dwelling unit, occupied by one family, either as owners or tenants. One year later, Pablo converted the house he bought into a three-unit apartment building. He lives in one unit, and rents the other two units to tenants. Serena sues Pablo, claiming he has violated the covenant. The most probable result is:

A. Serena prevails because Pablo is making a profit by renting apartments to tenants.
B. Serena prevails because Pablo's tenants are engaging in business.
C. Pablo prevails because public policy discourages restrictions that inhibit the creation of rental housing.
D. Pablo prevails because the "residential use" language should be construed strictly to protect Pablo's property rights.

ANALYSIS. Like many multiple choice questions, this one is structured to cause you to make two related decisions: who should win, and why. Choice **A** reflects an argument for Serena with some plausibility. Pablo arguably has gone into the business of developing and operating rental housing. This might be a type of commercial use, intended to be proscribed by the covenant.

Choice **B** proceeds along the same lines, but focuses on Pablo's tenants, rather than Pablo. This choice is flawed by the absence of support in the facts. Nothing indicates that Pablo's tenants are doing anything other than living in their apartments. There is no indication that they are selling goods or seeing customers on the premises, or doing anything that might be a "home business."

Choices **C** and **D**, then. predict Pablo will win, with two different explanations. Choice **C** posits a public policy favoring rental housing, and Choice **D** uses a rule of contract interpretation that resolves an ambiguity in favor of Pablo. Either one might work. This may be a close call, but I believe **D** is stronger. It is well understood that covenants may restrict or prohibit rental housing, so as to make a community largely or even completely owner occupied. So if there is a public policy favoring the creation of rental housing, it has not trumped the ability of parties to covenants to exclude that form of housing. **D** invokes a standard rule for interpreting covenants, even though courts sometimes do not follow it.

So now we must pick between Choices **A** and **D**. I believe Pablo is likely to win this case. Pablo's tenants are not engaging in business activities on the premises, and Pablo making a profit as a landlord would not detract from Serena's use and enjoyment of her house. So **D** is the better answer.

C.   Change of Circumstances and Abandonment

Many covenants are written with no express expiration dates. They may be perpetual, just like a standard right-of-way easement. There are rules, however, that serve to terminate covenants. A defendant in an action to enforce a covenant may raise an affirmative defense. When an affirmative defense is found to be meritorious, often the consequence is not only to deny relief to a particular plaintiff but also to terminate the covenant as a general matter.

The most important affirmative defense is the doctrine of *changed circumstances*, which applies when the conditions in the neighborhood have changed from the time the covenant was made so that the benefits of the covenant cannot be substantially realized. Generally, a change of conditions outside the subdivision is not sufficient to terminate the restrictions.

Other affirmative defenses often used as a shield from covenant enforcement are abandonment, waiver, estoppel, and laches. Covenants, like easements, are also subject to abandonment. For neighborhood covenants, abandonment or waiver may result if neighbors tolerate a significant number of violations of the covenants. Ordinarily, abandonment applies to all lots within the scheme, not a smaller area.

> **QUESTION 3.   Living next to a busy highway.** Covenants recorded 40 years ago restricted all of the lots in a 90-lot subdivision to residential use only. Homes were constructed on all the lots. Four lots at the edge of the subdivision adjoined Simpson Bridge Road, at the time a two-lane road with residences and small businesses on both sides. Commercial development gradually intensified along Simpson Bridge Road. Today the part of Simpson Bridge Road adjoining the four lots and near the subdivision is a divided eight-lane highway, lined with shopping centers, hotels, restaurants, automobile dealerships, and other businesses. Heavy automobile traffic and proximity to these businesses have made the four lots undesirable for residential purposes. These properties have a market value equal to approximately 60 percent of the value of equivalent properties in the subdivision with interior locations, away from Simpson Bridge Road. On four of the interior properties, homeowners conduct small-scale home businesses. No one has sued them, claiming that they have violated the covenant. The owners of the four lots recently granted a real estate developer an option to purchase their properties. The developer presently is exploring commercial development possibilities. Other homeowners in the subdivision have brought a declaratory judgment action against the four lot owners and the developers, seeking

a judgment that the restrictive covenant remains enforceable. Will the court hold that the "residential use only" covenant is still enforceable?

A. Yes, because the economic loss incurred by the four lot owners if they continue to abide by the covenant is not severe.

B. Yes, because the changes that have taken place during the past 40 years are external to the subdivision.

C. No, because the four lots are no longer suitable for residential use.

D. No, because no one has enforced the covenant against the four interior lot owners who conduct home businesses.

E. The outcome will depend upon whether horizontal privity was established when the covenants were created 40 years ago.

ANALYSIS. Let's start at the end by eliminating **E**, which fails to give a clear answer, claiming that horizontal privity is an issue. We can't tell from the facts whether horizontal privity between the original parties existed (although it probably did under the concept of "deed privity" because the original subdivision developer probably restricted the lots in connection with sales to lot purchasers). If there was horizontal privity, we have real covenants. If not, we have equitable servitudes. Either way, the same possible affirmative defenses apply.

A and **C** are a "pair." They both focus on the same point, the severity of the harm to the four lot owners if the covenant remains in place, but they come down on opposite sides. The 40 percent diminution in value certainly is substantial, but it indicates that the lots still have substantial value if occupied as residences. This means **A** is preferable to **C** unless we can find a better choice.

Choice **D** points to waiver or abandonment as affirmative defenses based on the home businesses that have been established on four interior lots. Either is possible, but there are two substantial weaknesses. First, four out of 90 is a low percentage. Eighty-six out of 90 lots are in compliance. This counsels against either waiver or abandonment, both of which typically are based on noncompliance that is to some degree extensive. Second and probably more importantly, the character of home businesses is different from what the developer no doubt intends to do with the four lots bordering on Simpson Bridge Road. Waiver or abandonment as to home businesses is distinguishable from waiver or abandonment as to full-scale commercial uses that do not take place within a residence.

We're left with **B**. The defendants' principal argument will be that the changed circumstances along Simpson Bridge Road justify releasing their four lots from the covenant. Most courts would disagree because all the changes have taken place outside the subdivision. Even though the defendants' homes are worth significantly less due to the external changes, courts would likely conclude that their properties ought to serve as a "buffer" to protect the interior lots from commercial infiltration. **B** is the best choice.

D.   The Closer: Single-Family Use

Many covenants that govern residential properties restrict the use to a "single family." This is a narrower concept than restricting the property to "residential use only." Plainly a "single-family" covenant is designed to prevent the landowner from constructing multi-family housing, such as an apartment building. But it may have a broader impact. The meaning of the "single-family" restriction is rarely explained by additional language in the covenants, with the consequence that courts often have had to determine its scope.

QUESTION 4.   Too many students? Hugo owns a four-bedroom house in the South Hills neighborhood in College City where almost all of the homes are owner-occupied. The neighborhood has a set of restrictive covenants, one of which provides that "each lot shall be used for a single-family dwelling only." The covenants do not define the term "single family." Hugo moves out in July and advertises his house for rent. On September 1 he signs a one-year lease with six college students who take possession. None of the students are related to each other. On December 1 the South Hills Homeowners Association sues Hugo and the six student tenants, seeking to enjoin their continued occupancy on the ground it violates the restrictive covenant. The students' best defense is:

A. They are living as a single household, which constitutes a "single family" for purposes of the covenants.

B. An injunction is not proper because vertical privity is not present.

C. An injunction is not proper because there is no proof that the South Hills Homeowners Association owns land that is benefitted by the covenant.

D. An injunction is not proper because the single-family covenant is a real covenant, not an equitable servitude.

E. The court would be engaging in state action, in violation of the students' constitutional rights, if it issued the injunction.

ANALYSIS.   Here you are not called upon to decide who will win this case. Instead the task is to determine which argument on the students' behalf is most likely to persuade a court. Choice **A** in effect states the six students are a "single family" even though they are unrelated. The facts do not indicate whether they are acting as one family due to activities such as eating meals together, sharing expenses and chores, and so forth. Many students who choose to live together often go their separate ways much of the time, not behaving like a biologically related family; but obviously if the court finds that these students are a "single family" they are in compliance with the covenant and they win.

The remaining choices all include statements about the remedy of injunction sought by the plaintiff homeowners association. Choice **B** is wrong because a court is highly likely to conclude that vertical privity is satisfied. Hugo is bound by the covenant, whether he is an original covenantor or a subsequent purchaser of a lot. The students are bound in equity even though they own a leasehold rather than the fee estate. For review, see Section G of Chapter 26.

Choice **C** is also unlikely. Even if the homeowners association does not own any real property, it acts as an agent for the other homeowners. For review, see Section G of Chapter 26.

Choice **D** focuses on the equitable nature of an injunction. Even if the court labels the restriction a real covenant and not an equitable servitude, it will issue an injunction if the plaintiff proves a material violation of the restriction. For review, see Section C of Chapter 26.

Choice **E** asserts that the students have a constitutional right to live as a group in Hugo's house. This is highly unlikely. It would represent a dramatic extension of *Shelley v. Kraemer*, 334 U.S. 1 (1948), which refused to enforce covenants prohibiting occupancy by "persons not of the Caucasian race." Subsequent decisions have not extended *Shelley* beyond situations of racial discrimination. So Choice **A** represents the students' best argument. Even though it may not be a winner, the other arguments are not plausible.

 ## Smith's Picks

1. Cellular tower next to the waterworks   **A**
2. Turning a house into apartments   **D**
3. Living next to a busy highway   **B**
4. Too many students?   **A**

28

Nuisance

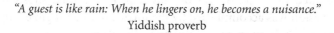

"A guest is like rain: When he lingers on, he becomes a nuisance."
Yiddish proverb

CHAPTER OVERVIEW
A. The Classic Perspective: Substantial Harm
B. Modern Balancing of Utilities
C. Nuisance Immunity
D. Nuisance Per Se
E. The "Coming to the Nuisance" Defense
F. The Closer: Priority in Time
◈ Smith's Picks

The law of nuisance is not covered in all property classes. Some property professors skip the subject, sometimes on the basis that it is covered in the torts course. (Sometimes that belief is misguided. When I was in law school, early in the fall semester the section's property professor told us that nuisance was a tort, and we would not study it in property because it would be covered in our torts class. Shortly thereafter in torts class, we finished the unit on intentional torts, and our torts professor told us that nuisance was defined as another type of intentional tort, but it was really about protecting property ownership. Thus he would not cover it, and we'd learn about it in property class. So much for coordination of subject matter among our section's faculty.)

Even if your property class does not include a unit on nuisance, the subject is foundational, and you will gain something of value by learning a few things about nuisance on your own. Many court opinions dealing with other property subjects discuss nuisance principles, looking to them for useful analogies and to justify certain propositions. For example, zoning laws are often justified on the basis that they suppress nuisances; in the law of takings, a regulation that greatly reduces property value is not likely to be considered an unconstitutional taking if the owner's proposed use has nuisance-like characteristics; in the law of waste, the duty of a present possessor not to impair the value of the future interest is sometimes analogized to a landowner's duty not to commit a nuisance.

A. The Classic Perspective: Substantial Harm

The classic view of nuisance, developed by English courts and applied by early American courts, imposed liability on a defendant landowner whose activity resulted in a non-trespassory invasion that caused substantial harm. If the invasion was accomplished by the intrusion of a tangible, physical object, the wrong lay in trespass, not nuisance. But if the invasion consisted of odor, smoke, or noise, nuisance provided a remedy.

In the nineteenth century, American courts began to depart from the classic view of nuisance, which held a defendant liable for all substantial harms caused by its invasions. Industrialization gave rise to a growing number of conflicts between industrial defendants and their neighbors. Judges became reluctant to assess damages against emerging industries. They avoided damage liability by refocusing nuisance doctrine. If the defendant was acting *reasonably* in devoting its land to an industrial activity, the defendant was privileged to continue without having to pay its neighbors. This new perspective led to the modern, expanded view of reasonableness. It was no longer enough for the plaintiff to prove that the defendant's invasive activity caused substantial harm — it had to cause *substantial unreasonable harm*. A nuisance exists only if the gravity of the harm outweighs the benefits flowing from the defendant's conduct.

> **QUESTION 1. A house next to a big mine.** Mining Company owns a large iron ore mine, which operates 24 hours a day, year round. Blasting operations take place at the mine three times a week, year round. Sarah owns a house that is located only 200 yards from the boundary of the Mining Company's property. Mine operations generate large quantities of airborne dust, which accumulates on Sarah's property, both inside and outside her house. Sarah also complains that the blasting sends tremors through her property. This impairs her use and enjoyment of her property, causing her to spend money to clean and repaint her house, replace windows, carpets, and drapes, and repair cracks in masonry. Sarah brings an action for damages against Mining Company. If she recovers, the most probable reason will be:

> **A.** The invasion of Sarah's property with airborne dust and blasting vibrations constitutes a trespass.
>
> **B.** Mining Company has not taken adequate precautions to minimize the harm caused by dust and blasting.
>
> **C.** Mining Company's activities have caused substantial injury to Sarah's property.
>
> **D.** The harm to Sarah's property is greater than the value of the Mining Company's activities.

ANALYSIS. Choice **A** is a weak answer. This problem is based on the facts in *Adams v. Cleveland-Cliffs Iron Co.*, 602 N.W.2d 215 (Mich. App. 1999), which considers claims brought by 55 homeowners against the Empire Mine, one of the largest mines in the United States. At trial the owners obtained a jury verdict based on trespass, but the appellate court reversed because trespass requires an invasion "in the form of a physical, tangible object." The court indicated that the plaintiffs might obtain relief for nuisance, but the jury had been unable to agree on a verdict regarding their nuisance claim.

Choice **B** is wrong because the facts contain no indication that Mining Company could conduct its operations so as to cause less dust and blasting vibration. The claim made in **D** — that the harm to Sarah is measurably greater than the mine's value — is highly unlikely. The mine is a valuable asset, employing many people and making a useful product. That leaves us with **C**, the best answer. Under modern nuisance balancing rules, Sarah might not win her damage action, but if she does, the reason will be that the court applies the historic view of nuisance that compensates a person in her position if she proves an invasion that causes substantial harm to her property interests.

B. Modern Balancing of Utilities

Under modern law, nuisance usually gives rise to relative and correlative property rights among neighboring landowners. When a nuisance claim is brought, the *gravity of the injury* to the plaintiff is weighed against the *utility of the defendant's conduct* to arrive at a judgment as to whether a nuisance has taken place. The defendant's conduct is found to be a nuisance if it is said to be *unreasonable*, considering all the facts and circumstances. Often but not always the decision maker is the jury or other trier of fact; whether a nuisance exists is said to be a mixed question of fact and law.

The Restatement follows the modern, post-industrial view and applies a reasonableness filter to both parties' conduct. With respect to the gravity of the harm, the Restatement (Second) of Torts §827 (1979) calls for evaluation of

(a) The extent of the harm involved;

(b) the character of the harm involved;

(c) the social value that the law attaches to the type of use or enjoyment invaded;

(d) the suitability of the particular use or enjoyment invaded to the character of the locality; and

(e) the burden on the person harmed of avoiding the harm.

With respect to the utility of the defendant's conduct, Restatement §828 points to

(a) the social value that the law attaches to the primary purpose of the conduct;

(b) the suitability of the conduct to the character of the locality; and

(c) the impracticability of preventing or avoiding the invasion.

The Restatement approach has the virtue of being flexible and adaptable, but this comes with a cost. Multifactor analysis incorporating these eight variables produces a level of indeterminacy that is difficult to surpass. Litigation outcomes are unpredictable. In almost all nuisance disputes, both parties can raise plausible arguments, with the law not compelling any particular judicial outcome.

QUESTION 2. "Ready, aim, fire." Clint owns and operates a firing range, which is open seven days a week, 9 AM to 10 PM, where patrons can hone their shooting skills using a wide variety of weapons, including handguns, high-powered rifles, and shotguns. Next door to Clint's firing range is the Sleepy Hollow Apartment Complex, a property with 80 dwelling units that is owned by Raul. No bullets have landed on the apartment complex, but the almost constant noise from firearms can be heard by the apartment tenants, especially by those with units closest to the boundary line between the two properties. Some of the tenants have complained to Raul about the noise, and they have also expressed fear that sooner or later, bullets from errant shooters will cross the boundary line. Raul has brought an action for nuisance, seeking to enjoin Clint's operation of his firing range. Which of the following facts or issues is LEAST likely to be relevant to the decision whether the firing range constitutes a nuisance?

A. The number of tenants who have complained to Raul about the firing range.

B. The tenants' subjective fears that misdirected bullets may escape from the firing range, entering the apartment complex property.

C. Noise levels at the apartment complex from other sources, such as automobile traffic on adjoining streets.

> **D.** The possibility that Clint can modify his firing range so that the discharge of weapons takes place further away from the boundary line.
> **E.** Whether there are other firing ranges in the community.
> **F.** Whether there are other apartment complexes in the community with vacant units similar to those in Sleepy Hollow Apartment Complex.

ANALYSIS. For the typical nuisance case like this one, numerous factors are inserted into the weighing process, with no single factor being determinative. All six of the factors discussed in the choices conceivably can come into play, and all can be tied to the Restatement criteria. **A**, **B**, and **C** all relate to the "extent of the harm" and the "character of the harm" inflicted by the shooting range. If the neighborhood is not quiet but for the firing range (**C**), then the harm from the firing range might not be very significant — it may only increase noise levels incrementally. The tenants' subjective fears about safety (**B**) can be considered in a nuisance case, even if this is not a harm that can be readily measured in economic terms.

Choice **D** raises the possibility that Clint may minimize the invasion by making changes to his firing range, so this is relevant. Choices **E** and **F** bear on the "social value" of the competing activities. Here we're considering community interests — the interests of third parties. If the court considers a firing range to be socially useful, it is more likely to issue an injunction that forces Clint to shut down if Clint's patrons may practice shooting elsewhere. Choice **F** is parallel in the sense that if Clint's firing range remains open and Sleepy Hollow is no longer suitable for many of its tenants, it might be feasible for Raul's tenants to move elsewhere. However, this is a sizeable apartment complex, meaning that relocation of many tenants is not likely to be practicable, and many decision makers are likely to attach a higher social value to housing than to firing ranges. On balance, **F** is the least likely consideration to influence the outcome.

C. Nuisance Immunity

Modern nuisance law usually balances the landowners' competing interests, but it is not all about balancing. Nuisance has two other zones, each lying on opposite sides of the balancing core. These zones may ultimately either insulate the defendant from liability, or may impose liability on the defendant regardless of the reasonableness of the activity. Both of these zones give us bright-line rules.

Nuisance Immunity	Nuisance Balancing	Nuisance Per Se
No Liability	Weighing Harm and Utility	Strict Liability

The first zone is what we may call nuisance immunity. Certain landowner activities are regarded as sufficiently beneficial or benign that courts virtually never castigate them as nuisances. Such activities are privileged and are not subject to nuisance balancing. An important caveat is that for some types of activities the landowner must conduct the activity in a non-negligent fashion. In a case falling within the nuisance immunity zone, the defendant is free from nuisance liability.

Different types of activities qualify for nuisance immunity. One example is the refusal of American courts to grant relief for improvements that block views or deprive a neighbor of sunlight or air. Another is the doctrine of *aesthetic nuisance*, which holds that improvements or landscape modifications cannot constitute a nuisance if the only harm to neighbors is aesthetic blight. Thus, the ugliest grain silo in the world, even when located next to a neighbor's boundary and shadowing her sundeck, is not actionable.

QUESTION 3.   Is it "natural landscaping" or "weeds"? Greenlawn, a residential subdivision, consists of 140 single-family homes, all of which were improved with traditional suburban landscaping, including spacious, attractive lawns. Greenlawn has recorded covenants and servitudes, which apply to all the lots, but they do not address landscaping standards. Six months ago, Harry bought a home in Greenlawn and removed all of the landscaping, replacing it with what he calls "natural landscaping." His new landscaping consists of wild grasses, wildflowers, and bushes, which he claims are indigenous to the state. Harry's closest neighbors, all of whom have retained traditional, manicured yards, are indignant. They claim Harry is only growing "invasive weeds," which attract rodents and other undesirable wildlife and emit pollen, which threatens to propagate the undesirable plants on their beautiful properties. They can prove that their property values are diminished by $15,000 per house due to their proximity to Harry's property. The neighbors sue Harry for nuisance. The probable result is

A. The neighbors will prevail if the court concludes that the gravity of their injury outweighs the value of Harry's "natural landscaping."
B. The neighbors will prevail if the court concludes that Harry's "natural landscaping" is out of character for the neighborhood.
C. Harry will prevail because his activity is considered to be privileged.
D. Harry will prevail because his activity produces significant environmental benefits.

ANALYSIS.   Students will tend to prefer choices **A** and **B** because they reflect the analysis used in the vast majority of nuisance disputes, which weighs multiple factors to determine whose property claim merits protection. This is unlikely to happen in the case because Harry is engaging in a type of activity that traditionally is considered to not be a nuisance. In essence, the neighbors are complaining only about aesthetic harm. The fact that they can prove a real loss of market value for their properties does not show that the harm is something other than aesthetic. All this demonstrates is that the local market of potential homebuyers generally shares the neighbors' aesthetic values rather than Harry's aesthetic values. Thus, **A** and **B** are wrong.

Choice **D** is also wrong because a court is not likely to protect Harry only if it concludes that his activity is socially or environmentally valuable. Even if his landscaping preferences are idiosyncratic, his property is not likely to be considered a nuisance. This is a case of nuisance immunity for which the court will probably say he can grow whatever he wants on his property as long as no other law prohibits this (e.g., he is not growing marijuana) and he has created no genuine health or safety hazards. **C** is the best answer.

D.   Nuisance Per Se

The zone lying on the opposite side of nuisance balancing is represented by the nuisance per se doctrine. Sometimes, a distinction is made between *nuisance per se*, where the action constitutes a nuisance no matter what the circumstances or where it occurs, and a *nuisance per accidens*, where the action becomes a nuisance because of the surroundings in which it occurs. Certain conduct, perceived as generally undesirable or high risk, is always wrongful. If an owner or possessor of land has engaged in that conduct, a neighbor can get relief (enjoin the nuisance or collect damages) without the need to prove that the conduct is unreasonable. Nuisance per se has two prongs, one common law and the other statutory. Under the common law branch, courts have repeatedly labeled certain activities as nuisances, with the consequence that due to stare decisis, subsequent courts find them to be nuisances without inquiring into the specifics of the facts. Under the statutory approach, when a land use activity violates a statute or an ordinance and the proscribed conduct is of a type that often produces nuisance-like harms, the court may find a nuisance per se. This is analogous to the negligence per se doctrine in tort law.

Nuisance per se is properly seen as a species of strict liability, even though many courts choose not to discuss it in those terms. When nuisance per se is found, the defendant's conduct is deemed wrongful, with no need to balance the utility of that conduct against the harm to the plaintiff.

There is some confusion in the cases as to whether the nuisance per se doctrine sanctions only conduct that is bad everywhere—no matter where the defendant's property is located—or whether it includes conduct that is wrongful because of the nature of the neighborhood where it takes place. For example, a crack house is a nuisance per se due to its illegality in all neighborhoods. In contrast, a dynamite factory located in a residential neighborhood would constitute a nuisance per se, but probably not if that same factory were located in an industrial zone.

QUESTION 4. Zoning students out of a campus neighborhood. West End is an older neighborhood in College City, located near the campus of a major state university. All of the properties in West End are improved with detached, single-family houses, almost all occupied by homeowners. Under the zoning ordinance of College City, West End is in the R-1 Zone, which provides

> Each dwelling unit may be occupied only by a single family, consisting of one or more persons related by blood, adoption, or marriage, living together as a single housekeeping unit; provided, two persons who live together as a single housekeeping unit and who are not related shall be deemed to constitute a family.

Sharon owns a home in West End, which she occupies personally. She moves out in July and advertises her home for rent. On August 1, she signs a one-year lease with six college students who take possession. None of the students are related to each other. The week after the students take possession, Paul, the owner and resident of the house across the street from Sharon's property, sues Sharon and the six student tenants, seeking to enjoin their continued occupancy on the ground it constitutes a nuisance. No evidence is introduced that bears on the students' conduct as residents. The most probable result is:

A. Plaintiff prevails because occupancy by six adults is not allowed under the zoning code.
B. Plaintiff prevails because the benefits of preserving the family character of West End substantially outweigh the defendants' interests.
C. Defendants prevail because the students have a constitutional right to live in a neighborhood of their choosing.
D. Defendants prevail because there is no proof they have substantially interfered with the neighbors' use and enjoyment of their properties.

ANALYSIS. Two of the choices, **B** and **D**, reflect the application of common law balancing principles. Under this approach, Paul prevails if the gravity of the harm outweighs the utility of the defendants' conduct (**B**). Given the lack of evidence that the students' occupancy has caused an actual interference with Paul's enjoyment of his home (by causing noise, excessive vehicular traffic, etc.), **D** is much more likely.

Choice **C** is incorrect because zoning ordinances may impose restrictions on the occupancy of homes provided those restrictions are reasonably related to police power objectives such as health, safety, and welfare. The zoning code restrictions probably do not impair the students' constitutional rights.

Choice **A** is the best answer because it reflects the nuisance per se doctrine. The students' occupancy is in violation of the zoning code, which is designed to protect the residential character of the neighborhood for the benefit of residents such as Paul.

E.   The "Coming to the Nuisance" Defense

Courts from time to time have applied a "coming to the nuisance" doctrine. When the plaintiff moved to a neighborhood after the defendant began her activity, the plaintiff is said to have "come to the nuisance." The defendant pleads "coming to the nuisance" as an affirmative defense, arguing that the plaintiff should not prevail.

Barring a plaintiff from suing based on "coming to the nuisance" has a great degree of intrinsic appeal. It is compatible with the often-followed property principle of "first in time, first in right." It seems unfair to force a defendant to stop her long-standing activity when the plaintiff could have avoided the harm by simply not buying the property or commencing the use that has turned out to be incompatible with the defendant's use. Moreover, the plaintiff may have purchased the property at a price that was discounted due to its proximity to the defendant's property, in which case granting a remedy for nuisance might amount to a windfall.

Modern courts, however, often refuse to apply the "coming to the nuisance" defense, especially in the context of residential owners confronted with problems emanating from industrial or commercial sources. An example is *Spur Industries Inc. v. Del E. Webb Development Co.*, 494 P.2d 700 (Ariz. 1972), in which a developer placed a retirement community near cattle feedlots. To protect the residents, the court ordered the feedlots to close but adopted an innovative remedy, conditioning relief on the developer's payment of the costs of closing or relocating the feedlots.

Applying the "coming to the nuisance" doctrine expansively means that the first occupant of a community has the ability to determine the character of that community, despite the desires of the latecomers, who may be more numerous and may propose to make economically valuable uses. The doctrine may represent a forced transfer of a servitude, a criticism recognized by the New York Court of Appeals long ago, when it observed, "One cannot erect a nuisance upon his land adjoining vacant lands owned by another and thus measurably control the uses to which his neighbor's land may in the future be subjected." *Campbell v. Seaman*, 63 N.Y. 568, 584 (1876).

The most typically expressed law and economics approach to nuisance also eschews priority in time as the basis for awarding entitlements. With respect to nuisance disputes, Ronald Coase noted, "The economic problem in all cases of harmful effects is how to maximize the value of production . . . courts have often recognized the economic implications of their decision and are aware (as many economists are not) of the reciprocal nature of the problem." Ronald H. Coase, *The Problem of Social Cost*, 3 J.L. & Econs. 1 (1960).

Based on such considerations, the Restatement has taken a soft approach with respect to "coming to the nuisance":

> The fact that the plaintiff has acquired or improved his land after a nuisance interfering with it has come into existence is not in itself sufficient to bar his action, but it is a factor to be considered in determining whether the nuisance is actionable.

Restatement (Second) of Torts §840D (1979).

QUESTION 5. The store is too close to the stadium. Ten months ago Linda purchased a small grocery store located two city blocks away from a major league baseball stadium. During the baseball season, her regular customers find it very difficult to shop at her store when home games are scheduled. Before and after the game, traffic clogs the street where her store is located. Also, many of her regular customers avail themselves of on-street parking near her store, and during games no spaces convenient to her store are available. She sues the owner of the stadium and the baseball club for nuisance, seeking to recover damages based on her lost sales. If defendants prevail, the most likely reason will be:

A. At the time Linda bought her store, she should have realized that the stadium would affect neighborhood traffic and parking conditions.
B. Defendants are not responsible for the conduct of fans who attend baseball games.
C. Linda does not have a property right in the public streets.
D. Lost profits cannot be recovered in a nuisance action.
E. Defendants did not intend to interfere with Linda's store.

ANALYSIS. This question tests understanding of the "coming to the nuisance" defense. Linda's nuisance action against the defendants has a number of potential weaknesses, but none of them are identified by Choices **B** through **E**. Defendants can be responsible for the conduct of their invitees when, as here, it is foreseeable that they would behave as they are. Linda's ownership interest in the store is sufficient; she does not need to prove that she has a property right in the streets to recover. If Linda proves lost profits with reasonable certainty, they are recoverable, just as they are in other cases of tort and contract. Although an "intent" of the defendant to cause harm is sometimes mentioned as an element for nuisance, modern courts that require "intent" find it to be satisfied if the defendant intentionally engages in the activity that happens to cause the nuisance. Here the defendants intended to hold baseball games at the stadium, knowing that large numbers of fans would drive to the stadium vicinity.

Because Linda purchased the store after the stadium was in operation, she can be charged with knowledge that a large number of fans would drive down her street on game days and that this could impact the access her customers have to her store. Courts generally treat "coming to the nuisance" as one factor when weighing the equities in a nuisance action. While this time sequence does not absolutely bar an otherwise meritorious nuisance action, it is likely to count against her on these facts. Choice **A** is the best answer.

F. The Closer: Priority in Time

The "coming to the nuisance" doctrine reflects the idea that property rights are sometimes acquired or vested based on prior use. What should happen when the first established use does not have nuisance-like characteristics and it is threatened by a newer, arguably incompatible use? Consider the following problem.

> **QUESTION 6. A restaurant opens next door.** Larry bought a house located on a lot at the intersection of two streets in a neighborhood zoned for small retail businesses, apartment buildings, and one- and two-family residences. The zoning code specifies that "small retail businesses" include "businesses where food and drink are dispensed for consumption on the premises." Larry demolished the house and built a restaurant with indoor and outdoor seating. Two months ago he opened the restaurant, with business hours from 9:00 AM to midnight. Next door is a single-family house owned by the Neighbors, where they have lived for 18 years. Noise from the restaurant has bothered them considerably, and they assert a claim based on nuisance. In the litigation, what is the most likely effect of the fact that Neighbors were in the area before Larry?
>
> **A.** Neighbors have a prior right and therefore Larry is liable for committing a nuisance.
> **B.** Neighbors have a prior right because Larry has "come to the nuisance."
> **C.** Neighbors' priority in time is irrelevant because of the zoning ordinance.
> **D.** Neighbors' priority in time is irrelevant because commercial uses have a higher economic value than residential uses.
> **E.** Neighbors' priority in time supports their claim but is not controlling.

ANALYSIS. Choice **B** is not a strong answer because Neighbors are claiming Larry is committing a nuisance, and he is the newcomer in the neighborhood. Although the economic view of nuisance that asserts the problem is reciprocal might provide some justification for this answer, Larry did not "come to the nuisance"—he is the alleged nuisance maker.

It counts in Larry's favor that he has not violated the zoning ordinance, but zoning compliance does not insulate him from liability for committing a nuisance if his operation of the restaurant is considered a nuisance under common law principles. More to the point, this inquiry has nothing to do with the question whether priority of usage is relevant. Choice **C** is incorrect.

Choice **D** relates to nuisance balancing, suggesting a comparison of the economic value of the competing uses. This is wrong for the same reason **C** is wrong. This is a factor that may be considered, but it does not preclude consideration of the Neighbors' priority in time.

That leaves us with **A** and **E**. Choice **A** reflects application of the "first in time, first in right" idea. This is a plausible answer—Neighbors might win for this reason—but **E** is better because it is nuanced. For the same reason that most states consider "coming to the nuisance" to be one factor that courts will consider, but not a controlling factor, priority in time of use is some evidence that will assist the Neighbors, but by itself it is not sufficient for them to prevail.

✴ Smith's Picks

1.	A house next to a big mine	C
2.	"Ready, aim, fire"	F
3.	Is it "natural landscaping" or "weeds"?	C
4.	Zoning students out of a campus neighborhood	A
5.	The store is too close to the stadium	A
6.	A restaurant opens next door	E

29

Zoning

"I've often thought that if our zoning boards could be put in charge of botanists, of zoologists and geologists, and people who know about the earth, we would have much more wisdom in such planning than we have when we leave it to the engineers."
Justice William Orville Douglas, in *Government and the Democratic Process; A Symposium by American and Israeli Experts* 16 (Judd L. Teller, ed. 1969)

CHAPTER OVERVIEW
A. The Constitutionality of Zoning
B. The Separation of Land Uses
C. Zoning Ordinance Amendments
D. Nonconforming Uses
E. Variances
F. Special Exceptions and Special Permits
G. Performance Zoning
H. The Closer: A New, Tough Tree Ordinance
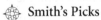 Smith's Picks

Zoning regulations have a dramatic impact on land ownership. While zoning originated in large metropolises, it has spread beyond the confines of those urban areas. Almost all American cities, large and small, have zoning ordinances, which apply to all tracts of land within their jurisdiction. Among major cities, only Houston, Texas, lacks a zoning code. Much rural land is subject to zoning pursuant to county ordinances. Although landowners tend to view zoning only from the perspective of restrictions placed on their property—zoning being a form of government control—it also adds value to private property. Property values are enhanced because an owner has the assurance that neighboring tracts of land must be used in compliance with zoning.

Zoning as a form of property regulation is relatively new. Traditionally most land use regulation was accomplished through private ordering. Owners entered into agreements that specified restrictions, using devices such as leases, defeasible fee conveyances, and licenses. The use of real covenants and equitable servitudes accelerated when American law freed these tools from a number of the restrictions inherent in English common law. Covenants and servitudes have the advantage of durability, enabling burdens and benefits to pass to new owners of the affected properties. All of these vehicles for controlling land use, however, have significant limitations. Generally, they have allowed individuals to control limited aspects of land use, rather than impose comprehensive regulation. Procedurally, only owners who agree to the restrictions are bound, thus precluding widespread territorial coverage. In the absence of agreement, some private ordering takes place through the application of nuisance law, which controls or prohibits particular types of land use in given locations or in the context of specific factual settings. But nuisance depends upon litigation, thus resulting in sporadic control, similar to contract-based land use restrictions.

What is distinctive about zoning is its comprehensive nature. For centuries dating back to the Middle Ages in England and the American colonies, governments have promulgated some regulations and restrictions on land use. Early regulations generally focused on such things as building height restrictions and spacing of buildings to reduce fire hazards. For a long period in American history, governmental land use regulation was not pervasive. There were only limited public intrusions on an individual's ability to use her land as she wished.

The modern comprehensive zoning system is a distinctly American phenomenon, inaugurated in New York City in 1916. The federal government played a significant role in its expansion. The Department of Commerce prepared and published the Standard State Zoning Enabling Act (SZEA) in 1926. The SZEA was extremely influential. Most states passed zoning enabling statutes closely patterned on this model act. The acceptance of zoning fostered a rebirth of the profession of city planning. A second model law, the Standard City Planning Enabling Act issued by the Department of Commerce in 1928, encouraged the widespread formation of city planning commissions.

Zoning is authorized by state law, but it is adopted and implemented by local governments. Cities, towns, counties, and other local governmental bodies enact zoning ordinances. This results in a great amount of diversity in the content of zoning laws. Local governments have considerable flexibility in drafting zoning ordinances with features that are appropriate to their local circumstances. A consequence of the local nature of zoning is the introduction of delegation problems concerning the zoning power. Zoning is a valid use of the police power of the state, but the state does not implement zoning directly by enactment of the state legislature. Local governments do not possess the entire police power of the state. Instead, they can only enact laws that are within their scope of authority. For certain zoning controls, even though the state could enact the measure, it is not clear whether the local government has the authority to do so. Usually the issue is one of statutory interpretation of the zoning enabling act, which is often modeled on the SZEA, but occasionally state constitutional provisions and other state laws must be consulted.

A. The Constitutionality of Zoning

The adoption of comprehensive zoning was controversial at first. From the outset it was clear that zoning signified a sharp break from past real estate development practices, which proceeded from the principle that the private market should control the location and type of improvements to private property. Opponents of zoning sought invalidation on several grounds, the principal ones being violations of due process and takings of property without just compensation. State supreme courts came down on both sides of the constitutional issues. In *Village of Euclid v. Amber Realty Co.*, 272 U.S. 365 (1926), the United States Supreme Court tackled the problem, holding that as a general matter the imposition of comprehensive zoning does not infringe the constitutional rights of landowners. *Euclid* proved to be a catalyst for the zoning and planning movement, prompting many local governments that had been holding back to initiate zoning. State courts that had previously rejected zoning reversed their stance to follow the *Euclid* decision.

Although *Euclid* sanctioned zoning as a general principle, it did not immunize all zoning regulations from landowners' constitutional challenges. Only two years later, the Court struck down the application of residential use restrictions to a specific tract of land under the due process clause on the basis that such zoning interfered with private property without a substantial relation to community welfare. *Nectow v. City of Cambridge*, 277 U.S. 183 (1928). The *Nectow* Court distinguished *Euclid* on the basis that the earlier case addressed a general, "facial challenge" to a zoning ordinance, but in *Nectow* the plaintiff conceded the general legitimacy of zoning but claimed the ordinance substantially reduced the value of his particular property without a sufficient countervailing public purpose. Ever since *Nectow*, landowners have regularly brought actions challenging zoning regulations "as applied" to their properties, with many victories for landowners and for local governments.

> **QUESTION 1. Annexation with large-lot residential zoning.** Your client, Horatio, owns a 500-acre tract of undeveloped land, which until last year lay one-half mile outside the city limits of Big City. Last year, Big City annexed several square miles of land, including Horatio's property. Big City has had a zoning ordinance since 1938. Although Horatio requested that Big City place his land in a zone that permitted commercial use, Big City zoned his land RSF-1, which allows only single-family detached residences, with a minimum lot size of two acres. With

commercial zoning, Horatio's land would be worth $50 million. With the current residential zoning, it is worth only $8 million. Horatio brings an action to challenge the zoning classification for his property. Which of the following arguments is most likely to succeed?

A. The RSF-1 zoning classification is not reasonably related to a legitimate governmental objective.

B. The RSF-1 zoning classification deprives Horatio of a substantial portion of his property value.

C. Big City lacks the authority to apply the RSF-1 zoning classification to Horatio's property because the minimum lot size is unreasonably large.

D. The RSF-1 zoning classification is invalid because prior to the annexation Horatio had the right to develop his property for commercial uses.

ANALYSIS.   Choice **A** is a facial challenge to the RSF-1 zoning classification, which should fail due to the Supreme Court's decision in *Euclid*. Zoning is generally constitutional, and single-family use districts, with large minimum lot sizes, are a common ingredient of zoning ordinances. For the same reason, Choices **C** and **D** are flawed. Under certain circumstances, courts have sometimes held that large minimum lot sizes are unconstitutional or are not authorized under the scope of the zoning power because the supposed public benefits are insufficient, but such cases are exceptional, and here we have no facts suggesting that Big City lacks a sufficient reason for setting the minimum lot size at two acres. Likewise, **D** is contrary to the holding in *Euclid*. When local governments first enacted zoning ordinances, the effect was always to restrict the rights that landowners previously held.

Choice **B** reflects the best chance Horatio has in attacking the zoning classification applied to his property. He is claiming that the zoning ordinance, "as applied" to his property, deprives him of a large percentage of his property value without sufficient justification. A similar claim prevailed in *Nectow*. Horatio might not prevail, but this is his best argument.

B.   The Separation of Land Uses

The cornerstone of zoning is the spatial separation of different types of uses. Zoning is premised upon the belief that disparate uses ordinarily should not be located in close proximity to one another. Homes should not be next to offices; stores should not be next to factories. The separation of uses is not intrinsically a goal, but it is thought to be desirable in order to maximize the land values of the community. The value of any tract of land is influenced, positively or negatively, by the uses that are made of nearby land. A residential lot is more valuable when located next to a park or other well-maintained residences. The very same residential lot is worth less when it adjoins a factory or a store that draws hordes of shoppers.

The early zoning ordinances, which are still prevalent today, can be identified as the "as of right" approach. This approach accomplishes the separation of incompatible uses by a static model. The local government divides up its territory into a number of districts or "zones," each having a defined list of permitted and prohibited uses. These zones are typically categorized by a hierarchy of permitted uses. Thus, there might be a zone 1 for single-family residential; zone 2 for multi-family residential; zone 3 for light commercial, retail, and office space; and zone 4 for heavy industrial use. At the highest point are detached, single-family homes, often with minimum lot sizes that are quite large. A local government may establish as many or as few levels of zones as it feels necessary to best carry out the objective of protecting the public's health, safety, and welfare. The text of the zoning ordinance sets forth the use rules for each zone, and a zoning map of the entire community locates the particular zones on the ground. This zoning system is "as of right" because owners have the right to use their properties under the rules set forth in the existing zoning ordinance without the need to obtain any additional government approval. This system preserves private property rights by limiting government discretion, thus adding to the perceived legitimacy of zoning. In principle, zoning decisions are made by the local legislative body without reference to the identity of particular landowners or their particular development proposals.

The earliest system of comprehensive zoning is known as *cumulative zoning*. This system, which is still popular, ranks the use districts from most restrictive to least restrictive. The detached, single-family residential zone is most restrictive, with all other uses generally prohibited. All of the "lower" zones are defined by a selective relaxing of prohibitions. With cumulative zoning, single-family housing is permitted at the landowner's discretion in an apartment zone and, for that matter, in an industrial zone. If the separation of disparate uses is the sine qua non of zoning, it is difficult to see why a purely cumulative system is desirable. For this reason, many modern ordinances replace the traditional system of use restriction with *noncumulative zoning*, which does not allow housing to be built everywhere in the community. Instead, residential uses may be entirely prohibited in commercial zones, and vice versa.

QUESTION 2. Revising the zoning code. Lumpkin City, population 101,101 at the last census, presently has cumulative zoning, which establishes four types of zones: a single-family residential zone, a residential zone that allows apartments, a commercial zone, and an industrial zone. The city council is considering an amendment to its zoning ordinance that would make all the zones noncumulative. The council wants your advice as to the effects such an amendment would have. Which of the following consequences is likely?

A. The amendment would increase the likelihood that incompatible uses will be situated in close proximity to each other.

B. The amendment would decrease the likelihood that incompatible uses will be situated in close proximity to each other.

C. The amendment would increase the choices for development afforded to owners of land in the commercial and industrial zones.

D. The amendment would make the zoning ordinance more vulnerable to a challenge that it is facially invalid.

ANALYSIS. Choice **D** is improbable. Noncumulative zoning is common today, and although a particular application of noncumulative zoning to a specific parcel of land may be constitutionally suspect, a court is not likely to strike down a zoning ordinance simply because it is noncumulative.

Choice **C** is incorrect because noncumulative zoning reduces the market choices that are available to all owners except those who own land in the single-family zone. With cumulative zoning, an owner of commercially zoned land has the right not only to make commercial uses (for example, stores and office buildings) but also build single-family homes or apartment buildings. Choices **A** and **B** are symmetrically opposite. As indicated by the example in this paragraph, cumulative zoning allows an owner a "lower" zone to put houses or apartments near commercial or industrial uses. Thus, the right answer is **B**.

C.   Zoning Ordinance Amendments

A zoning ordinance contains two basic parts: (1) textual provisions defining the use districts and setting forth a multitude of regulations and (2) a zoning map displaying what land is in which districts. The initial adopting of a zoning code is legislative action, and so is any amendment. A zoning amendment may consist of a modification of the text by, for example, redefining what uses are permitted in each district or by adding new features such as an ordinance specifying parking requirements or a provision for Planned United Development (PUD) projects. A textual amendment may have the effect, as applied to a given tract of land, of permitting development or another type of activity that was previously prohibited. More common, however, are zoning amendments that revise the zoning map, leaving the ordinance text alone. A map amendment "rezones" certain land—perhaps many tracts or perhaps only one—by moving it to a different use district.

Zoning shapes private property rights, and zoning amendments inevitably affect those rights, making some properties more valuable and others less valuable or desirable. For any given zoning amendment proposal, there are three possible outcomes concerning its legitimacy vis-à-vis property rights. First, the owner of the land in question may have a legal right to the requested rezoning. Such a right usually will be constitutional in origin, based upon either takings analysis or police power limitations. The owner may demonstrate that the present zoning deprives the land of its economic value to such an extent that a refusal to rezone constitutes a taking of property without just compensation. Alternatively, the owner may claim that the present zoning is invalid because it is not substantially related to the public health, safety, or general welfare.

At the other end of the spectrum, a neighbor or a group of neighbors may have a legal right to block the proposed rezoning. Generally, this right will be derived from limits to the public power, the argument being the converse of the one described above employed by the proponent of the zoning change. Here, the neighbors contend that the rezoning harms their property rights and is intended primarily to benefit the developer or other landowner seeking the rezoning. Since such a zoning amendment benefits a private party without substantially furthering the public interest, it is beyond the scope of the police power and, therefore, unlawful. When this line of attack succeeds, the rezoning is often characterized by the court as *spot zoning*, a term that means the measure is unlawful.

The third possible outcome in a landowner-neighbor dispute reflects the absence of legal rights in either adversary. The landowner does not have the right to insist that the present zoning be altered, and the neighbors do not have the right to block the change. In this group of cases, the merits of the proposed change are often reasonably debatable, and the local legislature, with no vested rights on either side, has the legitimate discretion to decide the matter either way.

In attacks on rezoning, courts traditionally have applied a presumption of validity, treating the ordinance amendment the same as other exercises of legislative authority. Under this approach, judicial review is curtailed. The plaintiff must demonstrate that the legislation is arbitrary or patently unreasonable. One court explained the standard as follows:

> As a legislative act, a zoning or rezoning classification must be upheld unless opponents prove that the classification is unsupported by any rational basis related to promoting the public health, safety, morals, or general welfare, or that the classification amounts to taking without compensation. This rule applies regardless of the size of the tract of land involved. Our narrow scope of review reflects a policy decision that a legislative body can best determine which zoning classifications best serve the public welfare.

State ex rel. Rochester Association of Neighborhoods v. City of Rochester, 268 N.W.2d 885, 888 (Minn. 1978).

A number of jurisdictions have developed stricter standards of judicial review which replace the traditional presumption of validity in certain cases.

The most commonly followed tighter standard of judicial review treats certain zoning amendments as quasi-judicial or administrative, rather than legislative, in nature. A dual standard applies, depending upon the scope of the amendment to the ordinance. In the leading case of *Fasano v. Board of County Commissioners*, 507 P.2d 23, 29 (Or. 1973), the court stated

> [When] the action . . . is an exercise of judicial authority, the burden of proof should be placed, as is usual in judicial proceedings, upon the one seeking change. The more drastic the change, the greater will be the burden of showing that it is in conformance with the comprehensive plan as implemented by the ordinance, that there is a public need for the kind of change in question, and that the need is best met by the proposal under consideration. As the degree of change increases, the burden of showing that the potential impact upon the area in question was carefully considered and weighed will also increase. If other areas have previously been designed for the particular type of development, it must be shown why it is necessary to introduce it into an area not previously contemplated and why the property owners there should bear the burden of the departure.

QUESTION 3. **Rezoning to allow a convenience store.** Green Acres, a residential subdivision built 40 years ago, has 180 single-family homes located on a total area of 84 acres. From its inception the City has zoned Green Acres for single-family use only, prohibiting all commercial and business uses. The City has recently widened Lexington Road, the public street that adjoins Green Acres, and the substantial vehicular traffic makes homes fronting on that street less desirable. Ten years ago Amanda bought one of the properties fronting on Lexington Road, which is a corner lot. She has lived there since. Last year she bought the neighboring house. She has a good friend on the city council, and she persuaded him to introduce and support an amendment to the zoning ordinance. The City amended the zoning for Green Acres to place Amanda's two lots in a "neighborhood retail" zone, which allows convenience stores. Amanda has just signed a long-term lease with a convenience store chain, which plans to demolish the houses and build a "Food Movin' Fast" store. The neighbors file suit against the City, Amanda, and the store chain, claiming that the rezoning is invalid. The neighbors are more likely to prevail if the court evaluates the rezoning decision under

A. An arbitrary and capricious standard of review.
B. A business judgment standard of review.
C. A standard of review that treats the ordinance the same as normal legislation.
D. A standard of review that requires clear and convincing evidence.
E. Quasi-judicial standard of review.

ANALYSIS. This question tests your understanding of the two basic approaches to rezoning that affects small parcels of land. The traditional approach, which is most deferential to the government, treats the rezoning decision as legislation, applying a presumption of validity. The burden of proof is on the plaintiffs to show that the measure is arbitrary. Choices **A** and **C** both reflect this approach.

Choice **D** would not help the neighbors. They will have the burden of proof, and they hope the standard will be preponderance of the evidence, not the higher "clear and convincing" evidence standard.

Choice **B** is a red herring. The business judgment rule is a tenet of corporate law that insulates officers from liability for decisions that they make in good faith. It has no application to decisions made by legislative bodies or by administrative agencies.

Choice **E** is the right answer. The neighbors have the best chance for success if the court characterizes the rezoning decision as quasi-judicial. This treats the decision as if it were made by an administrative agency and requires that the government justify the decision by a showing that the public purpose is sufficient to outweigh the costs imposed on the neighbors.

D. Nonconforming Uses

When cities first adopted zoning, they had to define zones and map zones on top of communities that were already populated, with a multitude of existing uses in place. Inevitably, there were neighborhoods where owners had established land uses that were incompatible with the zone to which their properties were assigned. Somewhere, homes, stores, businesses, and other uses were intermingled. A nonconforming use describes such a property for which the use predates the zoning and does not conform to the zoning. Thus, a nonconforming use is a zoning violation, but the use was lawful when it commenced. Nonconforming uses also frequently result when a local government adopts zoning amendments and adds new restrictions in its zoning code.

There are two basic types of nonconforming uses: (1) those consisting of nonconforming improvements, such as a building or other structure, and (2) those consisting of a nonconforming use but with no building or structural violation. The distinction is important because a decision by the government to terminate a nonconforming use is generally more onerous on the owner when it requires the destruction or substantial alteration of existing improvements.

All zoning systems have had an appreciable degree of toleration for nonconforming uses. They have a protected status, often because state zoning enabling acts and local zoning ordinances expressly authorize their continuance. Considerations of fairness as well as pragmatism underlie such legislation. Landowners who have invested in lawful improvements to their property suffer hardship if new zoning forces them to stop. Popular support necessary to adopt and continue zoning might fade if numerous owners were forced to give up their established land uses. Moreover, governmental suppression of nonconforming uses is often questionable on constitutional grounds. Arguably, the state's destruction of existing nonconforming uses constitutes a taking of private property without just compensation, at least when the use cannot be classified as a nuisance.

Governments have used several approaches in an attempt to reduce and phase out nonconforming uses. First, governments have adopted limiting rules. The owner cannot extend the geographical boundaries of the area containing the nonconforming use. A change from a valid, existing nonconforming use to a new nonconforming use is not permitted. Discontinuance of a nonconforming use for a period of time can result in its abandonment, with the owner having no right to resume that use. The abandonment doctrine ordinarily implies some degree of voluntary cessation of use on the part of the owner and commonly does not apply to the destruction of nonconforming buildings by fire or other casualty. However, zoning ordinances often contain a provision prohibiting the restoration of nonconforming structures that are substantially destroyed by casualty.

Amortization of nonconforming uses is a more drastic measure used by some local governments. With this approach, a landowner is given a set period of time to continue her nonconforming use, and, when the period expires, the use must cease. In effect, the landowner receives a grace period and is put on notice as to the date in the future when the use or structure must comply with the zoning regulations. Ordinances generally provide different amortization periods for different types of nonconformities, with nonconforming buildings often receiving periods running from 20 to 40 years. Many communities have utilized amortization to compel the removal of billboards and other signs from certain locations, with shorter time periods. Amortization of nonconforming uses has generally been upheld by the courts, although there are some cases to the contrary. Amortization has not been used pervasively, primarily due to political opposition in many communities.

QUESTION 4.   Adding a "mother-in-law" suite to the garage. Tony owns a single-family residence with a detached garage located in City. The garage has a sizeable attic, and five years ago Tony improved it, converting it into a "mother-in-law" suite, complete with kitchenette and bathroom. Promptly his mother-in-law ("Mom") moved in to be close to her daughter, Tony, and their children. Mom did not sign a written lease, and she paid no rent. Prior to doing the work, Tony obtained a building permit from City. This improvement and Mom's occupancy of the space fully complied with the zoning ordinance and all applicable laws at the time. Eight months ago, Mom died. Tony decided to offer the suite for lease, and he placed an ad in the local newspaper. However, Tony just discovered that two years ago City amended its zoning code to prohibit any lot in his neighborhood from having more than one "dwelling unit," which is defined as space designed for and suitable for occupation by a family that is a "separate housekeeping unit." Under the zoning code as it now stands, Tony cannot rent the space to a tenant. Moreover, his improvements do not comply with the zoning code because he now has two "dwelling units" on his lot. Tony asserts that, notwithstanding the zoning code, he has the right to maintain the suite intact, with no modifications, and to rent the suite to a tenant. The court is likely to decide

A. Tony has the right to keep the suite intact and to rent it to a tenant.
B. Tony has the right to keep the suite intact but not the right to rent it to a tenant.
C. Tony does not have the right to keep the suite intact as a separate "dwelling unit."
D. Tony has the right to keep the suite intact and to rent it to a tenant unless City can prove that such actions would cause actual harm to the community.
E. Tony has the right to keep the suite intact and to rent it to a tenant unless City can prove that such actions would constitute a nuisance under generally accepted legal principles.

ANALYSIS. Zoning regulations are presumed to be valid. Therefore, normally the government can enforce them without the need to prove, on a case by case basis, that conduct proscribed by the zoning code will cause actual injury or will constitute a nuisance under common law principles. So **D** and **E** are incorrect.

Either a use of property or a structure can qualify as a nonconforming use under a zoning ordinance. When Tony built the garage suite, it fully complied with the zoning as it then existed. Thus, this is a nonconforming structure which, under the terms of most zoning enabling statutes and most zoning ordinances, he has the right to maintain. City cannot force Tony to remodel the space so that it no longer constitutes a separate "dwelling unit." Tony's proposed rental, however, is a different matter. He was not using the suite as rental property at the time of the zoning code amendment. Occupancy was by Mom, a member of his family; she did not sign a lease, and she paid no rent. Possibly she was a tenant at will, paying no rent; alternatively she may have been a licensee. In either event, her occupancy was very different from a normal market rate lease to a tenant. Thus, Tony should not be able to establish rental as a nonconforming use. Thus, **B** is a better choice than **A** or **C**.

E. Variances

Traditional comprehensive zoning tends to be rigid and mechanistic, with the mapping of a community into sharply defined districts, each having its own subset of zoning regulations. This scheme fails to take account of a primary characteristic of a tract of land: its uniqueness. Even in the most ordinary city, land varies substantially in topography and in proximity to the community infrastructure, other uses such as schools and employment centers, and physical features of the environment.

When zoning was first invented, two devices were developed to interject some flexibility into the system. In 1926, the SZEA provided for both *variances* and special exceptions, both of which were incorporated into zoning ordinances on a widespread basis. Variances are authorized by virtually all zoning ordinances, and, in terms of frequency of use, are granted more often than special exceptions. A variance relaxes one or more of the zoning regulations that apply to a particular lot. It functions like a nonconforming use provision in that it legitimates some activity that otherwise would be prohibited. The SZEA empowers a local administrative body (labeled the "board of adjustment" in the Act) to grant variances in the following cases:

> To authorize upon appeal in specific cases such variance from the terms of the ordinance as will not be contrary to the public interest, where, owing to special conditions, a literal enforcement of the provisions of the ordinance will result in unnecessary hardship, and so that the spirit of the ordinance shall be observed and substantial justice done.

SZEA §7(3) (1926).

Most local zoning ordinances, following the SZEA, require the variance applicant to prove that the existing zoning regulations, if not varied, will result in *unnecessary hardship*. Often the ordinance incorporates another element, permitting a variance when the landowner would suffer unnecessary hardship or would encounter "practical difficulties" in complying with the regulations. The hardship suffered by the landowner if the variance is denied must be substantial. Usually the hardship is economic in nature. The applicant should present evidence of a loss of value of the land if a variance is refused.

The requirement that the hardship be both substantial and "unnecessary" has produced two refinements. Some courts have denied variances on the basis that the hardship was self-inflicted. This reasoning often applies when the applicant purchases the property with notice of the existing zoning. Presumably, the buyer should have recognized the problem and purchased elsewhere, or else offered a discounted purchase price to reflect the impact of the difficulty.

Some courts indicate that the hardship must be unique to qualify for variance relief. This means that the problem should stem from some characteristic that is peculiar to the lot in question, not common to the neighborhood.

The requirement of uniqueness is in part a gloss on the meaning of hardship, confining it to a detriment that is not widely shared by many owners. Also, uniqueness has served to distinguish problems that should be handled by amendment to the zoning ordinance rather than by variance.

Variances may be classified according to the type of zoning regulation being modified. *Dimensional variances*, which alter the setback requirements, open space requirements, or height limits, are probably the most common. A *density variance* permits more intensive use of a parcel than ordinarily allowed: for example, an increase in the number of apartment units to be built on a given tract of a specified acreage.

Use variances, widely used in some localities, permit a use to be made that is otherwise prohibited in the district. Use variances are often controversial because they effect a more drastic zoning change than dimensional or density variances. The relief they furnish and the change they effect is indistinguishable from a zoning amendment that redraws district boundaries. For this reason, courts in a number of jurisdictions require stronger evidence of hardship before a use variance may be issued, and a few states prohibit use variances altogether.

QUESTION 5.   Squeezing in a new garage. Three years ago the Slaters bought a corner lot in a single-family neighborhood. Their lot contained one house, situated on a 0.6-acre tract, and was bounded by public streets on three sides. The lot was zoned R-1, a residential classification that contained a special provision relating to corner lots: "The side yard on the side facing the side street shall be at least 15 feet from both main and accessory structures." Their property had no garage, and the Slaters petitioned the board of zoning adjustment for a variance from the required 15-foot set back to zero feet, in order to construct a garage. Their proposed location would provide the easiest access to the street. The topography of the lot was difficult. The garage could be constructed closer to the house without the need for a variance, but this would require construction of a ramp that would add $12,000 to the expense of the project. Also, there was a stone retaining wall, five feet in height, behind the house that would be weakened or destroyed if the garage were to be built closer to the house. Neighbors objected, alleging that the construction of the garage so close to the corner would create a blind area that would be dangerous for traffic and that the proposed garage would be an "eyesore" and would destroy existing vegetation. If the Neighbors prevail, which of the following rationales is the best explanation for denying a variance for the Slaters?

A. Adding the garage to the Slaters' lot will cause the use of their property to violate the provisions of the zoning code.

> B. There is no hardship to the Slaters if they are required to build the garage in a location that complies with the set-back requirement.
> C. The hardship to the Slaters is self-inflicted because they purchased the house, knowing it did not have a garage.
> D. The Slaters' lot is not significantly different from their neighbors' lots.
> E. The Slaters' proposed location for the garage would have a negative impact on other persons.

ANALYSIS. Many states apply a stricter standard for the issuance of a use variance, but Choice **A** is wrong. The Slaters are seeking a dimensional variance, not a use variance. A garage is consistent with residential use.

Choice **B** is incorrect because the Slaters have established hardship. A garage that conforms to the setback will cost an additional $12,000 and will not be as valuable for them. Nor is the hardship self-inflicted, as **C** asserts. Had the Slaters built the house, choosing to locate it on the lot where they did, the hardship might be labeled self-inflicted, but they purchased the house after that decision had been made by a prior owner.

Choice **D** is also wrong. The Slaters have a special problem in adding a garage to their lot because they have a corner lot (actually, bounded on three sides by streets), plus "difficult topography." Presumably most of their neighbors' lots do not share these characteristics.

This leaves **E** as the best choice. The Slaters have demonstrated hardship if they are denied a variance, but it is not "unnecessary hardship" if granting the variance will cause harm to the neighbors or the community, creating a traffic risk or impairing the aesthetic appearance of the neighborhood.

F.   Special Exceptions and Special Permits

A *special exception*, like a variance, allows flexibility in zoning by allowing a landowner to do something that is ordinarily not allowed under the zoning regulations. The SZEA authorizes the board of adjustment "to hear and decide special exceptions to the terms of the ordinance upon which such board is required to pass under such ordinance." SZEA §7(2) (1926). The special exception signifies a use that is permitted in a particular district only if certain criteria set forth in the ordinance are satisfied, as certified by a permit issued by the board or by some other entity empowered by the ordinance to issue special exceptions. In some states, instead of "special exception" this device is called a special use, conditional use, or special permit.

The traditional zoning system produces a list of permitted uses and a list of prohibited uses for each zone, with no deviations. Use of the special exception technique reflects a legislative judgment that a particular use is sometimes appropriate within a district, depending upon location and other variables such as siting, architectural standards, landscaping, buffering from adjacent uses, and other protective measures designed to minimize possibly adverse neighborhood effects.

Disputes concerning special exceptions generally turn on whether the permitting entity properly applied the ordinance criteria to the facts concerning the proposed use. When a special exception is issued over the opposition of neighbors, a reviewing court will generally affirm if it finds that the criteria set forth in the ordinance are reasonable and that there is substantial evidence that the proposed use satisfies those criteria. It is clear that a local government need not utilize the special exception device, notwithstanding that it is authorized by state enabling legislation. Therefore, a landowner has a right to a special exception only to the extent she can come within the terms of a special exception provision in a zoning ordinance.

Often the permitting board grants a special exception subject to certain conditions that the applicant must satisfy. Courts generally uphold the imposition of conditions, provided that they are reasonably related to the protection of neighboring residents.

Sometimes the validity of the special exception criteria set forth in the zoning ordinance will be challenged. Although courts will require that the local legislature select reasonable criteria that promote the public health, safety, and welfare, the normal presumption of legislative validity applies, generally insulating the ordinance from serious judicial scrutiny.

Often the criteria specified in the ordinance, which must be satisfied, are quite specific, but sometimes the criteria are general, thus allowing a great deal of discretion for the government in their application. This can pose a problem when the permitting entity is the zoning board of adjustment or another administrative body. Legislative authority cannot be delegated to such a governmental entity. If the discretion to approve or deny special exceptions is too broad, with no ascertainable standards provided for the issuer to follow, then the special exception provision of the ordinance may be invalidated as an unlawful delegation of legislative power.

QUESTION 6. Can the church be built here? A church purchased a vacant two-acre lot in a suburban neighborhood, fronting on a county highway. The neighborhood was subject to county zoning, which placed the lot in the RS-2 zone, which restricted all the lots to residential use, with a minimum lot size of 1.5 acres. The zoning ordinance allowed use by special exception of lots in the RS-2 zone for cemetery, church, and restaurant purposes under the following provision:

> The County realizes that certain uses have operational characteristics that, depending on the locations and design, may have the potential to negatively impact adjoining properties

and uses. Such uses therefore require a more comprehensive review and approval procedure in order to evaluate and mitigate any potentially detrimental impacts. Special exceptions, which may be revocable, conditional, or valid for a term period, may be issued by the County Board of Commissioners for cemetery, church, and restaurant purposes.

As required by the ordinance, the church submitted a site plan for its proposed development of its lot along with an application for a special exception. The County Board of Commissioners, the legislative body for the county, approved the special exception but required modifications to the church's proposal. It added a variety of conditions regarding the environmental impact of the proposed use, including a 25-foot "no development" buffer along the north side of the property, a requirement that ceremonies remain indoors, and required landscaping. It also required that the church reduce the size of the proposed facility so it would accommodate religious services of no more than 80 people at a time. The best argument for the church that the conditions are invalid is:

A. The ordinance allows the Board of Commissioners too much discretion in deciding whether to grant or deny a request for a special exception.
B. The condition limiting the size of the church structure has no rational relationship to a legitimate governmental purpose.
C. The conditions imposed by the Board of Commissioners have reduced the value of the church's property to a nominal amount.
D. The conditions imposed by the Board of Commissioners are not supported by an adequate statement of facts.

ANALYSIS. The assertion presented by Choice **A**—that the special exception provision lacks ascertainable standards and is too indefinite—would have merit if the entity with decision-making authority was an administrative agency, such as a board of adjustment. But here the Board of Commissioners is the local legislative body, and there is nothing wrong with it having unbridled discretion to decide whether issuance of the special exception is in the public interest.

Choice **B** is also a weak answer. Although the Board of Commissioners did not explain why a smaller church structure would "mitigate. . .detrimental impacts" on nearby residents, it is easy to imagine reasons in support of a size limit. There will be less vehicular traffic, less noise, a smaller scale structure may be more in harmony with nearby structures, and so on.

Next up is **C**, which reflects a regulatory takings test. If the church's property has no economic value under either the existing zoning or the special exception alternative with the approved conditions, then the government's action might be a regulatory taking, but no evidence in our facts points to the unlikely conclusion that the property is valueless without approval of the church's request.

Last up is **D**, which is the best answer. A legislature, such as the Board of Commissioners, need not give reasons for its decision if it is acting in a legislative capacity, but if its decision is administrative in nature, courts sometimes require that the decision be supported by an adequate statement of the rationale, coupled with findings of fact. Here the board did not explain the factual predicate for the conditions it imposed—why they were necessary or desirable to protect the nearby properties.

G.   Performance Zoning

The special exception technique, which adds some flexibility to the traditional zoning system, is a predecessor of *performance zoning.* Under performance zoning, a landowner does not have a discrete list of permitted uses, all of which are available as a matter "of right." Instead, the owner may select from a list of potential uses, which the government will approve if the owner's plan meets published criteria that are designed to ensure that the use is in the public interest and protects the community from adverse impacts. Performance zoning may include discretionary use zones, such as Planned Unit Developments (PUDs), downtown development zones, enterprise zones, historic preservation districts, recreational and wildlife zones, and other districts that require specific case by case approval for particular land uses. No land use is necessarily permitted as of right within such districts. Instead, these districts require a collaborative effort between public officials and private parties. A private owner selects from a range of possible uses prescribed by statute or ordinance and submits an application for a specific use for individual approval. Often the application leads to extensive negotiation between public and private parties.

Under performance zoning, the owner may have to agree to undertake certain expenses for public improvements which will serve or benefit the owner's property and the surrounding neighborhood. These expenses might relate to providing for public road work, sewer improvements, or in the case of substantial residential development, for additions to public school or service facilities. All such districts and zones are heavily regulated and can involve specific controls on materials to be used in any construction as well as limitations on size, density, and use with respect to all improvements. Historic districts may have very specific requirements with respect to the preservation of original structures and the nature of any improvements or replacements. This can include all aspects of a building from its structural materials to the doors, windows, lights, and paint. Enterprise zones may even go one step further and require qualification as to not only the type of use but also the nature of the work force employed within the zone. Because many such zones are designed to enhance employment opportunities for targeted groups within an urban area, approval to operate within the zone can require specific hiring programs along with any other land use restrictions.

Performance zoning requires the developer of real estate to demonstrate compliance, or ability to comply, with stated goals for the use of the property. This may require a developer to show that the property and its improvements will be able to handle a stated amount of rainwater runoff within a given time frame or that a stated number of people or cars will be able to access, locate on, or otherwise visit the property without having an adverse impact on traffic flow to adjoining streets. Within the zone a variety of uses may be permitted as long as all of the standards are met. Consequently, zoning and land use approval typically depend on the development and presentation of expert evidence of compliance with complex standards for noise abatement, traffic control, and air and water purity. These performance standards can also address local, regional, and environmental impacts requiring expert certification as to compliance with community standards as to availability of services to the property and manageability as to third-party impacts or externalities resulting from a proposed use.

QUESTION 7.   Regulation of building on steep slopes. Thomas owns a 90-acre tract of undeveloped land, which he bought for $450,000 three years ago. The land topography is uneven, with a significant part consisting of sloped elevations. The land is subject to the zoning ordinance of Pride County. When Thomas bought the land, it was zoned C-2, which permitted commercial uses under a cumulative zoning approach. Two months ago, Pride County rezoned the land, placing it within a brand new P-2 zone, which provides the following provision applicable to land with steep slopes:

A "steep slope" is defined as land area where the inclination of the land's surface from the horizontal is twelve (12) percent or greater. The following building restrictions apply to areas of steep slopes:

(1) Twelve (12) to less than fifteen (15) percent slope: no more than forty (40) percent of such areas shall be developed and/or regraded or stripped of vegetation.

(2) Fifteen (15) to twenty-five (25) percent slope: no more than thirty (30) percent of such areas shall be developed and/or regraded or stripped of vegetation, with the exception that no more than twenty (20) percent of such areas may be disturbed in the case of landslide prone area.

(3) More than twenty-five (25) percent slope: no more than fifteen (15) percent of such areas shall be developed and/or

regraded or stripped of vegetation, with the exception that no
more than five (5) percent of such areas may be disturbed in the
case of landslide prone area.

In addition to satisfying these steep slope restrictions, Thomas must
meet specified technical standards for the channeling of water runoff if he
develops the property.

Thomas brings an action challenging the rezoning, claiming that
it deprives him of a viable use of his property because he will not be
permitted to build on about 70 percent of his property as a result of the
ordinance. The evidence indicates that before the ordinance, he could
develop his land into 140 town home residential units or 200,000 square
feet of commercial space. Under the new "steep slope" ordinance,
capacity is limited to 89 town home residential units or 150,000 square
feet of commercial space. This has the effect of precluding Thomas
from building on about 70 percent of his property, whereas before he
could build on 50 percent of his property. The probable outcome of the
litigation is:

A. Pride County prevails because Thomas is entitled to a variance to
   build most residential units or commercial space if he applies for one.
B. Pride County prevails because the zoning restrictions substantially
   advance legitimate public interests.
C. Thomas prevails because the ordinance denies him the right to
   develop his property under clear, unambiguous standards.
D. Thomas prevails because his development rights were vested prior to
   Pride County's enactment of the "steep slope" ordinance.

ANALYSIS. Choice **A** is premised on a conclusion that if Thomas applies for
a variance, which he has not done, Pride County must issue the variance. This
is wrong because there is no evidence that he can prove that he meets the usual
variance standard — that under the existing "steep slope" zoning, he will suffer
unnecessary hardship if a variance is denied.

Choice **C** is wrong because Thomas has no right to insist that Pride County
apply traditional zoning to his property, which affords him the opportunity to
develop as a "matter of right." Thomas has to meet flexible standards with
respect to the quantity of development based on the slope of his land and the
need to control surface water runoff, and it is within the state's police power to
impose such requirements.

Choice **D** is incorrect whether Thomas is claiming he established a nonconforming use or has a "vested right." He did not install improvements or
commence a use before the zoning change, and he does not have a permit
to build which might invoke the "vested right" doctrine as it is commonly
applied.

Choice **B** is the correct answer. Although it does not use the term "performance zoning," it reflects the idea that performance zoning criteria, when reasonably crafted, are within the scope of the zoning power and are constitutionally valid. This problem is based on *Jones v. Zoning Hearing Board of Town of McCandless*, 578 A.2d 1369 (Pa. Commw. 1990), which upheld the steep slope regulations quoted in this problem.

H.   The Closer: A New, Tough Tree Ordinance

During the past several decades, many local governments have passed tree ordinances. Sometimes the ordinance is a new section of the zoning code, and other times it is free standing. Here is a particularly tough new ordinance for you to evaluate. In the context of this problem, it does not matter whether the tree ordinance is part of the zoning code, and thus must be justified as an exercise of the city's power to zone, or whether it's free standing.

> **QUESTION 8.   Save our trees.** The City of Trees just added a tree ordinance to its zoning code, which prohibits landowners from removing any tree eight inches in diameter and larger unless the owner first obtains a permit from the city arborist. The ordinance authorizes the arborist to issue a permit for removal only if the applicant demonstrates that retention of the tree(s) will cause "unnecessary hardship." In order to apply for a permit, the owner must submit a site plan that accurately locates all such trees on the applicant's property. Daisy owns a 40-acre tract of undeveloped land, which is heavily wooded. Her property is presently zoned RS-2, which allows single-family homes and townhouses at a density of up to three dwelling units per acre. Daisy brings an action claiming that the City's new tree ordinance is unconstitutional on its face. If she prevails, the most likely rationale will be:
>
> A.   The burden placed on landowners in City of Trees substantially outweighs the public benefits likely to accrue from the ordinance.
> B.   It is not practicable for Daisy to develop her 40 acres as residential property unless she removes a substantial number of trees protected by the ordinance.
> C.   A landowner's removal of healthy trees is not a nuisance at common law.
> D.   Daisy had a vested right to remove her trees, which the ordinance cannot lawfully impair.
> E.   Daisy's trees qualify as a nonconforming use, which she is entitled to continue.

ANALYSIS.   Choice **C** is true. At common law, a landowner may remove trees from her property with no risk that a court will consider the mere removal to constitute a private or public nuisance. But ordinances may lawfully prohibit many forms of conduct that are not common law nuisances.

Choice **D** refers to "vested rights." In a certain sense, if the ordinance is unconstitutional, Daisy could be said to have a vested right to remove trees, but this is conclusory, and the vested rights doctrine is usually employed in a different context when an owner relies on an existing permit or government-conferred right, which the government subsequently revokes.

Nor does Daisy have a "nonconforming use," so **E** is incorrect. Prior to the tree ordinance, her trees were lawful, and they are still lawful. Her problem is not that the ordinance has made it unlawful for her to keep the trees. Instead, she wishes to change the status quo.

Choice **B** would be the correct answer if Daisy had claimed that the tree ordinance was invalid *as applied* to her property. Instead, she is making a claim that is harder to establish—that the ordinance is *facially invalid*. This means that the ordinance has such a harsh impact on property rights that the city cannot apply its terms to any landowner who owns trees large enough to be covered by the ordinance. Daisy is unlikely to win this case, but if she does, the court must conclude that the benefits of the ordinance, as applied to the entire community, are small as compared to the costs, and therefore the ordinance as a whole is unconstitutional. So **A** is the best answer.

Smith's Picks

1. Annexation with large-lot residential zoning	B
2. Revising the zoning code	B
3. Rezoning to allow a convenience store	E
4. Adding a "mother-in-law" suite to the garage	B
5. Squeezing in a new garage	E
6. Can the church be built here?	D
7. Regulation of building on steep slopes	B
8. Save our trees	A

30

Eminent Domain

"The property of subjects is under the eminent domain of the state, so that the state, or he who acts for it, may use, and even alienate and destroy such property . . . for ends of public utility, to which ends those who founded civil society must be supposed to have intended that private ends should give way. But it is to be added, that when this is done, the state is bound to make good the loss to those who lose their property."

Hugo Grotius, *The Rights of War and Peace*, book 3, chap. 20,
(1625; William Whewell trans. 1853).

CHAPTER OVERVIEW
A. Public Use Requirement
B. State-law Restrictions
C. Just Compensation
D. The Closer: Stopping the Stadium
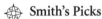 Smith's Picks

Governments at all levels — federal, state, and local — acquire property all the time. Governments buy automobiles, office supplies, computer software, and lots of other types of personal property. Frequently governments also purchase land for uses such as new schools or roads. Almost always, the government enters the market and buys from an owner who sells voluntarily. But on occasion a government wants to buy property that the owner refuses to sell. Then the government may invoke its power of *eminent domain*, forcing the owner to sell to the government. Eminent domain is also known as *condemnation*.

The scope of the eminent domain power is part of the general category of the law of "takings" under the Fifth Amendment to the federal Constitution. This chapter considers the rules that apply when the government expressly decides to exercise its *power of eminent domain*. The next chapter considers what is called *inverse condemnation*, when a property owner claims that government regulation or government activities have unconstitutionally impaired her property.

A.   Public Use Requirement

The Fifth Amendment to the Constitution provides: "Nor shall private property be taken for public use, without just compensation." This means that the government cannot take property for a private use or private purpose, even if it pays the owner the full measure of "just compensation." A line of Supreme Court cases has interpreted the public use requirement. The government has won almost all of those cases, with the Court interpreting "public use" broadly. Takings are permissible not only for traditional public facilities, such as schools, roads, and military bases, but also for government-sponsored development plans, in which the government transfers condemned properties to private parties who agree to develop the property in accordance with the approved plan.

In *Kelo v. City of New London*, 545 U.S. 469 (2005), in a five-to-four decision the Court held that the city could take single-family homes to develop an office park and to provide parking or other support facilities for an existing state park and marina. The majority followed the Court's longstanding rule that the government takes for a "public use" under the Fifth Amendment whenever its purpose is to provide a public benefit. After the taking, members of the general public need not have a right to enter the property, and title to the property need not remain in a public entity. The majority did state, however, that such an "economic development" taking must be pursuant to a "carefully considered development plan" that is not adopted simply to benefit one person or group at the expense of another.

QUESTION 1.   Land for a baseball stadium. The Blue City Clippers, a major league baseball team, played its games in an old stadium. The team wanted a new stadium in a better neighborhood, and City government feared that the franchise would relocate to another city if it did not assist the Clippers in getting a new stadium. The City owned 110 acres in an appropriate neighborhood, which it was willing to sell to the Clippers at a bargain price, but that tract was too small. Adjoining the 110-acre tract was a block of 30 homes, which were in good condition but of modest value. The Clippers negotiated to buy 22 of the homes, but homeowners who lived in the other eight homes refused to sell. The City brought an action against those owners, seeking to use its power of eminent domain. After completion of the eminent domain proceedings, the City plans to sell the properties to the Clippers. If the owners object to the condemnation on the basis of the federal constitution, the most likely outcome is:

A. The owners will prevail because the government is seeking to benefit a private entity.

B. The owners will prevail because eminent domain may not be used for the purpose of acquisition by a private entity.

C. The city will prevail because the city's plan can be characterized as seeking to provide community benefits.

D. The city will prevail because the owners' properties will be considered blighted.

E. The city will prevail because the Fifth Amendment takings clause restricts the federal government, not the state government.

ANALYSIS.   This question tests the students' understanding of *Kelo v. City of New London* and its Supreme Court precedents that afford substantial deference to the decisions made by governmental entities to exercise the power of eminent domain. The first two choices predict that the owners will win, and the last three predict that the government shall win. Given the Court's history of pronounced deference, you should lean toward selecting one of the last three—but of course it's necessary to study all the responses.

Choice **A** reflects the owners' best argument. The land is to be transferred after condemnation to the baseball team, a private entity. The *Kelo* majority opinion accepted the proposition that "the sovereign may not take the property of A for the sole purpose of transferring it to another private party B, even though A is paid just compensation." 545 U.S. at 477 (Stevens, J.).

Choice **B** on the other hand is plainly wrong. Kelo allowed the City of New London to condemn land for the stated purpose of transferring it to Pfizer Inc. and other private entities.

Let's examine the three "city wins" choices. Choice **C** looks good. The city's rebuttal to the owners' private benefit argument (Choice **A**) will contend that the new stadium will provide public benefits, including adding a new asset and preserving local employment and tourism. Choice **D** is factually wrong. The owners' homes are stated to be in "good condition" so they are not blighted. Choice **E** also fails. As *Kelo* plainly demonstrates, the Fifth Amendment restricts state governments as well as the federal government.

So Choice **C** is the best answer. I've used this question on my prior examinations, with 78 percent of the students getting it right. Most of the students who missed this one picked Choice **A**, the second best answer.

B.   State-law Restrictions

The *Kelo* decision was controversial from the moment the Court announced its decision in 2005, attracting substantial criticism in the media and from academics. Many observers had expected that the Court would rein in the power of eminent domain to protect the *Kelo* homeowners from the forced sale of their homes. Although *Kelo* remains intact as a statement of federal constitutional law, a backlash has taken place under state law. State constitutions, like the federal constitution, have takings clauses, and a number of state courts have interpreted their takings clauses more narrowly to prohibit takings in situations similar to the one in *Kelo*. Moreover, many state legislatures have passed statutes that restrict the use of eminent domain by state agencies and by local governments. A number of those statutes allow an "economic development" taking, which results in a transfer to a private party, only if the condemned property is "blighted." For example, Texas Govt. Code §2206.001(b) (enacted 2005) states in part:

> A governmental or private entity may not take private property through the use of eminent domain if the taking ... (3) is for economic development purposes, unless the economic development is a secondary purpose resulting from municipal community development or municipal urban renewal activities to eliminate an existing affirmative harm on society from slum or blighted areas. ...

QUESTION 2.   Land for a wilderness preserve. Dan owns 190 acres of undeveloped land in Lake County, which he plans to develop as a residential resort community. About half of the land is forested, and the remainder is wetlands. The land hosts a rich variety of native flora and fauna. Lake County wants to acquire the land and dedicate it for use as a wilderness area. It will allow minimal or no human activities on the property. Lake County offers to buy the land from Dan, but he refuses to sell. Lake County brings a condemnation action against Dan. He files an action claiming that the condemnation is improper under the federal constitution and the law of the state where the property is located. The most probable result is that

A. Lake County prevails because wilderness preservation is a higher use than residential development.

B. Lake County prevails because Dan's preferences cannot stand in the way of the public interest.

C. Dan prevails because the public will have no rights to use the property.

D. Dan prevails because the costs imposed on Dan outweigh the public benefits.

ANALYSIS. This question is basic, although the best answer might not leap right out at you. Choice **C** is wrong. Here Lake County plans to acquire title to Dan's property and hold it long term as a wilderness area. There is no indication that Lake County will subsequently transfer it to a private party, so there is no *Kelo* problem. Even if the court requires a strict showing of "public use" based on its state law, that element is satisfied here even though members of the public will not be allowed to enter the property, the same as if it were a public park. Public benefits flow from preserving environmentally valuable properties, and there are many types of government-owned property where members of the public have few or no rights to enter (such as military bases and jails).

Choices **A** and **D** are both incorrect for the same reason. If the government acquires the property for a public use and pays just compensation, the court will not make an independent judgment as to whether the government's plan or the private party's plan for the property is more valuable.

We're left with **B**. Although it sounds slightly lame, it reflects a truism. Provided that the government intends to devote the property to a public use, it has the right to condemn, notwithstanding the owner's preferences.

C. Just Compensation

The Fifth Amendment requires that the government pay "just compensation" for the property it condemns. This generally means the fair market value of the property at the time of condemnation. Under this standard, the owner is entitled to receive what a "willing buyer" would pay to a "willing seller" at the time of the taking. This means that a special value placed on the property by its owner is not compensable. In exceptional cases in which the property is of a type that is sold very infrequently, evidence of fair market value may be difficult to obtain. In that event, other measures of "just compensation," such as the replacement cost to the owner, may be appropriate.

> **QUESTION 3. A church closes.** Last year an inner city Catholic church, built 150 years ago, closed due to the lack of parishioners. The structure has significant historical value. As part of a plan to revitalize the neighborhood, the City seeks to acquire the church and demolish the building. Because the City and the Diocese are unable to agree to a price, the City commences an eminent domain action. The City's position is that it should pay only for the value of the land because the church's decision to close the parish demonstrates that the structure has no economic value. It claims the land value is $200,000. The Diocese's position is that the City should pay for the land value plus the cost today of rebuilding

the same structure, using stone, wood, sculptures, and other materials that are equivalent in quality and craftsmanship to that employed 150 years ago. The Diocese claims this value is $5.3 million (land value of $200,000 and structure replacement cost of $5.1 million). Evidence is submitted at trial that supports the values argued for by both parties ($200,000 land and $5.1 million structure). No other evidence of value is introduced. Who should prevail?

A. The City, because the structure has no market value.
B. The City, because the Diocese has abandoned its property.
C. The Diocese, because all buildings have some value, regardless of their present use.
D. The Diocese, because the structure has economic value even though it is difficult to ascertain.

ANALYSIS. Here we can identify two weak responses. The Diocese has closed the church, but it has not abandoned ownership of the real property. Indeed, the law does not allow an owner of real property to abandon ownership, even if the owner evinces a clear intent to do so. Choice **B** is wrong.

Likewise, Choice **C** is wrong. Some buildings, due to poor physical condition or economic obsolescence, have no economic value. This means the land is worth more after the building is demolished and removed than it is with the building in place.

Should we pick **A** or **D**? The Diocese is entitled to "just compensation," which includes the value of both the land and the church building. The City's only basis for its statement that the building has no value is the fact that the parish has closed, but the building may have value for other reasons. Another religious organization or a secular entity may want to acquire the church, if given the opportunity. Due to its historical value, some organization may be interested in expending resources to save the church. The Church's method of valuation may not be as appropriate as some other alternative, such as the cost to replace the church with a modern structure of the same size using modern, less expensive materials, but neither party has proposed such a measure or introduced evidence that establishes such a possibility. The Diocese should recover $5.2 million; **D** is the right answer.

D. The Closer: Stopping the Stadium

As indicated above, presently federal law as interpreted by the U.S. Supreme Court seldom protects a property owner from the consequences of a governmental decision to take property in exchange for the payment of just compensation. But in many states when a state entity asserts the power of eminent domain, state law provides a basis for the property owner to challenge the action. This question asks you to consider which fact is most likely to help the owners' case.

QUESTION 4.   Land for a baseball stadium revisited. The Blue City Clippers, a major league baseball team, played its games in an old stadium. The team wanted a new stadium in a better neighborhood, and City government feared that the franchise would relocate to another city if it did not assist the Clippers in getting a new stadium. The City owned 110 acres in an appropriate neighborhood, which it was willing to sell to the Clippers at a bargain price, but that tract was too small. Adjoining the 110-acre tract was a block of 30 homes, which were in good condition but of modest value. The Clippers negotiated to buy 22 of the homes, but homeowners who lived in the other eight homes refused to sell. The City brought an action against those owners, seeking to use its power of eminent domain. After completion of the eminent domain proceedings, the City plans to sell the properties to the Clippers. If the owners object to the condemnation on the basis of state law, which of the following facts is most likely to support their case?

A. The properties will be transferred to an entity that is already identified.

B. The proposed stadium will be open to members of the public if they buy tickets to the baseball games.

C. The owners presently occupy their properties rather than leasing them to tenants.

D. The city's goal of retaining a major league baseball franchise is not an essential governmental function.

E. There are multiple property owners, rather than just a single owner, who refused to sell to the Clippers.

ANALYSIS.   Let's look at our choices in reverse order. Choice **E** correctly notes that eight homeowners refused to sell to the city, while 22 accepted the city's offer. So what? Each property owner has an individual right not be subjected to the illegal use of eminent domain. It doesn't matter that there are eight holdouts, rather than only one.

Choice **D** sounds good. The owners assert keeping a major league baseball franchise is not an essential governmental function. Let's assume this is accurate (though as a life-long baseball fan I'm more than willing to argue for the essentiality of baseball). As long as the government is advancing a public use, the level of importance of the public use does not matter. Many governmental functions (such as libraries and public parks) may be described by some people as non-essential, but the government is still allowed to provide those facilities, and to condemn property to do so.

Choice **C** identifies the homeowners as owner-occupiers rather than land-lords. Although this is a point they may emphasize, and it may perhaps seem harsher for the government to force them to find a new place to live (rather than evict their tenants), this has no bearing on whether the government's plan reflects a valid public use.

Choice **B** points out the members of the public will be able to enter the property after condemnation, but they must purchase tickets. Access by the general public counts in favor of the government, not the owners. Although the owners may say this is not free access, this is unlikely to matter much, if at all. The government often condemns land for uses that are not freely open to the public; for example, jails, government laboratories, and military installations.

Choice **A** is factually true. The city will transfer title to the owner of the baseball team. Just as in Question 1 above (analyzed under the federal Constitution) the owners may use this to support a claim that the City's primary motivation is to benefit the team owner by subsidizing a new stadium. This might not succeed, but it's the owners' best shot. When I last used this question on a prior examination, only 9 percent of the students picked **A**. A large majority, 79 percent, were enticed by Choice **D**, attacking baseball as non-essential.

 ## Smith's Picks

1.	Land for a baseball stadium	C
2.	Land for a wilderness preserve	B
3.	A church closes	D
4.	Land for a baseball stadium revisited	A

31

Takings

~

*"The general rule at least is, that while property may be regulated to
a certain extent, if regulation goes too far it will be recognized as a taking."*
Justice Oliver Wendell Holmes
Pennsylvania Coal Co. v. Mahon, 260 U.S. 393, 413 (1922)

~

CHAPTER OVERVIEW
A. Regulatory Takings
B. Physical Invasions
C. Exactions
D. Judicial Takings
E. The Closer: Transferable Development Rights
✦ Smith's Picks

A large body of law known as "takings" has developed under the Fifth
Amendment to the federal Constitution and under analogous takings clauses in state constitutions. Sometimes the government does
not expressly exercise its power of eminent domain, but government regulation or government activities substantially impair the utility and value of privately owned property. The owner may assert that the government's conduct
amounts to a *regulatory taking*, entitling the owner to compensation or other
relief. An action brought in court that raises this argument is called *inverse
condemnation*. It is "inverse" and unlike normal condemnation in the sense
that the owner, not the government, is the plaintiff who initiates the action.

A. Regulatory Takings

Government regulation that substantially reduces the value of a landowner's
property may violate the takings clause even though there is no physical entry

upon the property. In a long line of cases, the Supreme Court has identified a number of factors to consider. They include but are not limited to

- The economic impact of the regulation on the owner.
- Interference by the regulation with the owner's investment-backed expectations.
- The character of the governmental action.
- The degree to which the owner's proposed activity has nuisance-like characteristics.
- Whether the regulation seeks to prevent the owner from causing a nuisance.
- Whether the regulation secures an "average reciprocity of advantage" among a sizeable number of property owners.
- Whether the regulation destroys a recognized property right.

The first element, which asks how much the regulation decreases the value of the owner's property, appears to be the most important factor. In *Lucas v. South Carolina Coastal Commission*, 505 U.S. 1003 (1992), the Court fashioned a per se rule to handle one narrow category of regulatory takings. If a regulation deprives the owner of all economic value, it is a taking unless the regulation is justified on the basis that it prevents the owner from committing a nuisance under previously established "background principles of the State's law of property and nuisance." Thus, a total deprivation of value is a taking unless the government can establish that it is suppressing a nuisance.

QUESTION 1. Downzoning the farm. Eight months ago Laura, a real estate developer, bought a small farm consisting of 30 acres at the edge of suburbia for $900,000. She plans to build a neighborhood shopping center and an apartment complex on the property. At the time of her purchase, the zoning permitted these uses as well as farming. However, two months after Laura bought the farm the county amended the zoning to limit use of Laura's tract to farming or single-family homes with no lot smaller than two acres. This reduces the market value of her land to about $200,000. Laura brought an action in court to challenge the change in zoning. Which of the following statements is most accurate?

A. The zoning change is valid because Laura is allowed to continue farming the land.

B. The zoning change is valid because residential use is a higher use than commercial use.

C. The zoning change is invalid because of the extreme reduction in market value of the land.

D. The zoning change is invalid because Laura has a vested right to build the shopping center and apartment building.

E. The validity of the zoning change cannot be determined from the facts given.

ANALYSIS.   Let's go in order. Choice **A** makes a good point — the ability of Laura to continue the use existing when she bought, farming — is a plus for the government. However, this is not sufficient by itself to preclude her takings claim if the regulation is considered sufficiently harsh and not justified by public purposes that it might be said to promote.

Choice **B** is just plain wrong. Although in the hierarchy established in the typical zoning system residential uses are considered "higher" than commercial ones, this does not mean that residential use is more valuable economically or that a government can limit an owner to residential use under all circumstances with no risk of a meritorious takings challenge.

Choice **C** makes a good point — the zoning change has greatly diminished the market value of Laura's land and has interfered with her investment-backed expectations. Yet she still has positive economic value, so if the government advances sufficiently weighty reasons that explain why the change is necessary to protect the community, it might prevail.

Choice **D** is incorrect. Even if Laura has a regulatory takings claim, her relief will not necessarily consist of having the right to build the shopping center and apartment complex. The government may avoid liability by rezoning the property to another category, which gives Laura more opportunities to develop but less than her original plan. Moreover, the term "vested rights" typically refers to an owner's right under a government-issued permit or license to continue a development or an activity, not the right to challenge a law under the takings clause.

By now it should be clear that **E** is the best choice. The law of regulatory takings is highly uncertain, and cases turn on the analysis of a long list of factors. Here the facts don't give us nearly enough information to make an informed prediction as to outcome.

B.   Physical Invasions

When the government wants to take possession of land or improvements, it normally is seeking to acquire a recognized estate in land, such as a fee simple absolute or a leasehold. In the typical case, the government wants private land for purposes such as a library, school, or airport, and if the owner does not sell voluntarily, the government will initiate an eminent domain proceeding.

There are situations, however, in which the governmental conduct is not designed to transfer the right of possession (an estate) to the government, but it nevertheless has an effect on the owner's possessory rights. A regulation may allow government or a third party to enter privately owned land for a particular purpose. Alternatively, a government activity that takes place near privately owned land may interfere with the owner's right to possession. In such cases, the owner may bring an action asserting a taking.

The Supreme Court has developed a bright-line rule to handle some of the fact patterns. A taking is found if a physical invasion onto private property, by the government or pursuant to governmental authority, results in a permanent physical occupation. That physical invasion would constitute the tort of trespass if committed by a private individual. Governments, however, are generally immune from tort liability under the doctrine of sovereign immunity, but they can be liable to owners under the takings clause for equivalent conduct. Even if the intrusion does not occupy a significant percentage of the owner's property or cause a great loss in economic value, the action violates the federal takings clause.

QUESTION 2.   Cable lines across Rosey's Ranch. Rosey owns a 5,000-acre ranch, which is subject to an easement that allows the easement holder to install and maintain "an electric transmission or distribution line system." Two years ago, a dispute in the same state arose with respect to the scope of a utility easement that had substantially identical language. The easement holder had authorized a cable television provider to install cable lines within the easement, using the same poles. This dispute went to the state supreme court, which held that use of the easement for the transmission of cable signals was not permissible. Last year the state legislature passed a statute that authorized cable television providers to install their lines on all electric utility easements in the state, with no requirement that they obtain the landowners' consent. The statute, however, requires that the cable television provider pay each landowner an annual rent of one dollar. A cable television provider has installed its lines in the easement that crosses Rosey's ranch. If she brings an action against the provider and the state, the most probable outcome will be:

A. This is a taking because Rosey has been deprived of the opportunity of selling a cable easement to the provider.
B. This is a taking because the cable lines are on Rosey's property.
C. This is not a taking because the cable lines might not remain on Rosey's property permanently.
D. This is not a taking because the presence of the cable lines has not diminished the value of Rosey's property.
E. This is not a taking because the cable provider is paying consideration to Rosey.

ANALYSIS.   Choice **C** is a weak answer. Of course, no occupation or invasion is ever "permanent" in the literal sense. The rule that prohibits a permanent physical invasion calls for distinguishing between temporary invasions and those that are continuous for a substantial period. Here the state statute apparently has granted cable providers an easement right that has no set expiration date. That's permanent enough.

Choice **D** is wrong because the owner does not have to prove a reduction in market value if the government has authorized a permanent physical invasion.

Nor does the payment of an annual rent of one dollar make a difference, so **E** is incorrect. Clearly the dollar payment is nominal and cannot be considered the payment of "just compensation."

Choice **A** is plausible. It's true that the law has deprived Rosey of the opportunity of bargaining to sell a cable TV easement to the provider. Had such bargaining taken place, presumably the provider may have been willing to pay her the market value for such a right. However, to prevail on her takings claim Rosey does not have to prove that she in fact lost a valuable right to bargain for consideration. Thus, **B** is the right answer. There is a taking simply because the cable lines are on her property, pursuant to governmental authority and without her consent. This question is loosely based on *Loretto v. Teleprompter Manhattan CATV Corp.*, 458 U.S. 419 (1982) (ordinance requiring landlords of apartment buildings to allow cable companies to attach cable wires to their buildings is a taking).

C.   Exactions

In land use planning, the term "exactions" refers to a government requirement that a landowner dedicate land or contribute money as a condition for allowing the owner to develop her property or pursue some activity on her property. For example, early last century when cities began to regulate the development of residential subdivisions, they adopted regulations that required the developer to dedicate streets, sidewalks, and utility easements to the public. In exchange, the developer obtained approval for its subdivision. Obviously, the streets, sidewalks, and utilities were necessary in order for the subdivision to work.

Governments began to impose land exactions that were more far reaching. They also began to impose fees (called monetary exactions) as an alternative to land exactions. State courts developed tests to determine which exactions were valid, and which were unconstitutional. In a series of cases, the U.S. Supreme Court developed Fifth Amendment rules. First, there must be an "essential nexus" between the exaction and a legitimate state interest. Second, the degree of the exaction must be "roughly proportional" to the projected impact of the owner's development or activity. The Court also held that monetary exactions demanded as a condition of a land use permit must satisfy the nexus and rough proportionality requirements. *Koontz v. St. Johns River Water Management District*, 570 U.S. 595 (2013).

QUESTION 3.   Replacement trees. Three years ago Lorena bought a one-half acre undeveloped residential lot in the city of Treehaven. The lot is heavily wooded. Last year the city council passed a tree ordinance, which applies to all residential property within the city. Property owners are not allowed to remove trees without a permit from the city arborist. Even with a permit, removal is allowed only if the owner plants replacement trees so as to maintain a minimum tree canopy cover of 30 percent of the lot area. Lorena hired an architect to design a house to be built on her lot. Construction will require the removal of 10 existing trees on her lot. When Lorena applied for a building permit, the city informed her that she must plant 12 replacement trees on parts of her lot that are not presently wooded. Lorena brought an action to challenge the permit condition as a taking of her property. The most likely result is:

A. Lorena wins because there is no nexus between the permit condition and the city's objective.
B. Lorena wins because the tree replacement requirement is not roughly proportional to the impact of Lorena's house construction.
C. Lorena wins because the city is taking physical possession of part of her lot.
D. Lorena wins because the tree replacement requirement is not rationally related to a legitimate governmental objective.
E. The city wins.

ANALYSIS.   This is a straightforward question that tests your understanding of the Supreme Court's Fifth Amendment test for determining the validity of governmental exactions. By number the choices are stacked in favor of Lorena winning, four to one, but don't let this fool you. Choice **A** hits the first element, whether there is a nexus between the condition and the city's objective. Lorena cannot win on this point. Here the nexus is unassailable: the city's objective is to preserve trees, and the condition directly requires tree replacement for trees removed by a landowner.

Choice **B** turns to the second element. Lorena may complain that she is cutting down only 10 trees, but must plant 12 new trees, two more. Again, the city wins. Surely this is "roughly proportional." I'm not sure the city needs to justify the difference, but if it does, it might say that the newly planted trees will at first be smaller than the removed trees.

The next two choices depart from the wording of the Court's "exactions test" and reflect other constitutional doctrines. Choice **C** is implausible. The city is not taking possession of any of Lorena's lot. Although the required replacement trees will occupy space, they will be Lorena's trees, not the city's trees. Choice **D** leaves the realm of takings law. The due process clause requires that a law have a rational relationship to a legitimate state objective. Preserving trees is within the scope of the police power (there are environmental and aesthetic benefits), and the tree ordinance obviously advances this objective.

So we're done, Choice **E** is right, the city will win. Choice **E**, as I drafted it, does not tell you the reason why. But by now the reason should be clear. The city is making an exaction, so its conduct is subject to the Court's exaction test, but there is a nexus between the means (planting new trees) and the end (preserving existing trees) and the requirement imposed on Lorena (plant 12) is roughly proportional to the impact (removing 10).

D.   Judicial Takings

Almost all takings claims raised by property owners are directed to legislative or executive action. When if ever might judicial action unconstitutionally take property rights? In *Stop the Beach Renourishment, Inc. v. Florida Dep't of Environmental Protection*, 560 U.S. 702 (2010), oceanfront landowners challenged a government beach renourishment program, which would create fixed boundary lines between the privately-owned tracts and newly restored beaches. The owners alleged an infringement of their riparian rights to receive title to accretions (imperceptibly slow addition of sand) and to have their property remain in contact with the public waters. Traditional common law provides for a migrating or "floating" boundary between private tracts and the public beach, which adjusts to accretion and erosion. Overruling a lower court, the Florida supreme court held that the government program did not infringe their property rights. Before the U.S. Supreme Court, the owners claimed that the state court effected a "judicial taking" of their property rights. The Court affirmed, holding unanimously that the state judicial decision was not a taking because it did not violate established property rights. However, a four-justice plurality opinion written by Justice Scalia declared that, in an appropriate case, a judicial departure from established property law could violate the Takings Clause (*id.* at 713–715):

> The Takings Clause is not addressed to the action of a specific branch or branches. It is concerned simply with the act, and not with the governmental actor ("nor shall private property be taken.") There is no textual justification for saying that the existence or the scope of a State's power to expropriate private property without just compensation varies according to the branch of government effecting the expropriation. Nor does common sense recommend such a principle. It would be absurd to allow a State to do by judicial decree what the Takings Clause forbids it to do by legislative fiat. . . .
>
> In sum, the Takings Clause bars the State from taking private property without paying for it, no matter which branch is the instrument of the taking. To be sure, the manner of state action may matter: Condemnation by eminent domain, for example, is always a taking, while a legislative, executive, or judicial restriction of property use may or may not be, depending on its

nature and extent. But the particular state actor is irrelevant. If a legislature or a court declares that what was once an established right of private property no longer exists, it has taken that property, no less than if the State had physically appropriated it or destroyed its value by regulation.

QUESTION 4.   Overruling a traditional common law rule. In 1880 the supreme court of the State of Caledonia decided a case involving the property rights of the owners of oceanfront land, adopting the common law rule that granted to the landowner any additional land formed by the process of accretion.[1] In a 2014 case, the Supreme Court revisited the issue in a case between an owner of oceanfront land and the State Department of Natural Resources. The state agency argued that accreted lands should belong to the state, not the private landowner. The majority of the Supreme Court agreed, overruling its 1880 precedent by a six-to-three vote to hold that accreted lands belong to the state. The landowner who lost the case brought an action to challenge the court's decision on the ground that it violated the takings clause of the Fifth Amendment to the U.S. Constitution. The best defense for the state is that:

A. It is commonly understood that state supreme courts frequently reexamine old precedents to determine whether they still serve important contemporary purposes.

B. The landowner's claim is for a regulatory taking, which is allowed only for actions taken by the legislative or executive branch.

C. The change in the law does not amount to a significant economic loss because it only prevents the landowner from acquiring additional land.

D. The takings clause does not apply to judicial changes in the common law of property.

ANALYSIS.   This is a tough one, mainly because the law on "judicial takings" is in its infancy, with no consensus among U.S. Supreme Court justices and other legal scholars as to the guiding principles. All the choices have some plausibility. Your task is to reach a judgment as to which is more likely to be a persuasive argument for the state, taking into account the holding and analysis in *Stop the Beach Renourishment*, including the points made by Justice Scalia. Let's go in reverse order.

Choice **D**, were the Supreme Court to adopt it, is a home run for the state. If judicial changes in the law are never unconstitutional takings of property, then the extent of the change in the law, and the reasons for the change, become irrelevant. But given Scalia's arguments, it seems quite unlikely that the Court would adopt a bright-line rule that says courts are always immune from takings challenges.

Choice **C** focuses on the extent of the diminution, suggesting that the landowner's economic harm is not great because she keeps all of her existing oceanfront land, only losing the right to newly accreted land. This is a factor commonly used by courts in regulatory takings cases, so it's a decent argument.

Choice **B** does two things: first, it states that the landowner's claim is for a regulatory taking (not a physical invasion); second, it suggests a possible rule—that judicial takings should be cognizable for physical invasions, but not for regulatory takings. The second point may be plausible, but this defense founders on the first point. The state's claim of ownership of the accreted land looks much more like a physical invasion than a mere regulatory taking. Under the traditional common law rule, the landowner would have title and the right to possess the accreted land. Now under the new rule the state has title and the right of possession.

Turning to Choice **A**, the defense is that the landowner should expect judicial changes in property rights, especially when they involve the revisiting of old precedents. Its strength is that it speaks to the owner's reasonable expectations, a core theme in takings laws. Landowners should not expect that property rights established more than a century ago will endure forever, despite substantial social, cultural, and economic changes. Its weaknesses are that it is conclusory, and possibly overly broad—like Choice **D**, it may imply that judicial changes in property law never amount to unlawful takings. In my judgment, Choices **A** and **C** are the stronger two answers. I give the nod to Choice **A** because **C** implicitly rests on the assumption that the landowner is making a regulatory takings claim. It shares this flaw with Choice **B**. The extent of diminution in economic value does not matter for the government's permanent physical taking of part of the owner's land.

E.   The Closer: Transferable Development Rights

Some public land use controls establish an indirect system of compensation by giving a landowner development rights that can be used elsewhere. These rights are known as transferable development rights, or TDRs. In exchange for the government's imposition of a prohibition or limitation on development, the owner receives a right to transfer density to another site in the jurisdiction. The owner may use that right at another location or sell it to a buyer who will use it. In some instances, the grant of TDRs may influence a court to decide that the regulation does not effect a taking. In *Penn Central Transportation Co. v. New York City*, 438 U.S. 104 (1978), a historic landmarks law prevented the owner of Grand Central Terminal, a classic railroad station, from building an office tower on top of the terminal. The Court upheld the law, observing that the owner's rights

> to build above the Terminal. . .has not been abrogated; they are made transferable to at least eight parcels in the vicinity of the Terminal, one or two of which have been found suitable for the construction of new office buildings. Although appellants and others have argued that New York City's transferable development-rights program is far from ideal, the New York courts here supportably found that, at least in the case of the Terminal, the rights afforded are valuable. . . .

Id. at 137.

QUESTION 5.   Opening the park. French owned a residential housing complex. The site included a private park space, currently used by residents of the complex. The City's zoning allowed residential development of the park space. The City modified its zoning ordinance by declaring the park space and other similarly situated properties owned by other persons to be public parks. In so doing it eliminated all rights of future development on the property. The new ordinance included a transferable development rights (TDR) mechanism. It severed the air rights over the park from the surface rights of the land and allowed the owner of park spaces to sell the TDRs to developers in certain locations elsewhere in the City. The ordinance provided a formula that allowed the buyer of such rights to add extra stories to buildings, which would exceed the otherwise permitted levels in these other locations. French brought a claim of inverse condemnation against the City. The most likely result is

A. The City prevails because it exercised its right to zone and regulate land use for the public good.
B. The City prevails because the TDRs constitute just compensation.
C. French prevails because there is a permanent physical invasion of his property.
D. French prevails because the ordinance is not likely to produce significant public benefits.

ANALYSIS.   Choice **B** is wrong. Just compensation has to be paid in cash unless the owner otherwise agrees, and TDRs, even if they are valuable, are not cash.

Choice **D** is also wrong. The court is not going to second guess the City as to whether public park spaces are more valuable than private park spaces, which might either remain as private parks or subsequently be developed.

Which is better, **A** or **C**? In opening the private park spaces to the public, the government is making a permanent physical invasion of French's property. This is a per se taking, which overrides the City's claim that it is properly exercising its zoning power for the public good. This question is based on *Fred F. French Investing Co. v. City of New York*, 350 N.E.2d 381 (N.Y. 1976), which held for the landowners and found the regulation to be a taking of private property without just compensation. The court said that the right to regulate land use was a broad one but could not go so far as to eliminate all possible use and value. The court approved of the idea of TDRs but found that under this particular program there was no real market for these rights, and thus the owners did not receive real value. Choice **C** is the stronger answer.

Smith's Picks

1. Downzoning the farm   E
2. Cable lines across Rosey's Ranch   B
3. Replacement trees   E
4. Overruling a traditional common law rule   A
5. Opening the park   C

Closing Closers: Some Practice Questions

~

"It ain't over 'til it's over."
Yogi Berra, New York Yankees catcher

~

This chapter contains a short practice multiple-choice exam with 18 questions. Unlike the other chapters, here there are no topic headings to signal the subject matter and no text to lay out blackletter law. You're not given a "heads up" to alert you to what's coming. Just like real exams, it's up to you to decide what subject matter the professor is attempting to test with the question.

Professors often write multiple-choice questions that incorporate issues or concepts drawn from multiple topics. This makes the multiple-choice question more like a standard essay question, which requires the student to do a good job at issue spotting. The multiple-choice questions in this chapter fit this mold. This practice exam gives you the opportunity to review a number of different concepts and to see how they fit together.

At the end of the chapter under Smith's Picks, I've given short explanations of the questions along with the answers. To get the full value out of this chapter, you should take the exam from beginning to end, and then grade yourself by looking at my answers and analysis. And again, if any of my questions in this chapter or the others seems wrong or confusing, send me an email and I'll try to fix the problem for the next edition.

So, let's go.

QUESTION 1.   The Law of Tiddlywinks. Famous Law Professor wrote the Glannon Guide to Tiddlywinks Law, which was published in 1990 and became a bestseller. In their written contract the publisher generously allowed Famous Law Professor to retain the copyright. Famous Law Professor died in 2000, survived by his wife ("Wife") of 20 years. The will of Famous Law Professor devised "all of my personal property to Daughter and Son-in-Law." Famous Law Professor, Wife, Daughter, and Son-in-Law have always lived in a community property state. In the year 2022, who owns what interests in the copyright?

A.   Wife owns the entire copyright.
B.   Daughter and Son-in-Law each have an undivided one-half.
C.   Wife, Daughter, and Son-in-Law each have an undivided one-third.
D.   Wife has an undivided one-half, and Daughter and Son-in-Law each have an undivided one-fourth.
E.   No one, because the copyright has expired.
F.   The copyright has reverted to the publisher.

QUESTION 2.   Helping out the Girl Scouts. Jacy owns Lakeacre, a five-acre lakefront parcel of land that is ideal for swimming and camping. Her daughters had a great experience in scouting, so she decides to let the local Girl Scout council ("Newtown") use the property. Jacy has decided not to require any payment from the Council. Jacy and the Council sign the following writing:

> Jacy hereby leases the property known as "Lakeacre" to the Newtown Girl Scout Council for so long as the Council desires to use the property for Girl Scout purposes.

The Newtown Girl Scout Council probably has obtained which of the following interests in Lakeacre?

A.   Tenancy for years.
B.   Easement.
C.   Life estate.
D.   Fee simple subject to condition subsequent.
E.   Tenancy at will.

QUESTION 3.   Get off my cloud. Ann and Rick are two neighboring farmers. Due to a protracted drought that has seriously threatened Ann's crops, Ann has hired an aviation firm to seed clouds in an attempt to induce rain. Because cloud seeding must cover a wide area to be effective, Ann instructed the firm to seed the clouds over Rick's farm as well as her own farm. Rick grows a different type of crop than Ann, which needs far less rainfall, and cloud-seeding will damage his crop. If Rick sues Ann to enjoin cloud-seeding operations directly above Rick's farm, Rick's strongest argument would be:

A. The overflights are within navigable airspace recognized by federal legislation.
B. The overflights are a trespass because Rick has a property interest in the clouds over his land.
C. The overflights are a nuisance whether or not Rick can demonstrate harm to his real property.
D. The overflights are a taking of Rick's property under the doctrine of inverse condemnation.
E. Because Rick has the right to exclude others from the subsurface of his land, that right to exclude must also extend upward.

QUESTION 4. The government interferes with the cloud. In Question 3 above, assume that a state governmental agency, instead of Ann, proposes to seed the clouds. If Rick asserts a cause of action against that agency based on cloud seeding directly above Rick's land, Rick's strongest argument would be:

A. The overflights are within navigable airspace recognized by federal legislation.
B. The overflights are a trespass because Rick has a property interest in the clouds over his land.
C. The overflights are a nuisance whether or not Rick can demonstrate harm to his real property.
D. The overflights are a taking of Rick's property under the doctrine of inverse condemnation.
E. Because Rick has the right to exclude others from the subsurface of his land, that right to exclude must also extend upward.

QUESTION 5. Who gets the crop? In May, Farmer Jones plants corn in his field. The corn will be ready to harvest in September. On August 4, Farmer Jones makes an inter vivos gift of his farm to his relatives Maria and Jose. To document the gift, he signs and delivers a warranty deed, which conveys his entire farm "to Maria for life, then to Jose and his heirs." On September 10, the crop is ready to be harvested. Who owns the crop?

A. Farmer Jones.
B. Maria.

C. Jose.

D. Farmer Jones, Maria, and Jose each have a one-third interest as cotenants.

E. Maria and Jose each have a one-half interest as cotenants.

F. Maria owns a life estate in the corn and Jose has a remainder.

QUESTION 6. Walking to the pond. Cletus owns two adjoining lots (Lots 1 and 2) in a subdivision. The rear part of Lot 2 (but not Lot 1) borders on a pond. Cletus conveys Lot 2 to Lana, the deed to Lana stating in pertinent part, "The grantor reserves the right to cross the land hereby conveyed for access to the pond." One year later, Lana sells Lot 2 to Lucky. Six months after that sale, Cletus sells Lot 1 to Cornelia. Cornelia's best argument that she has the right to walk across Lot 2 to the pond is:

A. The deed provision created an appurtenant easement.

B. The deed provision created an easement in gross.

C. The deed provision created a license.

D. The deed provision created a real covenant.

E. Lucky cannot prove that Cornelia's walking across Lot 2 will cause actual harm.

QUESTION 7. A covenant followed by rezoning. Laura, a real estate developer, just bought a small farm consisting of 30 acres at the edge of suburbia, planning to develop a residential subdivision. She gave the seller a valid, enforceable real covenant promising that each lot would have a minimum size of two acres. At the time of her purchase, the zoning permitted this use with a two-acre minimum lot size, but two months thereafter the county amended the zoning to reduce the minimum lot size to only one acre. What effect did the rezoning by the county have on the real covenant?

A. Laura can build on one-acre lots because private arrangements cannot stand in the way of the police power.

B. Laura can build on one-acre lots because this will not create a nuisance.

C. Laura can build on one-acre lots, but the government may have to compensate the seller for the loss of benefit of the real covenant if the seller can prove damages.

D. Laura must observe the two-acre minimum because the real covenant was created before the zoning amendment passed.

E. Laura must observe the two-acre minimum because both the real covenant and the zoning ordinance are valid restrictions on the use of her tract.

QUESTION 8.   A residential subdivision. Daisy owns 40 acres of undeveloped land for which she files a subdivision plot showing 42 lots and several streets. Daisy sells all of the lots to individual purchasers, conveying to each a fee simple determinable estate, with the limitation being that the lot must be used solely for residential purposes. Assuming that Daisy and all of the purchasers desire a strictly residential subdivision, one drawback to this mechanism is:

A. Daisy can enforce the limitation only so long as Daisy continues to own benefited land.
B. Daisy can enforce the limitation only if the court finds a general plan or common scheme of development.
C. Both A and B.
D. Daisy can enforce the limitation only if the court finds that Daisy and her purchasers were in a relationship of horizontal privity by virtue of inclusion of the provision in the deeds of conveyance.
E. Purchasers of the lots will not be able to enforce the limitation against another purchaser who violates the residential-use-only provision.

QUESTION 9.   Stolen painting. Henrietta and Walter, husband and wife, owned a Van Ram painting, which they kept in their house. Six years ago, Walter died, survived by Henrietta as his sole heir. Eight years ago, Ted broke into their house and stole the painting. One month later, he sold the painting to Cindy at a price approximating the painting's fair market value. Six months ago, Cindy was diagnosed with a serious disease. She sent an email to her niece, Natalie, who attended college in another state far away. The email read, "You know my prognosis is not good. I want you to have my Van Ram painting, which is still hung in my dining room." Natalie thanked Cindy and printed a copy of the email, which Natalie has kept. Cindy died from her disease 20 days after sending the email note to Natalie. Through an online search, Henrietta learned that Cindy had possession of the Van Ram painting. Henrietta contacted Cindy's executor and persuaded the executor to deliver the painting to her, rather than to Natalie. The following statute is in force in the jurisdiction whose law applies to determine property rights in the painting:

> Actions of replevin and all other actions for taking, detaining, or injuring goods or chattels shall be commenced within four years after the cause of action accrues, and not afterwards.

Natalie has brought an action of trover against Henrietta. The most probable outcome is:

A. Henrietta should prevail because the statute can have no effect on her ownership rights.

B. Henrietta should prevail because a gift causa mortis requires actual delivery of the subject matter.

C. Natalie should prevail because Cindy validly transferred a property right to Natalie.

D. Natalie should prevail because she can tack her period of possession to Cindy's period of possession.

E. Natalie and Henrietta should each have an undivided one-half interest because Walter's interest was not capable of passing to Henrietta, as Walter died after Ted stole the painting.

QUESTION 10. Parking lot. The Hungry Hippo restaurant opened 16 years ago on a small lot immediately next to the Big City Mall, a large regional shopping center. The Hungry Hippo has a small parking lot on its lot, which is always full when the restaurant is busy with customers. Customers who cannot find parking spaces in the Hungry Hippo's lot regularly park nearby in the Big City Mall's parking lot. A few months ago, Big City Mall announced plans to lease the part of its parking lot adjacent to the Hungry Hippo to a company that will build a pet-boarding facility. As part of this transaction, Big City Mall plans to install fencing and cut off access for Hungry Hippo's customers to park in its parking lot. Hungry Hippo brings an action against Big City Mall for a judgment recognizing that Hungry Hippo has a right to continue to use Big City Mall's parking lot for customer parking. Is Hungry Hippo's claim more likely to succeed on the basis of the law of adverse possession or the law of prescriptive easements?

A. The law of prescriptive easements because adverse use of the mall parking lot is not required.

B. The law of prescriptive easements because proof of exclusive use by Hungry Hippo's customers of particular mall parking spaces is not required.

C. The law of adverse possession because the statute of limitations for adverse possession is usually shorter than the statute of limitations for prescriptive easements.

D. The law of adverse possession because proof of open use is not required.

QUESTION 11.   Parking lot revisited. In Question 10 above, if Hungry Hippo seeks a prescriptive easement for customer parking, the most probable outcome is:

A. Big City Mall prevails.

B. Hungry Hippo prevails because Big City Mall acquiesced to Hungry Hippo's customers parking in the mall parking lot.

C. Hungry Hippo prevails because its customers' use of the mall parking lot was continuous and open.
D. Hungry Hippo prevails because estoppel prevents Big City Mall from stopping the customers from using the mall parking lot.

QUESTION 12.   Death before the sale can close. Cooper leases a ranch to Tessa for 20 years pursuant to a written agreement, charging an annual rent of $40,000. Tessa takes possession of the ranch. Two years later Cooper dies. His will devises all of his real property to Doug and bequeaths all of his personal property to Ester. What property rights in the ranch do Doug and Ester acquire?

A. None because Tessa is in possession of the ranch.
B. Ester acquires fee simple title to the ranch, and Doug acquires nothing.
C. Doug acquires fee simple title to the ranch, and Ester acquires nothing.
D. Doug and Ester each take an undivided one-half interest in the ranch.

QUESTION 13.   Tenant wants out. In Question 12 above, assume that after Cooper's death Tessa decides that she no longer wants to continue leasing the ranch. She sends a notice to Doug and Ester, stating that she considers the lease not to be binding because she agreed to lease the ranch from Cooper, and not from anyone else. She is no longer willing to pay the annual rent. Doug and Ester respond that the lease is still binding. If Doug and Ester sue to collect the rent, the most probable result is:

A. Plaintiffs prevail because Cooper owned an interest in the ranch that was devisable.
B. Plaintiffs prevail because Cooper's will manifested his intent that his successors acquire the landlord's rights under the lease.
C. Defendant prevails because the covenant to pay the rent is personal.
D. Defendant prevails because paying a person other than Cooper would materially change the nature of her obligation.

QUESTION 14.   Protecting a lake view. Dora owns two lots. The downhill lot has lake frontage. The uphill lot, which does not border the lake, has fine views of the lake. Dora builds a house on the uphill lot, positioning it to take advantage of the lake views. Dora decides to sell the downhill lakefront lot, which is presently unimproved. She wants to ensure that the buyer will not build a house or another structure on the lot so as to block the lake views from her house on the uphill lot. The best way for her to accomplish this objective would be to do the following in the deed of conveyance to the buyer:

A. Grant a fee simple subject to executory limitation.
B. Reserve an appurtenant easement.
C. Reserve an easement in gross.
D. Create a real covenant for Dora's benefit.
E. Except airspace rights in the deed.

QUESTION 15.   Susan's will. Susan executed her will ten years ago, devising Blackacre, a highly valuable tract of real estate, "to my brother William for 50 years, then to my sister Abbie's heirs; but if William dies before said 50-year term expires, the property shall go immediately to Abbie's heirs." Abbie died five years ago, survived by her husband Garth and her sons, Gabe and Garry. Abbie's will devised all of her property to X Foundation. Susan died last year, survived by William, who was 90 years old when Susan died. At the time of Susan's death, William's interest in Blackacre is best described as:

A. A life estate.
B. A term of years.
C. A defeasible fee simple.
D. A cotenancy interest he shares with Abbie's heirs.
E. An easement.

QUESTION 16.   Susan's will after the present estate. In Question 15 above, at the time of Susan's death what interest in Blackacre is owned by Garth, Gabe, and Garry?

A. Garth owns a remainder.
B. Gabe and Garry own a remainder in fee simple.
C. Garth, Gabe, and Garry own a remainder in fee simple.
D. Nothing, because of the Doctrine of Worthier Title.
E. Nothing, because the future interest granted to Abbie's heirs violated the Rule against Perpetuities.
F. Nothing, because X Foundation now owns the future interest granted to Abbie's heirs.

QUESTION 17.   What's the state of title? Eleven years ago Ophelia bought Blackacre, a ten-acre tract of land, in fee simple from Sam. In the deed of conveyance, Sam reserved a right-of-way easement, not to exceed 20 feet in width, across the western boundary of Blackacre. Sam retained ownership of a tract, named Northacre, lying immediately to the north of Blackacre. The purpose of the easement was to allow Sam to have access from Northacre to a public highway that ran along the southern boundary of Blackacre. At the time of Ophelia's acquisition Blackacre was unimproved, largely covered with pine trees and brush. Eight years ago Crooker, purporting to be Ophelia, sold Blackacre to Paula for valuable consideration, conveying by a warranty deed. Paula immediately took possession of the eastern part of Blackacre, clearing a small area where she built a cabin which she occupied as her principal residence. Over the years Paula cut timber from the eastern half of Blackacre, and she left the western half alone. Five years ago Ophelia died, devising a life estate to Paul and a remainder to Quigley. Sam has never cut trees from the right-of-way location or used that easement in any way. Sam has lived on Northacre at all relevant times and has access to Northacre by means of a county road that adjoins Northacre near its northeast corner.

In the jurisdiction where the property is located, the statutory period for adverse possession is ten years unless the claimant has color of title, in which case it is seven years. Assuming that Paula has met the general requirements for adverse possession other than duration, she probably has obtained the following title:

A. Title in fee simple to all of Blackacre, subject to Sam's easement.
B. Title in fee simple to all of Blackacre, free of Sam's easement.
C. Title to a life estate in all of Blackacre, subject to Sam's easement.
D. Title to a life estate in all of Blackacre, free of Sam's easement.
E. Title in fee simple to the eastern part of Blackacre actually occupied by Paula.
F. Title to a life estate in the eastern part of Blackacre actually occupied by Paula.
G. Title to nothing, because Paula has been in possession for less than ten years.

QUESTION 18. Finding gold coins. Bonnie and Clyde, wife and husband, are hiking on a public trail that runs on the course of an abandoned railroad line. They have a metal detector that they're playing around with, and they get a strong reading as they're swinging the metal detector near the boundary that separates the trail from Farmer's cornfield. They dig three feet into the cornfield, on Farmer's land, and find 42 gold coins, dating from the 1880s. It seems that they had been contained in a wooden box, which is almost wholly rotted away. If the jurisdiction follows the traditional law of treasure trove, who owns what interests in the gold coins?

A. Farmer owns all the gold coins.
B. Bonnie and Clyde own all the gold coins as tenants in common.
C. Bonnie and Clyde own all the gold coins as joint tenants.

D. Bonnie and Clyde own all the gold coins as tenants by the entirety.

E. Farmer, Bonnie, and Clyde are tenants in common, Farmer with a one-half interest and Bonnie and Clyde each with a one-quarter interest.

QUESTION 19.   Arguing about adverse possession at closing. Sue contracts to sell a five-acre tract of land to Peg. Sue has good fee simple title of record to four acres, but Opal has record title to one acre. Sue claims she has acquired title to that one acre by adverse possession. The contract does not specify the quality of title Sue would convey. At closing, Peg raises an objection to Sue's title to the one acre. Sue insists that her title is good, and refuses Peg's demand for the return of her earnest money. Peg then sues Sue. Which of the following results is most likely?

A. Sue will win because the contract does not promise that Sue's title is marketable.

B. Sue will win because Peg did not order a survey of the property prior to closing.

C. Peg will win because Sue breached a duty to disclose a material latent defect.

D. Peg will win because this title would subject her to the risk of litigation.

QUESTION 20.   A burnt-orange bedroom. Leinart rented his condominium unit to Young for a term of two years, with Young promising to pay monthly rent of $1,300. In the written lease Leinart gave Young permission to repaint the walls of one bedroom the color burnt orange in exchange for his promise to repaint that room, by the end of the term, with the shade of boring off-white that matched the rest of the interior of the condominium. Right after taking possession Young accomplished the burnt-orange repainting. Sixteen months after the lease commenced, Young and Benson signed a writing denominated as a "sublease agreement," pursuant to which Benson obtained the right to possess the condominium for the remaining duration of Young's lease with Leinart in exchange for Benson's promise to pay monthly rent of $1,500 to Young. Benson took possession and vacated on the last day of the term of the two-year lease. Leinart retook possession and discovered that neither Young nor Benson had repainted the bedroom. Leinart has the right to bring an action based upon this failure to repaint against:

A. Young and Benson.

B. Young or Benson, but Leinart may not sue both.

C. Young but not Benson.

D. Benson but not Young.

E. Leinart may not recover from either Young or Benson.

Smith's Picks

1. THE LAW OF TIDDLYWINKS. Go with **D**. This question requires that you know something about copyrights and community property. This copyright has not expired. The term is the author's life plus 70 years since the Copyright Act of 1976. Because Famous Law Professor and Wife were married while he wrote the Glannon Guide, the copyright is the fruit of his work performed during the marriage and thus was community property. If the copyright were the separate property of Famous Law Professor, then Daughter and Son-in-law would be the only owners. When Famous Law Professor died, his will passed his one-half community property interest to Daughter and Son-in-law. Wife retained her one-half community property interest in the copyright.

2. HELPING OUT THE GIRL SCOUTS. Of the five alternatives given, **E** is the best choice. This question requires that you understand the distinctions between leaseholds, easements, and freehold estates. Because the grantee is an entity rather than a natural person, a life estate is not feasible. A fee simple subject to condition subsequent will not work because the writing uses fee simple determinable vocabulary ("for so long as") rather than the words that signal a fee simple subject to condition subsequent. A tenancy for years is not appropriate because that type of leasehold requires a fixed term, and we cannot tell how long the Council will "desire" to use the property. The second-best choice is **B**. Jacy might have granted the Council as easement for swimming and camping purposes, but what cuts against this is the word "leases" in the grant, which implies that the Council has the right to possess the property (an easement is a nonpossessory right to use another's land). Also, the grant does not expressly limit the Council's use rights to swimming and camping, which typically is done expressly in the grant of an easement. A tenancy at will honors the parties' intention that they should have a lease relationship, and it facilitates the idea that the Council's estate should continue at the will ("desire") of the Council.

3. GET OFF MY CLOUD. The right one is **B**. This question requires some understanding of trespass to land, nuisance, and takings (inverse condemnation). It is based on a Texas case reproduced in some property casebooks, *Southwest Weather Research Inc. v. Rounsaville*, 320 S.W.2d 211 (Tex. Civ. App. 1958), but a student can deduce the correct answer without having read this case. Rick may attempt to prevail in trespass or nuisance, but **C** is flawed because it has an incorrect statement of the law of nuisance. In nuisance, unlike trespass, the plaintiff must prove substantial injury. If the overflights are in navigable airspace, this helps Ann, not Rick. The action cannot succeed as inverse condemnation because the defendant is not a governmental entity. Choice **E** is wrong because a landowner does not have an unlimited right to exclude others from entering the airspace over his land, as the aviation cases demonstrate.

4. THE GOVERNMENT INTERFERES WITH THE CLOUD. Now it's **D** because a state governmental agency is proposing to seed the clouds over Rick's property. The government is not liable to a landowner in tort for trespass or nuisance except to the extent that the government has chosen to waive sovereign immunity. Actions of this type are typically brought against the government as a taking without compensation under the Fifth Amendment. This is what the term "inverse condemnation" means: the government by its action is condemning an interest in the plaintiff's property, but the government is not pursuing "direct condemnation" by filing an eminent domain action against the landowner.

5. WHO GETS THE CROP? Choice **B** is best. Maria, the life tenant, owns the crop. A life tenant has the right to annual revenues from the property for the duration of the life estate, with no duty to account to the remainderman. The crop represents annual income or revenue. In some states, a ripe crop, which is ready to harvest, is considered personal property rather than real property. There is a split of authority on this point. But here the deed is delivered in August, so the unmatured crop is part of the real estate, and ownership is not retained by Farmer Jones. There is no cotenancy because the deed evinces the clear intent to give Maria a life estate and Jose a remainder.

6. WALKING TO THE POND. Go with **A**. If the deed created an appurtenant easement, the benefited estate is Lot 1 and the burdened estate is Lot 2. The conveyance of Lot 1 to Cornelia automatically transferred ownership of any appurtenant easement to Cornelia as grantee of the fee estate. If the deed provision created an easement in gross, probably it's nontransferable, and in any event there's no evidence that Cletus intended to transfer an easement in gross to Cornelia. A license would not help Cornelia because typically it is nontransferable and revocable at the option of the licensor (Lana or Lucky as Lana's successor). The deed provision would not create a real covenant because the terms allow an entry onto Lot 2, something a real covenant or equitable servitude cannot do. E is "out in right field." Unless the deed provision created a property right now owned by Cornelia, she will be trespassing if she crosses Lot 2 to get to the pond, and a trespass results whether or not there is actual harm to the property.

7. A COVENANT FOLLOWED BY REZONING. The only correct statement of the relationship between covenants and zoning is **E**. When a tract of land is subject to both a private covenant (a real covenant or an equitable servitude) and zoning covering the same subject matter, the owner generally must comply with both the covenant and the zoning regulation. This means that when one of the regulations is more restrictive than the other, the owner must comply with the most restrictive regulation, whether it is the covenant or the zoning provision. It does not matter whether the covenant or the zoning was first in time.

8. A RESIDENTIAL SUBDIVISION. Take the last one, **E.** The point of this question is to distinguish between the requirements for a fee simple determinable, which is one type of defeasible fee, and the requirements for real covenants/equitable servitudes. Responses **A**, **B**, and **D** all state various requirements for real covenants equitable servitudes, but here we have a fee simple determinable. With a fee simple determinable, Daisy has retained a possibility of reverter. The only person who may enforce the limitation is the owner of the possibility of reverter, which is Daisy or her successors or assigns. Even if the possibility of reverter is transferable inter vivos (true in many jurisdictions today), the lot purchasers are not Daisy's successors and assigns with respect to the possibility of reverter.

9. STOLEN PAINTING. The better choice is **C.** This question combines the law of gifts of chattels with adverse possession of chattels. Either Henrietta or Natalie might win this case, with the outcome turning on what rule set the court applies for adverse possession — the traditional rules requiring open, continuous, and exclusive possession by Cindy; or the discovery rule requiring due diligence by Walter and Henrietta — and on what facts are found. So we have to examine the quality of the responses. **A** is flawed; even though Henrietta is defendant, not plaintiff, the statute will cut off her rights if the court determines she would be time-barred, had she sued, under adverse possession/discovery rule principles. Choice **B** is flawed; a court may uphold a gift causa mortis based on a symbolic delivery, and the email note should qualify. Choice **E** is flawed; Walter's undivided one-half passed to Henrietta at his death, even though he died after the theft and lacked possession and knowledge as to the painting's whereabouts. Choice **C** is the better explanation of why Natalie could win. Cindy made a valid transfer of whatever rights she had by effecting a gift causa mortis. Tacking, mentioned in **D**, is not necessary because Cindy's period of possession exceeded the four-year period specified by the statute.

10. Parking lot. Choice **B** is best. This question requires a comparison of the basic elements of adverse possession and prescriptive easements. In many cases, an adverse user of another person's land may be able to prevail on either theory, but it is harder to gain title by adverse possession than to gain use rights by a prescriptive easement. The main reason is that an adverse possessor must prove *exclusive possession* of the land in question, while the prescriptive user need only prove regular (continuous) use. Thus, evidence that the parking spaces regularly used by Hungry Hippo's customers were also sometimes used by persons who shopped at Big City Mall would prevent adverse possession, but not a prescriptive easement.

11. Parking lot revisited. Take Choice **A.** There are several reasons why Hungry Hippo probably will fail in its claim of prescriptive easement. Big City Mall will claim that, until now, it permitted Hungry Hippo's customers to use the mall shopping lot. Big City Mall did not post signs restricting parking and took no measures to stop it. A prescriptive easement, like an adverse-possession claim, requires *adverse* use. The landowner's permission defeats the claim. Big City Mall might also prevail on the basis that the customer parking was not sufficiently continuous or that Big City Mall lacked notice of Hungry Hippo's claim.

12. DEATH BEFORE THE SALE CAN CLOSE. The correct response is **C**. This question tests understanding of the distinction between real property and personal property. The ranch was real property before Cooper entered into the lease with Tessa, and the ranch remains real property with respect to the landlord's rights. This is true even though at common law, a leasehold from the tenant's point of view was considered personal property—historically, it was called a *chattel real*. Because Cooper's will devised all of his real property to Doug, he is now the sole owner of the ranch. Choice **C** could be more complete, if it said that he, Doug, acquired fee simple title subject to the lease, but it is still true as written.

13. TENANT WANTS OUT. A is the right choice. The facts don't say anything about the lease provisions, other than (1) specify that it applies to the ranch, (2) indicate the term of 20 years, and (3) state the amount of rent. So we assume that the lease is silent on whether it binds and benefits successors of landlord or tenant. Remember: never assume unstated facts. The rule is that leases run with the land—at least, all real covenants in lease agreements run with the land. Tessa's obligation to pay rent is a real covenant, not a personal covenant. So **C** is wrong. Likewise, **D** is wrong. It is no more burdensome that she now pay rent to Doug than before, when she had to pay Cooper. Both **A** and **B** reach the right result, but **A** is the better explanation. Cooper's actual intent, or presumed intent, when he executed his will with respect to continuation of the lease does not matter. It's easy to see this if you consider what would have happened had he died intestate—his heir (whether Doug, Ester, or someone else) would inherit both the ranch and the landlord's rights under the lease.

14. PROTECTING A LAKE VIEW. Choice **B** is best. Dora should reserve an appurtenant easement of view across the downhill lot. This will not only bind the immediate buyer, but unlike the typical easement in gross, it will bind the buyer's successors and benefit Dora's successors. A real covenant, by which the buyer promises not to build so as to obstruct Dora's views, is also plausible. But a covenant is subject to judicial termination if a court perceives a change in circumstances from the time of conveyance, whereas an appurtenant easement is not terminable under the change of circumstances doctrine. A fee simple subject to executory limitation may work but should be avoided. It makes the buyer's title unmarketable, and thus Dora may not be able to sell the downhill lot, or if she can, she'll get a lower price. Also, unlike an easement, courts strain to find reasons not to enforce a limitation that takes title away from a grantee. Likewise, an exception of airspace rights may work, but it is complicated and heavy-handed compared to the simple creation of an appurtenant easement.

15. SUSAN'S WILL. Take **B.** Form over substance applies to the labeling of estates and future interests. Students may properly conclude that William in effect owns a life estate in Blackacre. He is 90 years old when Susan dies, and it is inconceivable that he will live until 140, when the term is scheduled to expire. But Susan in her will used words that clearly gave William a leasehold estate for 50 years, defeasible if he dies before the term expires. That's how the court will interpret the will.

16. SUSAN'S WILL AFTER THE PRESENT ESTATE. Choice **C** is the right answer. In all states when a married person like Abbie dies, her heirs are her surviving spouse and children. The proportions that they take differ from state to state. So Garth, Gabe, and Garry share a remainder. Many states still apply the Doctrine of Worthier Title, but it would affect only a remainder created in the testatrix's (Susan) heirs, not a remainder created in the heirs of another person. X Foundation has nothing. Susan's gift was to "Abbie's heirs," not to Abbie, so Abbie has nothing she can devise. The Rule against Perpetuities does not invalidate the remainder because it is vested when it was created — it was certain to become possessory no later than 50 years after Susan's death.

17. WHAT'S THE STATE OF TITLE? The first choice, **A**, is it. I tried to wear you out by giving you a total of seven choices — well beyond the normal allotment. But I expect you know enough about taking multiple-choice exams to be sure to read all the choices, even if you feel certain that **A** is the right answer as soon as you read it. You may read something in the latter responses that changes your mind, despite your previous certainty.

This is on the long side for a multiple-choice question, by my taste. It's the type of question I'd usually draft for a short-to-medium-length essay question. You have to deal with four variables or issues: (1) Does the easement run with the land to bind Paula? (2) Should Paula get adverse possession title to all of Blackacre or just the part that she has actually taken and used? (3) Is Paula claiming under the seven-year statute or the ten-year statute? (4) Does Ophelia's devise of Blackacre, dividing ownership between a life estate and a remainder, affect Paula's title by adverse possession?

The answers are (1) yes, (2) all of Blackacre, (3) the seven-year statute, and (4) no. A few details: The easement is appurtenant, so it generally binds Ophelia's successors. The fact that Sam has not used it and that he has alternative access for Northacre is not relevant. This is not sufficient to demonstrate that Sam has abandoned ownership of the easement. The deed Paula obtained from Crooker is color of title, which does two things. She gains title to all of Blackacre under the doctrine of constructive adverse possession, and she may use the seven-year limitations period rather than the normal ten-year period. Ophelia's will doesn't matter. This severance of title took place after Paula began her adverse possession, so the running of the period extinguishes both the life estate and the remainder.

18. FINDING GOLD COINS. You should pick **B**. The traditional law of treasure trove, as applied in the United States, awards the treasure trove to the finder who unearths it, even if the finder trespassed to locate and retrieve the trove. Bonnie and Clyde must be cofinders. There's nothing in the facts to suggest that one was more responsible than the other in finding the coins. Modern law presumes a tenancy in common, rather than a joint tenancy. Approximately half the states recognize the tenancy by the entirety for real property, but many of those states do not allow it for personal property, which the coins are after they are unearthed. Thus, **D** is not a likely answer in the absence of a prompt in the question telling you that the jurisdiction allows a tenancy by the entirety for personal property.

19. ARGUING ABOUT ADVERSE POSSESSION AT CLOSING. Take the final one, Choice **D**. In some states, Sue will win this litigation if she is able to prove that she has clearly satisfied all of her jurisdiction's requirements for adverse possession. But neither **A** nor **B** capture this idea. **A** is wrong because Peg as buyer has the implied right to marketable, which means she may rescind and recover her earnest money if Sue's title in unmarketable. **B** misses the point. Ordering a survey before closing might have revealed the adverse possession problem, but Peg's failure to do so does not impair her right to marketable title. **C** suggests that the adverse possession problem is a "material latent defect" that Sue should have disclosed prior to the closing. This has some plausibility, but it's weak because Peg learned about the problem prior to the completion of closing. Thus, Sue's failure to disclose did not harm Peg. **D** reflects the reason why Peg would win in many states. Many states require the seller to have a marketable title based on recorded documents. The reason for this rule is to protect the buyer from the risk of having to litigate to quiet title.

20. A BURNT-ORANGE BEDROOM.[1] The winner is **A**. Leinart may sue both the original tenant, Young, and the assignee of the leasehold, Benson, for breach of the lease covenant to repaint the bedroom off-white. Of course, Leinart is entitled to only one satisfaction for nonperformance of the covenant (i.e., if he sues for damages, he may collect the judgment from either defendant but may not get a double recovery by collecting the *entire* amount from *both* defendants). Young is liable because he made the promise to repaint and Leinart has not released him from his obligation to perform.

---

1. Your author would consider a burnt-orange bedroom a thing of beauty as he is an alumnus of the University of Texas, whose school color is burnt orange. However, he resisted the impulse to integrate explicitly into this question something about UT or one of its sports teams. Hook 'em Horns!

Why is Benson liable? The promise to repaint is a covenant running with the land. It's an affirmative covenant that touches and concerns the tenant's estate and the landlord's estate, so Benson became liable on that real covenant when he took possession. If Benson really were a sublessee, as the parties' agreement stated, he would be off the hook. But Benson is an assignee because the transfer from Young to Benson was for the entire remaining time period of the original two-year lease.

Index